A Guide to Crisis Intervention

Fifth Edition

KRISTI KANEL

California State University, Fullerton

CENGAGE
Learning·

Australia • Brazil • Mexico • Singapore • United Kingdom • United States

CENGAGE
Learning®

A Guide to Crisis Intervention, **Fifth Edition**
Kristi Kanel

Product Director: Jon-David Hague

Product Manager: Julie Martinez

Content Coordinator: Sean Cronin

Product Assistant: Kyra Kane

Media Developer: Audrey Espey

Associate Marketing Manager: Shanna Shelton

Art and Cover Direction, Production
Management, and Composition:
PreMediaGlobal

Manufacturing Planner: Judy Inouye

Rights Acquisitions Specialist: Roberta Broyer

Cover Image: © iStockphoto/Thinkstock

Library of Congress Control Number: 2013944596

ISBN-13: 978-1-285-73990-8

ISBN-10: 1-285-73990-6

Cengage Learning
200 First Stamford Place, 4th Floor
Stamford, CT 06902
USA

Cengage Learning is a leading provider of customized learning solutions
with office locations around the globe, including Singapore, the United
Kingdom, Australia, Mexico, Brazil, and Japan. Locate your local office at
www.cengage.com/global.

Cengage Learning products are represented in Canada by
Nelson Education, Ltd.

To learn more about Cengage Learning Solutions, visit
www.cengage.com.

Purchase any of our products at your local college store or at our
preferred online store **www.cengagebrain.com**.

Printed in the United States of America
5 6 7 17 16

This book is dedicated to the many human service students
who have given me their feedback over the years and to
all the brave individuals who have survived
and grown through their crises.

Brief Contents

Preface xv

About the Author xix

CHAPTER 1
What Is a Crisis and Crisis Intervention?   1

CHAPTER 2
Ethical, Legal, and Professional Issues   27

CHAPTER 3
The ABC Model of Crisis Intervention   48

CHAPTER 4
**When a Crisis Leads to Danger to Self, Others,
or Psychotic Decompensation**   82

CHAPTER 5
**Developmental Crises and Special Issues
of Adolescence (Bullying, Pregnancy, Teens Who
Run Away from Home, and Eating Disorders)**   109

CHAPTER 6
**Crises of Loss: Death, Relationship Breakups,
and Economic Loss**   133

CHAPTER 7
PTSD, Trauma, and Community Disasters   154

CHAPTER 8
Veteran's Issues   **176**

CHAPTER 9
Sexual Assault and Rape   **199**

CHAPTER 10
**Crises of Personal Victimization: Child Abuse,
Elder Abuse, and Intimate Partner Abuse**   **210**

CHAPTER 11
Crises Related to Substance Abuse   **243**

CHAPTER 12
Crises Related to Serious Illness and Disabilities   **270**

Name Index   299

Subject Index   305

Contents

Preface xv
About the Author xix

CHAPTER 1
What Is a Crisis and Crisis Intervention?   1

Crisis Defined   2

Crisis as Both Danger and Opportunity   3
  Crisis as Opportunity   5
  Crisis as Danger: Becoming a Crisis-Prone Person   6
  Other Factors Determining Danger or Opportunity   7

Precipitating Events   9

Developmental Crises   10

Situational Crises   10

Emotional Distress   10

Failure of Coping Methods and Impairment in Functioning   12

The Wellesley Project: The Development of Crisis
Intervention   12

Crisis Intervention and Suicide Prevention Strengthen
Nationwide   14

Community Mental Health Act of 1963   14
  The Rise of Managed Care   15

Contributions from Other Theoretical Modalities   17
  Psychoanalytic Theory   17
  Existential Theory   18
  Humanistic Approach   18
  Cognitive-Behavioral Theories   19

Brief Therapy   19
Critical Incident Debriefing   20
The ABC Model of Crisis Intervention   20

Chapter Review   21
Answers to Pre-Chapter Quiz   22
Key Terms for Study   22
References   25

CHAPTER 2
Ethical, Legal, and Professional Issues   27

Introduction   28

The Need for Ethics   28

What Are Ethics?   28

Defining Law   28

Controversies   29

Use of Paraprofessionals   30

Ethical Issues   31

Self-Awareness   31

Dual Relationships   32

Confidentiality   32
Elder Abuse Reporting Act   33
Child Abuse Reporting Act   34
Client's Rights   36
Virtual or e-Therapy   36

Multicultural Competence   36
Development of Cultural Sensitivity   37
Etic vs. Emic Issues   38
Latinos   39

African American Families   40

Asian American Families   41
Asian American Family Structure   41
Shame and Obligation in Asian American Culture   41
Communication Process in Asian American Culture   42

The Subculture of Lesbians, Gays, Bisexuals, and
Transgenders (LGBT)   42

Chapter Review   44
Answers to Pre-Chapter Quiz   44
Key Terms for Study   44
References   46

CHAPTER 3
The ABC Model of Crisis Intervention   48

Introduction   49

A: Developing and Maintaining Rapport: Follow the Client   50
Attending Behavior   52
Questioning   53
Clarifying   55
Paraphrasing   56
Reflection of Feelings   56
Summarization   58

B: Identifying the Problem: Follow the Model   59
Identifying the Precipitating Event   62
Recognizing the Meaning or Perception of the Precipitating Event   63
Identifying Emotional Distress and Functioning Level   64
Making Ethical Checks   65
Substance Abuse Issues   66
Therapeutic Interaction   66

C: Coping   69
Exploring the Client's Own Attempts at Coping   70
Encouraging the Development of New Coping Behaviors   70
Presenting Alternative Coping Behaviors   70
Commitment and Follow Up   73

Case Example: Using the ABC Model of Crisis
Intervention with a Survivor of Military Sexual Trauma   74
Chapter Review   79
Answers to Pre-Chapter Quiz   79
Key Terms for Study   79
References   81

CHAPTER 4
When a Crisis Leads to Danger to Self, Others,
or Psychotic Decompensation   82

Introduction   83

A Brief History of Suicide   83

Introduction to Suicide   84
Symptoms and Clues   84
Suicide Assessment   85
Interventions   88
A Phenomenological Look at Suicide   92

Two Philosophies of Suicide Prevention   94

Nonsuicidal Self-Injury (NSSI) and Self-Mutilative
Behavior (SMB)   95

Assessment of NSSI   96
Interventions for NSSI   97

Managing a Client Who Is a Danger to Others   97
Risk Factors for Violence Against Others   98

Psychotic Breakdowns and Gravely Disabled Mentally Ill Persons   100

The Mental Status Exam   100

Chapter Review   104
Answers to Pre-Chapter Quiz   104
Key Terms for Study   105
References   106

CHAPTER 5
Developmental Crises and Special Issues of Adolescence (Bullying, Pregnancy, Teens Who Run Away from Home, and Eating Disorders)   109

Introduction   110

A Brief Review of the Life Cycle Crises   110

Family Systems Theory   114

Runaways   114

Structural Family Therapy   115

Evolutional Crises   116
First Stage of a Family: Creating a Marital Subsystem   116
Creating a Parental Subsystem   118
Creating Sibling Subsystems   118
Creating Grandparent Subsystems   119

Special Issues of Adolescence   119
Bullying   120
Teen Pregnancy   121
Teens Who Run Away from Home   123
Eating Disorders   124

Chapter Review   128
Answers to Pre-Chapter Quiz   129
Key Terms for Study   129
References   130

CHAPTER 6
Crises of Loss: Death, Relationship Breakups, and Economic Loss   133

Death and Dying   134
Kübler-Ross's Five Stages of Death and Dying   134

Definitions Related to Loss   135
Tasks of Mourning   136
Manifestations of Normal Grief   138
Determinants of Grief   138
Intervention   139
Counseling Principles and Procedures   140
Losing a Child   140

Divorce and Separation   143
Intervention   144
Children and Divorce   144
Crises Related to Blended Families   145

Job Loss   146
The Role of Perceptions   147
Interventions   147

Chapter Review   151
Answers to Pre-Chapter Quiz   151
Key Terms for Study   151
References   152

CHAPTER 7
PTSD, Trauma, and Community Disasters   154

Posttraumatic Stress Disorder (PTSD)   154
Effects on Young Children   156
Military Service   156
Personal and Family Victimization   157
Natural Disasters   157
Four Phases of Community Disasters   158
Man-Made Disasters   159
Gun Violence and Shootings   160

Interventions   162
Critical Incident and Debriefing   163

Burnout and Secondary Posttraumatic Stress Disorder   165
Definitions of Burnout   165
Symptoms of Burnout   165
Causes of Burnout   166
Secondary Traumatic Stress   167
Study of Community Crisis Workers as Related
to Secondary PTSD and Burnout   167
Debriefing Process   169
Other Therapeutic Approaches Commonly Used to Treat PTSD   170

Chapter Review   172
Answers to Pre-Chapter Quiz   172
Key Terms for Study   173
References   173

CHAPTER 8

Veteran's Issues   176

Serving in the Military: An Historical View   176
Introduction to the Population of OIF and OEF Veterans   177
Statistics   178
Military Culture   178
Issues Particular to These Veterans   178

Invisible Wounds   179
PTSD   179
Depression and Suicide   179
Anger Issues   180
Treatment of PTSD   180
Alcohol Misuse   180
Traumatic Brain Injury   181
Issues Facing the Families of Veterans   182
Issues Facing College Enrolled Veterans   183
A 2008–2009 Research Study of OIF and OEF Veterans and PTSD   183
General Interventions   191

Chapter Review   194
Answers to Pre-Chapter Quiz   194
Key Terms for Study   194
References   195

CHAPTER 9

Sexual Assault and Rape   199

What Is Rape?   200

Rape Trauma Syndrome   201

Interventions with a Rape Victim   202

The Empowerment Model with Sexual Assault Survivors   202

Date and Acquaintance Rape   203

Military Sexual Assault   204

Chapter Review   207
Answers to Pre-Chapter Quiz   207
Key Terms for Study   207
References   208

CHAPTER 10

**Crises of Personal Victimization: Child Abuse,
Elder Abuse, and Intimate Partner Abuse**   210

Child Abuse   211
Prevalence   211
Types of Child Abuse   212
How to Detect Child Abuse and Neglect   213

Prevalence of Child Sexual Abuse   213
Infant Whiplash Syndrome   215
Association of Child Abuse with Posttraumatic Stress Disorder   215
Reporting Child Abuse   216
Interventions with an Abused Child   217
The Battering Parent   219
Interventions for Adults Who Were Sexually Abused as Children   221
Intervention for Perpetrators of Sexual Abuse   221

Elder Abuse   222
Interventions with Abused Elderly People   223

Intimate Partner Abuse/Domestic Violence   224
A Historical Perspective   224
Cultural Factors and Universal Factors Related to Intimate Partner
Abuse   225
Cultural Considerations   226
Prevalence of Intimate Partner Abuse   227
How Are Children Affected?   228
Why Do Women Stay?   228
The Battering Cycle   229
Battered Woman Syndrome   230
Intervening with Battered Women   232
The Batterer   234
A Phenomenological View of the Batterer   235
Interventions with the Batterer   236

Chapter Review   239
Answers to Pre-Chapter Quiz   239
Key Terms for Study   239
References   240

CHAPTER 11
Crises Related to Substance Abuse   243

Drug Use Statistics in the Twenty-First Century
for the United States   244

What Is Substance Abuse?   244
Types of Drug Abuse Crises   245
Family Crises   245
Medical Crises   245
Legal Crises   246
Psychological Crises   247

Alcohol: The Most Common Drug of Abuse   247
The Alcoholic   248
Intervention   248
The Codependent   254

Illicit Drug Misuse   257
Speed: Cocaine, Crack, and Crystal Meth   257

Effects of Cocaine and Speed on the Family   259
Marijuana   259
LSD (lysergic acid diethylamide)   261
Heroin   262
Nonmedical Use or Abuse of Prescription Drugs   262

Chapter Review   263
Answers to Pre-Chapter Quiz   266
Key Terms for Study   266
References   268

CHAPTER 12
Crises Related to Serious Illness and Disabilities   270

Palliative Care   270

The Biopsychosocial Model   271

Serious Illnesses   272

AIDS and HIV   272
What Is AIDS?   274
Misconceptions About AIDS   275
Modes of Transmission   275
Progression of HIV Infection to AIDS   276
AIDS Testing   276
Treatment   277
Social Aspects   278
Type of Clients Who May Seek Crisis Intervention
Related to HIV/AIDS   279
Interventions   281

Alzheimer's Disease   283
What Is Alzheimer's Disease?   283
Effects on the Caretaker   284

Issues Related to Disabilities   285
A Brief History of Disabilities   285
The Disabled Population and the ADA   287
Vulnerable Subgroups Within the Disabled Population   288
Disabled Elderly People   288
Mentally Disabled People   289
Developmentally Disabled People   290
Crisis Intervention Strategies for Persons with Disabilities   291

Chapter Review   294
Answers to Pre-Chapter Quiz   294
Key Terms for Study   294
References   295

Name Index   299
Subject Index   305

Preface

When I first wrote this book, my intent was to create a student-friendly text that would guide both new and more experienced counselors through specific procedures when conducting brief crisis intervention sessions with a variety of client populations. Although I have included much research and theory throughout the book, the focus has stayed the course—how to conduct interviews in a structured fashion.

In general, this book is written for college students and beginning mental health professionals who might benefit from a step-by-step practical guide on how to work effectively with clients in a variety of settings. There are many case examples and practice opportunities woven throughout the text. This text works great in courses in which students are given opportunities to practice what they are reading through role-plays with one another, or with actual clients, under the supervision of the instructor or other mental health counselors. It has been useful for professionals such as police, firefighters, military personnel, as well as mental health counselors.

Organizing Features

I have included many real-world examples and sample scripts for students throughout the text. Over the years, I have found that students benefit from seeing what others actually say during counseling sessions. They can then practice similar types of comments when they conduct role-play sessions.

I have also presented the major theory behind crises, and then how the theory is utilized when conducting crisis intervention. Connecting theory with practice helps students better understand both and systematically learn how theoretical constructs are put into practice. Once theory is presented, students are provided with a detailed description of the ABC Model of Crisis Intervention. In order to practice that model, students are then provided with various chapters that deal with specific client populations, their needs, and how to implement the ABC Model with that type of client.

Pedagogical Aids

Each chapter includes a brief pre-chapter quiz. Students will be able to assess their knowledge of the material prior to reading the chapter and then again after they have studied the material. These quizzes also introduce the students to the chapter itself. At the end of each chapter is a chapter review and key terms for study that will aid in preparing for exams.

Boxes have been inserted through the book to highlight interesting new case examples and scripts. Tables, diagrams, and figures have also been inserted to keep students focused on essential theoretical and clinical material.

In chapters dealing with client populations, case vignettes to practice are placed at the end of the chapter. Included with these are specific ideas such as precipitating events, cognitions, emotional distress, impairments in functioning, suicidality, and therapeutic interaction statements so that the student can more easily practice the ABC Model with other students.

New to This Edition

As I have revised the text over the years, I have included new information as the world has changed, and as various traumas have been experienced by many of us. For example, my second edition included the issues surrounding the effects of 9/11, and the third edition included information about the Katrina disaster. In this fourth edition, I had included data based on my own research study related to the types of crisis experiences described by the returning military personnel who were stationed in Iraq and Afghanistan. This fifth edition has an entire chapter devoted to just veteran issues since the drawdown of troops will no doubt create a need for mental health workers to help this population. This will be a group that more and more mental health counselors will be working with in the coming decade.

I have also separated out sexual assault from child abuse, elder abuse, and intimate partner abuse. Chapter 9 deals with sexual assault in general as well as Military Sexual Trauma. I have condensed the introductory chapter with the chapter related to the history of crisis intervention and have included multicultural issues in the chapter on ethics. The chapter on loss includes a section on financial loss and job loss.

I have included a section on bullying in the developmental crises chapter as it relates to adolescence as well. In the chapter on community disaster, I have included much information on gun violence.

Ancillaries to Accompany the Text

There is an instructor's manual that includes a section on how to teach the course I have taught for 27 years, test items for instructors to use (both multiple choice and essay style) and a description of the lectures for each chapter. Also available is a PowerPoint slide presentation and quiz items for students. These materials can be accessed through the instructor's companion site at login.cengage.com. For access, please contact your Cengage Learning sales representative.

Acknowledgments

I so appreciate the energy and efforts of the many reviewers of this text over the years. For this edition I would like to thank Cecile Brennan, John Carroll University; Julie Hayden, Southern California Seminary; Lisa Marucci, Ryerson University, Toronto; Lindee Petersen Wilson, Avila University; Michael Poulakis, University of Indianapolis; Christopher Roseman, University of Toledo; and Scharie Tavcer, Mount Royal University.

Lastly, I give much appreciation to my students who have provided me with invaluable feedback over the years about what aspects of the text help and hinder them. I have tried to eliminate any hindering aspects and strengthen the helping aspect.

About the Author

Dr. Kristi Kanel has been a teacher, practitioner, and scholar of human services for over 30 years. She has been a college professor for the past 30 years. She helped create the first crisis intervention course at California State University, Fullerton, in 1986 and has been teaching the course since then. She also teaches several courses in counseling theory and client populations.

Throughout her career as a human services practitioner, Dr. Kanel has worked at a free clinic as a counselor, interned with the Orange County Board of Supervisors as an executive assistant, worked as a mental health worker and specialist for the County Mental Health agency, worked as a clinical supervisor at a battered women's shelter, and provided psychotherapy for individuals, families, and groups in private practice and at a large health maintenance organization. She has worked extensively with victims of child abuse, partner violence, and sexual assault. Additionally, she has worked with Spanish-speaking Latinos and has conducted research related to the needs of this population. She specializes in crisis intervention and has conducted research on the most effective approach to working with people in crisis.

Dr. Kanel earned her Ph.D. in Counseling Psychology from the University of Southern California, her Master of Counseling degree from California State University, Fullerton, and her Bachelor of Science degree in Human Services from California State University, Fullerton.

She enjoys the outdoors, zumba dancing, biking, Rollerblading, spinning, singing, and beaching.

Chapter

1

What Is a Crisis and Crisis Intervention?

At the beginning of each chapter, the reader is encouraged to respond to 10 or more quiz items that provide a brief introduction to the chapter. Place a T if the item is true and an F if it is false. The correct responses are at the end of the chapter following the chapter summaries.

_____ 1. The cognitive key refers to the emotions one deals with during a crisis.

_____ 2. A stressor that triggers a crisis is often referred to as a precipitating event.

_____ 3. There is no possible benefit when one goes through a crisis.

_____ 4. It is always best to stifle emotions during a crisis.

_____ 5. Some anxiety helps motivate people to work through a crisis.

_____ 6. Ego strength refers to how vain someone is.

_____ 7. A major goal of crisis intervention is to increase functioning.

_____ 8. Stress is a natural occurrence in most people's lives.

_____ 9. Crisis intervention began during the HMO movement of the 1980s.

_____ 10. Nonprofessionals were used to provide crisis intervention at the Wellesley Project.

_____ 11. Crisis intervention has long been considered an inferior form of treatment by county mental health centers.

_____ 12. Cognitive-behavioral models have contributed much to the practice of crisis intervention.

_____ 13. Brief therapy is synonymous with crisis intervention.

_____ 14. Humanistic models have very little impact on the practice of crisis intervention.

Crisis Defined

The term **crisis** can be defined in a variety of ways. **Gerald Caplan**, often referred to as the Father of Modern Crisis Intervention, described a crisis as "an obstacle that is, for a time, insurmountable by the use of customary methods of problem solving. A period of disorganization ensues, a period of upset, during which many abortive attempts at a solution are made" (1961, p. 18). In its simplest form, according to Caplan, "it is an upset in the steady state of the individual" (p. 18). James and Gilliland (2013) offer nine definitions for an individual crisis. Most of these focus on a situation that an individual cannot respond to in an effective way leaving the person in a state of emotional and psychological imbalance. The definition of a crisis referred to throughout this book contains four components based on Caplan's definition and on more modern cognitive-behavioral approaches such as Ellis's Rational Emotive Behavior Therapy (Ellis, 1994) and Beck's Cognitive Therapy (Beck, 1976). These aspects will be essential when conducting the ABC Model of Crisis Intervention to be described in detail in Chapter 3 and mentioned briefly in this chapter. The four parts of a crisis as used in this text are: (1) a precipitating event occurs; (2) a person has a perception of the event as threatening or damaging; (3) this perception leads to **emotional distress**; and (4) the emotional distress leads to impairment in functioning due to failure of an individual's usual **coping methods** that previously have prevented a crisis from occurring.

These components of a crisis must be recognized and understood because they are the elements the crisis counselor will be identifying and helping the client to overcome. The perception of the event is by far the most crucial part to identify, for it is the part that can be most easily and quickly altered by the counselor. It is the focus in this definition, and the point that differentiates crisis intervention from most other forms of counseling.

By keeping this particular definition in mind, the crisis worker can perform the necessary services in a brief time. Whereas other forms of counseling may focus on building self-esteem, personality modification, or even extinguishing maladaptive behaviors, in crisis intervention the focus is on increasing the client's functioning. This is addressed in detail in Chapter 3; for now, two useful formulas for the crisis interventionist are provided: Figure 1.1 provides the essential definition of how a crisis state occurs, and Figure 1.2 presents the process for leading a client out of a crisis. It will be shown later in this chapter how Caplan's characteristics of effective coping people corresponds with the formula in Figure 1.2.

FIGURE 1.1   Formula for Understanding the Process of Crisis Formation

Precipitating event	$\longrightarrow$	Perception	$\longrightarrow$	Emotional distress	$\longrightarrow$	Lowered functioning when coping fails

FIGURE 1.2   Formula for Increasing Functioning

Change in perception of the precipitating event and acquiring new coping skills	$\longrightarrow$	Decrease in emotional distress	$\longrightarrow$	Increase in functioning

(Both figures developed by K. Kanel, 2013)

Notice that the method involves changing the perception of the precipitating event. Obviously, it is not possible to change the precipitating event. The best one can do is work at changing or altering the client's cognitions and perceptions of the event, offer referrals to supportive agencies, and suggest other coping strategies. These ideas are explored further in subsequent chapters.

One additional thought about crises in general: The word *crisis* often conjures images of panic, emergency, and feeling out of control. Sometimes this is true as in the case of natural disasters, bombing, shootings, and personal attacks. However at other times, crises may be viewed as a normal part of life. Crises occur in the lives of normal, average individuals who are just having difficulty coping with **stress**; therefore, they represent a state to which most of us can relate.

Crisis as Both Danger and Opportunity

Some crisis states are seen by many as somewhat normal developments that occur episodically during "the normal life span of individuals" (Janosik, 1986, p. 3). Whether the individual comes out of any crisis state productively or unproductively depends on how he or she deals with it. In Chinese, crisis means both danger and opportunity (see Figure 1.3). This dichotomous meaning highlights the potentially beneficial as well as the potentially hazardous aspects of a crisis state. A person might face the challenge of the precipitating event adaptively, or might respond with a neurotic disturbance, psychotic illness, or even death.

FIGURE 1.3 Danger or Opportunity

DANGER

or

OPPORTUNITY

(Obusnsha's Handy English-Japanese Dictionary, 1983)

According to Caplan (1961, p. 19), "Growth is preceded by a state of imbalance or crisis that serves as the basis for future development. Without crisis, development is not possible. As a person strives to achieve stability during a crisis, the coping process itself can help him or her reach a qualitatively different level of stability. This state of stability may be either a higher or lower **functioning level** than the person had before the crisis occurred" (see Figure 1.4).

Box 1.1 provides an example of how a rape victim's crisis might create a lowered level of functioning if she doesn't receive help; hence *danger*.

FIGURE 1.4 Crisis as Both Opportunity and Danger

OPPORTUNITY

Help ⟶ Higher level of functioning

⟶ Growth, insight, coping skills

Normal functioning interrupted by
1. Precipitating event
2. Perceived as threatening
3. Emotional distress
4. Impairment in functioning due to failure of coping

⟶ Drop in level of functioning

DANGER

1. **No help** ⟶ Lower level of functioning
   or
2. **No help** ⟶ Nonfunctioning level

⟶ Greater vulnerability, disequilibrium

⟶ Suicide, homicide, psychosis

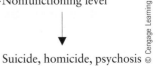

Box 1.1   Example of Crisis as Danger

After having been raped, a woman might not seek help or even tell anyone about the trauma. About a month after the violation, she may slip into a state of denial, with reduced contact with the world, lowered trust levels, increased substance abuse, poor interpersonal relations, and a state of dissociation. However, she may continue to be able to work, go to school, put on a front with family and friends, and appear to function normally. In reality, however, she is functioning at a lower level than she did before the rape and will be somewhat impaired until she gets intervention. The longer she waits to get help, the more resistant she will be to it because of the amount of energy she will have invested in the denial process. She may exist in a chronic state of depression, lowered trust toward people, and anxiety, which would affect interpersonal functioning.

Crisis as Opportunity

Even if a person receives no outside intervention or help, the crisis state will eventually cease, usually within four to six weeks. A crisis is by nature a time-limited event because a person cannot tolerate extreme tension and psychological disequilibrium for more than a few weeks (Caplan, 1964; Janosik, 1986, p. 9; Roberts, 1990; Slaikeu, 1990, p. 21). Although a person's character influences how he or she emerges from a crisis, that is, either stronger or weaker, seeking and receiving focused help during the crisis state has a much bigger impact on the person. In the midst of a crisis, a person is more receptive to suggestions and help than he or she is in a steady state. A crisis worker can gain significant leverage at this time because of greater client vulnerability. Instead of stabilizing at a lowered level of functioning, an individual who receives help is likely to stabilize at a higher, more adaptive level of functioning, learning coping skills that might prepare him or her for future stresses.

An example of how receiving help soon after a trauma would be more beneficial than waiting years or getting no help at all might be in the case of sexual abuse of a child. It seems fairly obvious that a 3-year-old girl brought in for counseling after being molested one time will respond better than a 30-year-old woman who was molested at age three and perhaps longer due to lack of reporting it and has repressed acknowledgment of the molestation for 27 years.

An important aspect of client vulnerability during crises is the ethics and integrity of the crisis worker. It would be easy for an unscrupulous worker to take advantage of a client in crisis. There are many other ethical concerns that a crisis worker may face besides client vulnerability. Chapter 2 is devoted to a multitude of ethical issues.

Once a client has returned to a previous, or higher, level of functioning, he or she may opt to continue with therapy. Brief therapy is a reasonably cost-effective approach for dealing with aspects of life that have plagued a person regularly but have not necessarily caused a crisis state. A counselor may work with an individual for 6 to 20 sessions and obtain excellent results in behavioral and emotional changes. Once a person has benefited from crisis intervention, he or she is often more open to continuing work on additional in-depth personal issues because of increased trust in the therapeutic process and the therapist. The choice to continue in postcrisis counseling will of course depend on financial resources and time availability.

Crisis as Danger: Becoming a Crisis-Prone Person

Not everyone who experiences a stressor in life will succumb to a crisis state. No one is certain why some people cope with stress easily, whereas others deteriorate into disequilibrium. Several explanations seem plausible. Figure 1.5 expands on Figure 1.4 to include the crisis-prone person. If a person does not

FIGURE 1.5   Crisis as Danger: The Development of the Crisis-Prone Person

Higher functioning level:
growth, coping skills learned for use with future stressors

↑

Receives help

State of disequilibrium

Receives no help

↓

Lower functioning:
defense mechanisms

New stressor hits; lack of ego strength
to cope with it leads to new crisis state

↓

NO HELP
Lower functioning than before, fewer coping
skills for future stressors

New stressor hits

↓

Another state of disequilibrium

↓

Lower level of functioning, death or psychosis,
severe personality disorder

(Developed by K. Kanel, 2013)

© Cengage Learning

receive adequate crisis intervention during a crisis state but instead comes out of the crisis by using ego defense mechanisms such as repression, denial, or dissociation, the person is likely to function at a lower level than he or she did before the stressful event. The ego, which has been hypothesized to be the part of the mind that masters reality in order to function (Gabbard, 2000), must then use its strength to maintain the denial of the anxiety or pain associated with the precipitating event. Such effort takes away the individual's strength to deal with future stressors, so that another crisis state may develop the next time a stressor hits. This next crisis state may be resolved by more ego defense mechanisms after several weeks, leading to an even lower level of functioning if the person does not receive adequate crisis intervention.

This pattern may go on for many years until the person's ego is completely drained of its capacity to deal with reality. Such people often commit suicide, harm others, or have psychotic breakdowns. These individuals are sometimes viewed as having personality disorders. People with personality disorders are usually seen as suffering from emotional instability, an inability to master reality, poor interpersonal and occupational functioning, and chronic depression (Gabbard, 2000). Defense mechanisms and substance abuse are common behaviors people use to overcome crisis states instead of seeking professional help. People who receive help before resorting to defense mechanisms may avoid developing a personality disorder.

Traditional psychotherapy has usually been the course of counseling implemented with people suffering from personality disorders. In today's economy and with health maintenance organizations (HMOs) dictating mental health treatment, clinicians often cannot take the traditional road with crisis-prone people. Because short-term treatment is the only service offered in most settings, it is essential to begin working with people as soon as possible after the crisis state sets in to prevent a chronic cycle from developing.

Other Factors Determining Danger or Opportunity

Other factors may also determine whether a crisis presents a danger or an opportunity. These factors are generally found in the client's own environment. In addition to receiving outside help, having access to (1) material resources, (2) personal resources, and (3) social resources seems to determine the level an individual reaches after a crisis.

Material Resources   **Material resources** include things such as money, shelter, food, transportation, and clothing. Money may not buy love, but it does make life easier during a crisis. For example, a battered woman with minimal material resources (money, food, housing, and transportation) may suffer more in a crisis than a woman with her own income and transportation. A woman with material resources has the choice of staying at a hotel or moving into her own apartment. She can drive to work, to counseling sessions, and to court. The woman with no material resources will struggle to travel to sessions and will have to be dependent on others. Her freedom to choose wherever and whenever she goes will be largely decided by those on whom she depends. According to Maslow's (1970) hierarchy of needs, material needs must be met before the other needs of personal integration and social contact can receive attention. Not until she is housed, fed, and safe can the battered woman begin to resolve the psychological aspect of the crisis.

It is important to remember that despite financial and other material resources, people with material resources are not immune to suffering. They may at times suffer more than those with fewer resources because of various psychological and social factors, the duration and severity of the victimization, or other precipitating events.

Personal Resources   After her material needs are met, the woman can begin to work through the crisis. Her **personal resources**, such as ego strength, previous history of coping with stressful situations, absence of personality problems, and physical well-being, will help determine how well she copes on her own and how she accepts and implements intervention.

If the ego is the part of our mind that carries the ability to understand the world realistically and act on that understanding to get one's needs and wishes met, then **ego strength** refers to how well one can do this on a regular basis and in times of stress. At times a crisis worker will serve as a client's ego strength (as when a person is psychotic or severely depressed) until the client can take over for himself or herself. These clients can neither see reality clearly nor put into action realistic coping behaviors. They need someone to structure their behavior until the crisis is managed successfully, often with medication, family intervention, and individual counseling. When someone has coped successfully in the past with various stressors, then usually his or her ego strength is high. However, when someone does not cope successfully with stressors, the person's ego strength is lowered (see Figure 1.5). A crisis worker must "tune into" a client's level of mastering reality in order to set up realistic goals and problem-solving strategies.

Certain personality traits may interfere with coping and also with accepting intervention. Some people have problems accepting help or being strong. Others are paranoid or avoid conflict. These people present challenges to counselors, in contrast to clients who are open and trusting.

A client's physical well-being also affects how well he or she deals with crises. Healthy people have more energy and greater ability to use personal and social resources. The ability to move about and exercise is essential in coping with stress. Disabled and sick clients must constantly cope with their conditions, and so when stress occurs, they simply do not have as much psychological energy to deal with it as physically healthy individuals do.

A person's level of intelligence and education also affects the outcome of a crisis state. Well-educated people are better able to use cognitive reframes and logical arguments to help them integrate traumas psychologically. People with lower IQs have more difficulty understanding events and their reactions to events, and may be less flexible when solving problems.

Social Resources   A person's **social resources** also affect the outcome of a crisis. A person with strong support from family, friends, church, work, and school has natural help available, provided these support systems are healthy. A lone individual struggles more during a crisis and tends to depend on outside support systems such as professional counselors, hotlines, emergency rooms, and physicians. Part of the crisis worker's responsibility is to link clients with their natural support systems so their dependency on mental health workers is reduced. Knowledge of support groups such as twelve-step self-help groups is vital to a counselor's effective intervention. Clients without much natural support can participate in these groups indefinitely, and the twelve-step group may become a natural support resource. The use of twelve-step groups will be explored in Chapter 3.

Precipitating Events

Personal crises have identifiable beginnings or **precipitating events**. These can be new adjustments in the family, loss of a loved one, loss of one's health, contradictions and stresses involved in acculturation, normal psychosocial stages of development, or unexpected situational stressors. Perhaps the most important aspect of any crisis is how the person perceives the situation. The meaning given to the event or adjustment determines whether the person can cope with the added stress. This meaning has been termed the **cognitive key** (Slaikeu, 1990, p. 18). It is the key with which the counselor unlocks the door to understanding the nature of the client's crisis. Once the helper identifies the cognitive meanings the client ascribes to the precipitating events, the helper can work actively to reframe these cognitions. This new way of perceiving the event aids the client in reducing emotional distress and increasing coping abilities.

The way the precipitating event interacts with the person's life view is what makes a situation critical. If people cannot cope with new situations by using their usual mechanisms, a state of disequilibrium will occur. However, if their cognitive perspective of a potential hazard or precipitating event allows people to relieve the stress effectively and resolve the problem, the crisis will not occur in the first place.

Stress is different from crisis, though the two terms are often confused. When a person experiences a negative precipitating event, suffers from negative emotions, but does not experience impairment in functioning due to being able to cope with it, he or she is probably suffering from daily or normal stress. Stress is part of modern life; in fact, it is part of daily life. This does not mean that crises are part of daily life, however, because people typically cope with stress without falling apart emotionally. Even if people undergoing stress experience some emotional distress, if they have the coping skills to master the stress, their functioning level will not be impaired, and hence, a crisis state will not ensue.

For conceptual purposes, we can describe two types of crises: developmental and situational.

Developmental Crises

Developmental crises are normal, transitional phases that are expected as people move from one stage of life to another. They take years to develop and require adjustments from the family as members take on new roles. James and Gilliland (2013) suggest that developmental crises are part of the normal flow of human growth in which change occurs and people respond abnormally. Developmental crises will be explored in a subsequent chapter. Clients often seek counseling because of their inability to cope with the evolving needs of one or more family members. Effective crisis workers are sensitive to the special issues surrounding this type of precipitating event.

Situational Crises

Situational crises "emerge when uncommon and extraordinary events occur that an individual has no way of forecasting or controlling" (James & Gilliland, 2013, p. 16). Some examples of situational crises are crime, rape, death, divorce, illness, and community disaster. The chief characteristics that differentiate these from developmental crises are their (1) sudden onset, (2) unexpectedness, (3) emergency quality, and (4) potential impact on the community (Slaikeu, 1990, pp. 64–65). Situational crises are discussed in detail in the second half of this book.

Emotional Distress

A rise in anxiety is a typical reaction to the initial impact of a hazardous event. A person may experience shock, disbelief, distress, and panic (e.g., stage 1 of Rape Trauma Syndrome, stage 1 of Kübler-Ross's stages of death and dying). If this initial anxiety is not resolved, the person may experience a period of disorganization (e.g., stage 2 of Rape Trauma Syndrome). During this phase, a rape victim, for instance, often experiences feelings of guilt, anger, helplessness, hopelessness, dissociation, confusion, and fatigue, leaving her in a vulnerable state. She is unable to function at her previous level at work, school, or home. Ironically, in certain circumstances anxiety has the power to generate energy and increase coping abilities, as when a child is in danger and a parent has a surge of adrenaline that helps him or her rescue the child, or when a natural disaster hits and people have the increased physical strength and endurance to carry bodies and sandbags.

Anxiety, however, seems to fit the **curvilinear model** (see Figure 1.6) in that too much or too little leaves a person in a state of inertia or with undirected and disintegrative energy (Janosik, 1986, p. 30).

When the anxiety level is moderate and manageable, the crisis worker can use it to help motivate the client to make changes. In sum, anxiety is not always a bad thing; it is considered necessary, at moderate levels, to spur people to make changes in their lives.

FIGURE 1.6 Curvilinear Model of Anxiety as Motivator for Change

Moderate anxiety
(highest level of performance)
(optimal motivation)

Low/very little anxiety **High anxiety**
(inertia/low motivation) (overwhelmed paralysis)

© Cengage Learning

Anxiety is an internal experience; therefore, interventions might first be aimed at alleviating the internal component of stress. This action makes sense because the external component of a crisis often cannot be undone. The only remedy for emotional distress is to change the internal experience.

Changing the internal experience as a remedy for distress can be done in several ways. One would be to medicate the person (e.g., inject a tranquilizer) to relieve the anxiety or grief. The benefit of this intervention is immediate reduction in emotional distress. Sometimes clients cannot benefit from cognitive crisis intervention because their anxiety or grief is too great; in these cases, medication can provide temporary relief until their cognitions can be altered. Crisis workers often work jointly with psychiatrists when medication is necessary. The crisis worker might call a psychiatrist or physician that he or she has worked with in the past to create a bridge for the client with the psychiatrist. At other times, the crisis worker might consult over the phone with a physician and set up a relationship in which the psychiatrist and crisis worker feel comfortable having ongoing communication while both are working with the client. Some agencies employ both counselors and psychiatrists. In these cases, it is rather simple for the crisis worker to work jointly with the psychiatrist because both workers generally get together during regularly scheduled staff meetings. It is not uncommon for colleagues at agencies to "pop" into each others' offices from time to time to engage in "informal" communication about the progress of mutual clients. No matter which way crisis workers choose to engage with a psychiatrist or a client's primary care physician, it is wise to be knowledgeable about the medications being prescribed and to let the physician take the lead in medication management.

Unfortunately, some of the medications given for distress do not take effect for 10 days to 3 weeks (i.e., antidepressants). Expecting a "magical" cure from medication must be discouraged, although if clients believe medication will eventually help, they may have increased hope, which in itself may lower the emotional distress. Kirsch (2010) suggests that the placebo effect is probably just as beneficial for mild or moderate depression as taking an antidepressant, so an individual might feel better soon after taking a pill if they believe it will help them.

The crisis worker, however, would not want to rid clients of all emotional distress too soon without helping them change their perception of the precipitating event or without encouraging coping behaviors. Without discomfort, clients are not as motivated to change. The crisis counselor depends on clients to be in a state of disequilibrium and vulnerability if cognitive change and behavioral change are to occur. Clients with good ego strength and no history of mental illness can often work through a crisis without any medication. Some people, though, absolutely need medication, and knowing when the situation calls for more than just talk therapy is a helpful skill for crisis workers.

The decision of whether medication is needed is up to a psychiatrist or even a primary care physician. The crisis worker can discuss his or her treatment plan with the psychiatrist and how medication fits into it. Often, the psychiatrist will have suggestions for the counselor and can be a valuable resource for clients. Keeping an open mind about medication can benefit your clients.

For clients who do not seem to need medication to relieve emotional distress, the internal experience is best changed through cognitive restructuring, discussed in subsequent chapters. Some clients may also be able to implement recommended behavioral changes, which can be done in a number of ways.

The essential idea to remember is to keep the focus not on changing precipitating events but rather the way in which clients experience them. Changing perceptions will lower clients' emotional distress and increase their functioning levels. Offering coping strategies also aids in lowering emotional distress and increases functioning.

Failure of Coping Methods and Impairment in Functioning

The final component of a crisis state refers to a person's inability to cope with the emotional distress leading to a decrease in functioning. When people in crisis are experiencing feelings of bewilderment, confusion, and conflict, they are in a vulnerable position. They lack skills to improve their situation. The ability to perform at work, at school, and in social situations may be impaired. Likewise, there may be a change in one's eating, sleeping, and everyday tasks, which are often referred to as "tasks of daily living." People sometimes try to fix these impairments on their own, but when they cannot, they may seek help, adapt through the use of ego defenses, dive into a deep depression, or unfortunately, attempt or succeed at killing themselves. Thus, the urgency to get them intervention as soon as possible when they enter a crisis state is clear.

The Wellesley Project: The Development of Crisis Intervention

Eric Lindemann (1944) introduced the first major community mental health program that focused on crisis intervention. He studied the grief reactions experienced by relatives of victims injured or killed in the **Coconut Grove fire** in Boston, on November 28, 1942. On that night, 493 people perished as the Coconut Grove nightclub burned. It was the single largest building fire in U.S. history. As Lindemann joined others from Massachusetts General Hospital to help survivors who had lost loved ones, he came to believe that clergy and other community caretakers could help people with **grief work.** Before this time, only psychiatrists and psychologists had provided services for those with anxiety and depression, symptoms that were thought to stem from personality disorders or biochemical illnesses.

After his study, Lindemann worked with **Gerald Caplan** to establish a communitywide mental health program in Cambridge, Massachusetts, that became known as the **Wellesley Project.** They worked at first with individuals who had suffered traumatic events such as sudden bereavement or the birth of a premature child. This focus on working with women dealing with the grief of either the death of an infant or the birth of an infant with abnormalities was most likely influenced by the baby boom, which began during the late 1940s, after World War II had ended. Millions of women were pregnant, and some had complications with their pregnancies. Physicians were experimenting with a new drug, thalidomide, that prevented morning sickness. Unfortunately, the drug also led to birth defects and other complications. Women who had taken the drug and whose babies had birth defects needed a way to deal with their trauma.

Caplan's focus on **preventive psychiatry,** in which early intervention was provided to promote positive growth and minimize the chance of psychological impairment, led to an emphasis on mental health consultation (Slaikeu, 1990, p. 7). It may seem hard to believe that the term *crisis intervention* hadn't even been thought of at that time in history. Caplan's approach began a trend toward short-term, directive, and focused crisis intervention. Interestingly, much of current-day crisis intervention theory has come from the Wellesley Project.

In his research at the Wellesley Project, Caplan (1964, p. 18) discovered certain people were able to cope with the situation better than others. He describes **seven characteristics of effective coping behavior** that were displayed by those who were able to climb out of their crisis state and of those who didn't enter into a crisis (see Table 1.1).

TABLE 1.1 Caplan's Seven Characteristics of Effective Coping Behavior

1. Actively exploring reality issues and searching for information
2. Freely expressing both positive and negative feelings and tolerating frustration
3. Actively invoking help from others
4. Breaking problems into manageable bits and working through them one at a time
5. Being aware of fatigue and pacing coping efforts while maintaining control in as many areas of functioning as possible
6. Mastering feelings where possible; being flexible and willing to change
7. Trusting in oneself and others and having a basic optimism about the outcome

Source: Caplan, G. (1964). Principles of preventive psychiatry. New York: Basic Books.

Once a client's emotional distress has been lowered to a manageable level, the crisis worker may offer coping strategies. These range from referrals to agencies, groups, doctors, and lawyers, to reading, journaling, and exercising. Caplan's seven characteristics of effective coping behavior can guide the counselor in creatively constructing a treatment plan that changes cognitions, lowers emotional distress, and increases functioning. Throughout this book references will be made to these characteristics as they relate to the ABC Model of Crisis Intervention.

Crisis Intervention and Suicide Prevention Strengthen Nationwide

In the early 1960s, the crisis intervention trend gave rise to the suicide prevention movement. This movement grew rapidly, and many community centers offered 24-hour hotlines. These centers developed out of the social-activist mentality of the 1960s and Caplan's theory. They relied on nonprofessional volunteers for their telephone counseling programs. Caplan's focus on critical life crises attracted nontraditionalists, who were dissatisfied with medical-model and psychoanalytic treatments. Many nonprofit organizations specializing in the treatment of certain personal crises evolved from such **grassroots programs** as free clinics for abortion of unwanted pregnancies, battered women's shelters, rape centers, and AIDS centers.

Parallel to the suicide prevention movement was the community mental health movement in the United States. In 1955, there were over 500,000 patients in mental hospitals, which was the highest in U.S. history. With the introduction and widespread use of psychiatric medications such as Thorazine and lithium in the 1950s, patients who suffered from chronic mental illness could be managed in the community, which led to the deinstitutionalization of the mentally ill over the ensuing two decades. Consequently, the same population of the mentally ill was down to about 200,000 (Cutler, Bevilacqua, & McFarland, 2003). In 1955 Congress established a Joint Commission on Mental Illness and Health and found that three out of every four individuals treated for mental illness were in public mental hospitals, and by 1960, the Joint Commission recommended that the mentally ill be cared for in the community and that federal financial assistance would be provided to the states to accomplish this (Library of Congress, retrieved 12/20/2012). President Kennedy was very interested in community mental health as there was someone in his own family with a mental disability, and in 1963 he proposed a new National Mental Health Program.

Community Mental Health Act of 1963

The goal of **Community Mental Health Act of 1963** was that by 1980 there would be one community mental health center per 100,000 individuals, or 2,000 such centers nationwide. In 1967 Congress reaffirmed the goal of having

2,000 community mental health centers built, but by 1980 there were only 768 centers, which may have been the cause of the high homeless population among the mentally ill. Kennedy also emphasized the need to provide services to children, families, and adults suffering from the effect of stress and programs were to be comprehensive and available to anyone (Cutler et al., 2003). In subsequent years, states have developed their own laws and ethical standards to implement community mental health programs, and not without controversy in some areas. Some of the specific natures of these controversies (including involuntary confinement and the definition of "dangerous") will be explored in Chapter 2, which deals with ethics, laws, and the mentally ill. A major part of the community effort was the development of the 24-hour emergency service, which became known as **Psychiatric Emergency Treatment (PET)** services. Most community mental health services are still based on the 1963 act. Procedures for dealing with psychotic, suicidal, and homicidal crises and the ways such crises relate to community mental health are discussed in Chapter 4.

In the late 1960s and early 1970s, journals such as *Crisis Intervention* and *Journal of Life-Threatening Behavior*, which dealt specifically with crisis topics, were published. Crisis intervention became more valued in the 1970s as economic conditions led to greater use of community resources (Slaiku, 1990, p. 8). In the 1970s, there was a growing antimedical attitude in mental health centers. There was an increase in the number of psychologists, nurses, and master's-level workers serving in mental health. Psychiatrists were leaving these centers and being replaced by other types of mental health workers (Cutler et al., 2003) who could be paid at lower rates than psychiatrists and could efficiently provide crisis management and case management services.

During this time, the country also saw an increase in university and college programs in which curricula focused on psychology and counseling. Many **paraprofessionals** who had previously staffed community mental health centers went to college to become professional therapists. Soon, the profession of licensed therapy was big business. Insurance companies paid for counseling services offered by individuals with master's degrees; this led to a rise in the number of people seeking mental health counseling as well as to complaints by insurance companies about the financial burden.

The Rise of Managed Care

The complaints resulted in managed care by indemnity insurance companies. Insurance companies no longer paid for patients to stay in therapy as long as clinicians felt necessary.

The short-term crisis intervention model is by far the most cost effective and, thus, the approach sought by most **health maintenance organizations (HMOs)**, preferred provider organizations (PPOs), and other insurance carriers in today's mental health treatment community. This type of payment for services became confusing as state-operated Medicaid programs began to emerge. Public funding and private funding became integrated and although many poor people were eligible for public welfare, an estimated 40 million people had no coverage at all, leaving them without any third-party payer for health services. By the 1990s, community mental health programs came under government scrutiny. Once the Clinton initiative for a single-payer system failed, finding fraud seemed to be the main purpose of the federal government in dealing with mental health services. In 1969, Gerald Caplan stated, "In a democratic capitalist country, individual psychiatrists have the freedom to decide how they will use their skills and make a living, but as corporate professionals, they must either be responsive to organized communal demands to deal with formally recognized population needs or they will incur sanctions and eventually be pushed aside in favor of some other profession, the development of which will be fostered in order to deal with the neglected problem" (Caplan & Caplan, 1969, p. 320). Currently, most managed care facilities, insurance companies, nonprofit agencies, and public mental health agencies (which have been relabeled as behavioral health agencies), focus on providing short-term, crisis, and emergency services. Understanding how to conduct crisis intervention is vital for modern-day counselors at all educational levels.

The Need for Nonprofessionals   A continuing controversy in the field of crisis intervention centers on the use of paraprofessionals to provide services to clients. Some licensed professionals believe that these workers, who have traditionally provided crisis intervention, do not have enough training to do intervention. Some professionals have proposed that only those with at least a master's degree should be allowed to provide services to those in crisis. Beigel (1984) suggested we should remedicalize community mental health centers, which has indeed happened in recent years because it is more cost effective to medicate than offer ongoing psychotherapy. One can often hear terms like "treat 'em and street 'em" on television shows and it is quite a negative approach to serving the mentally ill.

Such a move could have a negative impact on poorer communities that cannot afford the costs of this level of expertise, however, and it is a fact that not everyone needs medication to heal. Volunteer workers seem vital, especially during times of economic downturn. Understandably, politics and perhaps professional jealousy and fear play a part in the opposition to paraprofessional counseling. But, it is without doubt that many clients in need would go untreated if these workers were prohibited from practicing crisis intervention.

Many professional therapists are not aware of the historical foundations of crisis intervention, which was based on paraprofessional services during the Wellesley Project period. Although crisis intervention is used in most mental health offices, not all mental health workers have received specific training in the field. It is often included in other courses in graduate schools and other counseling preparatory colleges. Hence, students must provide crisis intervention based on their interpretation of how to shorten the traditional therapy process. Because crisis intervention is not often emphasized in traditional

TABLE 1.2 Time Line in the Development of Crisis Intervention

Time Frame	Development
1942	Coconut Grove nightclub fire; use of nonprofessionals to provide counseling
1946–1964	Baby boom; increase in stillbirths, birth defects, and miscarriages caused by thalidomide; WWII Shell Shock Syndrome
1950s	Psychotropic medications introduced; deinstitutionalization of the mentally ill
1963	Community Mental Health Act
1960s	Publication of professional journals related to suicide prevention and crisis intervention; increase in professional studies in psychology and counseling
1960s–1970s	Civil rights movement; grassroots movements; rise in nonprofit agencies; use of paraprofessionals
1970s–1980s	Increase in college programs offering psychology and counseling courses; professionalization of mental health; proliferation of licensed counselors; movement away from crisis intervention and toward traditional longer-term mental health counseling
1980s–1990s	Managed-care takeover of medical field, including mental health; return to crisis intervention in private industry and in community mental health

counseling and psychology graduate schools, many nonprofit agencies provide specific training in crisis intervention to ensure that nonprofessional volunteers can work effectively with clients.

One cannot say that traditional models have had no influence on crisis work. In fact, each traditional counseling approach has contributed to the field of crisis intervention. This seems reasonable considering that the founders of crisis intervention were themselves trained in these models. Table 1.2 provides an historical outline of events leading up to modern day crisis intervention.

Contributions from Other Theoretical Modalities

No single discipline or school of thought can claim crisis theory as its own, for this theory has been derived from a variety of sources. The result, therefore, is an eclectic mixture drawn from psychoanalytic, existential, humanistic, and cognitive-behavioral theories.

Psychoanalytic Theory

Psychoanalytic theory has contributed to the treatment of people in crisis. Sigmund Freud postulated an idea that is applicable to crisis intervention and crisis theory in his assumption that psychic energy is finite and that only a limited amount exists for each person. This assumption helps explain the disequilibrium that develops when customary coping skills fail and a person's psychological energy is depleted. It also helps explain why people with personality disorders, neuroses, and psychoses react poorly in a crisis: Much of their psychic energy is being used to maintain their disorder; they do not have the "spare" energy to combat unforeseen emergencies (Brenner, 1974, pp. 31–80).

In crisis theory, probably more than in any other psychological theory, the counselor is advised to assess the client's ego strength and at times take over the function of the ego. The concept of ego strength is directly related to psychic energy. People with personality disorders or psychotic disorders usually cannot cope effectively with precipitating events because their psychic energy is being used to deal with previous stressors, losses, and traumas.

Existential Theory

Existential theory has contributed to crisis treatment. Although true existential psychotherapy is a long-term therapy with the goal of basic revision of life perspective (Bugental, 1978, p. 13), some ideas are also useful in a short-term adjustment model. Certainly, the existential thought that anxiety is a normal part of existence and can help self-development is useful to the crisis worker. This idea coincides with the Chinese idea of **danger and opportunity**. Without anxieties caused by new life situations, people would never grow. Therefore, anxiety as a motivator for risk taking and growth is a key concept from existential theory that has contributed to crisis theory. The belief that all people will suffer in life at one time or another and that suffering can strengthen people can be used to reframe a crisis for the person experiencing it.

Another useful concept from existential theory relates to the acceptance of personal responsibility and realization that many problems are self-caused. Choice then becomes a major focus for the person in crisis. Empowering clients with choices and encouraging them to accept responsibility are useful strategies in many crisis situations. A person who has recently been confronted about his or her cocaine abuse can be helped to accept responsibility for his or her addiction. The worker can offer alternative choices and be supportive while the client struggles with the anxiety of withdrawing from the cocaine habit.

Humanistic Approach

The **humanistic approach** and person-centered therapies have much to offer crisis intervention. This style of helping stresses the importance of trusting clients to realize their potential in the context of a therapeutic relationship. Optimism and hope that clients will recognize and overcome blocks to growth are the foundations for trying to help someone work through a difficult situation (Bugental, 1978, pp. 35–36). If the crisis interventionist does not truly believe that his clients can work through their problems, why would he waste his efforts on them? True, clients may not resolve their difficulties his way, or in his time frame exactly, but he needs to respect clients at their level and work from there.

Carl Rogers, the founder of person-centered counseling (considered a humanistic therapy), has contributed to the field of crisis intervention by his focus on reflective and empathetic techniques. These techniques, shown to be effective in treatment outcome, help clients acknowledge and freely express their emotions (Corsini & Wedding, 1989, pp. 175–179). In addition to these outcomes, humanistic techniques create an environment that is special.

Practitioners of person-centered counseling believe that people can grow in a beneficial direction if they can experience a relationship of true acceptance, genuineness, and empathetic understanding. Crises are seen as blocks to growth and the potential for growth. By their presence, counselors help clients begin to accept themselves, trust in themselves, and make new choices based on this self-acceptance and trust.

Cognitive-Behavioral Theories

Every crisis model is based on the **behavioral problem-solving model**, which involves the following steps:

1. Define the problem
2. Review ways that you have already tried to correct the problem
3. Decide what you want when the problem is solved
4. Brainstorm alternatives
5. Select alternatives and commit to following through with them
6. Follow up

The **cognitive approaches** that blossomed in the 1970s and 1980s are also important in crisis work. As has previously been stated, a person's cognitions, meanings, and perspectives about the precipitating event are important in the counselor's determining the key to the crisis state. Cognitive approaches are largely based on Albert Ellis's Rational Emotive Behavior Therapy (Ellis, 1994), Beck's Cognitive Therapy (Beck, 1976), and Meichenbaum's Self-Instructional Training and Stress Inoculation Training (Meichenbaum, 1985). These approaches are concerned with understanding the person's cognitive view of the problem and then restructuring and reframing any maladaptive cognitions (Peake, Borduin, & Archer, 1988, pp. 69–71). Cognitive approaches stress homework assignments and follow-up.

Brief Therapy

Brief therapy may be confused with crisis intervention. It may be short term, but the focus is not only on increasing functioning. In this approach, clients explore past patterns of behavior and how the patterns have prevented them from succeeding in life in the way they have wanted to succeed. They may explore interpersonal relationships, self-concept, and family patterns. The focus is on creative change and incorporating new styles of relating to the world. Sometimes the precipitating event is the best thing that could happen to a person because it leads him or her to a counselor's office, where some chronic debilitating patterns can be identified. If past ineffective patterns can be recognized, they can be eliminated and the client can learn more effective behaviors for dealing with current as well as future stressors.

Brief therapy seems to be as effective as long-term therapy. According to Garfield (1980, p. 282), "The evidence to date suggests that time-limited marital family therapy is not inferior to open-ended treatment." The average length reported in his research was seven sessions, a number that certainly fits with crisis intervention philosophy.

Critical Incident Debriefing

Community disasters have been dealt with throughout the nation by a process referred to as **critical incident debriefing**. The Red Cross and state and county departments of mental health usually work in tandem to aid victims of unexpected trauma. Many of the coping strategies involved in this process are similar to the ABC Model of Crisis Intervention. The issues and interventions used in critical incident debriefing are presented in detail in a later chapter that deals with posttraumatic stress disorder in victims of natural disasters and other traumatic stressors.

The ABC Model of Crisis Intervention

The **ABC Model of Crisis Intervention** is useful in most nonprofit agencies, county agencies, hospitals, and HMOs and with most insurance plans. It is a convenient crisis interviewing technique that can be used either face-to-face or over the phone. It can be completed in a ten-minute phone conversation, in one session, or over six sessions.

The ABC model, developed by the author, is loosely based on Jones's (1968) ABC method of crisis management as well as on lecture notes from, and discussions with, Mary Moline at California State University, Fullerton, in the 1980s. Chapter 3 explores in detail the different aspects of the model. In general, the crisis intervention model is an action-oriented effort between a helper and a person immobilized by an emergency situation; the purpose is to provide temporary, but immediate, relief. This treatment differs from psychotherapy, which is usually a more intensive, introspective analysis between a professional therapist and a client; psychotherapy's goal is to provide self-understanding and reconstruction of long-standing personality traits and behavior (Cormier, Cormier, & Weisser, 1986, p. 19).

The focus of the ABC model is to identify the precipitating event, the client's cognitions about the precipitating event, emotional distress, failed coping mechanisms, and impaired function. Remember that these are the aspects of a crisis. The goal is to help the client integrate the precipitating event into his or her daily functioning and return to precrisis levels of emotional, occupational, and interpersonal functioning. Table 1.3 provides the contributions that various therapeutic approaches have given to crisis intervention.

TABLE 1.3 **Contributions from Counseling Models to the ABC Model of Crisis**

Intervention	
Theoretical Model	Contribution
Psychoanalytic	Finite psychic energy and ego strength
Existential	Responsibility; empowerment; choices; crisis as danger and opportunity for growth; anxiety as motivation
Humanistic	Rapport; safe climate; hope and optimism; basic attending skills
Cognitive-Behavioral	Focus on perceptions; reframing; goal setting; problem solving; follow-up

© Cengage Learning

Chapter Review

A crisis can be defined as a state in which a person is faced with a stressful event that precipitates emotional distress. The way in which a person perceives the event dictates whether negative emotions will be experienced. If the person cannot cope with the emotions and the thoughts about the event, impairment in daily functioning occurs. When a person cannot cope and return to normal functioning, he or she is in a crisis. The goal of crisis intervention is to increase the functioning level back to its normal level or higher, usually by helping the client perceive things differently and by offering the client coping skills. If a client doesn't seek help during a crisis state, there is a danger that he or she will come out of the crisis state and function at a lower level than before and is at risk of becoming **crisis prone**, suicidal, homicidal, or psychotic. When help is sought, the client often comes out of the crisis with increased coping skills and is often better prepared to cope with future stressors. Gerald Caplan is referred to as the Father of Modern Crisis Intervention and has identified seven characteristics of effective coping behaviors that crisis workers use to guide them in understanding people in crisis. Modern-day crisis intervention has its roots in the preventive psychiatry work developed by Gerald Caplan and Eric Lindemann after the Coconut Grove nightclub fire in the 1940s. They focused on the grief reactions of survivors and developed a model for brief, focused intervention using nonprofessionals at their Wellesley Project. The 1963 Community Mental Health Act funded centers throughout the country, which allowed for the deinstitutionalization of the mentally ill from public hospitals. During the 1960s and 1970s, the nation saw a proliferation of professional counseling programs and a tremendous increase in professional counselors staffing these mental health centers and setting up private offices to conduct more traditional, long-term therapies. Insurance companies and government agencies put a halt to this practice and insisted on a return to short-term, crisis-oriented therapy in both private and public mental health agencies. Crisis intervention has been influenced by the more traditional approaches to counseling such as the psychoanalytic, existential, humanistic, cognitive-behavioral, and brief therapy models. Modern-day trauma response interventions also have their roots in crisis work.

Answers to Pre-Chapter Quiz

1. F 2. T 3. F 4. F 5. T 6. F 7. T 8. T 9. F 10. T 11. F

12. T 13. F 14. F

Key Terms for Study

ABC Model of Crisis Intervention: One way to structure crisis intervention that includes (A) developing and maintaining contact, (B) identifying the problem, and (C) coping.

behavioral problem-solving model: Approach focusing on goal setting, problem solving, and brainstorming alternatives.

brief therapy: May be confused with crisis intervention, but focuses on changing longer-standing behavior patterns rather than on only the current precipitating event.

Caplan, Gerald: Known as the Father of Crisis Intervention. Worked with Eric Lindemann on the Wellesley Project after the Coconut Grove fire.

Caplan's Seven Characteristics of Effective Coping Behavior: Behaviors proposed by Gerald Caplan (1964) as essential for getting through a crisis state. They can be learned through formal crisis intervention, through experience, or while growing up. In any case, the crisis worker needs to acknowledge these characteristics and to transmit them to clients when possible.

Coconut Grove fire: Nightclub fire in 1942 in which over 400 people died, leaving many survivors in crisis; considered one of the major events leading to the development of crisis intervention as a form of mental health treatment.

cognitive approaches: Approaches focusing on a person's perceptions and thinking processes and how these lead to crisis states.

cognitive key: The perception a person has of the precipitating events that led to emotional distress. The crisis worker must identify the perception if he or she is to help the client change it and thereby increase functioning.

Community Mental Health Act of 1963: Legislation enacted during the Kennedy administration directing all states to provide mental health treatment for people in crisis.

coping methods: The behaviors, thinking, and emotional processes that a person uses to handle stress and continue to function.

crisis: A state of disequilibrium that occurs after a stressor (precipitating event). The person is then unable to function in one or more areas of his or her life because customary coping mechanisms have failed.

crisis prone: The condition that persists when people fail to grow from a crisis experience and instead deal with the crisis state by using ego defense mechanisms. They will be crisis prone because their ego strength will be weakened, leaving them unable to cope with future stresses.

critical incident debriefing: A process of helping victims of natural disasters and other unexpected trauma deal with loss and stress reactions.

curvilinear model of anxiety: Model showing that anxiety has the potential to be either a positive or a negative influence for someone in crisis. Too much anxiety may overwhelm the person and lead to lowered functioning. However, moderate anxiety may offer an opportunity for growth and transition from one stage of life to another or may motivate the person to grow from the experience of trauma. People who have no anxiety tend not to be motivated to make any changes at all.

danger and opportunity: Dichotomy associated with a crisis. A crisis can be an opportunity when the person grows by developing new coping skills and altering perceptions. It can be a danger when the person does not seek help and instead copes with the crisis state by using defense mechanisms, resulting in a lowered functioning level and possibly psychosis or even death.

developmental crises: Normal transitional stages that often trigger crisis states, which all people pass through while growing through the life span.

ego strength: The degree to which people can see reality clearly and meet their needs realistically. People with strong egos usually cope with stress better than people with weaker egos.

emotional distress: Painful and uncomfortable feelings experienced by a person in crisis.

existential theory: Theory from which crisis intervention took the ideas of choice and anxiety. The crisis worker believes that anxiety can be a motivator for change and encourages the client to master anxiety realistically by making choices and accepting responsibility for the choices.

Father of Modern Crisis Intervention: Title given to Gerald Caplan.

functioning level: The way a person behaves socially, occupationally, academically, and emotionally. The functioning level is impaired when a person is in a crisis. The goal of crisis intervention is to increase functioning to precrisis levels or higher.

grassroots programs: Upward movement from local groups that led to the creation in the 1960s and 1970s of many agencies to meet the needs of various populations not being helped by traditional governmental agencies.

grief work: Crisis intervention largely based on working with survivors and family members of victims of the Coconut Grove fire. It was with this population that Caplan and Lindemann learned how to conduct short-term interventions.

health maintenance organizations (HMOs): The current trend in health insurance. These organizations focus on maintaining health rather than curing illness. The orientation of mental health care under this style of management is definitely crisis intervention.

humanistic approach: Model using a person-centered approach in developing rapport with clients; counselor uses basic attending skills to focus on the inherent growth potential in the client.

Lindemann, Eric: Worked with Gerald Caplan on the Wellesley Project and helped create crisis intervention as it is known today; recognized for his contributions to grief work.

material resources: Tangible things such as money, transportation, clothes, and food. They constitute one determinant of how well a person is able to deal with a crisis.

paraprofessionals: Originally community volunteers. Because of the tremendous number of clients needing help at the same time after the Coconut Grove fire, it was necessary to employ community volunteers who were not professionally trained, to conduct crisis intervention sessions. These paraprofessionals became part of many agencies in later decades.

personal resources: Determinants of how well a person will deal with a crisis. They include intelligence, ego strength, and physical health.

precipitating event: An actual event in a person's life that triggers a crisis state that can be either situational or developmental.

preventive psychiatry: The term Caplan originally used to describe his work with the survivors of the Coconut Grove fire and others going through crises.

Psychiatric Emergency Team (PET): The professionals designated by a county/hospital to assess whether someone should be involuntarily hospitalized due to a mental disorder.

psychoanalytic theory: An approach considered the opposite of crisis intervention but with certain ideas useful for the crisis worker. The notion that we have only a certain amount of psychic energy to deal with life stressors leads us to keep our clients proceeding at a slow pace so they don't deplete this energy. Also, ego strength is a useful concept.

Rogers, Carl: Founder of person-centered therapy and well-known contributor to the humanistic approaches to counseling.

situational crises: Unexpected traumas having a sudden onset that impair one's functioning level.

social resources: A person's friends, family, and coworkers. The more resources one has, the better will one weather a crisis.

stress: A natural, though trying, part of life. A reaction to difficult events usually involving feelings of anxiety. Stressful events do not become crises if a person can cope with them and functioning is not impaired.

Wellesley Project: Developed by Caplan and Lindemann, the first organized attempt at introducing crisis intervention into a community.

References

Beck, A. T. (1976). *Cognitive therapy and emotional disorders.* New York: International Universities Press.

Beigel, A. (1984). The re-medicalization of community mental health. *Hospital and Community Psychiatry, 35,* 1114–1117.

Brenner, C. (1974). *An elementary textbook of psychoanalysis.* Garden City, NY: Anchor Books.

Bugental, J. F. T. (1978). *Psychotherapy and process: The fundamentals of an existential-humanistic approach.* New York: Random House.

Caplan, G. (1961). *An approach to community mental health.* New York: Grune & Stratton.

Caplan, G. (1964). *Principles of preventive psychiatry.* New York: Basic Books.

Caplan, R., & Caplan, G. (1969). *History of psychiatry in the 19th century.* New York: Basic Books.

Cormier, L. S., Cormier, W. H., & Weisser, R. J., Jr. (1986). *Interviewing and helping skills for health professionals.* Portola Valley, CA: Jones and Bartlett.

Corsini, R. J., & Wedding, D. (1989). *Current psychotherapies.* Itasca, IL: F. E. Peacock.

Cutler, D., Bevilacqua, J., & McFarland, B. (2003). Four decades of community mental health: A symphony in four movements. *Community Mental Health Journal, 39*(5), 381–398.

Ellis, A. (1994). *Reason and emotion in psychotherapy revised.* New York: Kensington.

Gabbard, G. O. (2000). *Psychodynamic psychiatry in clinical practice* (3rd ed.). Washington, DC: American Psychiatric Press, Inc.

Garfield, S. L. (1980). *Psychotherapy: An eclectic approach.* New York: John Wiley.

James, R. K., & Gilliland, B. E. (2013). *Crisis intervention strategies* (7th ed.). Pacific Grove, CA: Brooks/Cole.

Janosik, E. H. (1986). *Crisis counseling: A contemporary approach.* Monterey, CA: Jones and Bartlett.

Jones, W. (1968). The A-B-C method of crisis management. *Mental Hygiene, 52*, 87–89.

Kirsch, I. (2010). *The emperor's new drugs: Exploding the antidepressant myth*. New York, NY: Basic Books.

Library of Congress. (1989–1990) *Community mental health centers construction act of 1989*. Author.

Maslow, H . A. (1970). *Motivation and personality* (revised ed.). New York: Harper & Row.

Meichenbaum, D. (1985). *Stress inoculation training*. New York: Pergamon Press.

Obusnsha's Handy English-Japanese Dictionary. (1983).

Peake, T. H., Borduin, C. M., & Archer, R. P. (1988). *Brief psychotherapies: Changing frames of mind*. Newbury Park, CA: Sage.

Roberts, A. R. (1990). *Crisis intervention handbook: Assessment, treatment, and research*. Belmont, CA: Wadsworth.

Slaikeu, K. A. (1990). *Crisis intervention: A handbook for practice and research* (2nd ed.). Boston: Allyn & Bacon.

Chapter

2

Ethical, Legal, and Professional Issues

_____ 1. Professional ethics are based on each state's penal code.

_____ 2. Dual relationships are considered unethical in the counseling profession.

_____ 3. Crisis workers should not engage in a social or business relationship with clients.

_____ 4. Counselors should continuously monitor their countertransference reactions.

_____ 5. Crisis workers must report suicidal ideation to the police.

_____ 6. Confidentiality must be broken if a client is a danger to others.

_____ 7. Ataque de nervios is an example of a culture-bound syndrome.

_____ 8. Etic issues refer to behaviors particular to a cultural group.

_____ 9. Emic issues refer to universal issues.

_____ 10. Asians often deal with issues related to shame and obligation.

_____ 11. African Americans have suffered from racism due to salient differences from mainstream physical appearances.

_____ 12. People within the LGBT subculture are usually seriously mentally ill.

_____ 13. Learning to be culturally sensitive comes naturally to most counselors.

_____ 14. Enmeshed family structures are normal in most Latino families.

_____ 15. Coming out is often a crisis point for a gay individual.

Introduction

I have been a mental health practitioner for the past 35 years at the paraprofessional, master's level, and doctoral level in nonprofit agencies, county mental health centers, managed care facilities, and in a private practice setting. Over time, I have developed my version of appropriate ethical standards that allow for effective clinical practice and that follow guidelines of almost all of the various professional associations and state legislation and regulations.

Basically, ethics assure the public that counselors operate with the best interest of their clients and we mindfully try to do no harm (an idea that has its roots as far back as the ancient Greek physician Hippocrates and his "oath"). This concept of **nonmaleficence** guides most of the ethical standards to be presented in this chapter.

The Need for Ethics

Strong ethical practice is especially important in the field of crisis intervention, because clients in crisis come to a counselor in a vulnerable state of disequilibrium and instability. To take advantage of someone in such an unsteady state would be easy. At the outset of counseling, clients often feel hopeless and scared. They may view a counselor who reaches out with empathy with seemingly all the answers as a hero or savior of some type. Crisis interventionists adhere to strong ethical behaviors to help clients see them and their abilities in a realistic light.

What Are Ethics?

The term *ethics* is derived from the Greek word *ethos*, meaning character, and the Latin word *mores* that means customs. They guide behaviors that are deemed good for society and each individual (Elite CME, 2012). When someone identifies as a mental health professional, he or she should uphold the ethical standards put forth by the profession. In 1947, the social work profession adopted a code of ethics and many revisions have been created over the ensuing years by the National Association of Social Work, which was formed in 1960 (Elite CME, 2012). This process of revising standards is common to most mental health associations such as the American Psychiatric Association, the American Psychological Association, the American Association of Marital and Family Therapists, and the American Counseling Association. The reader is invited to visit the many websites that describe the specific ethical standards for each association. It will be no surprise to see the similarities among all of these groups.

Defining Law

Law is not exactly the same thing as ethics, though they sometimes overlap. Saltzman and Furman (1999) define *law* as "standards, principles, processes, and rules adopted, administered and enforced by governmental authority that regulate behaviors." Some laws regulate mental health practice by requiring certain education, experience, and examination completion to receive government standing as a professional. Other laws impose mandatory reporting practices such as child abuse reporting (Elite CME, 2012). Some general laws such as the sexual harassment laws created by the Equal Employment Opportunity Commission and the laws put forth by the Americans with Disability Act apply to mental health practice as well. An important law created by Congress in 1996 established national standards for the protection of certain health information. This Health Insurance Portability and Accountability Act (HIPAA) addressed who can use, look at, and receive individuals' health information, including mental health providers. In 2009, the Department of Health and Human Services created penalties for violations of this privacy rule making it imperative that all mental health providers adhere to the HIPAA law.

Since the inception of the Community Mental Health Act, various states have implemented laws and regulations about the rights of clients who utilize the mental health centers. This has led to controversies in the field.

Controversies

When mental health service centers were built in the community, they became places of specialty for psychiatry. The Community Mental Health Act was originally intended to serve chronically ill mental patients, but soon mental health workers began seeing healthier, less dysfunctional patients suffering from emotional disorders that had typically been treated in private psychologists' offices. As a result, the chronically mentally ill were receiving less care than intended. The **Lanterman-Petris-Short Act**, passed in 1968 in California, established more specific requirements for the provision of mental health services in the community. It set up the conditions of involuntary detention by peace officers or an individual designated by the Act. If an individual was determined to be gravely disabled or a danger to themselves or to others, they could be taken into custody for 72 hours if this was a result of a mental disorder. These conditions have been reviewed and are not without controversy. Some see this act as vague and may lead to unfair consequences to the poor and minorities. Moore (2000) found that at least one-third of blacks receiving psychiatric care in various California facilities were given twice the dosage of antipsychotic drugs compared to other races. He expresses concern about current pending legislation in the California legislature (Assembly Bill 1800 authored by Thomson and Peralta) that would expand forced treatment because it would lead to more racial bias and strengthen the mistrust of the mental health system by people of color. His studies suggest that African Americans are misdiagnosed and overrepresented as schizophrenic by many mental health providers.

Interestingly, "The primary motivations for this act (Lanterman Petris Short Act) were the abolition of indeterminate commitment and the removal of legal disabilities suffered by individuals adjudged mentally disordered" (Lenell, 2010, p. 733).

Lenell suggests that the concept of preventive detention, which is what these conditions deal with, may raise constitutional questions. If it is to be allowed, there must be a high probability of serious harm. She proposes that research indicates that psychiatrists consistently err in their prediction of violence and often individuals who are involuntarily detained may have lost their Fourteenth Amendment right to due process (2010). The Supreme Court stated in *Jackson v. Indiana* that "at the least, due process requires that the nature and duration of commitment bear some reasonable relation to the purpose for which the individual is committed" (p. 751). This refers to the idea that patients have the right to effective treatment if they are to be detained. Another Supreme Court decision, *O'Connor v. Donaldson*, stated that states may not confine a nondangerous individual who is capable of surviving safely by himself or with help of others. The "gravely disabled" condition doesn't apply if a person with a mental illness can properly survive even if others believe his clothing and food habits are not adequate. One last notable controversy is the case of *Humphrey v. Cady* in which the Supreme Court decided that evidence of an individual's harm to others must be high and the probability of danger must exist before confinement. Controversies like these are important to ensure that those suffering from mental illness and other forms of crises receive the effective treatment they need and that mental health practitioners operate in the most diligent and ethical manner possible. It is a good thing that "watchdogs" exist.

Use of Paraprofessionals

Another controversy has to do with the use of nonprofessionals in the provision of crisis intervention. Some mental health professionals may think that crisis intervention should only be provided by counselors with at least a master's degree or a license. However, as discussed in Chapter 1, crisis intervention began with the use of community workers, sometimes referred to as nonprofessionals or paraprofessionals. These workers often functioned in multidisciplinary team settings such as county agencies and grassroots nonprofit organizations. Effective crisis intervention can be conducted by undergraduate student trainees or community volunteers as well as by graduate-level students and professional counselors if their training is appropriate, and they are properly supervised.

The use of paraprofessional crisis workers has continued to be especially important as the world has moved into the twenty-first century. The economic recession of the early 1990s plus a decided shift in governmental policies during the beginning of the twenty-first century has led to cutbacks in government spending on human services programs, which has meant less money or no money to pay mental health workers. Under these circumstances, the use of volunteers and paraprofessionals makes excellent economic sense because most professional therapists will not provide crisis intervention consistently for the lowered fees often paid to many paraprofessionals. Also, many situations—including the wars in Iraq and Afghanistan, terrorism, continuing experiences of family deterioration, child and spousal abuse, and loss—ensure that crises will be plentiful and intervention desired. When immediate low-cost help is needed, using paraprofessionals makes the community stronger by ensuring that its population is functioning and coping with stress.

Ethical Issues

Most professional associations have created ethical standards around similar issues. These usually include issues related to boundary violations, improper and incompetent practice and record keeping, lack of honesty, breach of confidentiality, financial fraud, and failure to report inappropriate violations by others. By maintaining self-awareness and proactively monitoring ourselves, we will typically succeed in honoring ethical standards and engaging in minimal violations of ethical and legal codes.

Self-Awareness

"In addition to external ethics guidelines, mental health professionals must also rely on their internal cues through personal character" (Elite CME, 2012, p. 1). Therapeutic self-awareness means being conscious of one's own emotions, values, opinions, and behavior. Understanding one's own psychological processes and dynamics can help one guide others through their processes (Corey, Corey, & Callanan, 2010). Students can learn therapeutic self-awareness in crisis intervention classes; such training can help students take an honest, in-depth look at themselves in relation to the crisis of interest. It can be a valuable learning experience, enhancing the crisis worker's skills in helping clients. If workers learn to deal with all the issues surrounding death, for example, they have a better chance of helping a client deal with bereavement. It also helps counselors monitor reactions to situations that might trigger inappropriate reactions and lead to unethical behaviors. Additionally, without ongoing self-reflection and awareness, counselors may be prone to developing **countertransference** with clients. In these situations, the counselor intervenes inappropriately with the client because the client has triggered an emotional issue within the counselor based on the counselor's history with significant others.

Countertransference must often be addressed in the helping professions and has been formally defined as an "unconsciously determined attitudinal set held by the therapist which interferes with his work" (Singer, 1970, p. 290). It can be worked through effectively with personal therapy, lab sessions, and active self-exploration. Students new to crisis intervention have often experienced one or more of the situational crises practiced in coaching sessions. If students have not worked through the crisis completely, their feelings may interfere with their ability to remain calm, objective, and client-focused. However, once students' unresolved issues are discovered and processed, both in their own counseling and in lab group, they often are able to work quite effectively with clients going through that same type of crisis. Countertransference is not restricted to students in training. In actuality, this concept was first developed by Carl Jung in his training of analysts. Even the highly trained professional is liable to experience countertransference from time to time. This is the primary reason that personal analysis has been encouraged for psychoanalysts from the very beginning of the discipline.

Dual Relationships

Another ethical issue involves **dual relationships**—that is, a counselor's having more than one kind of relationship with a client. When counselors are providing crisis intervention to a client, they are prohibited from being involved with that client on a personal level of any kind. This includes prohibition of any relationship—sexual, social, employment, or financial—that is not directly related to the provision of crisis intervention. Such a separation is necessary because a person in crisis is often in a vulnerable state and could be taken advantage of quite easily by a counselor (who is viewed as an expert). Another reason to avoid a dual relationship is because of the possible emotional damage clients may sustain if they experience the counselor in a different role and then are disillusioned or disappointed. Also, the power differential between counselor and client is enormous. The counselor knows quite a bit about the client, and this knowledge can be a source of awkwardness for the client when he or she is out of the therapeutic situation. The most potent word on the subject is this: *Don't make friends or lovers of your clients. It is unethical and in some cases illegal.*

Confidentiality

Confidentiality is one of the hallmarks of any trusting relationship. It is also an important part of the ethical code for mental health providers. A broad concept that refers to safeguarding clients from unauthorized disclosures of information made in the therapeutic relationship, confidentiality is an explicit promise by the counselor to reveal nothing unless the client has agreed to it. **Privileged communication**, which is sometimes confused with confidentiality, is the statutory right that protects clients from having their confidences revealed publicly (Corey et al., 2010).

However, some **exceptions to privilege and confidentiality** do exist, as they relate to crisis intervention. Privilege is waived if the client signs a document giving the helper permission to disclose the communications between the client and the counselor. Clients may be asked to waive privilege to ensure continuity of care among mental health professionals, to provide for appropriate supervision, when access to records is needed for court testimony, and when information is needed for submitting health insurance claims. Confidentiality must be broken in cases of child abuse or elder abuse, when clients are a **danger to others**, and it may be broken when clients are a danger to themselves or are **gravely disabled**. Sometimes, a client's mental condition will be the focus of a lawsuit, and in some of those cases confidentiality can be ethically and legally broken. For example, a client who sues a therapist for malpractice and claims to have suffered emotional damage because of the therapist's incompetence gives up privileged communications from the therapy sessions. The therapist may use case notes to defend against the malpractice charge. A similar example in which a client would forfeit the protection of privilege is a case in which the client is attempting to prove emotional injury in a workers' compensation.

In order to remember these exceptions to confidentiality, the following philosophy offered by Justice Mathew O. Tobriner of the California Supreme Court, after the court heard *Tarasoff v. Regents of the University of California* and created the "duty to warn mandate," is often applied: "Privileged communication ends where public peril begins." (Buckner & Firestone, 2000). This includes peril to clients if they endanger themselves because of a mental disorder. If clients are considered suicidal or gravely disabled and unable to care for themselves, helpers may breach confidentiality to protect them. The spirit of this allowance is that sharing information is meant to be among professionals, family, and friends, and not for frivolous purposes. Gravely disabled clients are those who, because of a mental disorder, cannot take care of their daily needs for food, shelter, medical care, clothing, and so on. Clearly, it is more important to break confidentiality to save someone with Alzheimer's disease from starving because he is delusional about having food in the house than it is to maintain confidentiality.

The other situations in which privileged communications should be broken involve trying to prevent clients from harming others. These conditions include elder abuse, child abuse, and the possibility that clients might cause different kinds of danger to others. Specifics of mandatory reporting are presented next.

Elder Abuse Reporting Act

The department of social services in some states has an adult protective services program that responds to reports of abuse of the elderly (i.e., adults over 65 years old). **Elder abuse** refers to any of the following acts inflicted by other than accidental means on an elder by another person: physical abuse, fiduciary abuse (involves trust and money), and neglect or abandonment. In many states, knowledge of such abuse must be reported to social services, the police, or a nursing home ombudsman (governmental investigator). Some agencies have also begun taking reports of abuse of the disabled adult population. This could cover any adult who suffers from a mental or physical disability such as mental retardation or blindness.

Child Abuse Reporting Act

Since passage by Congress of the National Child Abuse Prevention and Treatment Act in 1974, many states have enacted laws requiring professionals to report child abuse. This act provided federal funding to states in support of prevention, assessment, investigation, prosecution, and treatment activities. It was amended several times and was most recently amended and reauthorized in 2003 by the Keeping Children and Families Safe Act (P.L. 108-36) (U.S. Department of Health and Human Services, 2010). States differ on the indicators for reporting and whether sanctions will be imposed on individuals for not reporting. **Child abuse reporting** includes suspicions of physical abuse, sexual abuse, general neglect, and emotional abuse.

In many states, child abuse must be reported within 36 hours of its discovery to the department of social services or the police. The child protective services program will then investigate the suspicion. Remember that there is no requirement to have evidence of abuse before it can be reported; suspicion alone is enough evidence. If abuse is suspected that is later proved, and it is not reported, there may be fines by the state. On the other hand, more and more states are ensuring immunity from suit for false reports. Each crisis worker is encouraged to know the requirements of reporting in his or her state.

The *Tarasoff* Case   The consequences of failing to warn an individual of possible danger to him or her by another are dramatically illustrated in the *Tarasoff* case. In 1969, Prosenjit Poddar was seeing a therapist at the campus counseling center of the University of California, Berkeley. Poddar confided to the therapist that he intended to kill Tatiana Tarasoff when she returned from Brazil. The therapist considered Poddar dangerous and called campus police, requesting that Poddar be confined. He was not confined. To complicate matters, the therapist's supervisor ordered that all case notes be destroyed. Tarasoff was later killed by Poddar, and her parents filed suit against the University of California's Board of Regents. The decision from this case requires a therapist to notify the police and the intended victim when possible if the therapist has reasonable belief that a client is dangerous toward others (duty to warn) (California State Case Law, 2010).

Informed consent is a way of providing clients with information they need to become active participants in the therapeutic relationship (Corey et al., 2010). Although no specific rules exist governing how much information a therapist is to provide, three legal elements to informed consent do exist. First, clinicians must make sure clients have the ability to make rational decisions and, if not, must ensure that a parent or guardian takes responsibility for giving consent. Second, therapists must give clients information in a clear way and check their understanding of the risks and benefits of treatment and alternate procedures available. Third, clients must consent freely to treatment. The exceptions to these elements occur when clients are dangerous to themselves and others or are gravely disabled. Electroconvulsive shock treatments and psychosurgery (lobotomies) cannot be done without consent; however, there are times when medication is given without client consent.

Competence   There is a growing model to ensure clients receive the most competent and effective service possible often referred to as *evidence-based practice*. Evidence-based practice takes into account the current state of knowledge regarding a variety of clinical needs.

Another way in which competence is increased and monitored is the requiring of counselors to receive appropriate supervision and training. Unless paraprofessionals are supervised by a licensed professional, most agencies—county, state, and nonprofit—do not let them provide crisis intervention and counseling. Even seasoned therapists often consult with colleagues about cases for which they have minimal training or experience. Crisis workers sometimes refer a client to another helper because the worker's duties mainly involve assessment and brokering out clients—tasks requiring a sound knowledge of community resources for a variety of problems.

Knowing one's limitations is essential for ethical practice. When a helper is conducting a crisis interview, being able to make an assessment for organic illnesses and severe mental illness is especially important. Some cases require a multidisciplinary team approach with a medical doctor involved; any serious mental illness or neurological impairment must be identified if the patient is to receive the total help needed. Even though making technical diagnoses is not usually considered appropriate for paraprofessionals, knowledge of the *Diagnostic and Statistical Manual of Mental Disorders* IV-TR (American Psychiatric Association, 2000) is helpful in ensuring that clients receive services from the type of professional appropriate to their needs. This manual provides information about very serious mental disorders that require intervention by physicians. Crisis workers should review this manual when possible to gain a beginning understanding of the types of presenting complaints that usually necessitate physician involvement. Box 2.1 provides an example of necessary physician involvement due to a client suffering from an organic illness.

Box 2.1   Example of an Organic Illness Necessitating Physician Intervention

Suppose that a 45-year-old woman comes to a community center because her 70-year-old mother has been behaving strangely, does not recognize her family members, and leaves the gas stove burners on all day. Knowing that these symptoms are indicative of Alzheimer's disease or other organic brain disorders helps the crisis worker develop treatment strategies. Most important is having the mother examined neurologically to rule out any medical cause for her unusual behavior.

Client's Rights

In addition to rights for privacy, a client also has the right to give consent for treatment unless he or she is considered incompetent to refuse. Clients must also be given information about the service so he or she may weigh the benefits and risks of treatment. They must be informed of the fee structure, the counselors' qualifications, and termination rights.

Virtual or e-Therapy

One of the newest practices is conducting counseling services via email, the Internet, teleconferencing, or videoconferencing. Some support this practice saying it allows people to be served who otherwise could not, due to their living location or due to fears of stigma, or conditions such as agoraphobia (Kanani & Regehr, 2003). They also have some concerns such as risks to security and confidentiality, lack of legal recourse for malpractice, and inappropriate counseling due to lack of observation of facial expressions. This practice is certain to come under more scrutiny in the future due to the global trend to "cyber everything."

Multicultural Competence

The idea that counselors should be sensitive to various cultural norms and behaviors when helping clients work through crises is nearly universally accepted. Crisis workers are encouraged to be open and knowledgeable toward subgroups that may differ from mainstream culture. Counselors must not impose personal values on clients, but instead be aware of how their values may be a part of the problems that exist. Of course, one can't help but sometimes expose one's values to others, but it is considered unethical to assume that everyone should believe and act the way counselors think they should.

This interest in the sensitivity of counselors and therapists to culturally diverse clients has been growing in the past few decades. It began in the 1960s when the civil rights and affirmative action movements emerged, and became a part of formal education in the late 1980s and 1990s. Arredondo and colleagues (1996, p. 43) describe specific behaviors and attitudes of culturally aware counselors: "Multicultural counseling refers to preparation and practices that integrate multicultural and culture-specific awareness, knowledge, and skills into counseling interactions." They suggest that multicultural refers to five major cultural groups in the United States: African Americans, Asian Americans, Caucasians, Latinos, and Native Americans. The reader is encouraged to obtain a copy of their article and keep it for reference. Although these groups have been the main focus of multicultural studies, other subgroups such as people with disabilities; gays, lesbians, bisexuals, and transgenders; and certain religious groups also have special needs.

Cultural sensitivity is an ethical mandate, and it helps to strengthen clinical practice.

Development of Cultural Sensitivity

As part of a course in a doctoral program at the University of Southern California during the mid 1980s, seven students coauthored an article that describes the **development of cultural sensitivity** in therapists. The students and their professor found similar patterns as all of them struggled with the gender and ethnic issues involved in diagnosing and treating various groups. At that time, very little emphasis had been placed on cultural sensitivity training in graduate programs, so this topic was somewhat novel to most of the students. Based on case vignettes and class discussion, a model of developmental stages was created and is shown in Table 2.1. What was discovered was that learning to be a culturally sensitive counselor is not an easy task. It is normal for counselors to struggle with developing this type of sensitivity. Counselors do not have to be perfect models of cultural sensitivity, but they are encouraged to be aware of cultural, ethnic, religious, and gender issues that may affect the crisis intervention process.

Knowing about various cultures before meeting with clients can be helpful. It is more important, however, to follow a client's lead in these matters, in order to help the client feel understood and validated. If a counselor fails to

TABLE 2.1 Proposed Stages and State-Specific Consequences in Therapists' Development of Cultural Sensitivity

Stage	Description	Consequence
Unawareness of cultural issues	Therapist does not consider a cultural hypothesis in diagnosis.	Therapist does not understand the significance of the clients' cultural background to their functioning.
Heightened awareness of culture	Therapist is aware that cultural factors are important in fully understanding clients.	Therapist feels unprepared to work with culturally different clients; frequently applies own perception of clients' cultural background and therefore fails to understand the cultural significance for a specific client; can at times accurately recognize the influence of clients' cultural background on their functioning.
Burden of considering culture	Therapist is hypervigilant in identifying cultural factors and is, at times, confused in determining the cultural significance of clients' actions.	Therapist believes that consideration of culture is perceived as detracting from his or her clinical effectiveness.
Movement toward cultural sensitivity	Therapist entertains cultural hypotheses and carefully tests these hypotheses from multiple sources before accepting cultural explanations.	Therapist has increased likelihood of accurately understanding the role of culture on clients' functioning.

Source: Lopez et al. (1989). © 1989 by the American Psychological Association. Adapted with permission.

Box 2.2   Example of Lack of Cultural Sensitivity

Example: "A 41-year-old man requested an emergency session regarding his marriage. At his request, I saw him Saturday morning. The man spoke with an Asian accent and said that he was half-Chinese and half-Spanish and had been born in China. As we discussed his presenting problem, the client resisted any of my suggestions that part of his problem might be that his wife was Caucasian, and her parents and siblings disapproved of him. He had come to my office to appease his wife, who said she would leave him unless he sought counseling. The couple had a poor sex life, but he resisted discussing this openly. He kept insisting that the problem was him, and he described himself as a cold person who did not like to be around people.

I noticed myself becoming very frustrated. The client refused to accept the idea that he and his wife had a relationship problem. I guess the client sensed my frustration because he asked if I could refer him to another therapist. He had many demands regarding the times he was available for appointments. He refused marital therapy, which I recommended. I guessed that some of his issues were cultural in nature, but, unfortunately, I will not have the opportunity to explore these issues with him." (Lopez et al., 1989, p. 370)

This vignette indicated that the therapist did not consider cultural factors in her work with this ethnic minority client. She appears to be defining the problem for the client without considering the client's definition of the problem and working from there. This is not to say that the therapist is wrong in her assessment; the client is likely having marital problems. However, her failure to validate his explanatory model or interpretation of the problem may have led to his request for another therapist. (p. 371)

respect cultural differences, the crisis intervention may come to an end. In the following case example, the therapist did not show cultural sensitivity, with the consequence that the client dropped out of therapy prematurely.

Unfortunately, counselors are not always culturally sensitive and this can have deleterious effects on the therapeutic relationship. Box 2.2 presents a case in which the counselor did not use cultural sensitivity.

Etic vs. Emic Issues

In order to help reduce this struggle, various theories regarding how to conceptualize the needs of various cultural groups have been discussed. One way in which to conceptualize how to become culturally sensitive is to understand the difference between *etic* and *emic* issues for various cultural groups. **Etic** refers to behaviors and traditions of all or most humans regardless of race, ethnicity, or culture. **Emic** refers to behaviors and traditions particular to a certain cultural group. The goal is not to use cultural norms to justify behaviors, especially if they are abusive, but to understand and find effective interventions that won't be resisted by the clients. Lastly, it is important to keep in mind that just because certain behaviors and traditions are culturally normal and accepted, it doesn't mean that people in that culture approve of them. In fact, these traditions may be the source of a crisis. This becomes particularly evident when individuals in a family are at different levels of acculturation to mainstream culture. The emic and etic issues related to domestic violence and three ethnic groups will be presented in a later chapter dealing with intimate partner abuse.

Because there are so many excellent texts that describe the various issues of cultural groups, this section only defines certain emic patterns so that the reader may remember to keep these in mind when conducting crisis intervention. However, the reader is strongly urged to review as much literature as possible for strong multicultural competent practice. McGoldrick, Pearce, and Giordana (2005) is recommended as an excellent beginning.

Latinos

Personalismo   This is a cultural pattern of relating to others in a manner that may include exaggerated warmth and emotions and a strong need for rapport in order to feel safe or trust others. It is particularly useful to create this relationship when working with Latinos.

Marianisma   is a tradition in which the Latina female is expected to be pure and self-sacrificing, focusing more on her children and spouse than her own needs. This contradicts mainstream culture in which women are encouraged to be equal to men and to embrace their own womanhood and personal identity. Sometimes Latina girls raised in the United States reject this quality, creating conflict with their mothers who strongly teach these daughters to be more traditional mothers, wives, and housekeepers. When the daughters do not speak up to their mothers about how this makes them feel depressed, they may be prone to suicide. According to a 2007 Centers for Disease Control and Prevention survey (Yager, 2009), one out of every seven Latina teens attempts suicide. This is higher than Caucasians (7%) and African Americans (9%).

Machismo   is the tradition of the male Latino taking pride in being virile and protective of his family. Many misdefine this quality and think of it as the right for Latino males to be abusive to their wives. True, there may be a strong sense of male privilege in this culture, but true machismo means that the man takes care of his wife, not abuses her. This is an effective reframe when a Latino male attempts to justify spousal abuse. It might also be the reason for high rates of drinking, domestic violence, teen pregnancy, and sexual abuse of daughters found in this culture.

Catholicism   This is still the religion of choice for most Latinos, though many are choosing more fundamental Christian religions than in the past. This Catholic tradition has in part been a contributing factor to the high rates of teen pregnancy, large families, and very few divorces found in this cultural group. Crisis workers should not assume every Latino is Catholic however.

Familismo   This refers to the value of family above all. This may cause resistance in some Latinos to talk negatively about their family. Also, they may not have many outside support people, and may feel awkward in support groups. Family counseling is an effective style for Latinos when family issues cause the crisis.

Enmeshed family structure   This style of relating gives very little independence to children. Although much emotional support might be present, teens may rebel against this lack of privacy and act out through joining gangs, engaging in sexual activities, or attempting suicide.

Emotionalism   One last characteristic of Latinos is their tendency toward emotionalism, even exaggerated expression that borders on the dramatic. If given the chance, and if they feel safe, they often express their feelings openly in counseling. This expression of affect (emotion) may allow them to master their feelings. Caplan discussed this process when he proposed seven characteristics of people coping effectively. At times, crisis workers may just want to allow clients to express their feelings and not pressure them to solve a problem.

Issues Related to Different Rates of Acculturation   Other crises that may emerge in Mexican American families may reflect patterns that developed and were functional when the family first immigrated to the United States, but have since become restrictive for certain family members. For example, many parents depend on their children to be their intermediaries with the larger culture. When the children grow up and want to separate from their parents, the parents may find it difficult to let them go (McGoldrick, Pearce, & Giordana, 2005).

Ataque de Nervios   One Latino phenomenon that may come to the crisis worker's attention is **ataque de nervios (los nervios)**, which literally means "attack of nerves." This is a culture-bound, self-labeled syndrome found only in Latinos. It is often a reaction to trauma, death, marital infidelity, or family conflict. A person suffering from this may seek help from a physician, counselor, or *curandero* (folk healer). Symptoms include panic attacks, fits of violent agitation with self-mutilation and suicidal behavior (Schechter et al., 2000, p. 530), shaking, heart palpitations, numbness, shouting, swearing, striking others, falling, convulsions (Liebowitz et al., 1994, p. 871), and signs of dissociation (Oquendo, 1995).

African American Families

When working with this subgroup, counselors may wish to keep in mind a few ideas. Because most **African Americans** speak English, the differences in any cultural traditions aren't related to language. In fact, African Americans have lived in the United States longer than many other ethnic groups who immigrated during the late 1800s, so they are usually acculturated to mainstream values such as independence, self-reliance, rights, and equality as much as most Caucasians. Nonetheless, their history of slavery, racism, and discrimination have set up some differences from mainstream culture that we should consider.

Religion   Slaves found solace in the view that God would provide a better world for them after they had left this world of suffering. This tradition of strong religious beliefs and practices has been passed down through the generations and must be kept in mind by the crisis worker. For the crisis interventionist, incorporating the church into therapy, either by seeking support from a minister or by encouraging the client to become involved in church activities, is valuable. Many African Americans do not place much trust in mainstream, middle-class mental health counselors. African American ministers, however, often do trust counselors and may be able to allay the fears of parishioners who would benefit from counseling.

Racism   The worker must always acknowledge that racism is present in our society and must try to understand the world of a client who deals with racism every day.

As stated earlier, there has been a tendency to overdiagnose this group with schizophrenia and involuntarily detain them, most likely due to lack of cultural competence. Distrust of a racist society may be perceived by some clinicians as paranoia, when, in fact, there is some basis in reality to be afraid.

Asian American Families

In his work with **Asian Americans**, Hong (1988) has found that mental health workers would do well to adopt a general family practice model whereby they maintain an ongoing interaction with the family and serve as a resource that the family can consult when they are in difficulty. A counselor should use knowledge of the client as well as knowledge of the client's family, community, and social environment. This approach seems particularly suitable for Asian Americans whose culture emphasizes the role of the family.

Asian American Family Structure

In most traditional Asian families, males are respected more than females. The oldest son has more privileges than his own mother, though he must respect her at certain levels. The mother plays the stereotypical role of nurturer, providing domestic structure, whereas the father dictates all family decisions. The daughter contributes to the household until she marries; then she belongs to her husband's household and family. The concept of individualism is not part of this culture.

Shame and Obligation in Asian American Culture

If the norms are not followed, an individual and the family will experience a sense of shame, not only for their own actions but also for the entire family line. This factor makes it necessary at times to reject a family member completely so as not to bring shame on the family. Differentiation between the family as a whole and its members often does not exist as it does in European cultures.

Obligation arises in any situation in which the rules of family structure come into play. The child is obligated to respect the structure. If the child does not, he or she will bring shame on the family. Having to choose between obligation and individual freedom often brings on feelings of depression and anxiety. The crisis worker needs to be sensitive to these struggles and search for ways to negotiate compromises when possible.

Kashiwagi (1993, p. 46) provides an example of how "certain traditional Asian cultural influences, such as bringing shame to the family and losing face in the community," have an effect on mental health problems and intervention. He asserts that when an Asian American teenager has a drug or alcohol addiction, the family often denies the condition and perpetuates the problem. This denial results in large part from the lack of connection, communication, and understanding in the parent–child relationship. If the counselor recommends a tough love approach—that is, tells the parents to refuse to continue being enablers for the teenager's behavior and set standards that he must meet—the parents probably will not follow through adequately because of the cultural tendency to care for family members at a surface level.

Communication Process in Asian American Culture

Another area in which sensitivity is helpful is communication style. Asian Americans have been conditioned to avoid eye contact and direct confrontations, especially with doctors and authority figures. This trait may create complications during an interview if the counselor is not aware of this cultural style. Whereas mainstream Americans may consider avoiding eye contact to be rude, Asians may feel that looking someone in the eye is rude. Also, Asian clients may feel that they cannot disagree with the counselor because of respect for the authority position. The counselor may have to encourage disagreement and define it as part of the interview process at times.

Also, if a crisis counselor is working with a family, the tendency to ask family members to confront each other directly may be culturally insensitive. They will probably do best with more educational, problem-solving approaches that focus on a presenting problem. Reframing the solution as strengthening the family unit will probably be well received by Asian American clients. The crisis worker might try to be aware of the hierarchy in the family and include the most powerful family members in making decisions.

The Subculture of Lesbians, Gays, Bisexuals, and Transgenders (LGBT)

Terms that are commonly used in discussions of the lesbian, gay, bisexual, and transgender population are listed next. These individuals are sometimes referred to as the l/g/b/t population.

bisexual: A person who experiences social and romantic attraction to both genders.

closet gay: A person who is unaware of his or her homosexuality or is unwilling to publicly acknowledge it; such a person may be described as "being in the closet."

coming out: The process of identifying and coming to terms with one's homosexuality. The term is also used to describe a homosexual person who tells another person or persons that he or she is gay.

gay: A man who is mostly sexually attracted to men.

heterosexism: The attitude of overt or covert bias against homosexuals based on the belief that heterosexuality is superior.

homophobia: Unreasonable fear or hatred of a homosexual.

homosexuality: Sexual desires primarily for a person of the same sex.

lesbian: A woman who feels sexual desire predominantly for other women.

transgender: A person who has experienced himself or herself socially, emotionally, and psychologically as male if the person was born female, or female if the person was born male.

There seems to be a trend among adults toward more acceptance of gays and lesbians in society (Yang, 1999). This is evident in the ratings of television shows that have been nominated for and won Emmy awards, such as Modern Family, and in the open disclosure by some celebrities of their homosexual identity. However, many people still have negative feelings toward individuals who live openly gay and lesbian lifestyles. Adults who present themselves to the world as gay make themselves open to criticism and rejection by family, friends, and coworkers. Recent political discussions have highlighted the ongoing debate about whether gays should be allowed to be legally married with the same rights as heterosexual married couples. Proponents of gay marriage believe that not allowing gay marriage is a form of discrimination. This is such an important issue that it has become a platform upon which certain major political parties run.

Keeping one's homosexuality hidden can lead to mental health problems such as anxiety and depression. The closet gay must always worry about keeping his or her true sexual orientation concealed. Often these people must lie to those they care about, and this duplicity leads to negative feelings. Coming out to oneself and others is often a crisis precipitating event, depending on the reactions from loved ones.

Crisis hotlines and centers have been established to help this population live healthy gay and lesbian lifestyles, disclose their orientation to others, and learn how to handle rejection from society. Suicide is a big risk for individuals in the beginning stages of discovering their gay sexual orientation as well as for gay persons who experience societal discrimination. The news media often has reports of hate crimes against gays. Gay persons have been socialized in a culture that fears homosexuality on moral grounds. Judeo-Christian culture has emphasized that sodomy is a sin. Therefore, gay individuals often experience self-loathing for a time until they can come to terms with the reality of their sexuality.

Chapter Review

Ethics are guidelines of acceptable behaviors within a profession, usually determined by those in the profession themselves. The counseling profession has very specific standards regarding confidentiality, dual relationships, mandatory reporting of abuse, informed consent, and counselor training and supervision. Because clients are thought to be vulnerable, counselors adhere to these standards to protect clients from being exploited. Part of being in a helping profession is to monitor one's own emotional well-being. The importance of cultural sensitivity in the field of crisis intervention is essential for effective management of a crisis. It is not an easy task, and most beginning counselors struggle with learning how to use the etic and emic issues presented by clients. Although no ethnic group is homogeneous in its makeup, there are certain emic characteristics of certain groups that, when kept in mind, make the task of counseling more effective.

Answers to Pre-Chapter Quiz

1. F   2. T   3. T   4. T   5. F   6. T   7. T   8. F   9. F   10. T
11. T   12. F   13. F   14. T   15. T

Key Terms for Study

(Terms already specifically defined within the chapter will not be redefined in this section)

African Americans: Counselors should keep in mind the history of slavery and ongoing racism and how this group while highly acculturated to mainstream values, often turns to the church for solace and leadership and may distrust mainstream institutions.

Asian Americans: Issues such as family lineage, obligation and shame are emic considerations for this subgroup.

ataque de nervios (los nervios): A self-labeled syndrome found in Latinos in which they experience a mixture of anxiety, panic, depression, and anger.

child abuse reporting: Reporting required of anyone working with children as a counselor, doctor, teacher, or in any other capacity since passage of the 1974 Child Abuse Prevention and Treatment Act by Congress. These people must report any suspicions of child abuse to the child protective services agency in their state. The requirement is mandatory and in many states overrides the client's right to confidentiality.

confidentiality: An ethical standard providing the client with the right for all disclosures in counseling to be kept private.

countertransference: A situation in a counseling relationship that arises from unresolved feelings experienced by a counselor in a session with a client. These feelings come out of the counselor's personal life and cause him or her to act out these feelings with a client, behavior that may cause emotional harm to the client.

danger to others: Condition in which a client is deemed to be a threat to others. At this time, the counselor must breach confidentiality and report his or her concerns to the police or the intended victim, or both. This is called the "duty to warn."

development of cultural sensitivity: A four-stage process during which counselors learn to consider cultural factors when they are conducting counseling sessions. The stages are (1) lack of awareness of cultural issues; (2) heightened awareness of culture; (3) realization of the burden of considering culture; and (4) beginnings of cultural sensitivity.

dual relationship: A relationship that a counselor engages in with the client outside the professional one—for example, a social, sexual, or business relationship.

elder abuse: Physical abuse, fiduciary abuse, neglect, or abandonment of someone 65 years old or older. In many states, anyone working with clients over 65 years of age must report suspected cases of elder abuse to the state's adult protective services agency. This reporting is often mandatory and grounds for breaching confidentiality.

emic: This refers to behaviors and traditions particular to a certain cultural group.

etic: This refers to behaviors and traditions of all or most humans regardless of race, ethnicity, or culture.

exceptions to privilege and confidentiality: Situations in which communications between therapist and client can be legally and ethically shared with others. In the case of confidentiality, these include elder abuse and child abuse, grave disability of the client, and danger posed by the client to self or others. In the case of privilege, these include voluntary waivers given by the client for information to be shared in a limited forum as well as some involuntary disclosures, as in certain court cases.

gravely disabled: Condition in which a client is psychotic or suffering from a severe organic brain disorder. People with such disorders are often incapable of meeting basic needs such as obtaining food or shelter and managing finances. Grave disability is often a reason for involuntary hospitalization of a person.

informed consent: Permission for treatment given by a client to a therapist after the client has been thoroughly informed about all aspects of the treatment. Anyone entering a counseling relationship has the right to understand the nature of therapy, give his or her consent for it, understand that it is voluntary, and be told the limits of confidentiality.

Lanterman-Petris-Short Act: This legislation was created to set up conditions for the involuntary hospitalization of the mentally ill and define patient rights in California.

Latino: An alternative term used to describe people whose family holds the traditions of Spanish-speaking countries.

nonmaleficence: The ethical guideline that focuses on doing no harm to clients based on the Hippocratic oath.

privileged communication: The legal counterpart of confidentiality. Clients may waive the right to privilege if they wish the counselor to share certain information in court or other limited venues.

References

American Psychiatric Association. (2000). *Diagnostic and statistical manual of mental disorders, fourth edition, text revision (DSM-IV-TR)*. Washington, DC: Author.

Arredondo, P., Toporek, R., Brown, S. P., Jones, J., Locke, D. C., Sanchez, J., et al. (1996). Operationalization of the multicultural counseling competencies. *Journal of Multicultural Counseling and Development, 24*, 42–78.

Buckner, F., & Firestone, M. (2000). Where the public peril begins. *The Journal of Legal Medicine, 21*, 2.

California State Case Law. (2010). *Tarasoff v. Regents of the University of California*. Retrieved May 21, 2010, from http://en.wikipedia.org/wiki/Tarasoff_v._Regents_of_the_University_of_California

Corey, G., Corey, M. S., & Callanan, P. (2010). *Issues and ethics in the helping professions* (3rd ed.). Pacific Grove, CA: Brooks/Cole.

Elite Continuing Education (2012). Telephone: 1-866-653-2119. Retrieved from www.elitecme.com

Hong, G. K. (1988). A general family practitioner approach for Asian-American mental health services. *Professional Psychology: Research and Practice, 19*(6), 600–605.

Kanani, K., & Regehr, C. (2003). Clinical, ethical, and legal issues in e-therapy. *Families in Society: The Journal of Contemporary Human Services, 84*, 155.

Kashiwagi, S. (1993, April). Addiction and the Asian family. *Treatment Today*, 43–76.

Lenell, M. (2010). The Lanterman-Petris-Short Act: A review after ten years. *Golden Gate University Law Review, 7*(3), 733–764.

Liebowitz, M. R., Salman, E., Jusion, C. M., Garfinkel, R., Street, L., Cardenas, D. L., et al. (1994). Ataque de nervios and panic disorder. *American Journal of Psychiatry, 151*(6), 871–875.

Lopez, S. R., Grover, K. P., Holland, D., Johnson, M. J., Kain, C. D., Kanel, K., et al. (1989). Development of culturally sensitive psychotherapists. *Professional Psychology: Research and Practice, 20*(6), 369–376.

McGoldrick, M., Pearce, J. K., & Giordano, J. (2005). *Ethnicity and family therapy*. New York: Guilford Press.

Moore, L. F. (2000). The color of trust: The impact of AB1800 on African American mental health consumers. *Poor Magazine*. Retrieved December 13, 2012, from http://poormagazine.org/node/2895

Oquendo, M. A. (1995). Differential diagnosis of ataque de nervios. *American Journal of Orthopsychiatry*, 65(1), 60–64.

Saltzman, A., & Furman, D. M. (1999). *Law in social work practice*. Belmont, CA: Wadsworth Group.

Schechter, D. S., Marshall, R., Salman, E., Goetz, D., Davies, S., & Liebowitz, M. R. (2000). Ataque de nervios and history of childhood trauma. *Journal of Traumatic Stress*, 13(3), 529–534.

Singer, E. (1970). *Key concepts in psychotherapy*. New York: Basic Books.

U.S. Department of Health and Human Services. Administration for Children and Families. (2010). *Child Abuse Prevention and Treatment Act*. Retrieved May 21, 2010, from http://en.wikipedia.org/wiki/Child_Abuse_Prevention _and_Treatment_Act

Yager, C. (2009). Trapped between worlds, some Latina teens consider suicide. *CNN.com*. Retrieved from http://www.cnn.com/2009/LIVING/10 /20/lia.latina.suicides/index.html

Yang, A. (1999). *Wrongs to rights: Public opinion on gay and lesbian Americans moves toward equality*. Washington, DC: Policy Institute of the National Gay and Lesbian Task Force.

The ABC Model of Crisis Intervention

_____ 1. Basic attending skills help develop and maintain rapport.

_____ 2. Reflection of feelings is contraindicated for clients in crisis.

_____ 3. It is usually best to ask a series of close-ended questions during crisis intervention.

_____ 4. The ABC Model of Crisis Intervention tends to have more structure than long-term therapy.

_____ 5. Educational statements provide clients with information about their situation.

_____ 6. Crisis workers try to identify the precipitating event, perceptions, and impairments in functioning.

_____ 7. Validation statements let clients know that the counselor approves of their decisions.

_____ 8. In the coping phase, the counselor tells the client what to do.

_____ 9. Twelve-step groups are a great resource because they are readily available and free.

_____ 10. Clients in crisis should not be expected to come up with ideas about how to improve their situation.

Introduction

The ABC Model of Crisis Intervention is a method of conducting very brief mental-health interviews with clients whose functioning level has decreased following a psychosocial stressor. This model follows the formula presented in Chapter 1 regarding the process of crisis formation. It is a problem-focused approach and is most effectively applied within four to six weeks of the stressor. The focus of this method is identifying the cognitions of the client as they relate to the precipitating event and then altering them to help decrease unmanageable feelings. In addition, providing community referrals and other resources such as reading material is essential in applying this model.

Caplan and Lindemann first conceptualized the crisis intervention approach in the 1940s (Caplan, 1964; Lindemann, 1944) while others have since developed models that use the principles and techniques of these founders. The ABC model of crisis intervention presented in this text has its origins in a variety of sources. It is loosely based on Jones's (1968) A-B-C method of crisis management, with its three-stage process: A, achieving rapport; B, boiling the problem down to basics; and C, coping. Moline (1986), a former professor at California State University, Fullerton, developed a course called Crisis Intervention in which she used a modified version of Jones's model. From her lecture notes and from discussions with her about how she organized the course, the author (Kristi Kanel) developed the ABC model of crisis intervention discussed in this book. Over a period of 27 years, the author has expanded and revised the ABC model. Revisions are based on current information from experts in the community who provide crisis intervention for a variety of populations, current research in professional literature, the author's experiences in teaching the model to students and community counselors, feedback from these students, and the author's experiences as a counselor in public, private, and nonprofit agency settings.

Other models have also influenced the ABC model of crisis intervention in terms of its particular structure and stages. Structuring the counseling process around certain phases or stages is not a new phenomenon. This has been done by mental health practitioners since the days of such founding theorists as Sullivan (1954) and Adler (Corey, 2008). The structure of Adlerian counseling follows four central objectives that correspond to four phases. These phases do not progress in rigid steps but are best understood as a weaving that leads to a tapestry (Dreikurs, 1967). The phases that Adler developed are:

1. Establishing the Relationship
2. Exploring Individual Psychological Dynamics
3. Encouraging Self-Understanding and Insight
4. Reorientation and Re-education

Figure 3.1 describes how Adler's four phases are similar to the ABC Model.

FIGURE 3.1   The ABC Model as Related to Adler's Four-Phase Model Here

A. Developing and maintaining rapport (corresponds with Adler's phase 1)
B. Identifying the problem and providing therapeutic interaction (corresponds with Adler's phase 2 and phase 3)
C. Coping (corresponds with Adler's phase 4)

Sullivan (1954) also used a phase model to structure psychiatric interviews. His stages can also be viewed as corresponding with the stages of the ABC model: Phase 1, the formal inception (analogous to A of the ABC model); Phase 2, the reconnaissance, and Phase 3, the detailed inquiry (analogous to B); and Phase 4, termination (analogous to C).

Although the ABC model of crisis intervention has a three-stage approach, in an actual interview the components of any one stage could be used at any time. Readers are strongly encouraged to keep this thought in mind during the discussion of each stage that follows. The crisis worker will learn how to integrate the stages through practice and experience.

A: Developing and Maintaining Rapport: Follow the Client

The foundation of crisis intervention is the development of **rapport**—a state of understanding and comfort—between client and counselor. As a client begins to feel the rapport, trust and openness follow, allowing the interview to proceed. Before delving into the client's personal world, the counselor must achieve this personal rapport. The counseling relationship is unique in this regard; before any work can be done, the client must feel understood and accepted by the counselor. A student of the author summed up this need quite appropriately: "People don't care what you know, until they know that you care." Everything the counselor asks or says to the client should be related to something the client has just said so the client can experience that the counselor is actually listening and not just thinking of things to say.

By learning several basic attending skills, the beginning crisis counselor can develop the self-confidence needed to develop rapport with someone in crisis. Use of these basic rapport-building communication skills invites clients to talk, brings calm control to the situation, allows them to talk about the facts of the situation, helps the counselor to hear and empathize with the client's feelings, and lets the client know that the counselor is concerned and respectful. Remember that the interview process does not proceed in a linear fashion; the various attending skills can be interwoven as appropriate. For example, the counselor may ask a question before reflecting or may reflect before asking a question.

Unlike other approaches to counseling, crisis intervention does not typically include the use of such techniques as interpretation or giving direct advice. These techniques generally require a therapeutic relationship of long duration before they are effective; in crisis intervention, developing such a relationship is not practical. Although it may be tempting to jump in and tell clients what is wrong with them and what to do about it, the crisis interventionist is encouraged not to do this. The basic attending skills are a useful alternative to the sometimes rote practice of asking routine questions and giving routine advice and interpretations.

The primary purpose of using the basic attending skills is to gain a clear understanding of the internal experience of the crisis as the client sees it. The focus should be on the client's feelings and thoughts about his or her situation. Too much exploration of others involved and the actual precipitating event often takes the client away from his or her self and blocks the flow of the interview. Only when the counselor truly understands can he or she help bring change to the client's emotional distress and assist the client in improving his or her functioning.

Table 3.1 can be used as a guide for the beginning counselor. It is not meant to be followed as a linear script but rather as a reminder of the skills the counselor is to use throughout the interview.

TABLE 3.1 Basic Attending Skills

	Skill Proficiency		
	Good	Fair	Poor
Attending behavior			
Eye contact			
Warmth			
Body posture			
Vocal style			
Verbal following			
Overall empathy (focus on client)			
Questioning			
Open-ended			
Close-ended			
Paraphrasing			
Restating in own words			
Clarifying			
A close-ended question that serves to clarify what the client just said			

(Continued)

TABLE 3.1   Basic Attending Skills (*Continued*)

	Skill Proficiency		
	Good	**Fair**	**Poor**
Reflection			
Painful feelings			
Positive feelings			
Ambivalent feelings			
Nonverbal feelings			
Summarization			
Tying together			
precipitating event,			
emotional distress, and cognitive elements			

Source: From *Basic Attending Skills*, Third Edition, by A.E. Ivey, N.B. Gluckstern, and M.B. Ivey, pp. 19–21, 35, 56, and 92. Copyright © 1997 Microtraining Associates. Reprinted with permission.

Attending Behavior

Of all the skills a counselor must learn, listening is probably the most essential for effective identification of the nature of the crisis. Appropriate verbal and nonverbal behavior—that is, **attending behavior**—is the hallmark of a helping interview. Good eye contact, attentive body language, expressive vocal style, and verbal following are valuable listening tools, but they are not always present in everyday conversations. The next time you carry on a conversation with a friend, observe whether these behaviors are in evidence. Using a soft, soothing voice, showing an interested face, having a relaxed posture, leaning toward the client, making direct eye contact, and maintaining close physical proximity (Cormier, Cormier, & Weisser, 1986, p. 30) are all ways to convey warmth and are part of active listening. These attending behaviors "demonstrate to the client that you are with him or her and indeed are listening," enabling the client to talk more freely (Ivey, Gluckstern, & Ivey, 1997, p. 19).

Active listening requires the ability to observe the client and at the same time pay attention to how one should best react to the client. Try the following exercise presented in Box 3.1.

Box 3.1   Basic Attending Behaviors Exercise

Break into groups of three or four. Using the basic attending skills evaluation sheet in Table 3.1, rate each other on attending behaviors. One person can play the client and another can be a crisis worker. A third can be the rater. The rater also enhances his or her skills of observation while giving feedback to the counselor. After this exercise, have some fun exaggerating an interview in which the crisis worker does not employ these behaviors (i.e., has poor eye contact, is cold, keeps arms folded, does not pay attention verbally). This behavior will impress on everyone what not to do!

Crisis workers should keep in mind that the attending behavior of different cultural and ethnic groups may vary in style, and these helpers may need to adapt when working with various subgroups as mentioned in Chapter 2. Ivey and colleagues (1997, pp. 20–21) have summarized typical variations:

- *Eye Contact:* African Americans, Latin Americans, and Native Americans may avoid eye contact as a sign of respect. With Latinos, direct, sustained eye contact can represent a challenge to authority. A bowed head may be a sign of respect from Native Americans.
- *Body Language:* The public behavior of African Americans may seem emotionally intense and demonstrative to European Americans. A slap on the back may be insulting to an Asian American or a Latin American.
- *Vocal Style:* Latin Americans often begin meetings with lengthy greetings and pleasant talk before addressing key issues. European Americans tend to value a quiet, controlled vocal style; other groups may see this as manipulative or cold.
- *Verbal Following:* Asian Americans may prefer a more indirect and subtle communication and consider the African American or European American style too direct and confrontational. Personal questions may be especially offensive to Native Americans.

Source: Reprinted with permission from Ivey, A. E., Gluckstern, N. B., & Ivey, M. B. *Basic Attending Skills,* Third Edition. pp. 19, 20–21, 35, 56, and 92. © 1997 by Microtraining Associates.

Questioning

Asking clients pertinent questions invites them to explore more of what they have spontaneously shared. **Open-ended questions** provide room for clients to express their real selves without categories imposed by the interviewer. They allow clients an opportunity to explore their thoughts and feelings without feeling interrogated by the interviewer. **Close-ended questions** can help the interviewer gather factual information such as age or marital status. However, clients frequently feel attacked or defensive with certain close-ended questions (such as "why" "do you" "are you" "have you" and "did you" questions), which should be used sparingly if at all (Ivey et al., 1997, p. 35).

Beginning counseling students tend to ask "do you," "have you," "could you," and "would you" questions. These types of close-ended questions can be answered with a "yes" or "no" by clients, with the result of a bogged-down interview. Counselors might try to avoid these types of close-ended questions, asking more specific open-ended questions instead.

Try to tie your open-ended questions to what the client has just said. Questions that begin with "what" and "how" are very effective in allowing the client to explore his or her ideas and feelings. When the question is posed effectively, it helps move the interview along and allows the gathering of essential information about the nature of the crisis. Remember, it is effective and appropriate to ask pointed open-ended questions when they relate to what the client has just said, and, hence, verbal following is extremely important to proper questioning. Whenever a client offers a new word or expresses energy behind what he or she says, the counselor can ask a question that helps him or her better understand the meaning of the word or the energy. Never assume that you know what the client means. Inquire!

The following dialogue between a client and a crisis worker shows appropriate use of questions.

> CLIENT: "I am so angry at my husband. He won't talk to me anymore and we just don't communicate at all."
>
> CRISIS WORKER: "What do you mean by communicate?"
>
> CLIENT: "He refuses to sit down and listen to me. I have no idea what his problem is. I can't get him to tell me anything. He obviously doesn't want to be around, but I don't know why."
>
> CRISIS WORKER: "What makes you think he doesn't want to be around?"
>
> CLIENT: "He is never home. He stays late at work, out with his friends every night, and is gone on the weekends. I don't know how long I can stand it."
>
> CRISIS WORKER: "What do you mean by you don't know how long you can stand it?"
>
> CLIENT: "Well, I am crying every night, my kids wonder where their dad is, and I am miserable and don't want to live like this."

(At this point, a reflection of feelings would be helpful, as would some close-ended questions about the kids' ages.)

Of course, these are not the only questions that could be asked. But notice that each question relates to what the client has just said, which has the effect of unrolling the client's cognitive and emotional experience. A useful metaphor is to think of the client's cognitive schema as a tree. The client presents the counselor with the trunk in the beginning. As the interview progresses, there is movement up the trunk and onto the branches. Each question allows movement onto the smaller branches and twigs, until the entire tree has been explored and is viewed in its totality. All branches, twigs, and leaves are connected to the trunk, whether directly or indirectly. When the counselor can see the tree fully, the nature of the crisis can be fully understood, and movement into offering coping strategies and altering cognitions can be accomplished.

Below are some examples of poorly worded questions and appropriately worded questions.

Poorly Worded Counselor Questions	Appropriately Worded Counselor Questions
Do you feel sad about losing your husband?	How do you feel about losing your husband?
Have you tried to talk to your father?	What have you done?
Could you tell me more about your sadness?	What is your sadness like for you?

Providing information in response to open-ended questions is generally more comfortable for clients than giving answers to 20 close-ended intake questions. There is a time and place for close-ended questions, usually when a fact is needed and during suicide assessments. Although it is true that many counselors must complete forms for their agencies, this does not mean that the interview should be a series of close-ended questions. Interweaving close-ended questions with open-ended questions, reflection, and paraphrasing usually allow a counselor to complete intake forms in most agencies. This takes practice, but clients benefit from this style.

Following are some examples of effective open-ended and close-ended questions. Included are suggestions for changing "why" questions into open-ended questions. Role-play these questions with friends.

Effective Open-Ended Questions	Appropriate Close-Ended Questions
How have you been feeling?	How long have you been married?
What is the worst part of being raped for you?	Have you been checked by a doctor yet?
What is it like for you to be diagnosed with AIDS?	Are you taking any medications?
How are you doing at work lately?	How old are your children?
What are your thoughts about death?	Has your husband ever abused the kids?
	Are you thinking of hurting yourself?

"Why" Questions	Open-Ended Questions That Replace "Why" Questions
Why did you ask him into your apartment?	How did things get out of control in your apartment?
Why did you smoke crack?	What was it like to decide to smoke crack?
Why did you try to kill yourself?	What was going through your mind when you took the pills?
How do these questions make you feel?	

Clarifying

Clarification questions are a form of soft closed-ended questions. Counselors use this basic attending skill when they aren't quite sure of what the client just said. Maybe they missed a piece of information because the client was speaking too fast, or presented so much information at once that the crisis worker just couldn't grasp it all. In clarifying, counselors restate in their own words what they thought they heard clients say in a questioning manner, beginning the statement with "are you saying," or "did you mean." The clarifying technique is used to clear up confusion or ambiguity and thus avoid misunderstanding and confirm the accuracy of what counselors heard. Clients might then be asked to rephrase or restate a previous message. The question is not meant to encourage clients to explore more of what was said, but simply to help counselors make sure that they understood what was said. Sometimes, clients talk in such a fragmented manner or so rapidly that important facts and ideas may not be heard accurately, and clarifying aids counselors in clearly understanding what was said.

Paraphrasing

Paraphrasing is when counselors restate in their own words what they thought they heard clients say. The crisis worker does not seek to parrot or simply repeat exactly what the client said, but instead the goal is to share with the client what was heard by the counselor. The focus is on the cognitive and factual part of the client's message. The intent is to encourage elaboration of the statements to let the client know that you, the counselor, have understood or heard the message; to help the client focus on a specific situation, idea, or action; and to highlight content when attention to affect would be premature or inappropriate (Slaikeu, 1990, p. 38). Try the paraphrase/clarification exercise provided in Box 3.2.

Reflection of Feelings

Empathy is integral to achieving and maintaining rapport with clients. This means being able to let clients know you understand their feelings. The technique of **reflection**, which is a statement that reflects the affective part or emotional tone of the client's message, whether verbal or nonverbal, is a powerful

---

Box 3.2   Paraphrasing and Clarifying Exercise

Choose a partner, and ask a third person to be an observer. One person plays the crisis interviewer, and one plays a client in crisis. After the client tells the counselor about the crisis, the counselor is to restate in his or her own words what was heard. Do not parrot or repeat exactly what was said. Sometimes it is helpful for the counselor to break out of the role and tell the observer, in the third person, what he or she heard the client say. The counselor can then go back into the role and talk directly to the client, paraphrasing what he or she heard the client say. The following dialogue shows how this might work:

CLIENT: "I've been depressed since I had to have my dog put to sleep last week. I can't sleep or concentrate at work and everyone thinks I'm a big baby."

CRISIS WORKER: "Are you saying that you have felt very bad since your dog died and aren't receiving any support from your coworkers?" (Clarifying)

CRISIS WORKER: "I hear you saying that since putting your dog to sleep last week, you've been unable to sleep and feel depressed, and no one at work seems to understand your feelings." (Paraphrasing)

tool in creating an empathic environment. Not only does it help clarify the client's feelings in a particular situation, but it also helps the client feel understood. Clients can then express their own feelings about a situation; learn to manage their feelings, especially negative ones; and express their feelings toward the mental health care provider and agency. As we saw in Chapter 1, Caplan proposed that one characteristic of people who are coping effectively is their ability to express feelings freely and master them. Reflection of feelings allows such a process to occur.

Reflections that are short may be most effective in helping clients stay with their feelings and therefore master them. If the crisis worker adds cognitive or factual information after the reflection of a feeling, the client might then focus on something other than the emotion. Try to keep it simple. Here are some examples of simple versus complicated reflections:

Simple Reflection	Complicated Reflection
I see tears in your eyes.	I notice you are crying when you speak of your father and it seems like you don't want to talk about it.
You sound angry.	Yes I can see how mad your wife makes you when she nags at you.
I sense a lot of anxiety.	So you are afraid that you won't get into graduate school.

Notice that in the simple column, the client can really only focus on the emotion while in the complicated column the client might focus on the father, the wife, or graduate school, as the case may be. Keep in mind that in the English language, people often use the words, "feel like" and "feel that" in response to the question, "How does that make you feel?" However, those phrases do not indicate emotions. They are followed by cognitions and beliefs and overall experience. Here are some differences between true feelings or emotions and thoughts and beliefs.

Emotions	Thoughts and Beliefs
I feel sad.	I feel like *I don't want to live.*
I feel mad.	I feel that *my boss doesn't understand me.*
I feel scared.	I feel like *my world is coming apart.*
I feel happy.	I feel that *I am finally on the right track.*

Notice that the italicized phrases couldn't grammatically follow the phrase "I feel." They need the qualifiers "that" or "like" or it wouldn't make sense. Also, each phrase in the thought and belief column could end with "and I feel sad, mad, scared, or happy" (as the case may be) about that. If a client responds to your open-ended question, "How does that make you feel?" with a "thought" answer, you might paraphrase the cognitive

---

Box 3.3 Reflection of Feelings Exercise

In pairs or in a group, have someone role-play a client in crisis, who will tell the others of his or her problem and feelings. Each student counselor then reflects just the feelings to the client. Listen to the emotional tone and look for nonverbal cues, such as eyes watering or a fist pounding. Try using these openings: "You seem to feel...," "Sounds as though you feel...," "I sense you are...." Look for ambivalent and contradictory feelings as well as positive feelings.

© Cengage Learning

---

component clearly and then re-ask, "What emotions do you feel when you think that?" This will help the client tune into the "feeling" part of the crisis experience and make the connection between his or her cognitions and emotional distress.

Therapists from Freud to Rogers have believed that catharsis and experiential awareness of feelings are the curative factors in therapy. The crisis interview might be the only time the client has ever felt validated in her or his feelings, and that is usually a good experience in and of itself! Try the reflection exercise presented in Box 3.3.

Summarization

The key purpose of **summarization** is to help another individual pull his or her thoughts together. A secondary purpose is to check on whether you as a helper have distorted the client's frame of reference. Summarization may be helpful in beginning an interview if you've seen the client previously; it may help to bring together threads of data over several interviews, or simply clarify what has gone on in the present interview (Ivey et al., 1997, p. 92). An example of a summarization that includes the precipitating event, cognition, and emotions might be: "So, your husband beat you last night and this time hit your daughter as well. So you are thinking that he is now so out of control you must leave him. You are scared and lonely and don't know where to turn." Summarizations differ from paraphrasing because they include almost all of the information that has been discussed in the interview, not just the information most recently presented by the client. Sometimes, when the interview is stuck, a summarization will help move it along. It can allow the client to decide which part of their crisis state they wish to continue to explore at any given moment.

As will be discussed in the "B" section below, summarization can also help make a smooth transition from identifying the problem to finding coping strategies. Usually, the cognitive and affective content are restated as well as the precipitating event and coping efforts. These aspects are easy to remember if you keep in mind the three aspects of any crisis: (1) the precipitating event; (2) the perception of the event by the client, which leads to emotional distress; and (3) the failure of the client to cope successfully with the distress.

Now that you've learned the basic attending skills, practice them in seven- to ten-minute role-plays using the Table 3.1 to guide you. Once you have mastered these skills, you are ready to move on to more advanced communication skills. The basic attending skills will be used throughout every session. These skills help counselors maintain rapport and allow them access to delicate information about the client. Counselors will use these basic attending skills during both the "B" and "C" stages of the ABC model. Notice how the ABC model is presented as three stages, but that "A" covers both "B" and "C."

B: Identifying the Problem: Follow the Model

After demographic information has been gathered and as rapport is developing, the crisis worker starts to focus on the client's presenting crisis. Identifying the problem is the second step in the ABC method and is the most crucial one. Refer to the ABC model of crisis intervention outline in Table 3.2 for a look at the interview process. Each aspect is examined individually as well as in the context of the others in the process. The most effective counselors become so well-versed in the various aspects of this model that they do not appear mechanical to the client. Keeping in mind the definition of crisis helps counselors remember what to identify: precipitating events, perceptions, emotional distress, and functioning. When all else fails, following the ABC Model will assist a counselor in moving forward in an organized manner while maintaining a connection to the client.

Although the model is presented in a linear outline form, interviews do not have to be conducted in a linear fashion. At the end of this chapter is a sample script of various questions and statements a counselor might use. However, each counselor must use his or her own intuition and listening skills to adequately respond to any individual client. Subsequent chapters offer ideas on various statements and questions counselors might use with certain types of problems, but practice and experience truly are the best teachers. Each of the subsequent chapters gives examples for practice in role-playing. Do not be restricted to using only the ideas given. Create your own ideas whenever possible. The outlines can be used for a 10-minute phone call, a 50-minute session, or a six-week (or longer) series of crisis intervention sessions. Each week, new issues can be addressed and new coping strategies sought while changes in functioning can be assessed from week to week. Notice that the model has several areas to assess. This does not mean that on every visit the counselor must make an assessment for each area. Rather, each area should be addressed at least on the first or second visit and then reassessed thereafter as necessary to evaluate the client's progress.

Of particular importance in crisis intervention and in brief therapy is the ability to explore the client's perceptions. Most sessions will be spent in this process, and through these explorations clients gain knowledge of the source of their pain. Once clients' perceptions and frame of reference regarding various situations are understood, the crisis worker is in a position to guide clients into new ways of thinking and experiencing themselves and the world. Also,

TABLE 3.2 ABC Model of Crisis Intervention

A: Use of Basic Attending Skills to Develop and Maintain Rapport
Attending behaviors
Open-ended and appropriate close-ended questions
Paraphrasing and clarifying
Reflection of feelings
Summarizations

B: Identifying the Nature of the Crisis and Therapeutic Interaction
Identify the precipitating event
Identify and explore cognitions
Identify emotional distress
Identify impairments in functioning: behaviorally, socially, academically, occupationally

Ethical checks:
Suicide, homicide, organic issues, psychosis, substance abuse, child abuse, elder abuse

Therapeutic interaction statements:
Educational, empowerment, validation, reframes

C: Coping Strategies
Explore what client wants to do now to cope
Explore how client has tried in the past to cope
Explore other things client can do to cope

Offer alternative strategies for coping:
Support groups
Twelve-step groups
Marital or family therapy
Lawyer
Doctor
Bibliotherapy
Reel therapy
Assertion training
Stress management
Shelters or other agencies
Secure commitment and follow up

once clients' cognitions are changed, emotional distress will be reduced, coping skills can be implemented, and functioning will be increased. This, as you will recall, is the goal of crisis intervention (review the beginning of Chapter 1).

The interview process can be thought of as climbing a tree with the client (see Figure 3.2). The client will usually present with the precipitating event or emotional distress such as emotional pain or impairment in functioning. The goal of the B section is to "climb the tree" to explore how all the components are related to the cognitions.

FIGURE 3.2   The Cognition Tree

Cognition 1 Is a Branch
  [Twigs and leaves explore this cognition—leaves are brown (cognitive key)]

Cognition 2 Is a Branch
  [Twigs and leaves explore this cognition—leaves are brown (cognitive key)]

Cognition 3 Is a Branch
  [Twigs and leaves explore this cognition—leaves are brown (cognitive key)]

Clients present a trunk: a precipitating event, emotions, or impairments in functioning

© Cengage Learning

The counselor climbs up the trunk with the client by asking what the client's thoughts are about the trunk. These thoughts are explored by asking the client to further explain what the client means. Open-ended questions are used to help the client explore all related thoughts and perceptions until the leaves are understood—they are the cognitive key. The counselor can help change the leaves from brown to green with therapeutic interaction comments.

Examples of therapeutic interaction comments will be presented in many sections of subsequent chapters and will be defined clearly later in this chapter. Many times, several important cognitions are presented. Each one will have to be explored and new therapeutic comments then provided. Identifying cognitions and offering new ways of thinking about the situation is the main focus of crisis intervention sessions using the ABC Model.

By exploring the many limbs and twigs of the initial perception presented, the counselor and client gain a deeper understanding of what is really bothering the client most about the precipitating event. It often takes as many as six questions before the cognitive key can be established and therapeutic statements offered. If the counselor attempts to provide an educational statement, a reframe, a support statement, or an empowerment statement too soon, the client often resists. The client probably just needed more time to fully explain his or her cognitive tree. Below is a sample dialogue in which therapist and client climb the tree:

CLIENT: "My husband left me." (Presents a precipitating event)

COUNSELOR: "What does that mean to you?" (Asks open-ended question to explore perception)

CLIENT: "I will be alone forever." (First cognition presented; client thinks she'll be alone forever)

COUNSELOR: "In what way alone?" (Counselor tries to understand exactly what client means by "alone")

CLIENT: "No one will ever love me again." (New cognitive statement)

COUNSELOR: "What makes you think that?"

CLIENT: "He told me that he's the only one who could ever love me because I'm so ugly and stupid." (More new information about the original cognition)

COUNSELOR: "What are your thoughts about the idea of your being ugly and stupid?"

CLIENT: "Well, I don't think I'm really that stupid."

COUNSELOR: "What do you think?"

CLIENT: "I'm afraid to be alone and start all over."

COUNSELOR: "What is most scary for you about this?"

CLIENT: "I'm afraid to get close to someone else and feel hurt."

COUNSELOR: "It is often scary to start over." (Support statement that validates client's feelings and thoughts) "This scary feeling may at some point turn into excitement at the opportunity to have a more rewarding relationship." (A brief reframe of the scariness possibly being excitement)

At this point, the client may feel some hope and her cognitions will probably have changed to some extent. Notice how many questions were necessary to reach the deeper meanings behind her initial cognition.

Probably the most important reason for exploring the client's internal frame of reference is that changing internal perceptions is easier than changing external situations. If the crisis worker spends too much time focusing on the significant others and the details of the situation—elements that generally cannot be changed—the client may experience increased frustration.

At the end of this chapter, a "script" using the ABC model of crisis intervention is presented. It offers specific questions and statements a crisis worker might use. It is presented after readers have had a chance to learn about each section of the model individually. Then they should be able to understand how to integrate all the sections in a typical interview.

Identifying the Precipitating Event

Shortly after the interview begins, the counselor seeks to find out about the precipitating event. To ask, "What happened that made you call for an appointment?" is appropriate. It is an opening for clients to tell what is going on with them. If clients cannot think of any particular event that brought them to counseling, the crisis worker is encouraged to probe further, explaining that understanding the trigger of a client's crisis aids in relieving the crisis state.

The precipitating event may have happened yesterday or six weeks ago. A helpful strategy is learning when the client started to feel bad, which helps pinpoint the triggering event. "The straw that broke the camel's back" is a common expression that can help clients focus on the beginning of the crisis.

FIGURE 3.3   Formula for Understanding the Process of Crisis Formation

Precipitating event $\longrightarrow$ Perception $\longrightarrow$ Emotional distress $\longrightarrow$ Lowered functioning (when coping fails)

© Cengage Learning

Another reason for specifying the precipitating event is to be able, later on, to explore how the client has been trying to cope since it happened. When the client's denial is strong, the crisis worker can confront the client about why exactly the client decided to come for counseling. The reason is usually because of difficulty in coping with a precipitating event. If the event is not clearly defined, the counselor will have problems presenting alternative coping strategies to deal with the event. Last, identification of the precipitating event is vital because the crisis worker must identify the client's perceptions about the episode. If these cognitions are not identified properly, there can be no therapeutic interactive comments related to them. Remember, change in the way the event is perceived is essential to increasing the functioning level of clients. In Chapter 1, two formulas were presented and are repeated here in figures 3.3 and 3.4. Refer to them as you practice using the ABC model.

FIGURE 3.4   Formula to Increase Functioning

Change in perception of the precipitating event and acquiring new coping skills $\longrightarrow$ Decrease in emotional distress $\longrightarrow$ Increase in functioning

© Cengage Learning

No matter how much clients profess that "nothing has happened, really," something drove them to seek help. Squeeze it out of them! They need to see that their current state of emotional distress is tied to an actual event or fact.

Recognizing the Meaning or Perception of the Precipitating Event

In addition to identifying precipitating events, crisis workers actively explore the meaning clients ascribe to these events. It is clients' perceptions of stressful situations that cause them to be in a crisis state as well as the inability to cope with the stress. Usually, stress originates from one of four areas: loss of control, loss of self-esteem, loss of nurturance, or forced adjustment to a change in life or role. The meaning behind these losses is helpful to explore.

All aspects of the situation will be examined. For example, suppose a woman is raped. Not only does the actual rape cause stress, but her perception of how her husband will react also contributes to her stress as she struggles with her perceived new role with him.

Some questions the crisis worker may ask to elicit the client's frame of reference regarding the crisis situation include these:

- "How do you put it together in your head?"
- "What do you think about this?"
- "What does it mean to you that...?"
- "What are you telling yourself about...?"
- "What assumptions are you making about...?"

Cognitive restructuring or reframing is a valuable tool for the counselor but can be done only if the client's current cognitions are known. It is impossible to develop a coping plan for clients without examining the cognitive and perceptual experience. Think of yourself as a mechanic who needs to analyze and experience the trouble firsthand before tinkering with the engine. Crisis workers can think of themselves as "cognitive mechanics."

Assessing the client's perception of the precipitating event is one of the most important parts of the interview and is to be done thoroughly on every visit to check for changing views as well as long-standing views on a variety of issues.

Identifying Emotional Distress and Functioning Level

In addition to exploring stressors and clients' perceptions of them, counselors also inquire about clients' emotional distress and functioning levels and how the precipitating events are affecting them. Clients seem to benefit from expressing painful feelings and sharing other symptoms—symptoms that may impair clients' occupational, academic, behavioral, social, interpersonal, or family functioning. Counselors can ask how clients' perceptions about the precipitating event are affecting their functioning in each area and what thoughts they are having that are linked to various painful emotions. Keep in mind that the more emotional distress a person experiences, the more likely that functioning will be impaired so this link between feelings and functioning should also be explored.

Often each area in which the person is suffering distress is dealt with separately because a specific perception may be associated with that area and not another. The crisis worker is advised to explore each area affected during the crisis state in as much detail as possible. This probing gives the counselor a feel for the degree of impairment the client is experiencing and can be used later to help select coping strategies. When clients discuss their symptoms and impairments in functioning, they can receive feedback, education, and support from the counselor. In addition to identifying the client's current level of functioning, the crisis worker may wish to assess the client's precrisis level of functioning in order to compare the two. This will help the counselor determine the level of coping the client can realistically achieve; it also gives the counselor an idea of the severity of the crisis for the person. The comparison serves as a basis for evaluating the outcome of crisis intervention. Remember that the goal of crisis intervention is to bring the client back to the precrisis level of functioning.

Making Ethical Checks

Several other areas are usually identified in an initial interview. These have ethical implications and are assessed either directly or indirectly with every client. However, in order not to behave like a prosecuting attorney, the crisis worker is encouraged to extract this information in a fluid, relevant manner. This means waiting until the client says something spontaneously related to any of the following ethical issues. These ethical issues are very important and will be discussed in detail in subsequent chapters.

Suicide Check   Because people in crisis are vulnerable and often confused and overwhelmed, suicide sometimes becomes an alternative for them. Every crisis worker must assess for suicidality, particularly when the client is depressed or impulsive. Suicide assessment and prevention are discussed in detail in Chapter 4.

Homicidal or Abuse Issues   As discussed in Chapter 2, mental health workers in many states are required to report child and elder abuse and any suspicion that a client may harm someone. Assessment of these issues must be done during the course of an interview. Often, the counselor's intuition will provide the basis for detailed inquiry. Child abuse and elder abuse are dealt with in subsequent chapters; working with clients who are a danger to others is examined in Chapter 4. Two examples of appropriate ethical checks are provided below in Box 3.4.

Box 3.4   Examples of Homicidal/Abuse Issues

Example 1: A 43-year-old male may say that he hates his father for having beaten his mother and can see himself smashing the father's face. This statement alone does not warrant an attempt to take the client into custody. However, I would inquire how he deals with this anger, especially toward his wife and children. It is important for counselors to know that suspected abuse of children must be assessed in all cases. Sometimes, turning away and collaborating in denial with an abusive family is easier than facing the issue, but doing so is never in the best interest of the child. Such action is unethical and might be illegal, depending on the laws of the state where the action occurs.

Example 2: The mother of a 15-year-old boy and a 16-year-old girl is in a crisis state and seeks help from a counselor. Two weeks earlier, the husband whipped the boy with a belt and left welts on his back. The father also slapped the girl across the face. When the mother was informed by the crisis worker that a child abuse report would have to be made, she was very upset and pleaded with the therapist not to make the report. She thought that it would affect her getting a high-security job for which she was applying, would make the husband angry, and would cause anxiety for her son, who was worried that his dad would take his car away. The counselor explained that a report was mandatory in this situation. To alleviate the mother's concern, the counselor made the report in the presence of the clients, so they would know what would most likely happen according to the social worker taking the call.

Making clients part of the reporting process helped them deal with it in a less fearful manner. The counselor had no choice but to make the report, even though the clients did not want her to.

Organic or Other Concerns   If clients state that they suffer from a serious mental condition such as **depression, bipolar disorder, obsessive-compulsive disorder,** or **schizophrenia,** they should already be receiving medication. Crisis workers can assess for medication compliance for these cases and encourage noncompliant clients to continue with prescribed medication until they can schedule an appointment with their physician. In these situations, crisis workers may want to consult with the physician by phone to ensure that clients receive the most effective treatment. When clients describe or exhibit behaviors, symptoms, or complaints that may be due to biological factors such as Alzheimer's disease or attention deficit disorder with hyperactivity (ADHD) or any other **organic brain disorder** but have not yet been formally diagnosed with a serious disorder, ethical standards require crisis workers to refer them to a physician or psychiatrist for further assessment. Chapter 4 presents a brief discussion of how to use the Mental Status Exam to assess for these serious medical disorders.

Substance Abuse Issues

Checking for substance abuse on a regular basis is a good idea and is often part of the intake form in most agencies. Since clients involved with substance use and abuse often deny and minimize their use, the crisis worker might be a bit more assertive in gathering information about drug use. Following are some examples showing how to extract this information without offending clients:

> *"Tell me about your past and present drug and alcohol use."*
>
> *This statement assumes that use exists or existed and is stated matter-of-factly, as if you won't be shocked to hear of it. The person who has not used drugs can simply say, "None."*
>
> *"How much alcohol do you use a week?"*
>
> *"What other drugs besides cocaine do you use or have you used?"*
>
> *These questions do not seem to be as judgmental or grilling as the following do:*
>
> *"Do you use alcohol? Do you use cocaine? Do you smoke pot? Do you drink daily?"*

Using general, open-ended questions will save time and reduce defensiveness in clients.

Therapeutic Interaction

The main part of the session, and probably the most therapeutic part, will be spent in identifying the client's beliefs and feelings, and then providing validating statements, educational statements, empowering statements, and reframing statements that will aid the client in thinking differently about the situation and assist them in coping with it. Of course, active listening skills remain important, but once these are used to identify the nature of the crisis, the counselor is ready to use the more advanced skills discussed next to help clients improve their coping ability.

Validation Statements   The counselor may, from time to time, tell clients that their feelings are normal or suggest there is hope that things will get better. In response to a woman who has just found out that her husband has been molesting their daughter and feels as though the world has come to an end, a crisis worker might respond supportively by saying, "I know that right now you feel that everything is falling apart, but many people have gone through the same situation and have survived. You have every reason to believe you can survive, too." Other validation comments that are useful include, "It is understandable that you might feel that way," "Your pain is understandable considering how difficult your situation is," or "Many people going through this would also feel and think this way."

Validating statements are not false hopes or words like "It'll be okay," "Don't worry," or "Forget about it." These comments are typical of family and friends who mean well; however, they are not very useful. As crisis workers, we need to say things to people that others do not say. Because counselors have knowledge of a variety of traumatic situations based on experience of working with others and from training, they are able to provide validation to a client that what the client is experiencing has been experienced by others and that his or her reaction is not out of the ordinary. Also, because clients see counselors as experts in crisis situations, they will tend to take comfort in validating comments from these helpers, often adopting a more optimistic attitude. Receiving validation from a counselor about one's feelings can help clients not see themselves as sick, weak, or bad.

Educational Statements   Providing factual information, whether developmental or situational, is vital in every crisis. Clients often suffer merely because they lack or have incorrect knowledge about the precipitating event and aspects associated with it. Thus, it is imperative for crisis workers to gather as much information as possible about each crisis situation. Whether this is done through formal academic courses, books, experience, or supervision, it gives counselors an edge in helping clients work through their issues. General knowledge of statistics and prevalence rates of various traumas that often trigger crises states are vital for effective crisis intervention.

Educational statements may include psychological, social, and interpersonal dynamics, or statistics or frequency of the problem. In any case, when a counselor helps people in a crisis state increase their knowledge of facts, the clients will have stronger coping skills for the current crisis and future crises. You will remember from Chapter 1 that seeking reality and information was one of Caplan's characteristics of effective coping behavior. Box 3.5 gives an example of the use of an educational statement.

Box 3.5   Example of the Use of an Educational Statement

Picture a woman who has been completely isolated from others because she is in an ongoing battering relationship. She will most likely perceive herself as abnormal and bizarre. When she learns that about 30 percent of women live in such relationships, she may feel differently about herself and the abnormality of the situation. Without this issue to deal with, the counselor is now free to process other issues.

© Cengage Learning

Empowering Statements   Clients who are in certain crisis situations in which they feel violated, victimized, or helpless respond well to empowering statements. Clients are presented with choices and are encouraged to take back personal power by making helpful choices. Battered women, rape survivors, and survivors of child abuse often suffer from learned helplessness stemming from the abuse. They think that they cannot prevent bad things from happening because, in the past, they could not prevent abuse by a physically stronger (or in some other way stronger) perpetrator. This perception often motivates them to survive abuse rather than try and escape from it. A useful strategy is to let clients know that they may not have had the choice to stop the abuse from happening at an earlier time but that now they certainly can make choices to do something about the abuse (e.g., press charges, confront the perpetrator, talk about it). Also, the crisis worker can point out that they do not have to choose certain behaviors. It is important that they move from a position of feeling powerless to feeling that they have some control and choice in their life now. See Box 3.6 for an example of an empowerment statement.

Reframing Statements   In its simplest form, reframing is defining a situation differently from the way the client is defining it. It is a cognitive-restructuring tactic that aims at changing the crisis from danger to opportunity. American clichés such as, "Every cloud has a silver lining" and "When life gives you lemons, make lemonade" convey this idea quite clearly.

Reframing may seem like rationalizing away a problem to some. However, it is probably one of the strongest healing skills available to the crisis worker and for people in general. It allows us to acknowledge that life is a struggle, that we aren't perfect, and that dwelling on our failings is not necessary or helpful. Instead, if we can believe that something positive or beneficial will be an outcome or result of the problem, we can usually integrate the difficult episode more easily. The crisis worker's responsibility is to be creative in finding the right reframe, which means actively searching for the positive. Reframing is an advanced technique that puts problems in a solvable form

---

Box 3.6   Example of the Use of an Empowerment Statement

Example: A rape victim might be told, "You didn't have a choice in being raped, but now you do have a choice of what to do. You can call the police, go to counseling, tell a friend, or not do any of these things. Let's talk about your feelings and thoughts on each of these choices."

© Cengage Learning

Box 3.7   Example of the Use of a Reframing Statement

The author worked with a woman whose rape case was rejected by the district attorney after she had hoped for a year that it would go to court. The rapist was free, and her victimization had not been acknowledged because of a legal technicality. The counselor and client could have both thrown up their hands, called the judicial system names, and seethed internally. Alternatively, the counselor pointed out to the client that the rape prodded her to seek counseling that allowed her not only to work through the rape issues, but also to identify her codependency and its effects on her relationships. This knowledge led the way to better family relations and intimacy with her boyfriend. The reframe was that the rape, although terrifying, had been survived and indirectly allowed for an opportunity to gain self-understanding and growth. This client could tolerate this reframe because she had undergone one year of intensive therapy and had strong rapport with the counselor, who truly understood the client's frame of reference.

---

by changing the meanings of behaviors and situations and providing a new perspective that opens up new possibilities for change. Box 3.7 shows an example of reframing.

Reframing is possible only if the counselor first understands fully the client's current frame of reference. Otherwise, the counselor would not know what should be reframed. Counselors can learn the client's frame of reference by asking direct questions: "How do you perceive the situation?" "What does it mean to you?" "What runs through your head about it?" Reframing is not a technique to be taken lightly, and careful supervision is necessary in learning its effective use. Sometimes reframing is associated with a cold, strategic approach, but it can be done in an authentic, caring manner. The counselor does not deny the seriousness of the problem but instead offers a way out of a problem that allows the person to preserve the integrity of the self and often the family unit as well. Because reframes are usually offered with the person's self-identity in mind, shame is reduced and self-integrity is preserved. Because reframing is challenging for beginning counselors, examples of potential reframes are provided in subsequent chapters. It may take several years for a counselor to learn the art of reframing. Brainstorming with others is a useful way to learn how to formulate reframes.

In summary, the B section of the ABC model can be thought of as identifying issues one at a time and providing various forms of feedback as the process moves forward to a place where the client can accept coping as viable behavior. Periodically, the crisis worker summarizes the precipitating events, the client's perceptions of them, the client's functioning in several areas of life, and any major symptoms of concern.

C: Coping

The last step of the ABC model is concerned with the client's coping behavior—past, present, and future. Past coping success can be built on to help the person weather the present and future difficulties.

Exploring the Client's Own Attempts at Coping

Toward the conclusion of an interview, counselors begin summing up the problem and moving clients into a coping mode. To do this, crisis workers ask clients what they would like to do now to start coping with the problem. Often, the counselor will have seeded potential resources during the educational comments such as when a client is informed that support groups exist for rape survivors or twelve-step groups are usually the only thing that really helps an addict abstain long term. If these resonated with the client during the B section, it is probable that the client will mention it as something that might help. If clients cannot think of anything, they might be asked how they have managed crises in the past. All coping, whether it is helpful or not, should be examined. In this way, clients can make a mental list of what works and what does not.

If clients cannot think of any past coping behavior, the crisis worker can assertively encourage them. The counselor might say, "Well, you must have done something or you would not have made it this far." Remember that even sleeping and social withdrawal are coping strategies, and the counselor and client can talk about their helpfulness or unhelpfulness. Eliciting unhealthy attempts at coping is especially valuable as it helps the client see what has not worked in the past. The client will generally be more open to alternatives once the ineffectiveness of his or her current behavior is made evident.

Encouraging the Development of New Coping Behaviors

After current ideas about what the client might like to do now to cope and current and past coping attempts have been discussed, the counselor can prod clients to ponder other possible ways of coping. Remember that clients have already been presented with educational information, reframes, supportive comments, and empowerment statements. It is time for clients to do some of their own thinking. Clients are more likely to follow through with a plan they have developed themselves than with one suggested by the counselor. It is appropriate for a counselor to be challenging and persistent in getting clients to think of ways they could begin to cope better. This approach helps clients get in touch with their problem-solving abilities.

Presenting Alternative Coping Behaviors

Clients are first allowed to propose their own methods for coping with their problems. When they have reached the end of the resources they know, however, the counselor can then suggest other options. Many of these may be completely new to clients, offering them fresh insights. The suggestions offered by the counselor are best based on previous discussions with the client. The client will often provide the counselor with the best alternative for that particular client. For example, a client might have said that one of the things that made her feel better was talking to her girlfriends about her divorce. But now, she says, they are tired of listening. This might trigger in the counselor the idea that this client feels better talking to a group of women about her problem.

Getting the client to accept a referral to a support group should not be difficult, because the client herself has said that doing this type of thing has already made her feel better!

Support Groups and Twelve-Step Groups   If support systems haven't already been discussed, now is a good time to identify some existing natural support, such as coworkers, supervisors, relatives, friends, schoolmates, or church members. Clients may not have considered any of these people as helpers in getting through the crisis. With a little encouragement, they may be persuaded to reach out to others. This is not to suggest that crisis workers should avoid giving support to clients. However, it is often more comfortable for clients to receive help from natural **support systems** than to rely on mental health professionals during crises. As Caplan (1964) suggested earlier, people who are coping effectively with a situation will actively ask others for help, not necessarily mental health workers. The idea of encouraging clients to help themselves parallels the adage of teaching a man to fish versus just giving him fish. Self-sufficiency is more economical in the long run. The author has often felt that as a crisis interventionist, her job is to put herself out of a job by encouraging clients to function on their own and with the support of others in their life. A crisis worker is merely a beacon shedding light on these resources.

Some clients may need referrals to twelve-step groups such as Alcoholics Anonymous (AA), Al-Anon, Co-Dependents Anonymous, Cocaine Anonymous, or others. These mutual self-help groups are free and have no time limits for attendance; sessions can be found in every city at various hours of the day. The trend now is for insurance companies to pay for only six to twelve sessions of therapy, so twelve-step groups are a lifesaver for many people who cannot afford to pay for therapy out of their own pockets.

Long-Term Therapy, Marital Therapy, and Family Therapy   Some clients' problems have been going on for so long that crisis intervention cannot resolve them. Perhaps because of a personality disorder or other chronic emotional disorder, clients need ongoing therapy with a trained professional. This might be individual therapy or marital or family therapy. Often, a crisis is an opportunity for clients to resolve long-term problems that have been hidden for many years.

Shelters and Other Agencies   To address other problems, crisis workers need to be knowledgeable about community agencies and **resources**. Clients who are anxious and feeling overwhelmed are more likely to follow through with a referral when it is presented in written form with choices, addresses, phone numbers, and fees. Providing written information is much more effective than telling clients to look for certain services in the Yellow Pages. Even if you are conducting a phone interview, having these resources in hand, separated by the type of crisis, certainly aids the expediency of referral. Also, crisis workers will know whether an agency can actually help a client at an affordable rate if workers have recently updated their information about the agency.

Most communities have community resource directories that list various agencies, and local libraries also have listings available. One of the best ways to get names of agencies is by contacting an agency that has similar services. Most mental health and social service agencies are familiar with agencies in the community.

A useful assignment for beginning crisis intervention students is to do research on various community agencies and resources that regularly intervene in crisis situations. It is amazing to learn how many resources are available in most communities for almost any crisis situation. Community resources were developed during the grassroots era of the 1960s, and they have evolved over the years into an elaborate networking system of many different agencies. Large organizations often have nationwide toll-free phone numbers that workers can call to get information about many agencies. The organizations serve as clearinghouses for a variety of resources. Some examples of community resources include local churches, local community colleges, county mental health agencies, local AA groups, and private clubs such as the Sierra Club.

Some resources are more appropriate for certain crises than others. Suicidal clients should be given a list of hotlines to call, if necessary, between sessions. Persons suffering a loss from divorce might be referred to a divorce-recovery workshop through a church or support group. Clients dealing with issues related to HIV or AIDS should be referred to a local AIDS services foundation for support groups. It is widely known that substance abusers and their significant others benefit from twelve-step groups such as AA or Al-Anon. Sexual assault victims and battered women benefit from a referral to shelters or specialized support groups.

At times, crisis workers may want to contact an agency and let someone there know about a referral. It is quite reasonable to ask for a follow up call or note about whether the client used the resource. In other instances, a client may return to a crisis worker for another individual session and the crisis worker at that time can ask whether the client attended the support group or used the service recommended.

Medical and Legal Referrals   In some cases, **medical or legal referrals** are necessary. Even crisis workers who are considered paraprofessionals should have an understanding of the legal, political, and medical systems and how they will make an impact on various types of crises. For instance, workers should know the conditions under which a police officer may arrest a battering spouse. Also, they should have knowledge of restraining orders, which may be useful for a victim of abuse. How the court system generally deals with rape or child abuse is useful information as well. Though they are not expected to be lawyers, crisis workers need to keep abreast of recent laws that affect clients in crisis.

Similarly, though they are not expected or allowed to be physicians, crisis workers need to be able to refer someone to a doctor for an evaluation when medication or other treatment might be useful. Learning to consult and work with medical doctors is a skill worth developing, and knowing when to make a referral to a physician is vital.

Bibliotherapy, Journaling, and Reel Therapy   It would be optimal for every crisis worker to have some knowledge of reading material for clients in a variety of crisis situations. Using these materials with clients is called **bibliotherapy**. Reading often provides a new way of looking at the crisis (reframing) and gives the client information and support—especially books written by a person who has gone through a similar crisis. For example, reading a book by a woman who was raped will help the recently raped woman see that her feelings are normal; this knowledge should have a calming effect. Also, reading helps people think rather than feel, encouraging more productive problem-solving activity. Having clients keep a journal of their thoughts is also quite helpful; the clients may discover new feelings and thoughts as they jot them down on paper. The journal may be shared with the counselor or remain private.

Many therapists are also using movies to help move their clients toward breakthroughs more quickly. Viewing movies allows clients to "grow" in their own "free" time. For example, Nielsen (quoted in Hesley, 2000, pp. 55–57) has used the movie *Distant Thunder* for clients experiencing posttraumatic stress disorder. He states that many of his clients find it easier to explain their own "flashbacks" and "social phobia" after viewing this film. The use of films—so-called **reel therapy**—is likely to become more common because many future therapists watch films as part of their graduate school studies. Films do have limitations and should not take the place of personal discussion with the counselor. Movies should be selected carefully and thoughtfully (pp. 55–57).

Other Behavioral Activities   Some clients may benefit from assertiveness training, in which the counselor teaches them how to ask for what they want, express feelings and needs to others, or set boundaries with others. Other tasks may include having clients exercise, visit friends and family, or engage in a recreational activity such as going to the beach. Stress management classes may also be useful for helping clients organize their time and daily life activities.

All of these types of coping referrals provide ways for the client to cope and think differently about the precipitating event.

Commitment and Follow Up

Part of making any referral or suggestion is commitment and follow up; that is, counselors get a commitment from clients that they will indeed follow through with recommendations. This explains why it is best for clients to develop their own coping plans; they are more likely to follow through with a plan they have formulated themselves. In some cases, as with highly suicidal clients, a written contract may be prudent. The no-suicide contract is a useful intervention that will be discussed in Chapter 4. Written contracts are often used with clients who need to control their impulses or with acting-out teenagers. Both the therapist and the client keep a copy of the contract and discuss it at the next session.

In sum, the C part of the ABC model first asks clients to explore current, past, and possibly new coping strategies to deal with the crisis at hand. Then the crisis worker offers alternative ideas, makes referrals, and asks clients for a commitment to follow through on the plan. The worker's hope is that clients will move from a dysfunctional state to a higher level of functioning and perceived control over the precipitating event. At each visit, the crisis worker can verify and suggest connecting with these various coping aids, which gives clients something concrete to take home.

Case Example: Using the ABC Model of Crisis Intervention with a Survivor of Military Sexual Trauma

To sum up the ABC model, a sample script is presented in Table 3.3. This gives readers an idea of the types of questions to ask and statements to make when using the ABC model. CW refers to crisis worker and C refers to client.

In sum, follow the client and follow the model when all else fails!!

TABLE 3.3   ABC Model of Crisis Intervention (Sample Script)

A: BASIC ATTENDING SKILLS

CW: What brings you in today? (Open-ended question)
C: I've been feeling down and not myself lately.
CW: You look a bit tired and sad as you say that. (Reflection)
C: Yes, it's been hard for me to come back home.
CW: You've just come back home? (Clarification)
C: I was in Iraq for a year and came home last month.
CW: You served in Iraq for a year and recently returned. (Paraphrase)

B: IDENTIFYING THE PROBLEM AND THERAPEUTIC INTERACTION

Identify the Precipitating Event:

CW: What made you decide you needed to make this appointment right now?
C: My mom told me that I am acting weird.
CW: In what way weird? (Open-ended question)
C: Last week I got up in the middle of the night and ran around the house shouting. (Identified precipitating event)

Explore Meanings, Cognitions, and Perceptions:

CW: What are your thoughts about that happening? (First open-ended question to explore cognitions)

(Continued)

TABLE 3.3 ABC Model of Crisis Intervention (Sample Script) (*Continued*)

C: I must be a total looney.

CW: In what way do your mean looney? (Explores new term)

C: You know, crazy, normal people don't do that.

CW: What is your understanding of how you came to do something that you think of as crazy? (Continue to explore cognitions)

C: I think I woke up thinking I was in Iraq and someone was attacking me.

CW: What are your thoughts about that?

C: Maybe I'm re-living a sexual assault that happened to me over there.

CW: So you woke up in the middle of the night yelling and you thought you might be looney but now you think it might be related to a trauma you experienced in Iraq? (Clarifying summarization)

C: I don't want to talk about it.

CW: What makes you not want to talk about it?

C: I feel guilty, like it was my fault. I should have stopped it.

Identify Emotional Distress:

CW: Sounds scary (reflection)

C: You don't know the half of it.

CW: I'd like to. Especially if it prevents you from fully functioning. You said earlier that you've been feeling down too. It must be difficult to be around people feeling scared and sad. (Reflection of emotional distress)

C: Yes, I don't even want to hang out with my friends anymore.

Identify Impairments in Functioning in the Following Areas:

1. **Social**

   CW: So you aren't seeing your friends. (Paraphrase). Have you done anything socially lately at all? How are things going with your family?

   C: Well, I pretty much only talk with this girl that I served with and sometimes I talk with my mom. I started school and it's hard to talk with my classmates. I feel alienated and anxious a lot. No one understands me.

2. **Academic**

   CW: Oh, you're in school. How are classes going? How are your concentration skills? Sometimes it can be challenging to focus after returning from a war zone.

   C: Yes, it's hard. I have TBI (traumatic brain injury) because I was exposed to an intense explosion so my mind wanders at times. Sometimes I hear a noise and I get startled in class. It's embarrassing.

3. **Occupational**

   CW: Are you working too or just focusing on college right now?

   C: Just college, it's all I can handle.

4. **Behavioral:**

   CW: I know you said you are tired and depressed. Is this affecting your sleep pattern?

   C: Yeah, I can't get to sleep most nights, the doctor gave me sleeping pills.

   CW: How about your appetite? Are you eating OK?

(Continued)

TABLE 3.3 ABC Model of Crisis Intervention (Sample Script) (*Continued*)

C: I sometimes find myself overeating just to keep me numb.

Identify Any Ethical Concerns:

1. **Suicide assessment**

    CW: You mentioned you feel depressed and wish to keep numb. I'm concerned that you may be feeling sad and perhaps have had thoughts of suicide. Have you thought of harming yourself or ending things? (Assess ideation)

    C: Actually, yes. It would make things easier to just go to sleep and forget everything.

    CW: Do you have a plan as to when or how you would do this? (Assess plan)

    C: Maybe take all my sleeping pills with vodka.

    CW: Do you have the pills and vodka available? (Assess means)

    C: Yes of course.

    CW: What has stopped you?

    C: My mom has been through enough with me being deployed and all. It would kill her.

    CW: Yes it would most likely be devastating to her. I'm sure you have developed inner strength to bear your pain as part of military training. But I'm glad you have come to talk to me so you don't have to bear it alone.

2. **Child abuse, elder abuse, homicide**

    CW: You mentioned earlier that some things happened that you don't want to talk about. I'm concerned about how you are dealing with what seems like a pretty traumatic situation.

    C: It's not good. I have learned to really hate the military for how they handled things.

    CW: You sound pretty angry.

    C: Well they put the blame on the wrong person. As usual the jerk who caused the problem will get away with it. If I had my way, I'd handle him myself.

    CW: What do you mean you would handle him

    C: I'd like to make him suffer and feel my pain the way he made me feel.

    CW: Do you think you would ever take action against him physically?

    C: No, but I daydream about bashing his face in.

    CW: Sounds like you are very mad and want to hurt him, but that you won't act on it.

    C: Yeah, I am still battling this issue in court so I will behave, but that's why I came to see you.

3. **Organic or other medical concerns**

    CW: Sounds like your feelings to harm yourself and your wishes to hurt this man are under control for now. I am wondering about your sleep and eating however. Are you able to get out of bed, get ready, and function when you need to? Sometimes when people are depressed, they see a physician for an evaluation and possible medication.

    C: The doctor at the VA already suggested that I take antidepressants but I told him I only want the sleep aid for now. I can function OK.

    CW: Well let's monitor that and let me know if you change your mind and I can provide with you a referral to a physician or psychiatrist if need be.

(Continued)

TABLE 3.3   ABC Model of Crisis Intervention (Sample Script) (*Continued*)

4.   **Identify Substance Abuse Issues:**

   CW: You did mention earlier that your plan would be to drink vodka with those pills. I'm wondering if you have been drinking a bit more to help deal with your stress, or maybe using other types of drugs?

   C: Yes, I do like a cocktail at night, to get me through, you know. And sometimes me and my friends fire up a joint when we have weed.

   CW: Is this something that you think you need help with?

   C: Maybe, not sure if it's a problem, but yeah sometimes I pass out.

   CW: Well there are twelve-step groups for people struggling with drinking issues and I can give you a list of places if you like.

   C: Let me think about it.

Use Therapeutic Interactions:

1.   **Educational comments**

   CW: When someone is sexually assaulted, it is not uncommon to turn to drinking and drugging to help numb anxiety and feelings that are unpleasant. It takes time for the psyche to integrate a trauma like that. Additionally, you are also dealing with the trauma of being exposed to war, death, and other untold traumatic situations. Many of the symptoms you have mentioned are symptoms of Post Traumatic Stress Disorder. Researchers have suggested that these particular wars are incubators for PTSD because those serving never know when a fire fight will ensue or who the enemy is. It makes sense to feel helpless and get startled. The mind has to slowly learn to integrate these experiences. On top of this, you also have to integrate the sexual assault trauma.

   C: Yeah, I've heard about PTSD, but I don't really like to see myself as crazy. I'm strong and can usually handle anything.

   CW: I'm sure you are and when you were serving your mindset was one of strength for the team and survival. Now, though you are safe and the same behaviors that were necessary when serving are not necessary. Also, when someone is sexually assaulted they often feel like it is their fault, but I'd like you to consider that a felony crime was committed against you and that sexual assault is about power and control. It is entirely the perpetrator's fault.

2.   **Empowerment statements**

   CW: Being strong and not focusing on feelings gave you power while in combat. Now, it is stripping you of personal power because it prevents you from living fully. You can take back power and control of your life by learning to openly deal with your PTSD and your traumas. Taking back your feelings and learning to master them usually leads to increased feelings of control. Although you were a victim of sexual assault, by talking about it and feeling the pain, you become a survivor.

3.   **Support statements**

   *   *CW: This is an extremely difficult situation, and I don't take it lightly. I can only imagine the pain you are going through. I am so sorry this happened to you.*
   *   *Please, let me be there for you; I care. It must feel pretty bad if you have thoughts of harming yourself. These kinds of traumas often make people feel*

TABLE 3.3 ABC Model of Crisis Intervention (Sample Script) (*Continued*)

---

like giving up. It is understandable that you feel alienated from others since they didn't go through what you went through. However, there are people who have been sexually assaulted and understand that. There are many support groups that deal with sexual assault because it is so prevalent.

4. **Reframes**

   CW: It takes a lot of strength for you to feel this kind of pain. So all that strength you have been using to numb your pain can be harnessed to feel the pain and integrate it into your life. Instead of having a destructive effect, it can build you into a stronger person who has survived horrific trauma.

C. IDENTIFY CLIENT'S CURRENT COPING STRATEGIES AND ATTEMPTS

CW: At this point, what are some things you think you would like to do?
C: Well, maybe talk more about it.
CW: Great. Any ideas about where or with whom you'd like to talk?
C: I'm not sure, can I keep talking with you?
CW: Sure, I'd like that. Can you think of anything else that might help you?
C: One of my veteran friends went to a veteran's group. What do you think?
CW: That would be very helpful. Your campus has several groups. Why don't you try the Veteran's center there?
C: I think I will.

Present Alternative Coping Ideas:

1. **Refer to support groups, twelve-step groups**

   CW: What would you think about going to a support group for sexual assault survivors?
   C: I'm scared that it may affect my case.
   CW: How so?
   C: Well my attorney said not to tell people about it.
   CW: Well certainly with me, anything you say is confidential. Maybe the group could wait until you confer with your attorney about going. Do you think a twelve-step group like Alcoholics Anonymous would be something you could benefit from?
   C: Maybe, but I don't think I'm an alcoholic. I just drink when I'm really anxious.
   CW: OK, let's keep our eyes open on your drinking and if it seems to become a bigger issue, we can revisit AA.

2. **Refer to long-term therapy, family therapy**

   CW: It sounds like you are open to continuing in counseling with me. Let's keep that up for awhile and also you can visit the Vet center and see what services they think might be best for you. I know a therapist there who does Sand Tray therapy which is very helpful for PTSD and veterans.
   C: That sounds cool, I'll go talk to them.

3. **Refer to medical doctor or psychiatrist**

   CW: I do want to keep an open mind about seeing a physician. If your symptoms become more serious, you might wish to consider another evaluation.

(*Continued*)

TABLE 3.3 ABC Model of Crisis Intervention (Sample Script) (*Continued*)

4. **Legal referral**

   If you would like me to talk to your attorney I will. She needs to understand that you need to talk openly about what happened to you to help you overcome your suffering. Or you could inform her that you are in therapy and see what she says.

5. **Refer to shelter, other agency**

   If you want another referral, I suggest you look into the community vet center. They have many services provided by veterans who can truly understand your experiences.

6. **Recommend reading books and keeping a journal**

   CW: Do you like to read? I know of some really good books that help explain more about what you are going through. Here is a list of books I recommend for you to read. Also, many clients feel more under control if they keep a journal while going through difficult times.

Obtain Commitment; Do Follow up:

When can you make another appointment with me? I'd like you to let me know when you have visited the veteran's center at school.

© Cengage Learning

Chapter Review

The ABC model of crisis intervention is a structured short-term approach to help people work through a variety of situational and developmental crises. It is loosely based on Jones's ABC crisis management model, Adler's four stage model of therapy, and the current needs of nonprofit agencies, HMO centers, and public mental health agencies. The A section refers to the use of basic attending skills to develop and maintain rapport while the crisis worker begins the process of identifying the information in the B and C sections. Attending behavior, paraphrasing, clarifying, reflection, open-ended questions, and summarizations are the crux of these basic attending skills. During the B section, the nature of the crisis is identified, and therapeutic comments are presented by the counselor. After identifying the precipitating event, the cognitions associated with the event, the emotional distress, and impairments in functioning, the crisis worker is able to provide feedback such as reframes, empowerment statements, educational statements, and validation statements. In the C section, coping strategies are developed by the client and counselor together.

Answers to Pre-Chapter Quiz

1. T   2. F   3. F   4. T   5. T   6. T   7. F   8. F   9. T   10. F

Key Terms for Study

attending behavior: Behavior that has to do with following the client's lead, actively listening, and demonstrating presence.

bibliotherapy: The use of books as an alternative coping strategy.

bipolar disorder: A condition in which states of manic behavior (i.e., out-of-control, hyper, grandiose behavior) fluctuate with states of extreme depression. It is sometimes known as manic-depression.

close-ended question: A type of question that can be answered with a "yes" or a "no" or some other one-word answer. Its best use is for obtaining facts such as age, number of children, or number of years married. Forced-choice questions, or "do you," "have you," questions, are generally not effective. These types of questions can bring the interview to a dead end or sound like an interrogation.

depression: A state of being in which the client is sad, low in energy, and suicidal; he or she feels worthless, helpless, and hopeless; the person lacks desire, is socially withdrawn, and is slowed in processes such as thinking and concentrating. This person should be referred to a physician for an evaluation.

medical or legal referrals: Referrals made by the crisis worker if the client needs the services of other professionals, as when a person has been arrested, wants a restraining order, or has a severe mental or other illness.

Obsessive-compulsive disorder: This clinical syndrome is thought to be primarily due to chemical imbalance. Individuals suffering from this disorder engage in unwanted behaviors, often rituals that the person feels while the crisis worker begins the process of identifying the information in the B and C sections. He or she cannot control. Along with behavioral ritual, the person often has thoughts that are felt to be out of control as well. Some examples include compulsive hand washing, checking lights, and thinking constantly about running over children.

open-ended questions: The questions usually begin with "what" and "how" and allow clients to expand on material they have brought up on their own.

organic brain disorder: A condition resulting from a neurological disturbance, genetic abnormality, or tumor.

paraphrasing: A basic attending skill, or clarifying technique, in which counselors restate in their own words what was just said by the client.

rapport: A special type of bonding that a counselor seeks with a client. The more rapport there is between client and counselor, the greater the client's sense of trust and security.

reel therapy: The use of movies to aid clients in understanding and resolving their own issues.

reflection: The best way to show emotional empathy for a client; the counselor points out the client's emotions by stating them as either seen or heard.

resources: Sources of help in the community. A crisis worker must be knowledgeable about community resources to be able to connect a client in crisis with the appropriate support group or other service.

schizophrenia: A disorder usually requiring the attention of a psychiatrist and characterized by the following symptoms: hallucinations, delusions, loose associations, blunt affect, and poor appearance.

support statements: Therapeutic statements that make clients feel validated and also feel that the counselor truly understands and empathizes with their situation.

support systems: Networks of helping individuals and agencies. A crisis worker uses the client's natural support systems, such as family and friends, and also helps the client build new support systems.

summarization: A skill useful in tying ideas together, wrapping up a session, or moving from the B phase of the ABC model to the C phase; the skill is also useful when the counselor does not know where to go next. It is a statement that pulls together the various facts and feelings discussed in the session.

References

Caplan, G. (1964). *Principles of preventive psychiatry.* New York: Basic Books.

Corey, G. (2008). *Theory and practice of counseling and psychotherapy* (8th ed.). Pacific Grove, CA: Brooks/Cole.

Cormier, L. S., Cormier, W. H., & Weisser, R. J., Jr. (1986). *Interviewing and helping skills for health professionals.* Portola Valley, CA: Jones and Barlett.

Dreikurs, R. (1967). *Psychodynamics, psychotherapy and counseling. Collected papers.* Chicago: Alfred Adler Institute.

Hesley, J. W. (2000, February). Reel therapy. *Psychology Today, 33,* 55–57.

Ivey, A. E., Gluckstern, N. B., & Ivey, M. B. (1997). *Basic attending skills* (3rd ed.). North Amherst, MA: Mictrotraining Associates.

Jones, W. (1968). The A-B-C method of crisis management. *Mental Hygiene, 52,* 87–89.

Lindemann, E. (1944). Symptomatology and management of acute grief. *American Journal of Psychiatry, 101,* 141–148.

Moline, M. (1986). Lecture notes. California State University, Fullerton.

Sullivan, H. S. (1954). *The psychiatric interview.* New York: Norton.

When a Crisis Leads to Danger to Self, Others, or Psychotic Decompensation

_____ 1. One of the founders of suicidology was Norman Farberow.

_____ 2. Individuals who have been contemplating suicide, never tell anyone about their thoughts.

_____ 3. A high-risk suicidal client usually must be hospitalized for a brief time.

_____ 4. Individuals who engage in self-mutilative behavior are always at high risk for completing suicide.

_____ 5. If you ask someone if they are thinking of suicide, you run the risk of encouraging them to complete the act.

_____ 6. The Mental Status Exam is a way for clinicians to evaluate whether someone is psychotic.

_____ 7. It is common for depressed individuals to think about death.

_____ 8. Gravely disabled individuals are often just lazy.

_____ 9. A no-suicide contract is a good idea for a middle-risk client.

_____ 10. Mental health workers should not assess a client's danger to others.

Introduction

The responsibility of protecting society and its individuals from harm done by someone with a mental disorder has been delegated to the mental health community. Although law enforcement agencies, such as police and sheriff departments, may be called on at times to assist crisis counselors, it is the mental health worker who typically intervenes to manage life-threatening behavior. Frequently, persons with a mental disorder may pose a danger to themselves or others. In fact, threatening suicide, posing a danger to others, and being gravely disabled (which is often the result of a severe active **psychotic decompensation**) are often the grounds for involuntary hospitalization. Each state legislates the parameters of the duty to protect clients and potential victims. Guidelines are usually created to inform practitioners of ways to manage dangerous clients. Civil suits have been brought against therapists who failed to prevent suicide or homicide. It is essential for crisis workers to be familiar with the laws of the state in which they practice. Not all people who are suicidal, psychotic, or homicidal are detained in hospitals, however. Other interventions can be less costly and equally effective in managing these conditions.

When services are provided in an emergency setting, such as a hospital, to people with serious suicide attempts, life threatening substance-abuse conditions, vegetative depression, psychosis, and violence or other rapid changes in behavior, it is often referred to as **emergency psychiatry** (Allen & Currier, 2004). These emergency psychiatric services are rendered by professionals in the fields of medicine, nursing, psychology, and social work. We turn first to the issues involved in suicide, **suicide assessment**, and suicide prevention. Please note, that although in the past, people and even clinicians often used the phrase *commit suicide* when someone intentionally killed themselves, currently, the phrase *complete suicide* is considered a more sensitive term and doesn't imply things that often are associated with the word commit, such as *commit a sin* or *commit a crime*.

A Brief History of Suicide

One of the founding fathers of modern suicidology is Dr. **Norman L. Farberow** whose pioneering contributions to suicide research, treatment, and prevention spans the last 50 years in the United States (Litman & Farberow, 1961). His work began after World War II when suicide rates began to increase due to the disappearing sense of unity and shared purpose that the war had created in society (Shneidman, Farberow, & Leonard, 1961). Social and personal readjustments were often needed when the veterans returned home, and when inner turmoil couldn't be managed in healthy ways, it was expressed through suicidal acts and impulses. In 1958, Farberow and Shneidman launched the Los Angeles Suicide Prevention Center where they developed the L.A. Scale for Assessment of Suicidal Potential (Litman & Farberow 1961; Litman, Farberow, Wold, & Brown, 1974) and the crisis hotline (Litman, Farberow, Shneidman, Heilig, & Kramer, 1965). Their research found that more was needed than the newly introduced miracle antidepressant and antipsychotic medications in dealing with psychiatric emergencies.

Introduction to Suicide

Suicidal ideation often results when a client feels totally overwhelmed because of his or her perception of a variety of precipitating events (refer Chapter 1). Understanding suicidal thinking and intervention strategies is essential for counselors working with the situational and developmental crises presented in subsequent chapters. The crisis worker must be aware that suicide assessment will be a part of all crisis intervention interviews, even if suicidal ideation is not the presenting problem. The possibility that a suicidal person will kill himself or herself is quite high, and the threat must be taken seriously. Often, the media gives more attention to homicide, but, in actuality, more people die from suicide than murder. Factors often associated with a risk of suicide include unemployment, illness, impulsivity, rigid thinking (black and white, all or nothing), several stressful events, and release from hospitalization.

The burden caused by suicide and threats of suicide falls not only on suicidal persons and those closest to them but also on crisis workers. Flavin and Radcliff (2009) report that suicide affects more than a million people worldwide, about 11.5 per 100,000 in Canada, and about 12.9 per 100,000 in the United States. Kessler, Borges, and Walters (1999) report that 34 percent of those individuals who are "lifetime suicide ideators" will make a suicide plan, and that 72 percent with a plan attempt suicide. The effects spill over to crisis workers, also. Responding to a suicidal client can be intimidating for a counselor and is often a source of personal stress. When dealing with this population, crisis workers must seek and accept emotional support from colleagues, supervisors, and family. In a sample of 241 counselors, 71 percent reported that they had worked with persons who had attempted suicide, and 28 percent had worked with at least one client who had actually completed the suicide attempt (Rogers, Gueulette, Abby-Hines, Carney, & Werth, 2001).

Rogers et al. (2001) state that despite suicide prevention and intervention efforts over the past 40 years, suicide rates have remained relatively stable. One study indicates that 39,545 individuals in the United States completed suicide, and 765,000 individuals attempted suicide in 1997 (American Association of Suicidology, 1999).

Symptoms and Clues

Suicide is usually preceded by a warning. Almost always, persons considering it show symptoms of or provide clues to their intent.

Suicidal individuals do not always tell a crisis worker about their intent directly. Prudent workers learn to read between the lines when dealing with possible suicide risks in clients. Aguilera (1990) offers some typical signs of a suicidal person:

- Giving things away
- Putting things in order
- Writing a will
- Withdrawing from usual activities
- Being preoccupied with death
- The recent death of a friend or relative
- Feeling hopeless, helpless, or worthless
- Increasing drug and alcohol use
- Displaying psychotic behavior
- Giving verbal hints such as, "I'm of no use to anyone anymore"
- Showing agitated depression
- Living alone and being isolated

Of course, if someone shows just a couple of these signs, he or she may not necessarily be at high risk of completing suicide. However, it is not uncommon for mental health clinicians to routinely include some type of suicide question in an initial interview. On some suicidal hotlines, the first question asked of the caller is, "Are you having thoughts of hurting yourself?" Most clients will just figure it is simply a part of an intake to answer such questions. If the client is not suicidal, then he or she will simply move on. If the client is thinking of hurting him or herself, then at least it is out in the open, and the counselor can begin to conduct a more in-depth suicide assessment.

Suicide Assessment

The purpose of assessing for signs of suicide is to determine the risk level. When a client's risk level is determined, the appropriate intervention is easier to develop. The more signs, symptoms, and clues that a client presents, the higher the risk factor of actually attempting or completing a suicidal act. There are a variety of questionnaires and inventories that may be useful in determining a client's potential to attempt or complete suicide. The Beck Depression Inventory is a self-report consisting of 21 multiple questions, used widely for measuring depression (Beck, Ward, Mendelson, Mock, & Erbaugh, 1961). Since suicide is closely related to depression, this tool may be useful in establishing suicide risk as well as in understanding the thoughts that underlie the suicidal ideation. As this model focuses on the negative cognitions that play a major role in depression such as negativity about the world, the future, and the self, it may be useful when conducting the ABC model of crisis intervention, which focuses on such cognitions. In fact, Beck's Cognitive Therapy is extremely relevant to basic crisis intervention and has had a major impact in the field of cognitive therapy in general.

Another form of suicide assessment tool was created due to the high rates of teen suicide. TeenScreen National Center for Mental Health Checkups was developed to help communities in the United States establish early identification programs. There are over 500 active screening sites in 43 states which are for voluntary clients and are offered through schools, clinics, doctors' offices, juvenile justice facilities, and other youth serving organizations (Teenscreen Assessment, 2009; http://www.teenscreen.org/programs). Shaffer et al. (1998) examined young adults who had participated in TeenScreen programs in high school and found that two-thirds of those who made a later suicide attempt or suffered major depression had been identified as being at risk in high school, supporting the validity of this assessment program.

Nelson, Johnston, and Shrivastava (2010) investigated various assessment tools with the intent of understanding the effectiveness and importance of objective assessment tools. They describe the Suicide Status Form (SSF) as a prominent suicide risk assessment scale that has client's respond to questions regarding psychological pain, stress, perturbation, hopelessness, and self-hate. The focus of the SSF has been to measure suicidal intent, potential, and prediction of possible attempts in persons with personality disorders and with substance abusers (Jobes, Eyman, & Yufit, 1995). Although the SSF may prove to be reliable and valid, it may be limited due to its focus on only five constructs. As with the Beck inventory, it may not take into account the many complex factors that are related to suicide.

Nelson et al. (2010) suggest that clinicians may be reluctant to use objective suicide assessment tools because they may see them as having limited usefulness or that they might be inaccurate in predicting suicide risk (Jobes et al., 1995). Bisconer and Gross (2007) found that no single instrument was able to accurately predict suicide risk without significant amount of error.

A new scale to assess suicide risk has been developed by Shrivastava and Nelson (Nelson et al., 2010) called the Scale for Impact of Suicidality-Management, Assessment and Planning of Care (SIS-MAP). It was created to balance the risk and resilience factors and look at factors that contribute to suicide from a variety of domains. The standards of assessment used by the National Suicide Prevention Lifeline are consistent with the domains in the SIS-MAP. The following are the types of questions used in this instrument which includes items such as the protective factors that are not found in typical suicide assessment tools:

1. Demographics: age, gender, marital status.
2. Ideation: thoughts of hurting self, worthlessness of life
3. Management of suicidal ideation: Can you cope with these thoughts? Do you fear losing control and attempting suicide? Do you believe in seeking help for suicidal thoughts?
4. Current state of suicidality: Do you currently feel suicidal? Worthless? Have you attempted suicide?
5. Planning for subsequent attempt: Do you think you will get suicidal ideas in the future? Will you be able to cope with these thoughts? Do you think you need treatment and help?
6. Comorbidities: alcohol or drug abuse, sexual abuse, emotional abuse

7. Family history: attempts by others, mental illness, addictions
8. Biological: psychiatric illness, chronic medical illness, mood swings
9. Protective factors: Is your family supportive of your problems? Have you succeeded when faced with life challenges? Is home safe and stable?
10. Clinical ratings: personality disorder, psychosis, impulsivity
11. Psychosocial environmental problems: primary support group, economic problems, problems with access to health care services

This scale is in its preliminary evaluation stage, but it would certainly be appropriate to take all of these factors into consideration when conducting a suicide assessment.

Although special inventories and questionnaires are helpful in determining suicide risk, many clinicians often rely on clinical judgment and interview questions to conduct suicide assessments. Because of the emergency nature of this issue, there often isn't time to administer a test. Further, a client may not be willing to forego his time talking for a paper and pencil test. Fortunately, there are many solid and effective questions that crisis workers count on to guide a suicide assessment.

Steiner (1990) (a mental health therapist for 30 years) has developed an outline for assessing a person's potential for suicide, which might be useful for crisis workers in assessing suicide:

1. *Ask if the person has thought of killing himself or herself.*
   How often?
   How badly does the person want to die (on a scale from 1 to 3)?
   Does the person see suicide as a good solution or bad solution?
   Does the person perceive suicide as weak or strong?
   (A person is at high risk if he or she thinks about suicide often, has a score of 3, sees suicide as a good solution, and perceives suicide as a strong act.)
2. *Ask family members if they are concerned that the person will commit suicide.*
   (A person is at high risk if his or her family members say they don't believe it would happen and believe that the person is just acting.)
3. *Check the person's plan for suicide.*
   Is it detailed? General?
   Does the person have materials to carry it out?
   Does the person intend to do it soon?
   Has the person given away possessions or said good-bye, or both?
4. *Check the person's mental status.*
   Is the person confused? Intoxicated? Using street drugs? Hallucinating?
   Is the person in control of his or her faculties? Impulsive? Clinically depressed? Emerging from clinical depression?
5. *Check the history of suicide in a person's life.*
   Has the person made other attempts?
   Does the person have friends or family who killed themselves?

6. *Find out what the individual's support system is like by asking these questions:*
   What friends or relatives have you told about your intent?
   Who do you talk with when you are down?
   How does your family respond to your concerns?
7. *Find out how much control the person has by asking these questions:*
   Can anyone or anything stop you?
   What has been stopping you?
   What made you come for help?
8. *Ask the person for a commitment to talk with you, to see you in two days, or to give up all rights to suicide for a set period of time. Have the person tell you how he or she will do that.*

Table 4.1 provides a short and simple suicide risk assessment. It is based on a classification tree approach which reflects an interactive and contingent model of suicide risk. The particular questions to be asked depend on the answers given to prior questions. This type of model is also effective in assessing violence toward others (Steadman, et al., 2000). Basically, when a counselor hears that a client is depressed, feels hopeless, helpless, worthless, or that life is not worth living, it is vital to inquire about any suicidal ideation. If the client says, "Yes, I have thought about it," the next step is to ask if the client has a plan. If the client says, "No," then there is no need to continue the assessment. The client is determined to be low risk. If the client says, "Yes, I have a plan," then the next question is whether the client has the means to carry out the plan. If the client says, "No, I don't have a plan, just the thought of wanting to die," the client is assessed to be somewhat low risk, depending on other factors asked from Steiner's assessment guide. If the client says, "Yes, I have the pills, gun, rope, etc." the risk is moved up to middle risk. The next question is whether there is anything that could stop the client from killing himself or herself. If the client says, "Yes, my grandkids, my children, my job, etc." the risk is still middle. If the client responds, "No, nothing can stop me, I'm going to do it when I leave, or tonight, etc." the risk is deemed high.

Interventions

After a client has been assessed as suicidal, the crisis worker must determine the likelihood that the client will actually kill himself or herself. Some clients can be treated as outpatients while they are dealing with active suicidal feelings. Others may need to be hospitalized until the level of risk is lower. Whatever the risk level, the crisis worker frequently devotes more energy and time than usual to a suicidal client. Often, a suicidal client feels hopeless and by receiving a little extra attention the client may feel that someone really cares about him or her. This may give the client the idea that keeping the client alive is a true priority for the helper.

The key is to act quickly and decisively in a suicidal crisis. At times, the client must discard any potentially lethal instruments and amount of drugs.

TABLE 4.1 Suicide Assessments, Risk Level, and Intervention

Factor	Client Response	Level	Intervention
Ideation	No	Low	Supportive crisis intervention
	Yes		(Go to next factor to decide)
Plan	No	Low	Crisis intervention, verbal no-suicide contract
	Yes		(Go to next factor to decide)
Means	No	Low	Maintain regular contact throughout the crisis intervention, written no-suicide contract, ask about plan and means at each session
	Yes	Medium	Written no-suicide contract; frequent contact, family watch, give the means to counselor, refer for medication evaluation by physician. Possible brief voluntary hospitalization if very depressed
Can anything stop you now? What has stopped you?	Yes	Medium	Find out what has stopped them, encourage them to live for that reason and others, reframe, support, same interventions as above
	No	High (if angry, very high risk)	Involuntary hospitalization or voluntary hospitalization; possible medication

© Cengage Learning

It is helpful when counselors indicate that there is hope. Treating the client's depression or other emotional disorders is the only way to prevent suicide, so the sooner the counselor can assess the client for these disorders, the sooner and more effectively suicide can be prevented (Harvard Mental Health Letter, 1996). We have seen so far that there is not just one way to conduct a suicide assessment. Each counselor must use his or her own discretion and clinical intuition along with objective measurements. Table 4.1 provides the minimal questions and observations for a quick suicide assessment connecting risk factors with risk level with corresponding interventions based on risk level.

Low-Risk Suicidal Clients   **Low-risk suicidal clients** are those who have never tried suicide, have adequate support systems, and make comments such as, "I thought about it, but I'm not sure. It scares me to have feelings like these, and I need someone to talk to." These clients can usually be treated as outpatients and should be encouraged to make an appointment with a therapist if the crisis counselor cannot continue to see them (Wyman, 1982). They probably will respond well to educational interventions, such as reading books by others who have attempted suicide. Reframing the situation is also helpful. A crisis worker might say, "The fact that you are here is evidence you don't truly want to kill yourself. People who truly want to die usually don't go to a mental health worker, because they know we have an obligation to prevent suicide."

An empowering supportive comment might go like this: "The part of you that sought help is obviously very strong, and you can take comfort in knowing you have this inner strength that helps you choose to cope with your problems actively."

A client might be comforted to know that pondering suicide when things look bleak or stressful is a common human experience; it has been written about by the greatest novelists and philosophers from ancient to modern times. A helper can point out that pondering one's own death is not the equivalent of creating it and that the client appears to be in good control of this. Such thoughts will usually be a relief to low-risk suicidal clients.

Cole (1993) describes another type of low-risk suicidal case. Elderly people often consider suicide after the death of a spouse. Cole does not deny that this is a sad situation, but if the client can be brought to the clinic and stabilized on medication, or if other resources can be mobilized, the client can often be supported through outpatient services rather than hospitalization. Her goal is to empower clients and preserve their dignity by connecting them with medical services and other resources such as senior citizen centers or in-home support services provided by most county governments. The counselor should try to get at least a verbal agreement from clients that they won't harm themselves without first speaking to the helper. This informal, no-suicide contract can be very effective psychologically with low-risk clients.

Middle-Risk Suicidal Clients   The most common suicidal clients a crisis worker will probably see are **middle-risk suicidal clients**. These individuals can still function at work but are not feeling well and are often difficult to evaluate. They feel there is no way out of their situation. Family members of this type of client often report that the client has threatened to kill themselves. Unfortunately, these threats are ignored or not taken seriously. When this is the case, clients may need to be seen every day or hospitalized because they may carry out the threat just to get a reaction from the family. An intervention commonly used with middle-risk clients is a **no-suicide contract**. Clients agree that for two or three days they will give up the right to kill themselves while they see the crisis worker. Box 4.1 shows a sample pact.

Box 4.1   Sample No-Suicide Contract

I _____ agree not to harm myself for the next week. I promise to contact
(Client's name)

_____ when my suicidal feelings get too strong to control
(Crisis worker's name)

_____   _____   _____
(Client's signature)   (Date)   (Crisis worker's signature)

Shaking hands to seal the pact is a good idea. A no-suicide contract should not be used with a client who lives alone and has no support system because the client might not abide by it. This type of client should be monitored with a daily phone call. Most clients appreciate this type of concern. If possible, enlist family members to conduct a **suicide watch**. Family members accept a certain amount of responsibility for monitoring the suicidal person and commit to staying close to the person. In this way, the family helps assume some of the responsibility for the client's well-being. This behavior can show clients that family members do care enough about them to invest energy in helping them overcome their destructive feelings.

Hospitalizing the middle-risk client is done only as a last resort. According to family systems theory, keeping the family involved makes more sense than reinforcing a family myth that the client is an identified, sick person. Suicide says much about the family, and the most effective treatment includes the entire family. When a family member is hospitalized, that person loses credibility in the family, and family members begin to treat her or him differently.

In a crisis intervention session, the crisis worker has several options for working with middle-risk clients. Besides a no-suicide contract and suicide watch, the counselor often asks the client to bring in items that the client has planned to use for completing suicide and give them to the counselor. The counselor would most likely destroy or lock these items away so no one can be injured with them.

It is helpful for the counselor to address himself or herself to the ambivalence of the client and focus on the part that wants to live. Try to elicit from the client ideas for future plans and explore the things that have happened to make life no longer worth living.

High-Risk Suicidal Clients   **High-risk suicidal clients** say such things as, "I'm going to kill myself and you can't stop me." They are usually very depressed and angry, have tried suicide before, and lack support from loved ones. If pressed, they will admit to having a viable **plan** and the **means** for killing themselves, and that no one can stop them. Crisis workers should be familiar with the laws in their state that apply to the hospitalization of suicidal clients. If clients are hospitalized, crisis workers must see that they are admitted to a psychiatric hospital rather than a general acute hospital, because staff persons of a psychiatric unit are trained differently (Wyman, 1982).

If possible, crisis workers should convince clients to admit themselves voluntarily to a hospital. This empowers clients and reduces conflict. At times, however, calling the local police or psychiatric emergency team (PET) to request **involuntary hospitalization** becomes necessary. Doing this often causes unpleasant scenes and can be embarrassing, but according to mental health ethics, it must be done if it is legal under state law. When considering hospitalization for a high-risk suicidal client, the mental health worker explores the benefits and drawbacks. Current economic trends do not encourage hospitalization if maintaining someone out of the hospital is at all possible. Partial hospitalization is becoming popular, as it provides safety

---

Box 4.2   Example of a Situation Requiring Immediate Drastic Intervention

Cole (1993) received a call from the sister of a 22-year-old man who had doused himself with gasoline and was looking for matches. He wasn't doing well in college and couldn't get a job, and his fiancée had broken up with him recently. In this case, the police and ambulance were called immediately, and an involuntary 72-hour hold was placed on this man so he could be cared for in a hospital.

© Cengage Learning

---

for the client and is less costly than round-the-clock hospitalization. The example provided in Box 4.2 clarifies a situation requiring immediate drastic intervention.

Another instance requiring hospitalization is when schizophrenic clients are actively hearing voices telling them to hurt themselves. In this type of case, the individual needs to be medicated to control the hallucinations; this action should have the effect of removing the suicidal tendency.

A Phenomenological Look at Suicide

Once an objective assessment of suicide risk is fairly well completed, the crisis worker needs to understand the phenomenological aspects (i.e., the subjective, unique view) of the client's suicidal thoughts and behaviors, both past and present. This, of course, is part of the B section in the ABC model of crisis intervention. Remember that these assessments do not necessarily flow in a linear order. Counselors usually gather objective information and explore subjective perceptions of the client at the same time. This approach is presented in outline only to make clear what information needs to be extracted in the B part.

Steiner (1990), who counsels largely in a phenomenological style within the strategic systems model, has presented case examples and several ideas that clearly demonstrate the value of taking this position. By reviewing certain statistics, she theorizes that the reason teen suicide rates have increased is perhaps because teenagers' suicides in the past may have been mislabeled. It may have been too painful for parents to admit that their child had killed himself or herself. She suggests that today there are fewer taboos about dealing with pain and family problems; therefore, more teen suicides are labeled correctly.

Based on interviews with adult suicidal clients, Steiner proposes that suicide might seem to some troubled individuals to be a more viable alternative in times when the economy is slow, making jobs harder to find, and creating confused roles in the family and society. As she says, the American dream is no longer achievable for many people.

Two case examples presented by Steiner demonstrate her use of the systems model when teenagers' perceptions of their families have led to suicidal ideation. In general, Steiner has found that many teens consider suicide because of chronic family fighting. The teen is often made to feel responsible for the arguments and tensions. Some conflict is inevitable with a teenager in the home. If this conflict is not dealt with well, the family may exist in a crisis state for five to eight years. Teenagers who believe they alone are responsible for family conflicts may feel overwhelmed by the constant stress and may perceive suicide as the best solution for everyone. This is especially likely when parents blatantly tell the adolescent that family problems are completely the fault of the teenager. Of course, parents don't say this to encourage teens to kill themselves; the parents are in a crisis state and are ignorant about how to cope with the new demands of having an adolescent in the home.

Reframing a situation like this often helps everyone see the family differently and ease the tension. Some people need to be educated about the normal conflicts in families and shown that these are not one particular person's fault. Rather, they are the motivation that helps the family grow and adjust to the maturing child. Box 4.3 below gives two examples of the use of reframing for suicidal teens.

Box 4.3   Examples of Reframing Suicide

Example 1: For an English assignment, a 16-year-old girl wrote a poem describing her thoughts of suicide. After reading it, the English teacher sent her to see Steiner for counseling. Steiner interviewed the girl alone, and then asked the girl's mother to come to a counseling session. The mother complained about the daughter's disobedience and defiant behaviors. The parents were divorced, and the mother had threatened to send the daughter to live with her father if she didn't change her behavior. The daughter was frightened of her father. She interpreted this threat as complete rejection by her mother. She responded by entertaining thoughts of suicide. Steiner saw the daughter's oppositional behavior as symbolic of the ongoing conflict between her parents.

Steiner reframed the situation by stating that the suicidal behavior was evidence of the daughter's love for her mother and fear of her father. The intervention used by Steiner was an agreement in which the mother would give up the right to send her daughter to the father.

Steiner is a firm believer in allowing clients to maintain the perspective that suicide is their right. She avoids the conflicts that can result from telling a client, "You have no right to kill yourself." She interprets Nietzsche's words, "Suicide has saved many lives," to mean that sometimes clients' only control over themselves and their lives is the option of suicide. Simply having this option is often enough to reduce the pressure they feel to the point that it is bearable.

Example 2: A teenage boy felt lonely. People did not really know him and he did not express his feelings often. His parents had aspirations for him that he simply could not meet. They had filtered out his feelings of failure and had an unrealistic picture of what he could do. This boy was at high risk for suicide because he perceived his life as being very bleak and hopeless.

Including his parents in treatment was essential. Their expectations would have to be reframed as their own projections of what they expected of themselves, and the focus would be on them instead of the boy. This shift in attention would help release the tension in the teenager. His feelings of failure could be reframed as his unconscious identification with his parents' feelings of failure. Family therapy could focus on each member's realistic hopes for himself or herself instead of projected and introjected expectations.

Two Philosophies of Suicide Prevention

Although most mental health professionals assume it is their duty to prevent suicide, Szasz (1986) believes differently. Before examining mainstream suicide interventions, the reader may find it interesting to look at Szasz's somewhat radical perspective on suicide. Common sense suggests that suicide is a mental health problem, and that mental health practitioners have a duty to try to prevent it. Szasz (1986) believes that each individual is ultimately responsible for himself or herself, and that the nation's mental health policy on suicide "undermines the ethic of self-responsibility" (p. 806). Also, if this policy regarding the duty to prevent suicide were changed, it would reduce the number of malpractice suits against mental health professionals, because failure to prevent suicide is one of the leading reasons for successful lawsuits against these professionals.

Another interesting point made by Szasz concerns using the word *prevention* to describe a mental health worker's duty to suicidal clients. He asserts that this term is synonymous with coercion; it implies a paternalistic attitude toward the client and gives certain people (mental health professionals) privileges and powers to protect the suicidal individual. As an example, in California a counselor can breach the confidentiality of a suicidal client without the client's consent. Also, persons can be involuntarily detained in a psychiatric hospital for up to 72 hours if they are deemed uncontrollably suicidal; the detention is to prevent people from killing themselves. Szasz suggests that these acts of prevention undermine each individual's right to suicide. Szasz would not encourage suicide, but he believes that the decision not to take one's life is the client's responsibility, not the mental health worker's responsibility.

Szasz concludes his message by comparing suicide with other moral decisions such as abortion or marriage. Why, he asks, are mental health professionals held liable for a successful suicide but not for an abortion or a divorce? Part of the reason has to do with the philosophy that suicide is an insane behavior, and that if the mental disorder were treated, suicidality would cease to exist. In other words, suicide is never "desirable enough to justify it" (p. 811). This does not mean that Szasz accepts suicide as a legitimate option. Rather, Szasz believes that mental health professionals should be allowed to "treat it as an act that they may approve or disapprove in general and may choose to counsel for or against in any particular case" (p. 811), as they often do for clients who are considering having an abortion or getting a divorce. This philosophy would eliminate making counselors responsible and greatly reduce lawsuits. Most importantly, it places responsibility on the individual in a society that views doctors as having the wisdom of God.

Many examples exist that demonstrate sane suicidality. People with painful diseases or terminal illnesses (e.g., AIDS or cancer), or those who have suffered dishonor (in certain cultures), who feel that life is not worth living, point to suicide as a viable option. The Hemlock Society was created in support of situations in which individuals are seen as having the right to choose their own death.

Szasz and the Hemlock Society are in the minority, however, when it comes to suicide prevention. Most crisis workers with all types of licenses and in most agencies agree that it is their duty to prevent people from killing themselves. Szasz wonders about this, though, questioning whether this attitude would be so prevalent if suicide were not illegal, and if a worker were not liable to be sued for failing to prevent a client from killing himself or herself.

Taking an opposing view, Steiner (1990) claims that although she sometimes can understand how suicide might be a better option than to continue living for some people, she would still try to prevent it. She states her overall attitude clearly when she tells clients that she's in the business of helping people who will commit to being alive. These words tell clients that she opposes suicide and that she would not help them do it. When asked how she would deal with a dying AIDS patient who truly believed killing himself painlessly would be a better choice than dying in pain, Steiner suggested interesting questions to ask the patient: "What kind of example would you be for others who have AIDS or are just HIV positive? Can we find any meaning in your living it out until the end?" These questions may help the individual die in dignity through knowing he or she had contributed positively to others. Certainly, Magic Johnson's attitude about his HIV infection is considered exemplary, because he is basically saying that whatever time a person has left on earth is valuable, and each person should make the balance of that life productive.

Steiner also suggests asking clients to think of reasons for not killing themselves. Usually, the most severely depressed person can think of one or two reasons to live. In my own practice, I worked with a very suicidal client who was ready to be hospitalized by her psychiatrist. When I asked her for reasons to continue living, she said she loved her four-year-old grandson and enjoyed taking him to the park. By exploring this with her, I was able to join her phenomenological world and use this knowledge to show her that suicide might not be her only option, and certainly not the best one, if she wanted to continue going to the park with her grandson.

Nonsuicidal Self-Injury (NSSI) and Self-Mutilative Behavior (SMB)

Some people who visit counselors for crisis-related problems engage in self injurious behaviors without the intent of killing themselves. Deliberately damaging one's own body tissue without suicidal intent has been referred to as **self-mutilative behavior** (SMB) (Nock & Prinstein, 2004) and more recently as **nonsuicidal self-injury** (NSSI) (Goldman, 2010 and Whitlock, Purington & Gershkovich, 2009). Although those engaging in this behavior do not have a separate diagnosis, a proposed revision in the American Psychiatric Association *Diagnostic and Statistical Manual of Mental Disorders* (DSM) (2010), lists four criteria to consider when considering whether someone fits an NSSI syndrome: (1) engaging in five or more self-inflicted injuries to the body to induce bleeding or pain with absence of suicidal intent; (2) at least two of the following feelings: negative feelings and thoughts, period of preoccupation with the intended behavior that is difficult to resist, the urge to engage in self-injury that occurs frequently but may not always be acted upon, or behavior has the intended purpose such as relief from negative feelings; (3) behavior causes impairment and dysfunction; and (4) behavior does not occur during states of psychosis, delirium, or intoxication.

NSSI is typically an impulsive disorder prevalent in emotional and personality disorders such as anxiety, depression, borderline personality disorder, and eating disorders and is often the result of abuse, trauma, poor self-image, mood swings, and fears of abandonment (Brohl and Ledford, 2012). Historically speaking, inflicting pain and self-injury is not a new phenomenon. Some religions hold the belief that inflicting pain and human suffering will appease God. Self-flagellating was common among the religious who wandered through Europe in the Middle Ages lashing themselves to atone for society's sins and to stop the great plague (Conterio & Lader, 1998).

NSSI is seen in about 4 percent of the general adult population and 21 percent of adult psychiatric inpatient populations (Briere & Gil, 1998). Adolescents may be at increased risk for NSSI; this behavior has been seen in 40 to 61 percent of adolescents in psychiatric inpatient settings (Darche, 1990; Diclemente, Ponton, & Hartley, 1991) and 14 to 39 percent of adolescents in the community (Lloyd, 1998; Ross & Heath, 2002). Because NSSI is so prevalent in adolescents, it has been suggested that it may be a form of rebellion against parents and perhaps a way to get a parent's attention (Conterio & Lader, 1998).

In a recent study of adolescent psychiatric inpatients, Nock & Prinstein (2004) examined the most common methods of NSSI and self-reported reasons for engaging in NSSI. The top five methods of NSSI were cutting or carving one's skin, picking at a wound, hitting oneself, scraping one's skin to draw blood, and biting oneself. The top six reasons for engaging in NSSI were to stop bad feelings, to feel something even if it was pain, to punish oneself, to relieve feelings of numbness or emptiness, to feel relaxed, and to give oneself something to do when alone. These results indicate that the primary purpose of most adolescent NSSI is regulation of emotional or physiological experiences.

Assessment of NSSI

Simeon and Hollander (2001) offer some questions that can be used to identify and assess the severity of cutting and other forms of self-harm:

1. Have you intentionally hurt yourself in any way?
2. When you hurt yourself, were you trying to commit suicide?
3. How old were you when you first hurt yourself?
4. How often do you hurt yourself?
5. Have you had to seek medical treatment for hurting yourself?

6. How do you feel after you hurt yourself?
7. Do you ever have the urge to hurt yourself?
8. Do you want to stop hurting yourself?
9. Have you ever been able to stop right before you hurt yourself?
10. Do you use drugs or alcohol before you hurt yourself?
11. Is there a certain time of day that makes you feel like hurting yourself?
12. Is there a certain situation or place that makes you feel like hurting yourself?
13. Is there a certain person or people who make you feel like hurting yourself?
14. Do you know of anyone in your family who has hurt themselves?
15. Do you have friends or anyone you know who hurts themselves?

Interventions for NSSI

Once it is fairly well established that the person is indeed engaging in NSSI, the counseling may offer a variety of interventions. These range from creating a safe, nonthreatening and structured environment and implementing cognitive-behavioral components (Walsh, 2005) to psychodynamic psychotherapy (Veague, 2008) to group therapy where ground rules are created to promote healthy changes and focus on healing (Clark and Henslin, 2007). The S.A.F.E. (Self-Abuse Finally Ends) program created by Conterio and Lader (2008) in 1985 has been successfully implemented with teens for more than 25 years. It helps teens learn to face problems and communicate feelings to others. This program uses supportive, cognitive-behavioral and psychodynamic therapy approaches and uses four tools: the no-harm contract, an impulse-control log, a list of five safe alternatives to self-injury, and writing assignments designed to help clients build awareness and organize thoughts and feelings and focus energy in a constructive way.

Managing a Client Who Is a Danger to Others

Periodically, a crisis worker may come across a person who is homicidal or somehow a danger to others. As described in Chapter 2, the crisis worker has the duty to warn the intended victim when possible and to contact the police. Sometimes a person may be a threat to the public because of a psychosis (e.g., an individual hears the voice of God telling him to pour poison into the town water supply). Individuals who are angry and lacking impulse control may also be threats. *Homicidal ideation* is a common psychiatric term for thoughts about homicide which range from vague ideas of revenge to detailed and fully formulated plans without the act itself. Homicidal ideation accounts for about 10 to 17 percent of patient presentations to psychiatric facilities in the United States (Thienhaus & Piasecki, 1998). It often results from other illnesses such as psychosis and delirium and even personality disorders and substance-induced psychosis (Stern, Schwartz, Cremens & Mulley, 2005).

Homicidal ideation is an important risk factor when trying to assess some-one's risk for violence against others and is routine for people presenting to emergency psychiatric services.

Risk Factors for Violence Against Others

Some of the associated risk factors related to potential violence against others include:

- History of violence
- Thoughts of committing harm
- Poor impulse control and inability to delay gratification
- Impairment or loss of reality testing
- Delusions or command hallucinations
- Feeling of being controlled by an outside force
- Belief that other people wish to harm him or her
- Perception of rejection or humiliation at the hand of others
- Being under the influence of substances
- Past history of antisocial personality disorder
- Frontal lobe dysfunction or head injury (Thienhaus et. al, 1998).

The following six questions can be used to assess a person's potential for harming others:

1. Is the subject actively or passively engaged in violent or dangerous behavior?
2. Does the subject state that he or she is going to carry out violent or dangerous behavior?
3. Does the subject have a plan to follow through with this behavior?
4. Does the subject have the means to follow through with this plan?
5. Does the subject have a background of violent or dangerous behavior?
6. Has the subject acted on plans for violence in the past?

Answers to these questions can be obtained from an interview with either the client or relatives of the client. Try to get the client or relative to be as specific as possible about what the person has said or done and who the victims might be.

If the counselor believes the person is a threat and cannot comfortably end the session, the counselor must call for assistance. If permissible according to state law, the client should be involuntarily hospitalized until the client's violent impulses have been controlled either by medication or other forms of therapy.

In less volatile situations, crisis workers can try to help clients contain their violent urges by teaching them ways to manage their anger or referring them to a daily support group. If clients agree to refrain from acting out and intended victims have been warned, clients can be treated on an outpatient basis as long as any psychotic symptoms are controlled.

Certain psychotic states (e.g., mania or paranoia) may require clients to spend several days in a hospital receiving medication to control the delusions that lead to dangerous behaviors. Once individuals have been medicated and stabilized, they can often function appropriately with just a few counseling sessions to help them make the transition from hospital to outpatient living.

Some clients who are a danger to others may not be manic or psychotic but may have an impulse-control problem (e.g., spouse batterers and child abusers). These people seem to function normally in the larger society, but they control close interpersonal relationships by acting violently. In most states, crisis workers have a legal obligation to report suspected child abuse to the proper authorities. If the client has not abused a child but tells the crisis worker that he or she is on the verge of doing so, the crisis worker can suggest that the client call a child abuse hotline, go for a walk, count to ten, or temporarily move out of the house until he or she has cooled off.

Telling the client that counselors are required by state law to report violence against a child can be helpful in deterring this behavior. Impulsive people often need external controls because they feel so out of control internally. This holds true in cases of intimate partner abuse as well. Crisis workers are not required to report battering of another adult; however, if the batterer feels the police will be called in, this possibility will often act as a curb on the person's potentially violent behavior. Even so, the person may continue to verbally and emotionally abuse others.

Some people are a danger to others because of antisocial tendencies and anger. In certain cases, the police should be involved, especially when the person has no history of being mentally ill. Cole (1993) tells of an ex-convict who came to a psychiatrist at the mental health clinic saying he was mentally disabled and needed medication. When the doctor evaluated him and asked about his history, he discovered that the patient had no history of mental health treatment and was not mentally ill, so he prescribed no medication. The man pulled out a knife, held it to the doctor's throat, and forced him to write a prescription. As soon as the man left, the police were called, and the man was arrested and put in jail rather than being hospitalized under provisions for involuntary commitment of the mentally ill. Box 4.4 gives an example of danger to others in what Cole (1993) calls the "fatal attraction case."

Box 4.4   Example of a Client Who Was a Danger to Others

Example: A 23-year-old woman came to the mental health clinic complaining of being stressed out because her boyfriend had just broken up with her and was now with another woman. She was extremely angry and planned to wait until the man was asleep in his house and then pour gasoline all around the house and set fire to it. In evaluating the reality of such a plan, the mental health worker asked the client if she had any history of another man breaking up with her and what had happened at that time. The woman said that when her last boyfriend broke up with her, his car was wired so that it blew up when he got into it. In addition, she was discovered to have a history of mental health treatment going back ten years. The worker also observed that the woman had a row of safety pins in her ear as earrings. By combining all this information, the worker decided that the woman was a danger to her former boyfriend. The client was involuntarily hospitalized, and the intended victim and the police were made aware of the situation.

Psychotic Breakdowns and Gravely Disabled Mentally Ill Persons

Periodically, a crisis worker will come across a client suffering a **psychotic decompensation**. In essence, it is a state of active **delusions** and **hallucinations** during which the person is out of touch with reality. This condition causes extreme personality disorganization and heightened states of anxiety; the person cannot function in any way. People in this state cannot look after even their basic needs. They cannot provide themselves with food or water or keep themselves clean and therefore need someone to take care of them.

The term **gravely disabled** applies here. This condition may be grounds for involuntary hospitalization, depending on the laws of the state. While these clients are in the hospital, they usually can be stabilized on medication and become able to function more realistically within a few days. For some, however, the stabilization period may take up to two weeks or six months, depending on the severity of the psychosocial stressor, the person's premorbid functioning (i.e., before the breakdown), and the available support systems. Clients experiencing this type of distress can be diagnosed as schizophrenic, being in a paranoid state, or having an organic brain disorder such as Alzheimer's disease.

In some cases, people's psychotic thoughts leave them both gravely disabled and a danger to themselves or others. Cole (1993) tells of a 25-year-old man who had been completely catatonic (immobile and mute) for three days. His legs were turning purple because of poor circulation from lack of activity, and he was dehydrated. When he was informed by the mental health worker that he was going to be involuntarily hospitalized, he ran to the roof and threatened to jump off. Eventually, someone was able to coax him off the roof, and he was hospitalized as both gravely disabled and a danger to himself. In emergencies such as suicide and psychosis, family members need to be involved. In cases where there is no family, board and care homes and case managers serve as support systems for clients. The crisis worker must remain calm and not be afraid when working with these people. As pointed out previously, the worker may have to be the client's ego strength until he or she returns to a realistic state of functioning. Box 4.5 has three examples that demonstrate how someone who is gravely disabled might present to others.

The Mental Status Exam

The **Mental Status Exam** is a formal assessment tool that aids in determining if someone is psychotic and therefore gravely disabled, a danger to self, or to others. It is a structured way of describing a person's current state of mind under the domains of appearance, attitude, behavior, speech, mood and affect, thought process, thought content, perception, cognition, insight and judgment (Trzepacz & Baker, 1993). The Mental Status Exam should not be confused with the mini-mental state examination often used as a brief neuropsychological screening test for dementia. Table 4.2 presents the Mental Status Exam

---

Box 4.5   Examples of Cases in Which the Client Is Gravely Disabled

Example 1: A 17-year-old boy has become increasingly withdrawn and guarded at home. He no longer sees his friends, and his grades have dropped over the past year. He seems distant and shows little emotion (blunted affect). His mother brings him to a crisis counseling center because he has been suffering anxiety spells and believes extraterrestrials are watching him at night. When he is interviewed, he tells the counselor that he's been pacing at night and is afraid to sleep because he hears a strange whisper saying, "We're watching you."

This is a typical case of initial psychotic break. The young man will most likely be diagnosed as paranoid schizophrenic, hospitalized, and given antipsychotic medication that will reduce, if not eliminate, his symptoms. Unfortunately, he will probably have another breakdown at some time in the future.

Example 2: A man who has become belligerent on the job is sent to a counselor by his manager. During the interview, the counselor finds that he believes a white van is following him and tracking him with infrared sonar equipment. He brings in a magazine about hi-tech weapons and electrical devices to show the counselor. He is preoccupied with the information in the magazine and believes the equipment it describes is the type that is being used to spy on him. He seems connected to his family and friends, has a clear grasp of current events, and can still perform his job duties.

This man's condition may be diagnosed as a paranoid state; he might require hospitalization if it gets worse. Medication may or may not be effective in eliminating his delusions.

Example 3: A 70-year-old woman is brought to the mental health center by her 30-year-old granddaughter. The granddaughter found her sitting nude at home surrounded by newspapers and unopened Social Security checks. The woman had not eaten in several days because she believed the food was poisoned. She does not know what day it is, thinks she's still living in 1955, and believes that her granddaughter is her daughter.

The woman is probably suffering from Alzheimer's disease or senility. She is gravely disabled and needs someone to be her conservator (i.e., guardian of her finances).

© Cengage Learning

---

categories and potential observations or questions that might be asked or seen in an interview to assess for psychosis or other gravely disabled conditions. If a person being interviewed shows signs of the behaviors or observations presented in this exam, or responds inappropriately to the questions by giving "yes" responses, he or she may have a serious mental illness requiring physician involvement, at the very least. Potential psychotic and gravely disabled assessments are effectively done with the Mental Status Exam during interviews with clients and their families.

TABLE 4.2   The Mental Status Exam

Category	Question or Observation	Possible Diagnostic Considerations
Appearance	Observation: poorly groomed, unkempt, body odor, dirty, naked	Schizophrenia, substance-induced toxic state
Attitude	Observation: guarded when asked questions, hostile	Paranoid schizophrenia, substance-induced toxic state
Behavior	Observation: lacks physical boundaries, overly familiar, agitated pacing Observation: hand wringing, head down, slouched Observation: cataleptic, waxy flexibility, no movement	Bipolar mania Major depression Catatonia
Speech	Observation: rapid, forced, pressured Observation: slurred Observation: incoherent, lack of spontaneity	Bipolar mania Substance-induced toxic state Schizophrenia
Mood and affect	Observation: expansive, overly euphoric, inappropriate affect, silly, or hostile Observation: sad, agitated, desperate Observation: vacant eyes, lack of emotions, blunted	Bipolar mania Major depression Schizophrenia
Thought process	Observation: disorganized, tangential Observation: flight of ideas	Schizophrenia Bipolar mania
Thought Content	Delusions Questions: Do you think you have special powers? Can people read your mind? Are the telephone wires or the Internet sending you messages? Do you have a special code or message from the TV, radio, or computer? Are people out to get you? Can your thoughts be inserted elsewhere? Delusion of grandiosity	Schizophrenia Bipolar mania or paranoid schizophrenia
Perception	Visual, auditory hallucinations Questions: Do you hear voices or conversations that others don't seem to hear? Do you see people, characters, or other things others don't see? Do you experience strange or disturbing tastes or smells?(Olfactory or gustatory hallucinations) Questions: Does your food taste like it's been poisoned? Do you smell odd things?	Schizophrenia Dementia, brain tumors
Cognition: orientation	Questions: Do you know what day it is? Do you know where you are? Do you know who you are? Do you know who the president is? Can you name a current TV show or movie? What is the last thing you ate?	Schizophrenia, dementia
Insight	Question: Do you know why you have problems?	Schizophrenia, dementia, bipolar mania
Judgment	Observation: engaging in fights, inappropriate interpersonal behaviors, sexual promiscuity, handing out money, etc.	Bipolar mania

Box 4.6 below provides several cases for the reader to use in role plays practicing suicide assessment and the ABC Model.

Box 4.6   Cases to Role-Play

Now that you have been presented with the ABC Model of Crisis Intervention and suicide assessment, you will be given a variety of cases that may allow you to put into practice these interviewing skills. Each subsequent chapter will also have cases to role-play related to the material presented in that particular chapter. Various therapeutic statements have been provided to guide you when conducting these role plays.

Practice conducting a suicide assessment and intervention for the following clients. Use the ABC model of crisis intervention to identify the precipitating event, cognitions, emotional distress, and impairments in functioning. The person who is role-playing the client should be creative and embellish the situation based on knowledge of the emotional and cognitive elements typically found in suicidal people. The practicing counselor should use the suggested therapeutic comments included at the end of the case description. Feel free to be creative and create scenarios that include low-, middle-, and high-risk clients. Once you decide at which risk level the client is, discuss appropriate interventions. Any of these cases could be made into low, middle or high risk depending on the responses the client gives to the counselor's questions.

Case 1 A 19-year-old Asian boy has received two Ds on his college report card and feels he has shamed his family. He plans to kill himself by jumping off the highest building on campus. He knows that six other people have successfully ended their lives in this way over the past ten years.

Reframe: Point out the shame the family will suffer if he kills himself in such a public display. Grades can be hidden from others, but a suicide cannot.

Validation: Tell him that it is embarrassing and disappointing to receive low grades and it is difficult to face others when we don't succeed. It is understandable that he is feeling bad.

Empower: Although he cannot go back and change his scores, he does have the power to use this event as a motivator to change his behavior in the future to create consequences that will make him feel good about himself. Two Ds do not equal an entire life and there are ways for him to control his grades in the future.

Education: Many colleges have a policy whereby students can retake courses and change the grades on their transcripts. He can certainly look into this. Also, it is doubtful that his parents would prefer to see him dead rather than see a D on a report card.

Case 2 A 45-year-old woman is very depressed. All of her children are grown and married. She has been divorced for 20 years, and she is dissatisfied with her job. She sees no reason to live but has no specific plan to kill herself. She feels like a burden to her children.

Reframe: Show her that killing herself would be an even bigger burden on her children. Does she really want to traumatize them in this way?

Support: Let her know that many mothers feel sad when their children aren't around. Mothers love their children so much and often would love for them to come back home more frequently than their lives permit. Also, a job that is unsatisfying is very challenging to go to for most of us.

Education: Many woman have been returning to school for a midlife career change. Also, sometimes volunteer work provides the needed feelings of contribution that she may be missing.

Empowerment: While she cannot control her boss or job, she cannot even control her children, she does have control over her own behavior. She can make choices that help her create a life that is more rewarding.

(Continued)

Box 4.6   Cases to Role-Play (Continued)

Case 3 A 68-year-old man whose wife died six months ago is very depressed and wants to shoot himself. He has a loaded gun at home. His dog has just died.

Reframe: Does he believe his wife will rest in peace if he kills himself? Perhaps the extent of his grief is related to the extent of the love they had and he is fortunate to have had love like that; many people never get that in their life.

Support: Let him know that you understand his loneliness and that there are groups and other involvements he can focus on, though his life will probably never be the same. It is very difficult to lose a dog on top of losing his wife.

Education: Depression often causes people to think about killing themselves but it is often a temporary state and with counseling, his depression can go away and then he might be glad he is alive. He needs to grieve actively and with help he can learn to adjust to life without his wife and dog.

Empowerment: Death of a loved one often makes us feel powerless and it may seem that he can feel powerful by ending his own life. But there are other choices in which he can feel powerful.

Case 4 A 30-year-old woman feels hopeless and despondent. She thinks she is a bad mother and wife and can't manage her household. She has no appetite and can't sleep. She has little involvement with her children. She spends her days crying while the children are left to look after themselves. She has some vague thoughts that maybe it would be better if she weren't around.

Reframe: A bad mother wouldn't care if her children weren't being cared for. This mother is not bad; she is just depressed.

Support: Let her know that being a mother is hard. It is not necessarily easy to manage a home and children.

Education: From what she is describing, she sounds like she is suffering from depression. Many people experience these same symptoms and there are many medications and types of counseling that are very effective in alleviating depression.

Empowerment: She is in control of how she proceeds to manage the depression. Her first sign of being in control was coming to this appointment.

Chapter Review

When a person is experiencing a crisis, he or she may become in danger of attempting suicide, hurting someone else, or of decompensating into a gravely disabled state in which he or she cannot care for him or herself. These states often require assessment for risk level. Each risk level dictates the type of intervention that is most appropriate. The Mental Status Exam is often used to help guide crisis workers in terms of making ethical decisions about diagnosis and subsequent interventions. Sometimes, clients can be managed in an outpatient setting when suffering from these types of crises. Other times, clients may need to be managed in hospitals until they are stabilized.

Answers to Pre-Chapter Quiz

1. T   2. F   3. T   4. F   5. F   6. T   7. T   8. F   9. T   10. F

Key Terms for Study

delusions: Beliefs and thoughts often observed in individuals who are suffering from psychotic episodes due to schizophrenia, dementia, a manic episode, or substance intoxication. These beliefs have no basis in reality.

emergency psychiatry: When services are provided in an emergency setting such as a hospital to people with serious suicide attempts, life threatening substance abuse conditions, vegetative depression, psychosis, violence, or other rapid changes in behavior.

Norman L. Farberow: An American pioneer in the field of suicidology. Created the first suicide prevention center and hotline in Los Angeles.

gravely disabled: A term used to describe individuals who are unable to care for their own personal needs such as food, shelter, and clothing due to a mental disorder.

hallucinations: False sensory perceptions. Auditory hallucinations are associated with schizophrenia; visual and tactile ones with substance-abuse withdrawal; and gustatory and olfactory ones with organic brain disorders. Any hallucination is indicative of severe illness; when hallucinations are present, a doctor should be consulted.

high-risk suicidal clients: Clients who have a plan, the means, and the intent to complete suicide; they cannot be talked out of harming themselves. Hospitalization is often indicated for such clients.

involuntary hospitalization: Detaining clients against their will in a psychiatric facility for evaluation and observation when they have been deemed a danger to themselves or others, or are gravely disabled because of a mental disorder.

low-risk suicidal clients: Clients who have pondered but never attempted suicide. These clients have adequate support systems and can usually be treated as outpatients. Therapy and educational interventions are encouraged.

means: The actual physical implement, pills, or action that a suicidal person uses to kill himself or herself.

Mental Status Exam: A structured way of observing and interviewing clients to assess for possible psychotic states.

middle-risk suicidal clients: Clients who have been thinking about suicide and feel depressed. These clients probably still have some hope, but they might also have a suicide plan. A no-suicide contract works as well for such persons as does a suicide watch. Crisis intervention should be intense and frequent.

nonsuicidal self-injury/self-mutilative behavior: Intentionally causing tissue damage to oneself without desiring to kill oneself.

no-suicide contract: A formal written or verbal contract between the client and the crisis worker in which the client makes a commitment to speak to the counselor before harming himself or herself. It is considered an effective intervention for low- and middle-risk clients.

plan: A blueprint for action that clients have devised for killing themselves.

psychotic decompensation: A state in which the client is out of touch with reality and shows symptoms such as delusions and hallucinations. This often happens when a schizophrenic patient stops taking medication or at the beginning of a person's first schizophrenic episode. The state can also be associated with bipolar disorder and paranoid disorders. This person usually requires involuntary hospitalization.

suicidal ideation: The cognition component of suicide, the thinking involved.

suicide assessment: A process in which the crisis worker asks a series of directive questions to ascertain the seriousness of a client's suicidal intent and ideation. It includes identifying various risk factors, a means for suicide, a plan for suicide, and reasons for wanting to harm oneself.

suicide watch: Observation by family or friends of those who are at middle risk of hurting themselves. Someone stays by the client's side 24 hours a day to ensure that the person does no harm to himself or herself. Suicide watches are also conducted in psychiatric facilities for high-risk clients.

References

Aguilera, D. C. (1990). *Crisis intervention: Theory and methodology* (6th ed.). St. Louis: Mosby.

Allen, M., & Currier, G. (2004). Use of restraints and pharmacotherapy in academic psychiatric emergency services. *General Hospital Psychiatry, 26*(1), 42–49.

American Association of Suicidology. (1999). *U.S.A. suicide: 1997 official final data.* Washington, DC: Author.

American Psychiatric Association. (2010). Retrieved September 1, 2011, from http://www.dsm5.org/ProposedRevisions/Pages?proposedrevision.aspx?rid =443

Beck, A. T., Ward, C. H., Mendelson, M., Mock, J., & Erbaugh, J. (1961, June). An inventory for measuring depression. *Archives of General Psychiatry, 4,* 561–571.

Bisconer, S. W., & Gross, D. M. (2007). Assessment of suicide risk in psychiatric hospital. *Professional Psychology: Research and Practice, 38,* 143–149.

Briere, J., & Gil, E. (1998). Self-mutilation in clinical and general population samples: Prevalence, correlates, and functions. *American Journal of Orthopsychiatry, 68,* 609–620.

Brohl, K., & Ledford, R. (2012). Non-suicidal self-injury: Etiology, treatment and prevention of cutting. In *Continuing education for California social workers and marriage and family therapists.* Ormond Beach, FL: Elite Continuing Education.

Clark, J., & Henslin, E. (2007). *Inside a Cutter's Mind (211–215).* Colorado Springs, CO: Nav Press.

Cole, C. (1993). *Psychiatric emergencies*. Presentation at California State University, Fullerton, CA.

Conterio, K., & Lader, W. (2008). *Bodily harm: Breakthrough healing program for self-injurers*. New York: Hyperio Press.

Darche, M. A. (1990). Psychological factors differentiating self-mutilating and non–self-mutilating adolescent inpatient females. *The Psychiatric Hospital, 21*, 31–35.

DiClemente, R. J., Ponton, L. E., & Hartley, D. (1991). Prevalence and correlates of cutting behavior: Risk for HIV transmission. *Journal of the American Academy of Child and Adolescent Psychiatry, 30*, 735–739.

Flavin, P., & Radcliff, B. (2009). Public policies and suicide rates in the American states. *Social Indicators Research, 90*, 195–209.

Goldman, S. (2010). *Children's hospital Boston pediatric health blog*. Retrieved July 10, 2011, from http://childrenshospitalblog.org

Jobes, D. A., Eyman, J. R., & Yufit, R. I. (1995). How clinicians assess suicide risk in adolescents and adults. *Crisis Intervention and Time-Limited Treatment, 2*, 1–12.

Kessler, C., Jr., Borges, G., & Walters, E. E. (1999). Prevalence of and risk factors for lifetime suicide attempts in the National Comorbidity Survey. *Archives of General Psychiatry, 56*, 617–626.

Litman, R. E., & Farberow, N. L. (1961). Emergency evaluation of self-destructive potentiality. In N. L. Farberow & E. S. Shneidman (Eds.), *The cry for help* (pp. 48–59). New York: McGraw-Hill Book Company.

Litman, R. E., Farberow, N. L., Shneidman, E. S., Heilig, S. M., & Kramer, J. (1965). Suicide prevention telephone service. *Journal of the American Medical Association, 192*(1), 21–25.

Litman, R. E., Farberow, N. L., Wold, C. I., & Brown, T. R. (1974). Prediction models of suicidal behaviors. In A. Beck, H. L. P. Resnick, & D. J. Lettieri (Eds.), *Prediction of suicide* (Chapter X, pp. 141–159). Bowie, MD: Charles Press Publishers, Inc.

Lloyd, E. E. (1998). Self-mutilation in a community sample of adolescents (Doctoral dissertation, Louisiana State University, 1998). *Dissertation Abstracts International, 58*, 5127.

Nelson, C., Johnston, M., & Shrivastava, A. (2010). Improving risk assessment with suicidal patients: A preliminary evaluation of the clinical utility of the Scale for Impact of Suicidality-Management, Assessment and Planning of Care (SIS-MAP). *The Journal of Crisis Intervention and Suicide Prevention, 31*(5), 231–237.

Nock, M. K., & Prinstein, M. J. (2004). A functional approach to the assessment of self-mutilative behavior. *Journal of Counseling and Clinical Psychology, 72*(5), 885–890.

Rogers, J. R., Gueulette, C. M., Abbey-Hines, J., Carney, J. V., & Werth, J. L., Jr. (2001). Rational suicide: An empirical investigation of counselor attitudes. *Journal of Counseling and Development, 79*, 365–372.

Ross, S., & Heath, N. (2002). A study of the frequency of self-mutilation in a community sample of adolescents. *Journal of Youth and Adolescence, 31,* 67–77.

Shaffer, D., Restifo, K., Garfinkel, R., Wilcox, H., Ehrensaft, M., & Munfakh, J. (1998). *Screening for young-adult suicidality and mood disorders in high school.* Poster presented at the annual meeting of the American Academy of Child and Adolescent Psychiatry, Anaheim, CA.

Shneidman, E. S., Farberow, N. L., & Leonard, C. S. (1961). *Some facts about suicide* (Public health service publication no. 852). Washington, DC: Superintendent of Documents, U.S. Government Printing Office.

Simeon, D., & Hollander, E. (2001). *Self-injurious behavior: Assessment and treatment* (p. 22). Washington, DC: American Psychiatric Press.

Steadman, H. J., Silver, E., Monahan, J., Appelbaum, P. S., Robbins, P. C., Mulvey, E. P., et al. (2000). A classification tree approach to the development of actuarial violence risk assessment tools. *Law and Human Behavior, 24*(1), 83–100.

Steiner, L. (1990). *Suicide assessment and intervention.* Presentation at California State University, Fullerton.

Stern, T. F., Schwartz, J. H., Cremens, M. C., & Mulley, A. G. (2005). The evaluation of homicidal patients by psychiatric residents in the emergency room: A pilot study. *Psychiatric Quarterly, 62*(4), 333–344.

Suicide. (1996, December). *Harvard Mental Health Letter,* Part II, 1–4.

Szasz, T. (1986). The case against suicide prevention. *American Psychologist, 41*(7), 806–812.

Teenscreen Assessment. (2009). Retrieved November 5, 2009, from http://www.teenscreen.org/our-local-programs

Thienhaus, O. J., & Piasecki, M. (1998). Emergency psychiatry: Assessment of psychiatric patients' risk of violence toward others. *Psychiatric Services, 49*(9), 1129–1147.

Trzepacz, P. T., & Baker, R. (1993). *The psychiatric mental status examination.* Oxford: Oxford University Press.

Veague, H. B. (2008). *Cutting and self-harm.* New York: Chelsea House.

Walsh, B. W. (2005). *Treating self-injury: A practical guide.* New York: Guilford Press.

Whitlock, J., Purington, A., & Gershkovich, A. (2009). *Influence of the media on self-injurious behavior: Understanding non-suicidal self-injury.* New York: American Psychological Press.

Wyman, S. (1982). *Suicide evaluation and treatment.* Presentation at seminar sponsored by Orange County Chapter, California Association of Marriage and Family Therapists.

Chapter

5

Developmental Crises and Special Issues of Adolescence (Bullying, Pregnancy, Teens Who Run Away from Home, and Eating Disorders)

_____ 1. The psychosocial task for a toddler is to develop a sense of autonomy.

_____ 2. Learning how to feel industrious is usually the task of a young adult.

_____ 3. The midlife crisis often includes the "empty nest syndrome."

_____ 4. Cyberbullying is often done on social websites or through texting.

_____ 5. Adolescent problems like eating disorders, pregnancy, and running away often are a result of the adolescent's need for autonomy and nurturance from parents.

_____ 6. Teens run away from home because they are ready to start a career.

_____ 7. Developmental crises are often expected.

_____ 8. The elderly often struggle with the need for integrity versus despair.

_____ 9. Families often go into crisis states because of structural failings.

_____ 10. The need for intimacy is the task for preschoolers.

Introduction

The idea of developmental crises, proposed by Erik Erikson, is well documented and almost universally accepted by social scientists. Erikson spoke of developmental crises induced by special tasks and role changes required by each new stage in the sequence of psychosocial maturation. People are more vulnerable to crises at these stages in life. This normal process of growth and development occurs gradually as a person moves from one stage of psychological, biological, and social development to another. The short periods of psychological upset that occur during a critical transition point in the normal development of a person from birth to old age are frequently brought to a counselor's attention.

In working with developmental crises, crisis interventionists acknowledge that role development does not exist in a vacuum. If one person's role in the family changes, the roles of other family members change as well. Because of the involvement of the family in the completion of a role change, these crises can take years to complete.

A Brief Review of the Life Cycle Crises

Infancy: Having a baby is an example of a psychosocial stage that creates the need for accomplishing various tasks. The first year of a child's life creates many stresses in the home, and these often lead parents to seek out the services of a mental health provider. The baby needs unconditional love, attention, and **nurturance**. These traits do not come naturally to all parents. The addition of a baby definitely upsets the steady state that existed when the family consisted only of a husband and wife. If the mother is not married or is a teenager, other crises may occur. Providing the nurturance necessary for an infant to grow up trusting that all of his or her needs will be met is quite a task. Parenting education may prove to be helpful during this first year because most parents have not been systematically trained to take care of a baby. Many hospitals and health maintenance organizations offer classes on parenting in addition to the more traditional "birthing" classes. Most bookstores have an abundance of "how to" books for parents needing suggestions and knowledge. Parents also need support and encouragement to take care of themselves as a marital unit. New parents might benefit from the common-sense advice of counselors, nurses, social workers, or other professionals. For example, they need to take time to go out on a date, or ask grandparents to babysit so they can have a break from child care. Empathizing with parents on how difficult it is to be a good parent may help a couple during this stage of family development.

Toddlerhood: The next stage of parenting also brings in many families for counseling. Helping toddlers work through their needs to reach a balance of independence and dependence is quite a challenge. Parents often benefit from receiving instruction on how to implement structured behavior modification as they help their toddler work through this transitional process. Crisis workers can teach parents how to set boundaries and limits without shaming the child. It can be quite scary for a two-year-old to be in charge of a home. Parents need to take control without being tyrants.

Preschool and Middle School: Once children enter school, social acceptance, assertion, self-esteem, and identity become the tasks they must master. Children of school age often experience crises related to social rejection. The crisis worker can help by exploring suitable alternatives by which children can get their needs met. Parents are encouraged to be involved in these sessions and can be of great support to their children.

Adolescence: During this age period, teens are searching for an identity, autonomy, and differentiation from their parents. If they receive the sense of nurturance and boundaries they need from their parents, they will move on to young adulthood with a healthy foundation. They may also be at risk of engaging in illegal and potentially life threatening behaviors in search of autonomy. Crises during adolescence are so challenging that a separate section is devoted to this topic later in this chapter.

Young Adulthood: As individuals enter adulthood, new tasks arise. First, young adults must gain a sense of being economically and socially responsible for themselves. Young adults eventually seek partners to fulfill their emotional needs as they move away from their parents. Making the transition from parental affection to partner intimacy is no easy task. Generally, a decade is needed for young people to work through this stage. Relationship breakups are common during this period as young adults begin to engage in intimate relationships. Not only will crisis workers be dealing with young adults trying to find intimacy with peers, but also with those who are trying to separate emotionally from their parents.

Middle Adulthood: Another typical developmental crisis is often referred to as *midlife crisis*. It can occur over a period of several years as the middle-aged person's life starts to become routine. At this point, people usually have a stable career, their children are grown and independent, for the most part, and their marriage has lost its fire. To bring themselves out of this rut and reduce their feelings of boredom, many create circumstances that renew their youth, such as getting a sports car, having an affair, searching for a new job, or enrolling in college. The counselor can aid individuals at this time by showing them that their feelings are normal and helping them focus on productive ways to eliminate their depression. Marital counseling can be very useful at this point to help spouses grow together and create a relationship that does not depend on raising children but incorporates new activities into their lifestyle.

Maturity: The last psychosocial stage is often referred to as *integrity versus despair*. This is the time when older adults begin accepting the knowledge that life is approaching its climax. Retirement, illness, and death are some of the stressors normally found during this time. The crisis worker can help this age group adjust to a new way of life. Retirees can be encouraged to play golf, volunteer at charity organizations, or take classes at a recreation center. Also, couples may need marital therapy to help them find a new love for one another. They can then be at peace during their twilight years.

In Table 5.1, the author has used Erickson's eight stages of development as a beginning point, showing the particular changes occurring at each stage, as well as interventions that can be helpful to clients experiencing crises at each stage.

TABLE 5.1 Crisis Intervention as Related to Erickson's Psychosocial Stages of Development

Stage	Crisis	Possible Problematic Social Role Changes	Interventions
Infancy	Trust Versus Mistrust	Mother fails to bond or nurture infant	Teach mother proper parenting skills; discuss fears about intimacy
		Father fails to join in as a nurturer; father unable to maintain sense of belonging to family unit	Encourage communication and expression of sense of being left out with no function; educate mother on the need for father's involvement with infant including the daughter
Toddler Years	Autonomy Versus Shame and Self-Doubt	Parents fail to allow independence and are overcontrolling	Educate parents about the needs of toddler to feel powerful over self
		Parents fail to set appropriate boundaries and limits	Educate parents about ways to set limits without creating uncontrollable power struggles
Preschool Years	Initiative Versus Guilt	Child is unable to interact with children and initiate play	Support parents in their efforts to role model proper assertive behavior for their child within the family and with extrafamilial relationships
		Child is overly competitive and aggressive and unable to share or cooperate	Teach parents how to help child submit without feeling completely worthless
Childhood Years	Industry Versus Inferiority	Child fails to master skills at school, whether academic, physical, or social	Encourage child to develop competence at some task or game
		Child fails to demonstrate competence in areas parents perceive as appropriate	Teach parents about the need for child to develop an identity and skills appropriate for the child rather than expecting behaviors that meet the parents' emotional needs and desires
Adolescence	Identity Versus Role Confusion	Parents fail to allow child freedoms and responsibilities	Introduce family therapy that focuses on negotiation and compromise

(Continued)

TABLE 5.1   Crisis Intervention as Related to Erickson's Psychosocial Stages of Development (*Continued*)

Stage	Crisis	Possible Problematic Social Role Changes	Interventions
		Parents fail to listen to the child and understand his or her needs	Teach parents active listening and empathetic understanding skills
		Child fails to transfer emotional need fulfillment to peers	Support child to interact with peers and encourage social involvement
		Child fails to manage increased responsibilities and stress of growing up	Support child to accept reality of growing up, pointing out the advantages that go along with stress and responsibility
Young Adult Years	Intimacy Versus Isolation	Young adult fails to form intimate relationships; experiences loneliness	Teach healthy social interaction skills; help work through grief and depression
		Young adult fails to experience independence from parents emotionally, financially, or physically	Educate young adult about normalcy of fears regarding independence, adulthood and old age; give practical suggestions on how to manage daily stresses and let go of parents
		Parents fail to let go of young adult; attempt to control his or her life	Help parents grieve loss and focus on new involvements
Middle Adult Years	Generativity Versus Stagnation	Spouses fail to rekindle marital bond after children move out	Suggest marital counseling to address feelings of loss, increase marital interactions, and activities
		Adult fails to involve self in new and fulfilling activities	Encourage career change, enrolling in college, starting a hobby, doing volunteer work
		Adult fails to adapt to grandparental role appropriately	Teach appropriate role behaviors and boundaries for grandparents
		Parents fail to let go of adult children; experience profound depression because of their loss	Help parents grieve loss and work through depression
Mature Adult Years	Ego Integrity Versus Despair	Older adult fails to continue participation in life	Encourage involvement in senior centers and support groups
		Older person experiences depression about his or her life	Provide supportive counseling focusing on positives in life
		Older person experiences anger and shame about dependence on family	Use family therapy to address feelings and communicate needs

Source: Adapted from Erikson, 1963; expanded by author.

Family Systems Theory

Family systems theory is particularly useful when working with developmental crises and evolutional crises.

Family systems theory is loosely based on the concepts proposed by general systems theory that is based on Newton's third law of physics, which states that for every action there is an equal and opposite reaction. Terms like self-regulating mechanism, feedback, **counteraction**, and **calibration** can be used to describe an interpersonal system as well as a mechanical system. Family systems theory utilizes these ideas to understand how families undergo crises and how they cope with them.

The idea is that if a member in a family unit changes his or her behavior in a major way, others in the family will behave in ways to prevent the change from happening. This reaction is most likely due to fear of change which happens at a subconscious level. Change often makes people feel anxious. Counteractive behaviors lessen anxiety. Family members often do not realize what they are doing. Therapists point out these processes and make clients conscious of them. Counselors help contain a client's anxiety, ensure that the client is supported, and try to reframe the client's perceptions. Typical counteractive behaviors used by family members include shaming, threatening, excluding, or punishing the target person. The one who is behaving outside the family's calibrated (acceptable) range of behaviors may continue a behavior that is acceptable to the family even if it is **pathological**, rather than endure counteraction from the family. Family systems theory helps explain why pathologic interactions are so common in families and why change takes a long time to occur. People tend to prefer stability (**homeostasis**), even if the consequence is retention of painful symptoms.

Runaways

Runaway is the term used in the family systems model to describe a true family crisis. This term has a particular meaning in family systems theory. A runaway exists when the counteractive-negative feedback mechanisms fail to bring the situation back into calibration, that is, family members cannot create homeostasis with their normal coping mechanisms. The runaway state often causes a family to seek counseling.

Family therapy models have usually focused on brief interventions, much in keeping with the crisis model. Reframing and assigning positive connotations are two major intervention strategies in family systems approaches, particularly the strategic models. Both of these techniques aim at changing the internal cognitive experience of family members.

Just as a maintenance worker resets a thermostat if its mechanisms do not maintain temperature stability, a family worker resets the calibration of family rules after a runaway to help the family return to homeostasis, albeit a new stability. Crisis intervention often makes use of systems theory by employing techniques from structural and strategic problem-solving therapies (Peake, Borduin, & Archer, 1988, pp. 90–95).

Structural Family Therapy

Some families may inadvertently maintain a crisis state in a family member because they resist allowing the person to pass through a critical developmental stage. Structural family therapy attempts to help everyone in the family move through new developmental stages at the same time by learning new, more adaptive roles. The range of allowable behaviors is recalibrated, reducing counteractions (resistance). New boundaries are established that allow for age-appropriate independence and nurturance. Minuchin (1974) points out that these are the two main functions of a family: to provide support and nurturance and to create individuals who can function in society independent of the family of origin. Crisis workers keep this in mind when assessing the nature of a client's crisis, which could involve problems of closeness and support or distance and independence.

Certain terms may be helpful in identifying healthy versus unhealthy structures in families. They also shed light on why certain problems exist. These words describe boundaries which may need expansion or restriction. The crisis counselor often tries to create clearer boundaries that allow evolving needs to be met in family members.

Enmeshment: In an **enmeshed** situation, everyone in the family interferes and is overly involved in everyone else's decisions, feelings, wishes, and behaviors. Children may know too much about their parents, and vice versa. One sees a lack of independence of thought and feeling in family members. These families typically see themselves as very close or too close. A child may grow up feeling no sense of separateness and may have problems making decisions and functioning in other adult situations (Bowen, 1985). A crisis state may occur when someone attempts to break out of the enmeshment. Others may react by subtly punishing the individual, perhaps with the "silent treatment" or exclusion from family affairs. A healthy balance between closeness and separateness is the goal of counseling in these circumstances.

Diffusion: A family is diffuse when members are not clear about who is to do what. Roles are not well defined or are inconsistent. For example, when a 16-year-old girl raises a baby in her parents' home, the baby may be confused about the role of his mother, who is receiving parenting at the same time that she is parenting him.

A pathologic variation of diffusion is cross-generational coalition, where one parent and a child team up against the other parent, thereby crossing the parent-child boundary. Incest is one of the most harmful examples of cross-generational coalition. It results in moderate to severe disturbances of the victim throughout his or her life. Clear age-appropriate boundaries are essential for healthy emotional functioning.

Disengagement: In a disengaged family, distance is the pattern. The rule in these families is not to get too close emotionally or socially. The relationship between parents and children and between spouses tends to be more functional than in some other troubled families. Independence is encouraged. However, children may feel unsupported and unloved in families where

---

Box 5.1   Case Example of the Use of Family Systems Approach

A family seeks help to straighten out the thirteen-year-old daughter's behavior. She likes to be in her room alone, talks back to her parents, prefers her friends over her family, and is interested in boys. Her parents have been restricting her out-of-house activities, but that hasn't helped. A crisis interventionist might restructure and reframe the whole system. Instead of two adults and a child, the family consists of two adults and a maturing adolescent, who is behaving normally. The rules of behavior need to be changed to accommodate the change in structure, thereby lessening negative feedback. This less restrictive atmosphere encourages the 13-year-old to communicate more with her parents. The parents must be made aware of the family's enmeshment. They must see that their teenager needs a sense of independence to learn to function in the adult world she will soon be entering.

---

disengagement is strong. This feeling may lead to gang involvement, substance abuse, or teen pregnancy because children seek love and support outside the family or attempt not to feel anything (through substance abuse). Crisis workers can intervene by helping families learn how to show support for one another to increase a sense of belonging.

Rigidity: In families with rigid boundaries, spouses and children are treated only one way. There is no crossing over between generations: Children are to be seen and not heard. Wives clean; husbands work; children obey. Father disciplines; mother takes care of children. These rules are typical and can lead to rigid personality structures in children. Counselors need considerable skill to be able to reframe and educate parents with rigid boundaries. They carefully respect cultural factors. The following vignette shows a family with a problem. The approach used here combines structural family therapy with the family-systems model.

In the strategic family therapy model, the goal is to shift family rules to bring about a new homeostasis that does not include pathological behaviors. Insight into why the family behaves the way it does is not necessary. Short-term homeostatic systems therapy may require fewer than 10 sessions. Box 5.1 provides an example of a case of a family trying to manage normal adolescent developmental changes in a 13 year old girl and how to use the family systems model to intervene.

Evolutional Crises

Another way to understand crisis states is to look at the normal passages, or **evolutional crises**, through which typical families go as the years pass. This model is helpful for crisis workers who can explain it to clients when a crisis is clearly due to problems in adjusting to the growing family unit.

First Stage of a Family: Creating a Marital Subsystem

A typical nuclear family will be discussed here because Minuchin's (1974) original theoretical model was based on this type of family. This does not mean that other family structures are inadequate. In fact, if a marital subsystem is extremely pathological, it might be better to live in a nontraditional unit, such as a single mother unit. This model does suggest that families, whatever their structure, evolve based on the growing and changing needs of all of their members. This model may also explain why certain family structures might be more difficult or easier for children and other family members. Many of the problems that people face in a nonnuclear family are the result of societal values suggesting that being raised with one's biological mother and father who are married is best. This view is obviously biased. It still may cause discomfort and difficulties for people living in other types of families. Of course, people living in different family structures (e.g., lesbians or gay men raising adopted children, couples living together without being married, single-parent families) may experience structural difficulties in the same way that nuclear families do. Crisis workers dealing with these issues are challenged to apply the theoretical models in ways that are relevant for their clients. At times, crisis workers must be creative and offer interventions based on pure caring, intuition, and listening without judgment.

In a traditional nuclear family, the first adjustment must be made when a man and a woman decide to get married or move in together. Both the couple and their respective parents must change. Each member of the couple comes from a family in which certain values and behaviors are accepted and practiced. The new husband and wife need to create their own behavior patterns for their new home and their own marital subsystem. They will adjust to each other, try to change each other, and adapt. Sometimes conflicts occur because of the inability to adjust. At other times this conflict results from the interference of in-laws who discourage adjustment, albeit in subtle ways. Power struggles are common during this time. The parents may still want to control their adult child, and the adult child may be trying to assert independence without totally alienating the parents, a definite setup for a crisis.

Education and reframing are helpful here. The couple can be encouraged to set up their own home without completely negating their parents' wishes. Compromise is helpful when possible. Also, cultural considerations need to be explored.

The couple is encouraged to decide how each set of parents is going to influence their marriage. Also, it is beneficial for them to set boundaries that say, "We are united for each other" as opposed to "We are united against you." One way to prove to one's parents that one is truly an adult worthy of respect is to approach one's parents as an assertive, respectful adult. When a member of a newly formed couple wishes to behave in ways outside the norms of his or her family of origin, he or she can be encouraged to speak directly and lovingly to his or her parents. This can be done by reminding one's parents how scary and difficult it is to venture into adulthood and create a close, secure relationship with a mate. It may help ease tension if the young adult asks his or her own parents for tips on how to succeed. Of course, if someone has been brought up by parents who have been abusive, have substance abuse problems, or have other types of mental illness, this may not be the best strategy. The young adult may have to start understanding the emotional pain of the parents and deal with them not as parents on a pedestal, but rather as normal people with some emotional issues. It would be unrealistic for the young adult to pretend that the parents know everything and do not have any problems. The author has found that teaching clients to empathize with the issues of their parents goes a long way in helping to relieve the fear, anger, and guilt that clients often feel toward their parents when they first become intimately involved with a mate.

Some parents will be more accepting of their child's choice of a mate than others. When there is lack of acceptance, young adults may need encouragement to take care of their own emotional needs, and, if possible, still maintain some involvement with the parents. Sadly, some parents are incapable of interacting in a healthy way with a child who moves into adulthood because of their own sadness at losing control over the child, or losing the closeness that once existed with the child. Crisis workers might consider being just as empathic to these parents as to the young adult.

Creating a Parental Subsystem

The next potential for crisis in the evolving family occurs when a child is born. Now the parents have to adjust to a third individual, who will have a profound effect on the family unit they have been creating. Parental nurturance of the baby needs to be learned. This nurturance is different from the affection and intimacy between spouses. Each parent needs to develop skills and behaviors to help raise the child. Also, in-law involvement must be determined. Grandparents have a place in the lives of their grandchildren, and children benefit greatly from healthy grandparental involvement. If parents have not come to terms with their own parents, however, the birth of a child can create tension and conflict.

It is vital to have a strong marital subsystem before creating a parental subsystem. The crisis counselor works to help the couple strengthen their marriage before any real change in parenting function can be made.

Creating Sibling Subsystems

As children grow and new children are added to the family, new tasks of evolution are faced. It is helpful for parents to acknowledge that siblings share certain ideas and behaviors that belong to them and not to the parents. Good, strong, even conflictual sibling relationships are to be encouraged (though abuse should not be tolerated). These experiences are important to healthy interpersonal functioning later in life. If parents interfere too much, siblings do not learn how to cope interpersonally outside the family.

Also, healthy parenting styles demonstrate an understanding that there should be different expectations, responsibilities, and privileges for children of different ages. Healthy family structure dictates that a five-year-old be treated differently than a 15-year-old in regard to bedtime, curfews, eating habits, social activities, and household chores. Box 5.2 provides an example of a structural failing in a family and how incorporating the structural family therapy model would be useful.

> ### Box 5.2   Example of a Structural Dysfunction in the Sibling Subsystem
>
> **Example:** A 15-year-old girl was brought into counseling because she had been acting out against her parents, frequently opposing them, yelling at them, and demonstrating much unhappiness in general. Evidently, she had been required to come home from school every day and babysit her four younger siblings while her parents were at work. Not only did she have to do this, but she was also not allowed to be with her peers on weekends. She seemed to have all the responsibilities of an adult but the privileges of her four-year-old brother.
>
> Crisis intervention involved establishing a new role for her. Her parents were strongly encouraged to allow their daughter to join the volleyball team at school and to find someone else to watch their other children one night a week. The 15-year-old would also be allowed to be with her friends on weekends as long as she spent time with the family on Sundays. Though the parents were inconvenienced, in the long run the family functioned in a more stable fashion.

Creating Grandparent Subsystems

As children grow up and involve themselves in intimate relationships with peers outside the family, parents learn to relinquish control and move into a more collaborative relationship with their children. This means that the parents strengthen their marital unit and accept the boundaries that the adult children set. Also, when they become grandparents (i.e., a grandparent subsystem), they might learn to set boundaries so they are not taken advantage of by their children, either as babysitters or as financial contributors.

Grandparents often sit by quietly as they watch a child or child-in-law make mistakes with grandchildren. Interference is usually not appreciated and can cause problems in the family. The crisis worker might explain to well-meaning grandparents that their child and his or her spouse need to make their own mistakes, just as the grandparents themselves did. The counselor can also point out ways in which the grandparents can be supportive of their children without being intrusive.

In working with evolutional crises, counselors often seek to identify whether a crisis is related to unhealthy boundaries such as enmeshment, rigidity, diffusion, or disengagement as discussed previously. The goal would be to strengthen healthy boundaries that are clear and flexible between generations and within the marital relationship.

Special Issues of Adolescence

A number of situations that can become crises are unique to specific periods of life. Though these situations do not affect all adolescents, they are prevalent enough to warrant a closer look.

Adolescence can be a stormy period in which teenagers are struggling for independence, yet are still in need of guidance and emotional support. When a family system does not allow both **autonomy** and nurturance, teenagers may engage in self-destructive behaviors in order to meet one or both of these needs. Although individual or group therapy is effective with this population and is used widely in teen shelters and group homes, a look at the family structure and intervention with the family are vital for permanent resolution of the problems. For this reason, most adolescent treatment programs require family involvement.

Bullying

One cannot address issues facing adolescents without dealing with bullying. In the past decade, bullying has been discussed nationwide in the news, in movies and in television shows. Some have hypothesized that bullying not only causes negative consequences for those who are bullied, but may even be a cause of some of the recent incidences of shootings at elementary schools, high schools, and universities.

Definition   According to the American Psychiatric Association (as cited in Brohl & Ledford, 2012), bullying is characterized as aggressive behavior that is intended to cause distress or harm, involves an imbalance of power or strength between the bully and the victim, and occurs repeatedly over time. Bullying often takes place on school campuses, through email, cell-phone texting, instant messaging, blogging, and social networking sites.

Statistics   The data collected for the Report on the Condition of Children in Orange County (2012) shows that nearly 200,000 students stay home from school every day to avoid bullying. Data from this report also shows that 60 percent of middle-school students say they have been bullied. Interestingly, only 16 percent of school staff believe students are being bullied. This indicates where the problem and solution may lie.

Physical bullying may be easier to detect than other types such as cyberbullying which occurs online. However, **cyberbullying** may be more emotionally damaging because it can be broadcast to the youth's peers. Things like spreading rumors, threats, insults, hurtful messages, taking unflattering pictures, and forwarding sexual messages or pictures to third parties are considered cyberbullying (Bullying Statistics, 2009). Cyberbullying may be the reason why school staff do not perceive the amount of bullying that occurs. This is unfortunate because bullying can lead to serious consequences such as suicide, low self-esteem, mental health issues such as depression and eating disorders, substance abuse, and impaired academic achievement (UCLA Research Center, 2010; Swearer & Lembeck, 2012; Cooper, 2011; Nauert, 2012; and UCLA, 2010).

Intervention Strategies   Bullying prevention programs have been cropping up nationwide. They vary in size and scope, but the most promising seem to incorporate much of the following:

1. Creating schoolwide climate that discourages bullying
2. Surveying students to assess nature and extent of bullying and attitudes about bullying

3. Training staff to recognize and respond to bullying
4. Developing consistent rules against bullying
5. Reviewing and enhancing school's disciplinary code related to bullying
6. Discussing bullying issues in classrooms
7. Integrating bullying prevention themes across curriculum
8. Providing individual and group counseling to bullied children
9. Providing counseling to children who have bullied
10. Involving parents in bullying prevention
11. Using teachers and members of the school staff to increase staff knowledge and motivation related to bullying (U.S. Department of Health and Human Services, 2009)

Working with Families and Victims   Crisis workers might deal with parents of bullied children and the bullied child together or individually. The primary focus is keeping the child safe and protected. Discussing specific plans to ensure safety is useful (Brohl & Ledford, 2012). Victims may feel guilty and blame themselves and counselors can educate them on how it is the bully's emotional issues that's causing the problem and encourage their own power, resiliency and enjoyment of life. Solutions should be offered that are concrete and specific.

Working with Families and the Bully   Parents of bullies must learn certain disciplinary steps to take with their child who bullies others. They should be clear about what has happened and place the responsibility of the bullying on the bully, not the victim. The bully must solve the problem by some type of apology, restitution, reconciliation or resolution, but always ensuring the bully's dignity remains intact (Brohl & Ledford, 2012). Experienced counselors may also decide to explore parenting practice to ascertain if the parents themselves are bullies and are teaching their own children inadvertently or directly to bully others. This can be awkward and challenging, but often necessary.

Teen Pregnancy

The United States has the highest teen-pregnancy rate in the industrialized world, and California has the highest rate in the country (U.S. Census Bureau, *Statistical Abstract of the United States: 2004–2005*). Preliminary data for 2009 indicate that the birth rate for teens nationwide has decreased to 39.1 births per 1,000 females ages 15–19 from 47.7 per 1,000 in 2000. California teen-birth rates have decreased as well from 45.1 births per 1,000 in 2001 down to 29 births per 1,000 in 2010 (Centers for Disease Control and Prevention, 2010). So while the rates are decreasing, this problem still exists and remains a potential crisis situation for many. This data only reflects the number of infants born to teens, not the number of pregnancies that do not result in live birth. For example, in California, only 50 percent of teen pregnancies result in live birth, while the remaining 50 percent end with abortion (36%) or miscarriage (14%) (Alan Guttmacher Institute, 2010). Not only does teen pregnancy require crisis workers to deal with having a child, but also, how to deal with not continuing with the pregnancy.

When pregnant teens are compared with girls who did not become pregnant as teenagers, a number of social factors emerge. Teen mothers are less likely to get or stay married, less likely to complete high school or college, and more likely to require public assistance and live in poverty (Healthy People, 2012). Teen-childbearing costs taxpayers in the United States approximately $9 billion annually. Additionally, children of teen parents have a lower probability of obtaining the emotional and financial resources they need to develop into independent, productive, well-adjusted adults and are at greater risk for low birth weight, preterm birth and death in infancy (Centers for Disease Control, 2011). Simpson and colleagues (1997) have identified several common risk factors for adolescent pregnancy: being the daughter of a teen parent, poverty, poor academic achievement, low self-esteem, dating at an early age, dating boys or men five or six years older than oneself, and minority status. Others have suggested that certain family characteristics may also contribute to teen pregnancy. Jacobs (1994) proposes that teenagers' developmental needs of autonomy and attachment seem to be a factor in their desire to be sexually active. This behavior may be perceived by teens as a defiant act of **differentiation**.

In many families in which a daughter acts out sexually, the parents have not communicated with her about sexual matters and have put excessive restrictions on her. In these families, adolescents do not feel that they can talk to their parents, which increases their secrecy about their social activities. In addition to seeking autonomy, most of the girls seek a closeness that they do not have with their parents. Some choose to keep their babies instead of offering them for adoption because of their misguided belief that the baby will provide them with the nurturing they lacked at home. Of course, some teenage girls who become pregnant do not come from dysfunctional homes; they may have just made a mistake, or their birth control method failed.

Many clinics and shelters have been set up to address the problems peculiar to this group of teenagers. For example, pregnant teen girls can often be cared for in facilities in which they can go to school and learn how to parent the baby. The crisis worker might try to become aware of the availability of such options in the area. Parents are often willing to help out, and the crisis worker can help the entire family adjust to the pregnancy and the baby. This often means that the girl must drop out of school. More importantly, her social life will change. If the girl does not wish to keep the baby, the crisis counselor usually has knowledge of adoption agencies and abortion facilities and might present these options to the girl and her parents. When conducting crisis counseling with someone who is considering abortion or adoption, it is imperative to maintain a nonjudgmental attitude. It is not ethical for counselors to persuade a teen to either continue with the pregnancy or terminate it. Instead, counselors listen, help the girl clarify what she wants to do according to her value system, and provide education and referrals.

Teens Who Run Away from Home

Like teenagers experiencing other crises of adolescence, teens who run away from home are trying to meet their needs for both differentiation and nurturance. If a family prohibits **individuation**, the teen is unable to establish a mature identity and develop the capacity for intimacy that is needed to assume adult roles and responsibilities. Without the love and acceptance of their families, teens face much anxiety during this most stressful stage of development.

Running away from home is one way to achieve autonomy and independence, but it can be very dangerous. Runaway teens may be drawn into prostitution, pornography, and drug use. They are susceptible to the influence of others because of the sense of aloneness they feel. Often, they feel abandoned by their parents and seek the acceptance of anyone. They may at first think life on the streets will be glamorous and exciting. They might even relish the idea of making all their own decisions and being in total control of their lives. However, they will soon find that they are in no way prepared to truly control their lives.

According to Runawayteens.org and 1800runaway.org (Kennon, 2013), 1 in 7 minors between ages 10 and 18 will run away at some point and there are 1–3 million runaway and homeless youth living on the streets in the United States. It is estimated that 50 percent of runaway youth are male and 50 percent are female.

Motivations for Running Away   Interviews with runaway or homeless youth suggest a variety of reasons for the youth to run away from home. About 50 percent of these youth reported that they ran away due to conflicts with parents or that their parents actually told them to leave. In about 80 percent of the cases, the runaway girls reported having been sexually or physically abused, while 34 percent of girls and boys reported sexual abuse before leaving home and 43 percent of girls and boys reported physical abuse (Kennon, 2013). This unfortunately increases the likelihood of further victimization on the streets.

Interventions   More and more nonprofit agencies have been created to house teen runaways to prevent them from being preyed on while trying to live on the streets. These teen shelters usually provide brief crisis intervention and family counseling, either to find a permanent residence away from the family or to reunite the family. If the teen is abused, this will be reported, and attempts will be made to help the teen find a safe place to live with the assistance of the state social services department.

In effective intervention, families are taught more effective communication skills, and the counselor attempts to address the needs of the teen for autonomy and support. Cultural differences are recognized, and counselors are sensitive to parents' rights and values. This is not an easy task. A good idea is to seek consultation from others who have worked with adolescents and clients from other cultures. Once the crisis intervention is completed, most agencies offer ongoing support groups, continuing family therapy, and follow-up services. The stress in these families must be changed in order for the teen to return home and not act out again.

The past several decades have seen an increase in the need for runaway youth shelters. Casa Youth Shelter in Los Alamitos, California, is an example. Gary Zager (1998), the director of the program, describes the purpose of this shelter as a place to help calm down the crisis that began at home and get the minor back into his or her own home. He states that the counselors at the shelter attempt to define the client as "the entire family" rather than pin the label of "bad child" onto the teen in crisis. Extreme physical abuse is a major reason why teenagers run away from home. Zager says that about 20 percent of girls who run away are pregnant, and many others run away because they have been "kicked out." Unfortunately, the trend is for younger and younger children to be "thrown away" by their parents.

Sexual abuse is certainly another reason why teens run away from home. The teen may believe that leaving is the only way to make the sexual abuse stop, especially if he or she has attempted to get support from the nonperpetrating parent and has been ignored or scolded. Others are referred to the shelter by school counselors, juvenile probation workers, and social workers. Shelters such as the one in Los Alamitos are excellent resources for any crisis worker. Once the child is at the shelter, crisis intervention is provided for the child and the parents. In keeping with the theory of crises, a 45-day stay is typical. It is hoped that the crisis can be resolved in this period and reunification accomplished.

The goals of family therapy include creating more appropriate boundaries for the child, "deparentifying" the child, and respecting and encouraging the individuality of the child. In other words, an attempt is made to create an appropriate structure in the family, where parents are in charge, children get their needs met, and open communication is allowed. Often, the family is a single-parent one, and the mother needs support in developing an emotionally satisfying life for herself. The runaway often leaves so as not to be burdened with tasks normally ascribed to a second parent. Progress is made when the family can demonstrate appropriate communication processes in front of the crisis worker.

Eating Disorders

Approximately seven million females and one million males are afflicted with an eating disorder. Of the females, 86 percent developed it before the age of 20; 10 percent before the age of 10, and 33 percent between the ages of 11 and 15 (Radcliffe, 1999, as cited in AATBS, 2005).

Girls at highest risk for developing an eating disorder are white and middle or upper class. Unfortunately, these disorders are now becoming more prevalent among less-privileged girls of minority status as they assimilate into Anglo American culture, in which typical models weigh 25 percent less than the average woman. Sadly, the media usually present unrealistic body images to the public, not only by using ultrathin models in advertising, but by using extremely thin actresses in movies and television shows.

Anorexia Nervosa   The central features of **anorexia nervosa** syndrome include an intense fear of gaining weight, refusal to maintain adequate nutrition, erroneous complaints of being fat, loss of original body weight at least to a level 85 percent of that expected on the basis of height and weight norms, disturbance of body image, and absence of at least three menstrual periods (American Psychiatric Association, 2000).

Bulimia Nervosa   People with **bulimia nervosa** are distinguished from those with anorexia nervosa on the basis of relatively normal weight and the presence of binge eating and purging (Gabbard, 2000, p. 349). Bruch (1987) suggests that the two disorders contrast sharply with each other in that those with bulimia nervosa are more impulse-ridden, irresponsible, and undisciplined compared to the control and perfectionism found in those with anorexia nervosa.

Causes   Individuals who develop eating disorders have the following characteristics in common: (1) are highly emotionally reserved and cognitively inhibited; (2) prefer routine, orderly, predictable environments and adapt poorly to change; (3) show heightened conformity and deference to others; (4) avoid risk and react to appetitive or affectively stressful events with strong feelings of distress; and (5) focus on perfectionism, negative self-evaluation, and fears of becoming an adult.

Although it is easy to blame eating disorders on societal reinforcement of slimness in women, this is not the only cause. Evidence suggests that hereditary factors may play a role in the development of eating disorders, and that biochemical or structural abnormalities in the brain mechanism that control metabolism or eating may be a cause (Russell & Treasure, 1989; Walters & Kendler, 1995). Another way to understand eating disorders is to see them as a form of addiction. The person is addicted to the act of dieting or binging on food. A depressed or psychologically traumatized individual may use the eating disorder to soothe the self. Eventually, however, the disorder takes over and the person cannot stop it, similar to the process in drug addiction (Castillo, 1997, as cited in AATBS, 2005).

Treatment Considerations   Since eating disorders may have life-threatening implications, especially for those suffering from anorexia who weigh less then 70 pounds and for those suffering from bulimia who vomit daily, physician involvement must be considered by crisis counselors. The client may need medical care in a hospital if physical injuries are present, such as malnutrition, dehydration, or seizures caused by electrolyte imbalances. These patients may also be at risk for heart failure; the singer Karen Carpenter, who had an eating disorder for years, died of heart failure. A physician may prescribe various medications such as antidepressants or other mood stabilizers. Once the target weight has been achieved, psychological treatment can begin. In addition to needing medical care for eating disorder-related physical conditions, clients are at risk for self-mutilation and suicide. Crisis workers must assess for self-destructive ideation or behaviors. Some perceive the eating disorder behaviors as a form of self-destruction. These clients are often very depressed and suffer from low self-esteem. They often feel worthless, helpless, and hopeless—the perfect equation for suicidal ideation and behaviors.

The family is strongly persuaded to be involved in treatment because eating disorders affect the entire family unit. The parents often seek crisis intervention in the first place because of their fears about their daughter's health. A challenge encountered with anorexics is helping them face the seriousness of their condition and getting them to cooperate with treatment. They may tell counselors that it is their parents who have the problem and be thoroughly convinced that everyone is making a big deal out of nothing, even though they may only weigh 85 pounds and think that being a size 1 is too big! As with substance abusers, crisis workers begin by listening with nonjudgmental empathy to the client's side of the story and assess her frame of reference and cognitions about her body and eating habits. She will "hang herself" soon enough because her thoughts are usually illogical and are not supported by evidence. The key is to proceed slowly and kindly, but confrontations will eventually be given to help her see that she does need help.

Box 5.3 presents a case of an eating disorder highlighting the aspects of the ABC Model related to the case.

Box 5.3   Example of an Eating Disorder Case

Case A mother takes her 15-year-old daughter to counseling because *she refuses to eat* (precipitating event). The mother thinks the daughter has lost over 40 pounds this past year but is not sure. Last week, *the daughter fainted after she jogged five miles without eating anything all day* (impairment in functioning related to precipitating event). The daughter feels *sad and angry* (emotional distress) because she *thinks she is still fat and that her parents should stay out of her business* (cognition). She also *thinks that it is not a big deal* (cognition).

Crisis Intervention: Instead of focusing solely on her eating, it is wise to explore her role in the family, her identity as a growing woman, and her emotional needs for individuation and nurturance. It is easier to prove that these issues are a problem for her, because by the time her eating disorder has become such a problem that her parents seek professional help, she has usually *isolated herself socially* (impairment in functioning) and is *depressed* (emotional distress). Remembering that she is a teenager who needs to accept the process of growing up is helpful. Her behavior should be assessed to see how much is rebellion and an attempt to have control over her parents, and how much is due

(Continued)

Box 5.3   Example of an Eating Disorder Case (Continued)

to low self-esteem and lack of identity (need to explore these cognitions). Sometimes, the eating disorder can be *reframed* as a form of adolescent oppositional defiant disorder. She may *believe that she cannot openly disagree with her parents* (cognition), so the eating disorder can be a way to have power without openly defying her parents. The whole family should be *educated* about the seriousness of any eating disorder and that often physician involvement is recommended to ensure that she isn't suffering from any physiological problems. The parents might be *empowered* by letting them know that they cannot control what their daughter eats, but they can control how much they participate in professional intervention and the types of changes that are suggested to them by the counselors. *Validation* of the frustration that all are feeling should be offered and that even anger is understandable. Even fear and anxiety about giving up the anorexia is understandable.

Once therapeutic comments are offered, the family, including the daughter, will be asked how they think they should proceed. It is likely that the daughter will need several years of individual therapy, family therapy, and group therapy to overcome her disorder. Some individuals with eating disorders must attend twelve-step groups indefinitely. Others need to take medication indefinitely. Family members usually participate in treatment; therefore, it is vital to gain their trust and cooperation. If the individual suffering from the eating disorder is seen alone, as if she exists in a vacuum, family members may inadvertently sabotage intervention efforts. It is necessary to remain nonjudgmental toward parents who may seem overcontrolling and rigid. The crisis worker will help them work through the crisis of their teenage daughter growing up.

Box 5.4 provides several case vignettes involving developmental crises to use for role plays.

Box 5.4   Cases to Role-Play

In the following sample cases, the reader can apply the ABC model of crisis intervention, using knowledge about the type of crises presented in this chapter. Some hints are provided to assist the reader in providing educational statements, reframes, empowerment statements, and validation comments.

Case 1 A husband and wife seek help because they have been fighting all the time. They had their first baby one month ago and were so happy just after the birth, but now they are tense, angry with each other, and have no desire for sex or affection with each other.

Validation: It is often very stressful to have a newborn and to be deprived of sleep.

Education: Sexual drive is often reduced for the mother after birth due to hormonal changes and maternal preoccupation.

Reframe: The fact that they came to counseling together is evidence that they still love each other and want to regain the affectionate feelings they had. The fact that they take their stress out on each other instead of the baby is a positive thing because they can communicate with each other and modify their behaviors, whereas the infant is not capable of making changes yet.

Empowerment: Help them focus on what they can do to make changes that will lower stress, such as having the father help out more and having date nights for the husband and wife.

(Continued)

Box 5.4   Cases to Role-Play (Continued)

Case 2 A mother comes to you complaining that her two-year-old must be hyperactive. He makes noises all day, can't sit still, won't listen, bites his older sister when he's angry, says "no" all the time, and refuses to be "potty trained." His sister was potty trained by this age.

Education: It is quite normal for boys to take longer to be potty trained than girls. Educate about how one can't diagnose a two-year-old as hyperactive because much of the behavior is normal. Teach the parent how to talk to the child, how to set boundaries appropriately, and how to help the child be structured, yet also have some autonomy.

Offer some behavioral tips such as the use of positive reinforcement for good behaviors.

Reframe: Biting is his only way of communicating because he can't yet talk. His saying "no" is simply mimicking what is probably being said to him all day.

Case 3 A 20-year-old female becomes completely stressed out as she plans her wedding. Both sets of parents are trying to control the whole thing, and she is ready to elope tomorrow. Her soon-to-be husband seems to always take his mother's side and won't speak up to her. The bride-to-be is a nervous wreck. The wedding is in two weeks.

Education: A wedding is equally stressful for the parents because they have to let go of their children, which completely changes the dynamics of the family.

Reframe the parents' controlling behaviors as an attempt to maintain the role of parent, not just to be mean and nasty.

Reframe her fiancé not speaking up to his mother as possibly not so bad, because it could mean that he respects her and will most likely respect his new wife as well.

Reframe the situation as an opportunity for her and her fiancé to set the needed boundaries between them as a married unit and their families of origin.

Validate the fact that most weddings have a considerable degree of stress involved.

Empower her to take charge of the things that mean the most to her and not fight every battle. There is some power in letting go.

Case 5 A mother and father bring their 16-year-old son to you because he has been threatening to run away. This week they took his driver's license away from him because he is failing four classes. They don't want him on the streets but feel he must earn the privilege of having a car. The son is oppositional, defiant, and refuses to cooperate.

Reframe the running away as a last-ditch effort to feel some sense of control and independence.

Empower everyone by exploring what can be done to make everyone feel safe.

Validate everyone's feelings and recognize that adolescence is a stormy period in which parents and the teen often feel angry and sad.

Chapter Review

Certain crises are expected and develop as we progress through the normal life cycle within our families. **Erikson's eight stages of development** are widely accepted as the normal sequence that we go through while we try to complete certain tasks. Minuchin presented his model of evolutional crises as a family proceeds through various stages of development in which new roles and boundaries must be made. Adolescents experience many serious crises due to their need to differentiate while receiving optimal amounts of both nurturance and independence from their parents. Teen pregnancy, bullying, runaways, and eating disorders are some of the prevalent crises that teenagers face and with which crisis workers must often deal.

Answers to Pre-Chapter Quiz

1. T   2. F   3. T   4. T   5. T   6. F   7. T   8. T   9. T   10. F

Key Terms for Study

anorexia nervosa: An eating disorder in which the person becomes unhealthily thin by starving or overexercising.

autonomy: A state of independence and self-sufficiency needed to function as an adult in society. Adolescents often struggle to achieve this with their parents.

bulimia nervosa: An eating disorder in which the person binges on high-fat or high-calorie foods and then either purges by vomiting or by use of laxatives or excessive exercising.

calibration: This refers to the range of allowable behaviors in a family.

counteraction: This refers to behaviors that family members engage in when trying stop a family member from behaving outside family rules.

cyberbullying: A form of intimidation, threat, teasing, or humiliation that occurs on the Internet, through email, through texting, or social websites.

differentiation: A process whereby an adolescent or young adult establishes a mature identity and the capacity for intimacy needed to assume adult roles and responsibilities.

disengagement: Parental behavior in which parents do not relate to their child in a nurturing manner; the child feels little support or sense of belonging.

enmeshed: A state in which an individual lacks a sense of separateness from others with whom he or she has an emotionally intense relationship.

Erikson's eight stages of development: Often called the psychosocial stages of development. During each stage there are tasks that everyone must master. The inability for the family to adapt and guide each other through these tasks often lead to crisis states. Following are the stages and tasks for that stage:

1. Infancy: Trust versus mistrust
2. Toddler years: Autonomy versus shame and self-doubt
3. Preschool years: Initiative versus guilt
4. Childhood years: Industry versus inferiority

5. Adolescence: Identity versus role confusion
6. Young adult years: Intimacy versus isolation
7. Middle adult years: Generativity versus stagnation
8. Mature adult years: Ego integrity versus despair

evolutional crises: The normal stages a family experiences as it evolves through the life span of its members. The crises result from having to adjust to the formation of the following subsystems: marital, parental, sibling, and grandparent.

homeostasis: This is the steady, stable state of a family which is maintained when family members adhere to the acceptable rules and roles created verbally or nonverbally by the family.

individuation: See **differentiation.**

nurturance: A sense of emotional support and love.

runaway: This term is used by family therapists to indicate that a family is in crisis.

References

Alan Guttmacher Institute. (2010). *Contraception counts.* Retrieved June 10, 2012, from http://www.agi-usa.org

American Psychiatric Association. (2000). *Diagnostic and statistical manual of mental disorders, fourth edition, text revision* (DSM-IV-TR). Washington, DC: Author.

Association for Advanced Training in the Behavioral Sciences. (2005). *Eating disorders: A brief guide.* Author. Web site: http://www.aatbs.com

Bowen, M. (1985). *Family therapy in clinical practice.* Northvale, NJ: Jason Aronson.

Brohl, K., & Ledford, R. (2012). Bullying in children and youth. In *Continuing education for California social workers and marriage and family therapists.* Ormond Beach, FL: Elite Continuing Education, 1–122.

Bruch, H. (1987). *The changing picture of an illness: anorexia nervosa, in Attachment and the Therapeutic Process.* Edited by Sacksteder JL, Schwartz, D. P., Akabane, Y., Madison, C. T. International Universities Press, 205–222.

Bullying Statistics. (2009). Retrieved June 10, 2012, from http://www.bullyingstatistics.org/

Centers for Disease Control, MMWR. (2011). Vital signs: Teen pregnancy-United States, 1991–2009. *Morbidity and Mortality Weekly Report (MMWR), 60*(13), 414–420.

Centers for Disease Control and Prevention. (2010). *National vital statistics reports,* vol. 59, no. 3.

Cooper, R. (2011). *Link between bullying and eating disorders*. Retrieved July 2, 2012, from http://www.eatingdisordersblogs.com

Erikson, E. (1963). *Childhood and society*. New York, NY: W.W. Norton and Company.

Gabbard, G. O. (2000). *Psychodynamic Psychiatry in Clinical Practice*, 3rd ed. Washington, D.C.: American Psychiatric Press.

Healthy People (2012).Cited in the *Report on the Conditions of Children in Orange County* (2012).Orangewood Children's Foundation & the Center for Community Collaboration. Orange County, CA: Author. Page 59.

Jacobs, J. (1994). Gender, race, class, and the trend toward early motherhood. *Journal of Contemporary Ethnography*, 22(4), 442–462.

Kennon, M. (2013). *Runaway statistics and resources*. LLC: Kennon Transport. Retrieved April 24, 2013, from http://www.kennontransport.com /runaway.html

Minuchin, S. (1974). *Families and family therapy*. Cambridge, MA: Harvard University Press.

Nauert, R. (2012). Substance use linked to bully behavior. *Psych Central*. Retrieved July 26, 2012, from http://psychcentral.com/news/2012/03 /06substance-use-linked-to-bully-behavior/35608.html

Peake, T. H., Borduin, C. M., & Archer, R. P. (1988). *Brief psychotherapies: Changing frames of mind*. Newbury Park, CA: Sage.

Report on the Conditions of Children in Orange County. (2012). Orangewood Children's Foundation & the Center for Community Collaboration. Orange County, CA: Author. (CSUF at (657)278-5681 or hhd.fullerton. edu/ccc/ and Orangewood Children's Foundation at (714)704-8777)

Russell, G. & Treasure, J. (1989). The Modern History of Anorexia Nervosa, an Interpretation of why the Illness has changed. *Annual New York Academic Science*, 575, 13–27.

Simpson, C., Pruitt, R., Blackwell, D., & Sweringen, G. S. (1997, April). Preventing teen pregnancy: Early adolescence. *ADVANCE for Nurse Practitioners*, 24–29.

Swearer, S. & Lembeck, P. (2012). Bullying and depression. Education.com. Retrieved July 2, 2012, from http://www.education.com/reference/article /bullying-depression/

UCLA. (2010). *Victims of bullying suffer academically as well psychologists report*. Retrieved from http://www.sciencedaily.com/releases/2010/08 /100820101502.htm

UCLA Research Center. (2010). *Self-esteem and cyberbullying*. Cyberbullying Research Center. Retrieved June 28, 2012, from http://cyberbullying.us /blog/self-esteem-and-cyberbullying.html

U.S. Census Bureau. (2005). *Statistical abstract of the United States: 2004–2005. Vital statistics of the United States, annual: National vital statistics report*, and unpublished data. Retrieved from http://www.cdc.gov/inchs .htm

U.S. Department of Health and Human Services HRSA. (2009). The scope and the impact of bullying. *Stop Bullying Now!* Retrieved from http://www.education.com/reference/article/Ref_Scopre_Impact/

Walters, E. E. & Kendler, K. S. (1995). Anorexia Nervosa & Anorexic-like Syndromes in a population-based female twin sample. *American Journal of Psychiatry, 152*(1), 64–71.

Zager, G. (1998). *Teenage runaways: Life at a youth shelter.* Presentation given at California State University, Fullerton, CA.

Chapter 6

Crises of Loss: Death, Relationship Breakups, and Economic Loss

_____ 1. The first stage of mourning is denial and shock.

_____ 2. The first task of mourning is to quickly reinvest energy into someone else.

_____ 3. Loyalty is an issue that children in blended families often face.

_____ 4. The person who breaks off a relationship doesn't have to worry about experiencing a crisis state themselves.

_____ 5. Divorce is never as bad as losing someone to death.

_____ 6. Grief refers to feelings of sorrow and sadness after a loss.

_____ 7. About 26 percent of children in the United States live in a divorced family.

_____ 8. After a divorce, the individuals may suffer social loss.

_____ 9. The second task of mourning is the active expression and feeling of emotions.

_____ 10. The last stage of loss is bargaining.

When discussing death, dying and loss, Elisabeth Kübler-Ross's name is bound to be mentioned. She has provided an outline for understanding the different stages people go through when dealing with grief over death and dying. Whether a client is grieving the death of a loved one, a divorce, or loss of a body part or function, the issues are similar.

Death and Dying

Elisabeth Kübler-Ross, a Swiss-born psychiatrist is probably the most well-known person associated with death and dying. She began seminars on death and dying in the late 1960s. She had the courage to bring dying patients into the classroom and openly discuss with them their fears, concerns, and desires as part of the training process for psychiatrists. Until then, few doctors or medical schools openly discussed the need to deal honestly and openly with dying patients and their families (Kübler-Ross, 1969, pp. 35–36). From these courses, she extracted the five stages of grief that she believed were experienced by people who knew they were dying; these emotions are also felt by those who are emotionally close to dying individuals and can even be observed in individuals suffering a relationship break-up. **Kübler-Ross's five stages of death and dying** (1969) can serve as an introduction to the topic of loss.

Kübler-Ross's Five Stages of Death and Dying

1. **Denial and isolation**: Denial and isolation make up the first stage in the dying process. Denial is both a healthy and a familiar initial reaction. It cushions people from the initial shock and allows them to deal with both their hope and their despair.
2. **Anger**: Anger frequently follows denial as people and their loved ones begin to accept the real possibility of death. There may be rage, envy, resentment, and bitterness. This frequently includes the "Why me?" question that so often has no answer.
3. **Bargaining**: The third stage is bargaining. Usually, bargains are secret pacts made with God, regardless of whether an individual has been religious earlier in life. When bargaining fails, the next stage develops.
4. **Depression**: When death is recognized as inevitable, and feelings of loss become overwhelming, depression sets in. Depression often includes sadness, pessimism, gloominess, and feelings of guilt and worthlessness along with lethargy.
5. **Acceptance**: Eventually the depression lifts as people work through mourning the impending loss of their life or a loved one's life and come to accept the inevitable. At this stage, a person is described as being almost void of feelings. Individuals are in the process of disengaging from this life if they are dying or disengaging from a loved one if that person is dying or has died (pp. 35–77).

Understanding the stages of loss is vital for counselors who are helping clients through this process. In addition, these stages can be generalized to other forms of loss. A related issue is the triggering of suicidal thinking in a grieving person, especially after denial and anger pass, and depression sets in. This is one reason suicide is addressed in this book before crises of loss. Awareness of the possibility of suicide will help the counselor assess for it with any client, no matter what the presenting crisis.

The problem with Kübler-Ross's stages became apparent as her popularity increased. People were only too ready to talk about dying, death, grief, and mourning. Consequently, they frequently accepted the stages as truth with a capital T. Counselors tried to force all patients to move through the stages in the same sequence. They did not understand that the stages were no more than generalizations. Not every person goes through each stage and certainly does not go through the stages in a predictable, sequential order. People struggle back and forth, frequently experiencing other emotions or similar emotions in varying degrees. Although Kübler-Ross is often credited as the originator of the study and treatment of death and dying, others have dealt with this topic over the span of modern history. Ideas from other theorists may help you be more empathetic and offer more effective interventions when working with those who are terminally ill. The theories of Charles Darwin, Sigmund Freud, and John Bowlby preceded and contributed to Kübler-Ross's theories on death and dying.

As early as 1872, **Charles Darwin** commented that the separation reactions resulting from the loss of a loved one were innate. He observed similar body movements in grieving individuals, regardless of their cultural background (Darwin, 1965).

Sigmund Freud defined mourning as a period of gradual withdrawal of libido from the now-missed loved object. He described the reactions as dejection, disinterest in the environment, and detachment from others. He saw the process as self-limiting. The effects cease when the libido has completed its withdrawal from the loved object and is reinvested in a new object (Leick & Davidson-Nielsen, 1991, p. 9).

John Bowlby (1980), noted theorist in the area of attachment and separation, proposed four phases of mourning: (1) numbing, (2) yearning and searching for the lost figure, (3) disorganization and despair, and (4) reorganization (p. 85).

Since the beginnings of the study of death and dying issues, behavioral scientists have continued to develop their understanding of the various issues and of the intervention skills that are helpful with these clients.

Definitions Related to Loss

As with any topic, understanding is predicated on shared definitions. In this book, the following terms are used.

Bereavement: A state involving loss. To bereave means to take away from, to rob, to dispossess.

Grief: The feelings of sorrow, anger, guilt, and confusion that arise when one experiences a loss. It is the affect that accompanies bereavement. One can be bereaved without grief, although full recovery seems to include some affective experience of the bereavement, usually in terms of grief.

Mourning: The overt expression of grief and the usual response to bereavement. Frequently, it is culturally modified and influenced. Whether one wears white or black, dances or cries, drinks or prays is often the result of cultural tradition.

Tasks of Mourning

Rather than think solely in terms of stages of grieving, the crisis worker can consider **tasks of mourning**. Tasks imply no time sequence. Tasks can be experienced as they arise rather than in any particular order. In addition, tasks imply that some action must be taken by the bereaved person. There is a need to do or experience something, to work toward a concrete goal. Worden (1982) offers four tasks for the person working through the mourning process:

Task I: Accepting the Reality of the Loss   As Kübler-Ross discovered, most people have difficulty accepting death. After a loved one dies (or a body part is amputated), the defense mechanism of denial is typically used to cope until the person can assimilate the knowledge that the loss is real. Denial can take different forms. There can be denial of the facts of the loss, the meaning of the loss, or the irreversibility of the loss. Denial can be a buffer, but it can become pathological if it continues indefinitely. Worden's first task of mourning is for the person grieving to accept that the loss is real. Eventually, denial of permanent loss must be replaced by realization that the loss has happened, and that the person can survive the loss. The crisis worker can help by encouraging clients to release their denial slowly, accept the reality of the loss, and move toward the expression of grief. The time it takes for denial to lessen varies from person to person. When people do begin to feel anger and other aspects of grief, it is usually a sign that there is some acceptance that the loss is real. Crisis counselors can educate people about this and reframe the expression of feelings as a sign that the person is actively working toward surviving the loss and that the first step, lessening denial and facing the reality of the loss, has been accomplished.

Task II: Experiencing the Pain of Grief   The next step toward working through loss is for the person to fully experience the feelings associated with it. The broadest possible expression of pain is what is desired. This experiencing of the pain of grief may manifest itself in the form of crying, yelling, or ruminations. It may be more intense for some than others, but everyone is best served if they can come to the point of experiencing the void that is left in his or her life and the pain associated with that. One way to avoid experiencing the pain is not to feel. Our society has been good at fostering this avoidance in a subtle way. We are not comfortable around people who are in pain; therefore, we give a subtle message to them not to express their grief. More directly, we give the message, "It's time to get over this," after the socially acceptable mourning period of four weeks has elapsed. However, as was pointed out by Caplan (1964) (see Chapter 1), mastering one's feelings is one of seven characteristics of people who cope effectively and should be encouraged by crisis counselors.

Task III: Adjusting to an Environment from Which the Deceased Is Missing
For many widows and widowers, realizing that they must cope on their own

takes several months. Often, about three months after the loss, they realize that they can in fact manage to live in their new environment. It is helpful for them to look at all the roles the deceased played in their life and to develop ways to cope with new demands and new roles they must take on because of the loved one's absence. They often resist developing new skills at first, but eventually they become proud of their newfound abilities and feel the beginning of a new self-esteem. This process is also applicable for those dealing with any relationship loss, especially if the relationship was fairly long in duration.

Task IV: Withdrawing Emotional Energy from the Deceased and Reinvesting It in Another Relationship or Cause   For many, the idea of withdrawing their emotional energy from the dead loved one is seen as betrayal; the guilt that comes with this must be overcome. Working through this task means acknowledging that there are others to love. It does not take away from the earlier relationship; it is simply different. Mourning can be considered finished when the tasks of mourning are over. This certainly does not happen in four weeks. Mourning is an individual process; therefore, any attempt to set time limits is artificial and arbitrary. However, most literature supports the need for a year to pass before the loss is fully resolved. At least that much time is usually needed for a person to let go of old memories and begin to build new ones, which will help facilitate the grief process. Holidays, seasons, and family events all must come and go during the mourning period before resolution is complete. That does not mean that the expression of grief will be strong for the entire year, but the process of mourning continues and is experienced during all those events. One indication that mourning may be finished is when the person is able to think and talk about the deceased without pain. The sadness at this point lacks the tearing quality of loss. Studies of widows in particular find that a year is frequently not enough time for them to recover. Often, they need three to four years to find stability in life again. One thing is clear: Mourning can be a long-term process.

Table 6.1 below shows how Kübler-Ross's stages of death and dying and Worden's tasks of mourning can be understood in the context of the other.

TABLE 6.1   A Comparison of Kübler-Ross's Stages of Death and Dying and Worden's Tasks of Mourning

Kübler-Ross Stage	Worden Task
Denial	Accepting the reality of the loss
Anger, Bargaining, Depression	Feeling the pain and expressing grief
Acceptance	Adjusting to life without the deceased. Withdrawal of energy from the deceased and reinvestment of the energy into something or someone else

© Cengage Learning

Manifestations of Normal Grief

Regardless of the period required for mourning, people who experience normal grief share common manifestations. The ones seen most often are listed here:

Feelings: Sadness, anger, guilt, and self-reproach; anxiety, including death awareness and phobia; loneliness, fatigue, helplessness; shock—particularly with sudden death; yearning and pining; emancipation, which can be a positive response; relief, particularly from suffering; and numbness

Physical Sensations: Hollowness in the stomach, tightness in the chest and throat, sense of depersonalization, breathlessness, weakness in the muscles

Cognitions: Disbelief, confusion, preoccupation, sense of presence, hallucinations (usually transient)

Behaviors: Sleep disturbances, such as early morning awakenings; appetite disturbances; absent-minded behaviors; social withdrawal (usually short lived); dreams of the deceased; restless overactivity; sighing or crying; fear of losing memories; treasuring objects

Determinants of Grief

A person's response to loss will be influenced by several factors of the nature of the loss:

- Who the person was in relation to the survivor is important.
- The nature of the attachment—whether the deceased provided strength, security, or ambivalence in the relationship—will be influential.
- The mode of death will determine reactions. Natural death is easier to cope with than accidental death, suicide, or murder. At least one is somewhat prepared for the death of an 86-year-old grandfather who has been hospitalized on and off for several years. When a loved one is murdered or commits suicide, however, issues of blame and anger become very difficult to overcome.
- Prior grief experiences and mental health in general influence one's grief reactions.
- One's religious beliefs will affect the grieving process.

An individual may seek crisis intervention for grief issues at various points in the grieving process. As the counselor assesses the client's emotional distress, the counselor will determine the stage of grief and decide which interventions will be helpful. Many crisis workers are emotionally taxed when dealing with death and dying. Counselors who work with grief would be wise to come to terms with their own fears of death and beliefs about death and grieving. If the crisis worker is in denial about death and mortality, he or she may inadvertently send messages to clients that grieving and connecting fully with one's pain are not necessary. The crisis worker can learn to handle the pain involved in mourning for clients to grieve as needed. Learning to be both truly empathetic and objective and rational is beneficial for grieving clients. The counselor becomes a sort of emotional tranquilizer for clients in a bereaved state.

Intervention

As with any crisis state, workers watch for symptoms that may require the attention of a physician. If the emotions are so strong and out of control that they prevent clients from sleeping, working, eating, or taking care of themselves, medication may be necessary for a brief time. Remember that the counselor does not recommend medication; the counselor's responsibility is to refer the client to a physician if symptoms cause moderate to severe dysfunction. If the client's symptoms seem to be typical grieving reactions, then counseling can assist the mourning process and help the client work through the normal expression of grief.

Informing a person of a loss, whether it is a death or a serious, or terminal, illness often falls on the shoulders of doctors, lawyers, police officers, friends or family members. How the loss is presented may affect the person's ability to accept it. It may even determine the person's emotional reactions.

In general, most people do not like to be lied to or patronized. Such behavior is disrespectful and may lead to feelings of resentment beyond the normal anger involved in grieving. A direct, honest approach is best. Empathy skills are most helpful at this time. Following are some specific ways that professionals or family members might break the news of a death or loss:

PHYSICIAN: He didn't make it. I am very sorry for your loss. May I contact someone for you? Do you need some space to be alone?

LAWYER: I have been given the legal responsibility of informing you of some tragic news. Please accept my sympathy for the loss of your father, who has asked me to read you his will.

POLICE OFFICER: Mrs. Jones, I have come to you in person to ensure that you hear some tragic news with someone near you. Sadly, your child was fatally wounded in a car accident tonight. Please feel free to talk to me tonight about your grief. The loss of your child is a tragedy that no one else can understand but you, but I'd still like to assist you if I can.

FRIEND: Kathy, it's Jenny. I need to see you in person immediately. (After they meet.) Kathy, Margaret died today. We need to cry and talk together.

FAMILY MEMBER: Honey, your father became ill last night and didn't make it through the night. Please call your brother and sister for me. Let's all meet at my house as soon as possible.

If the person hearing the news loses control with grief, it is good to have another person available to help contain her or him. Emergency rooms are open 24 hours a day, and medical personnel there can give medication to someone who is a danger to himself or herself or others because of shock. However, people usually become numb after hearing the news of a death and just need to have someone around for emotional support and to help take care of any legal or business details. Uncontrollable emotions might come during the funeral or weeks later, when the person has had time to accept the loss.

Counseling Principles and Procedures

Counseling someone through a loss is difficult. However, knowing certain procedures and their underlying principles is helpful. The following list might be useful to workers counseling someone who is suffering a loss.

1. Help survivors actualize the loss. Talk about the loss. What happened? Ask.
2. Help them identify and express feelings. If they are dealing with anger, be indirect (what do you miss the most or least?). Four common difficult emotions are anger, guilt, anxiety, and helplessness.
3. Help survivors in living without the deceased. The problem-solving approach works well for this. Discourage major life changes for a while.
4. Facilitate emotional withdrawal from the deceased. Encourage survivors to go on.
5. Provide time to grieve. Crucial times include three months and one year after the death, anniversaries of the death, and holidays. Help clients prepare in advance for these.
6. Educate clients about customary grieving reactions of other individuals to help normalize the experience.
7. Allow for individual differences. Be sensitive to individual styles.
8. Provide for continuing support. Encourage clients to join support groups.

If a client's symptoms and grief reactions appear to be delayed, chronic (i.e., last longer than one year), exaggerated, or masked, longer-term therapy may be required. This individual may have an underlying pathologic disorder. In this type of grief therapy, the person's defenses and coping styles would be assessed; and most likely, issues about loss and abandonment will surface. The counselor can best assist this type of client to get through the most recent loss by helping her or him grieve previous losses first. If the previous losses are great, therapy will probably be a two- to five-year process.

Losing a Child

The interventions discussed thus far can be used with all grieving clients. When parents have lost a child, some special considerations are needed as well. Box 6.1 provides two examples of clients suffering from loss and subsequent interventions.

As Nancy Ludt (1993) said in her presentation, "Losing a child has a different meaning than losing a parent. When you lose a parent, you lose your past, but when you lose a child, you lose your future." It is this dream of the future that the crisis worker will need to discuss with the surviving parents.

If the parents are married at the time of the death, their relationship is usually weakened. This is especially true if the child died unexpectedly, as in an accident. After such trauma, most couples have a lot of trouble getting

---

Box 6.1   Examples of Two Clients' Responses to Loss and Subsequent Interventions

Example 1: A 45-year-old woman was referred to me for crisis intervention by the Victim Witness Assistance Program. Her 21-year-old daughter had been murdered horrifically four months earlier. The woman hadn't been able to work, continued to have nightmares, cried uncontrollably, and was having communication problems with her husband. Her grieving had continued to be strong and painful.

This client had a strong support system in her parents, who were still married; all of her other family members were still living; her own 25-year marriage was a loving one; and she had two other daughters who were 17 and 11. She had a very stable and appropriate childhood and responded well to the ABC crisis intervention model. In the B section, she was helped to discuss what her daughter's death meant to her, and how her life perspective had changed. Her functioning level was assessed for symptoms and behaviors at each session. In the C section, she was encouraged to consult with a physician because of a sleep disturbance; she was given medication for about six months. She was referred to a support group for parents of murdered children. This woman will do well with continuing crisis intervention that focuses on the current precipitating event—the death of her daughter. Her childhood does not have to be dealt with because she demonstrated excellent premorbid functioning. Her present symptoms can be assumed to be related strictly to the death of her daughter.

Example 2: A 35-year-old woman sought counseling after the death of her older sister. Before we were able to process her grief over her sister, we had to discuss her childhood and young-adulthood losses. This client's method of coping with trauma can best be described as a defensive style called denial. In her family, she was told not to be aware of her own feelings, that her mother and father knew her better than she knew herself. They beat her and degraded her, and then abandoned her. Her only ally was the older sister who had just died.

Not only did this client need to grieve her sister's death, she also had to deal with abandonment by her parents. Being without her sister caused unbearable feelings of aloneness and emptiness for her. She was completely emotionally dependent on this sister, who had offered the only nurturing the client had experienced in her life. The parents had offered no affection. As you can see, the complexity in this case would require a longer-term approach. The client would need to grieve her past losses and come to terms with her aloneness and her own death in addition to grieving the loss of her sister.

© Cengage Learning

---

along with each other as well as with their other children. They no longer feel like the same people they were before the tragedy occurred because their life has been so drastically changed. The divorce rate of bereaved parents is 92 percent if the couple does not receive some form of help. However, receiving help can make a measurable difference in helping a couple survive the loss of a child. Ludt said that of the 1,500 people who had attended her support group over the last 16 years, only two couples had later divorced. This is a great incentive for crisis workers to recommend to bereaved parents that they attend support groups. In these groups, the couple can say things to each other that they normally would not say at home. Also, the father has an opportunity to express his hurt as openly as the mother. This is helpful, considering society's perpetuation of the stereotype of the strong man: He can't cry but instead must be strong and go to work even after the death of a child. It is obvious that if the father has a forum where he can communicate openly and express his feelings, the marital relationship has a greater chance of working.

Societal norms also affect parents regarding working after the loss of a child. Many places of employment allow only three days of leave for a death. This is inadequate, considering that the attention span of a grieving parent is about a minute and a half. As a result, many parents may lose their jobs, further complicating their crisis state. It would be nice if people could grieve within tidy time frames, but this is not reality.

Crisis workers can ease the grieving parents' burden by listening. Because the parents' concentration is greatly affected, counselors might minimize their own talking, offering very brief educational and supportive comments. One reason that self-help groups are more popular than professional counseling groups is that parents feel they can just talk and be listened to, no matter what the topic. Structure will not be helpful, because the parents have changing needs, which may shift from one minute to the other. Guest speakers are usually not welcome, because group members want to talk. If a grieving client comes to you on an individual basis, don't be a guest speaker. Let the client be the speaker.

Another thing a counselor can do for grieving parents is help them feel normal about the severity of their grief and the normalcy of wanting to talk about their children. Eventually, they will focus on the child's life, not the child's death. Probably the best thing a crisis worker can do for parents whose child has died is to connect them to a **support** group. In the group, they can feel whatever is in their hearts and say whatever is on their minds with no fear of ridicule or invalidation. Many times, parents will laugh when talking about the death. To many people, this behavior would appear insensitive. In a group with other grieving parents, it would be understood and shared.

Ludt (1993) lists 10 reasons why grieving parents prefer a support group. Some parents may stay in a group for as long as 10 years after the loss of a child. According to the members of Ludt's support group, the group serves these functions:

1. It is a place of safety where it is all right to say anything. ("I'd trade my living son for my lost son.")
2. It fulfills the need to be with understanding people; even if members don't attend, they know it's available. ("Feelings change over the years, and although we don't need to come now, who knows when we will need to come?")
3. It is our child's space. ("We can talk about our child all night without any inhibitions. Often talking about memories hurts family members too much, but in group, our child is alive for two hours.")
4. It helps us to understand the death emotionally rather than just intellectually. ("If we say he's dead enough times, we begin to believe it.")
5. It allows a hope for socialization in the future. ("We often feel guilty when we have fun, but we learn here that we can have fun.")

6. It has no time frame. ("He's dead forever, so it will hurt forever.")
7. It allows parents to laugh or cry and not hurt anyone's feelings.
8. It allows parents to express their thoughts with no need to explain them.
9. It can save a parent's life. ("Suicidal thoughts are strong, and the group gives some hope and help.")
10. It is a place where I know that you know that I know that you know.

If the crisis worker cannot locate a group in the client's area, these ideas can be implemented during the course of counseling.

Divorce and Separation

Divorce, separation, and relationship breakups are extremely common presenting problems to counselors. Reactions to separations, whether the partners are married or not, may create dysfunctional states in an otherwise normally functioning person. The reactions range from severe depression to anxiety attacks. As with any situational crisis, how well the person copes with a breakup will depend on material, personal, and social resources. Why are relationship losses so devastating? Often, a person's entire life and self-concept is based on being part of a couple. After a breakup, major adjustments have to be made, sometimes even more than when a spouse dies. Divorce can be thought of as a failure of one or both spouses to live up to the projected expectations of the other. These expectations were established by the family of origin of each spouse, which created a sense of what a family was supposed to be. When a couple divorces, one or both spouses have realized that his or her emotional needs just haven't gotten met (Bell, 1999).

About 50 percent of marriages end in divorce, and probably more non-marital relationships than that end at some point. Since the issues surrounding loss and mourning have been covered previously, they are not repeated here. Crisis workers should know that each partner needs to complete the tasks of mourning as he or she passes through each stage. In general, the longer the couple was together, the stronger the feelings of loss. If children are involved, the suffering is increased and complicated. Parents often feel guilt and embarrassment when explaining divorce to the children. Rage and frustration are typical emotions that surface when parents are setting up custody arrangements. Crisis workers often step in to mediate these procedures.

There is also loss of financial status and social networks. Losing friends and in-laws often increases the partners' feelings of depression and loneliness. Financial problems create anxieties and often lead to a lowered standard of living. Adjusting to these losses is another focus of crisis intervention in these cases. The person who was "left" often seeks out crisis intervention and seems to suffer the most. This person may be at high risk for suicide and may have the potential for increased drug and alcohol abuse. These possibilities must be assessed, appropriate contracts developed, and twelve-step groups encouraged. This person in particular needs to rebuild a support system. Church, family, athletic organizations, and school ties can be helpful. Also, there are many excellent books available that can give solace.

The partner who "left" has different issues to face. This person may alternate between feelings of grief and resentment. At one moment, he or she may still try to take care of the spouse; the next, this person may be reckless and irresponsible as he or she goes out "partying" and living the much-missed single life. Although at first this crazy, wild fun seems great, eventually depression usually sets in. It is hard to be single when one has been used to companionship, even though it was miserable.

Intervention

The overall goal is to help the client grieve. This individual can be encouraged to cry, write, read, pray, and go to divorce support groups. The crisis worker, as usual, is soothing, comforting, and optimistic. Letting the person know that many people survive divorce and breakups is helpful. The counselor might remind the client that although he or she may not believe it now, things will eventually be better. Completing mourning can take up to five years for some people. Educating clients about the grief process will help normalize their experience. Other helpful educational statements that a counselor can offer deal with the client's concerns about children and in-laws.

Children and Divorce

Most parents are concerned about the effects of divorce on the children; many believe that divorce will damage the children. About 26 percent of children under 18 years of age (17 million) live with a divorced parent, separated parent, or stepparent. Careful attention must be given to the direct **effects of divorce on children**, such as changes in the child's living situations and economic status. In 1991, 39 percent of divorced women with children lived in poverty. Though divorce is difficult for children, they adjust fairly well to the situation. A small minority of children, however, will need mental health treatment. Findings indicate that the custodial parent's own adjustment is the best predictor of child adjustment (Johnston, 1994, pp. 174–175). Johnston's research also found that a history of physical aggression in the family was strongly associated with emotional, behavioral, and social problems in the children.

A crisis worker is often able to point out that whether children are hurt depends on how the parents deal with them and each other during the divorce. Civility and assurance that both still love the children help them greatly. Unfortunately, as a result of the tremendous pain they are enduring because of the divorce, many parents use the children to vent their anger at the other partner, which places children in the dangerous middle. Often, a worried parent may be told that more damage may be done to the children if parents stay together than if they divorce, especially if the marital relationship has been abusive, and love and affection has been lacking. This perspective allows them to reframe their perception that it is best to stay together no matter what. Another piece of information that may comfort a parent is that the average family is no longer a nuclear family, so their children need not feel weird or unusual compared with their friends.

Interventions for children may be child oriented or family oriented. Child-oriented interventions alleviate emotional and behavioral problems associated with adjustment to divorce. These interventions may include group sessions in which children meet on a regular basis to share their experiences, learn about problem-solving strategies, and offer mutual support. Individual therapy may include play therapy that allows free expression of feelings.

In regard to in-laws, it is probably best not to tell them everything. What if the couple decides to get back together? A spouse may be able to forgive, but an in-law may not. Also, after a divorce the children will still be involved with both sets of in-laws; therefore, the less the grandparents know, the better, so they are free to be completely supportive and nurturing to their grandchildren. Often, denial is very strong for the spouse being "left," and this partner must be helped gently to confront reality. The counselor can encourage this person to ask whether he or she truly wants someone who does not want him or her. Confronting such a question can give "discarded" partners some control over retaining their dignity. This is an example of empowerment. In a final note regarding legalities, it is good to be familiar with legal clinics and divorce lawyers in your area. Clients may need referrals to these professionals to avoid being taken advantage of or to obtain a restraining order.

Crises Related to Blended Families

Many families come in with crises stemming from the joining of two families when divorced parents have married. The Brady Bunch system is not as much fun as it was portrayed in the 1970s television show. Many of the conflicts in **blended families** arise because of the developmental stages of the children, the maturity level of each adult involved, and the stage of grieving over the divorce each adult is working through. It is rare for each biological parent to set aside his or her own personal power struggles and resentments for the sake of the children. When four adults are involved, at least one is bound to react dysfunctionally after the divorce and subsequent remarriage. Of course, in some cases, one of the persons marrying into a family with children has not been married before or has no children from an earlier marriage. This circumstance may disentangle the web slightly, but it certainly does not ensure complete cooperation and facility in adjustment.

Loyalty issues are common for children in cases where a stepparent becomes part of their home life. Children often feel guilty about bonding with another adult for fear it will make their natural parent angry or hurt. If possible, the crisis worker may bring in the natural parent to tell the child it is acceptable to be nice to the stepparent. This will not be an easy task, however, if the parent is still grieving over the divorce or has a serious personality disorder. Box 6.2 provides an example of a family dealing with a blended family crisis.

Incorporating the stepparent's rules and expectations into an existing system is another area in which a crisis worker may be needed. Here, a very brief

> **Box 6.2   Example of a Crisis Related to Blending a Family**
>
> A 45-year-old man comes to counseling because his girlfriend moved in with him and his 13-year-old daughter after he had been separated from his wife for five months. He was very stressed because his girlfriend complained about the amount of time he devoted to his daughter. The girlfriend felt deprived. Subsequent couples counseling brought out the girlfriend's perception of being disliked by the daughter and her feelings that her boyfriend was too focused on his daughter.
>
> Crisis counseling focused on educating the girlfriend about parental attachment and responsibility. This helped alter her view that the father was "overly devoted." She began to understand that his attention to his daughter was normal. The daughter was brought in as well to explore the girlfriend's perception that the daughter disliked her. The daughter said that she did not dislike the girlfriend, but that she felt awkward about liking her, considering that the girlfriend had now taken on her mother's former role. Crisis intervention explored loyalty issues and allowed each to clarify her expectations of the other.

© Cengage Learning

problem-solving approach is useful. Everyone is encouraged to speak up and give suggestions and can perceive himself or herself as validated.

In conclusion, as with all people in crisis, clients divorcing and forming blended families will fare worse if they have little ego strength and a low level of maturity. Although most people in this situation will suffer, not all will suffer in the same way.

Job Loss

Since the economic downturn which was largely precipitated by the housing crisis and the Wall Street crash beginning in 2008, many Americans have lost their jobs and have had to survive using unemployment and disability benefits. Although the unemployment rate has been decreasing since 2011 steadily from 9 percent to 7.6 percent, there are still 11.7 million unemployed persons nationwide as of March 2013. The unemployment rates for adult men is 6.9 percent, adult women is 7 percent, teenagers is 24.2 percent, whites is 6.7 percent, blacks is 13.3 percent, Hispanics is 9.2 percent and for Asians is 5 percent (Bureau of Labor Statistics, 2013). Job loss often leads to feelings of depression and low satisfaction with life. One frequently grieves the loss of a job in much the same way one might grieve the loss of a relationship. Much of one's identity and social life develops in the context of a job. In fact, many people spend more time at work than at home and learning to live without a job can be exhausting, especially when much of one's time is spent searching for a new job.

Losing one's job also has enduring health consequences. Researchers have found that people who lose their jobs have higher depressive symptoms and are at greater risk of chronic conditions than those with steady work (Catalano & Dooley, 1983; Gallo, Bradley, Siegel, & Kasl, 2000). However, not everyone who loses their job experiences these types of symptoms. It has been found that individuals with higher levels of education experienced fewer depressive symptoms and those with higher occupation prestige faced greater depressive symptoms (Berchick, Gallo, Maralani, & Kasl, 2012).

The Role of Perceptions

Of particular interest to crisis counselors is the part that one's perceptions play in determining how someone deals with job loss. Berchick et al. (2012) suggest that job loss affects health in part due to perceived loss of control. Those with higher education often have more social support and perceive themselves to have more control over their lives. Additionally, job loss simply cannot take away a person's educational attainment thereby keeping a sense of control intact (Berkman, 1995; Ross & Wu, 1995). However, job loss disrupts the status associated with high prestige positions and those in this category may perceive themselves as having farther to fall in the face of job loss. This may lead to a greater loss of power and prestige than those with lower status jobs (Strully, 2009).

Other factors involved in life satisfaction or dissatisfaction following job loss has to do with how much perceived control someone holds. Individuals with higher perceived control demonstrate a decrease in life satisfaction compared to those with a lower control belief. Additionally, higher levels of conscientiousness are also associated with a larger decrease in life satisfaction (Heidemeier & Gontz, 2013). Sometimes, it seems to be an adaptive quality to accept that one does not have control over everything. Crisis workers can use this knowledge to help empower clients by focusing on things that they do have control over and take action where possible.

Interventions

As with all clients, counselors should develop empathy and validate the challenge in securing new employment. Providing the statistics about the unemployment rate is helpful so the person doesn't perceive himself as a "loser." Accessing unemployment benefits may be necessary. If that is not an option, sometimes, people must borrow money to survive or seek temporary shelter at an agency for homeless individuals such as the Salvation Army or other non-profit homeless shelters. Learning how to navigate the financial-assistance resources can be quite taxing, embarrassing, and frustrating. Counselors can be a steady social support as someone begins dealing with these systems. Crisis workers can continually emphasize the temporary nature of the crisis and maintain optimism. Clients might even be encouraged to go back to school and focus on a new trade. There are school loans available as well as financial assistance that doesn't require the person to pay it back. Providing a broad framework regarding the financial challenges occurring in the world is often helpful so the person can save face and realize many others are in the same boat. Lastly, keeping the focus on the fact that unemployment rates are declining might be helpful. Box 6.3 presents case vignettes to assist the reader in conducting role plays using the ABC Model.

Box 6.3   Cases to Role-Play

Conduct role-play interviews using some of the following ideas and case vignettes. Use the ABC model of crisis intervention.

First, here are a few things *not* to say. These comments are often made by friends, family, and well-wishers who tend to discount the grief and seek to deny the experience:

"Cheer up."

"Don't be so depressed."

"Isn't it about time you got over this?"

"It'll get better."

"At least she's with God."

"Just think of the good things; don't dwell on it."

Now, here are some ideas that may be useful with the case vignettes and with your clients who are mourning. During the B section of the ABC model, crisis interventionists can offer various therapeutic statements as they explore the client's belief system, knowledge, support systems, and self-esteem.

Reframes will help the client think about a disturbing event differently:

"Rather than view yourself as weak and out of control when you cry, you might consider understanding this behavior as a sign of your love and part of the process it takes to learn to accept the loss strongly and boldly."

Educational statements will help normalize the client's experience and clear up confusions and misconceptions:

"The grieving process usually takes a full year. Every holiday, birthday, and anniversary of her death will need to be experienced without the person you have lost."

Supportive comments do not mean that you should take away the person's pain. Rather, they let the client know that you understand his or her feelings:

"I wish I could make the pain go away. But you and I both know that's impossible. I can be here to listen as you process your loss."

Empowerment comments will help show clients they have some control and choice despite not having control over the loss:

"You don't have control over the reality that your wife will die of cancer, but you can make choices about how you will live your life with her until that time comes."

Be creative and look for clients' strengths. Having some knowledge about death and dying will help you work meaningfully with your clients. This is also a good chance for you to become aware of your own issues of loss and feelings about death.

Case 1 A minister referred a 37-year-old woman to the crisis intervention center because she has just lost her husband. The minister is concerned because the woman and her two children have not cried since the death of her husband. She is still confused as to why she needs to come in. She tells the counselor that she does not think about his death. When probed a little more, she begins to cry. She has been left without any money, and has two children to feed. She was married for 10 years, and they were good years. Her husband died in an automobile accident, and the driver of the other car was drunk at the time.

Hints to help role play:

Precipitating event: Husband died three weeks ago.

(Continued)

Box 6.3   Cases to Role-Play (Continued)

Cognitions: "I shouldn't cry. It will upset my children. I must be strong and not think about it. God will take care of everything."

Emotional distress: "Confused, numb, flat."

Impairment in functioning: Poor concentration at work, lack of joy when playing and interacting with children, no social contacts, sleeps too much, lack of appetite.

Validation statement: Losing a husband is extremely challenging emotionally, especially when you have children to care for. Not only do you have to deal with grief, but also the shock of such an unexpected death. Being numb is normal at first.

Educational statement: This numbness and inability to cry is indicative of the first stage of loss which has been referred to as the denial and shock stage. It is normal because it allows your mind to slowly absorb the reality of this most difficult loss. As you begin to face the reality of the loss, then anger, sadness, and other emotions are likely to occur. These happen at different times for different people.

Reframe: While it is understandable that you think that not crying is strong, it may in fact be a stronger thing to let yourself cry and model for your children the necessity of grieving. If they see you cry, they may feel it is alright for them to cry as well.

Empowerment: Having your husband taken away from you so unexpectedly must make you feel a bit powerless. Unfortunately, we cannot control all events in the world. What you can do is focus on things you do have control over now. Your first step toward gaining power was coming in here today and taking the reins in working through this tragedy.

Case 2 A 39-year-old woman was referred to the counselor by her doctor. She lost her son to cancer. She feels she cannot go on living. Life seems worthless and meaningless. Her son died when he was only six years old. Her husband does not understand her feelings.

Precipitating event: Son died one month ago.

Cognitions: Cannot go on living. Life is worthless and meaningless. No one understands me. God is unfair. Doctors are useless.

Emotional distress: Sad, angry.

Impairments in functioning: Cannot work, cannot eat or sleep, no social contact, no intimacy with husband.

Validation: It is understandable how devastating it must have been to lose such a young child. Your feelings make sense and it is so hard to understand how this could have happened. Not many things in life are this difficult.

Empowerment: It is so hard to accept that we cannot control death. The only thing we can control is how to live.

Education: Your anger is a sign that you are working through this loss. These feelings suggest that you have accepted the death as real and your grief is necessary so that you can eventually work through it. It will take many years and will be difficult to adjust to. There is no set time frame for grief and it is valuable for you to express all your feelings and thoughts so you can actively work through the pain.

Reframe: The extent of your grief must be related to the depth of your love for your son.

C (Coping Strategies): Suicide assessment and referral to grief group for parents who have lost a child.

Case 3 A 45-year-old man comes to counseling feeling very confused. He cannot pinpoint the reason. He tells the interviewer that he wonders how she can possibly be of help to him. The counselor looks as though she has never experienced a separation. Two months ago, his lover of three years left him

(Continued)

Box 6.3   Cases to Role-Play (Continued)

suddenly, and he has been waiting for her to return. Yesterday, he saw her with another man; they were holding hands and acting very much in love.

Precipitating event: Seeing ex-girlfriend with another man.

Cognitions: This relationship is really over. I will never find anyone else to love. I will be alone forever. I am not good enough for her.

Emotional distress: Sad and angry.

Impairment in functioning: Cannot sleep or eat. Cannot drive or focus at work.

Validation: It is quite difficult to see a person you love with another man. Feeling angry and sad seems normal and expected in this situation.

Education: These feelings may be helpful for you in working through this loss. At least they mean that you have accepted the loss as real. It is hard to feel so sad, but at least you can talk about it and learn to adjust.

Empowerment: It seems like she has had control up to this point, but now that you have accepted the loss as real, you can take back some power and actively work through the grief by talking about your feelings and thoughts, and mastering them.

Reframe: Even though seeing them together feels devastating, it may be a positive thing because it might help you see the reality and then make decisions based on that and not on your wish to reunite.

Case 4 A friend has told a 35-year-old woman to come to the clinic. She has been yelling at everyone. She is not aware of how angry she feels. She tells the counselor that he looks like an inexperienced person and far too happy to be in touch with reality. The truth is she is very scared, because for the first time in her life she feels alone. Her spouse of seven years left her three months ago, and so far she has been saying, "Good riddance." The truth is that this is the first time she has ever been hurt by someone close to her.

Precipitating event: Yelling at her friend last week.

Cognitions: How dare he leave me? I don't need anybody anymore. No one understands my pain. I would rather live alone than feel this kind of hurt.

Emotional distress: Angry, hurt.

Impairments in functioning: Disturbed social relationships, unable to perform job duties appropriately, lack of enjoyable time with children.

Validation: Wow, getting divorced after seven years of marriage has got to be tough. It is hard to lose someone that you were so close to. It is normal to feel angry. Even being angry at me is a good sign that you are facing reality.

Education: Anger is a part of grief. Professionals have been studying loss for many years and have discovered that almost everyone going through a loss feels angry at some point. It is actually the way to move through the tasks of mourning. It shows that you have accepted this loss as real and now you can work through your feelings and eventually adjust to life without him.

Empowerment: People going through separations often feeling powerless, as if someone just pulled the rug out from under them. It is difficult to accept that you can't make someone love you or want to be with you. It helps to try to focus on that which you can control, such as how you wish to proceed in the divorce and how you wish to exist at work and with your friends and children.

Reframe: Underlying most anger is hurt and once you can explore this hurt, you can reduce some of that anger. But anger is not necessarily negative. It allows you to have energy to carry on during this most difficult time.

C (Coping Strategies): Divorce support group, reading.

Chapter Review

Elisabeth Kübler-Ross proposed the well-known stages of death and dying: denial, anger, bargaining, depression, and acceptance. Many helpers follow this a guide when working people going through grief. Worden's tasks of mourning: accepting the loss as real, expressing feelings, adjusting to life without the lost person, and withdrawing energy and reinvesting it are often used to understand how to assist people in their grief process. Divorce, like death, can lead people to feel pain which is best treated by allowing the person to talk openly. Divorce brings with it many other issues such as loyalty issues, financial issues, and social issues. Children's needs must also be dealt with when divorce arises in a family. Loss of employment often leads to depression when a person has a high-prestige job or feels a strong sense of control over life. Those with higher education levels tend to do better when unemployed.

Answers to Pre-Chapter Quiz

1. T   2. F   3. T   4. F   5. F   6. T   7. T   8. T   9. T   10. F

Key Terms for Study

bereavement: A state involving loss; a period of time when something has been taken away from someone.

blended families: The joining of two previously separate families. This often means that children have stepparents, a situation that leads to many conflicts and requires adjustment to new rules.

Charles Darwin: Commented that the separation reactions resulting from the loss of a loved one were innate.

effects of divorce on the children: Suffering is often experienced by the children of divorcing parents because of the power struggles and immaturity of their parents. This does not have to occur. Often, counseling is necessary to ensure that parents do not direct their feelings of anger and pain toward their children.

Elisabeth Kübler-Ross: A physician who developed the idea that people who have been diagnosed as terminally ill go through various stages as they mourn the loss. The stages are denial, anger, bargaining, depression, and acceptance.

grief: The feelings of sorrow and sadness that follow a loss.

John Bowlby: Noted theorist in the area of attachment and separation; proposed four phases of mourning.

Kübler-Ross's five stages of death and dying: Five stages that Kübler-Ross believes all people go through after the death of a loved one or while in the process of dying. They are as follows:

denial and isolation: The person is in shock or in a state of nonacceptance about the death or dying.

anger: The person becomes aware of feelings, especially about the unfairness of death, and feels rage and intense pain.

bargaining: The person may try to make deals with God, the doctors, or a loved one.

depression: The person experiences true mourning and grief, feeling sad, nonenergetic, and despondent.

acceptance: The person finally pulls out of the depression, accepts the death or loss, and is able to move on.

loyalty issues: Issues experienced in a blended family when the children sometimes feel guilty for loving or bonding with a stepparent. Their fear is that the natural parent will be angry or hurt. Unfortunately, it is often true. Crisis workers attempt to help both the children and natural parent come to terms with the reality of the blended family.

Sigmund Freud: Defined mourning as a period of gradual withdrawal of libido from the now-missed loved object.

support: Help that is considered essential for clients experiencing a loss. Validation of such clients' feelings of pain is an important function of the crisis worker. Support groups have also been found to be helpful.

tasks of mourning: Four proposed tasks a person needs to complete in order to grieve a loss fully. They are as follows:

1. Accepting the reality of the loss
2. Experiencing the pain of grief
3. Adjusting to an environment in which the deceased is missing
4. Withdrawing emotional energy from the deceased person and reinvesting it in another relationship or activity

References

Bell, T. (1999). *Divorce*. Presentation given at California State University, Fullerton, CA.

Berchick, E. R., Gallo, W. T., Maralani, V., & Kasl, S. V. (2012). Inequality and the association between involuntary job loss and depressive symptoms. *Social Science & Medicine, 75*(10), 1891–1894.

Berkman, L. F. (1995). The role of social relations in health promotion. *Psychosomatic Medicine, 57*, 245–254.

Bowlby, J. (1980). *Attachment and loss. Vol. 3: Loss, sadness, and depression*. New York: Basic Books.

Bureau of Labor Statistics. (2013). *The employment situation—March 2013*. U.S. Department of Labor. Released 8:30a.m. (ECT) Friday, April 5, 2013.

Caplan, G. (1964). *Principles of preventive psychiatry*. New York: Basic Books.

Catalano, R., & Dooley, D. (1983). Health effects of economic instability: A test of economic stress hypotheses. *Journal of Health and Social Behavior*, *24*, 46–60.

Darwin, C. (1965). *The expression of emotions in man and animals*. Chicago: University of Chicago Press. (Originally published in 1872).

Gallo, T., Bradley, E. H., Siegel, M., & Kasi, S. V. (2000). Health effects of involuntary job loss among older workers: Finding from the health and retirement survey. *Journal of Gerontology, Social Sciences*, *558*, S131–S140.

Heidemeier, H., & Gontz, A. S. (2013). Perceived control in low-control circumstances: Control beliefs predict a greater decrease in life satisfaction following job loss. *Journal of Research in Personality*, *47*(1), 52–56.

Johnston, J. R. (1994). High-conflict divorce. *The Future of Children*, *4*(1), 165–182.

Kübler-Ross, E. (1969). *On death and dying*. New York: Macmillan.

Leick, N., & Davidson-Nielson, M. (1991). *Healing pain, attachment, loss, and grief therapy*. London: Rutledge.

Ludt, N. (1993). *Bereaving parent support groups*. Presentation at California State University, Fullerton, CA.

Ross, C. E., & Wu, C. (1995). The links between education and health. *American Sociological Review*, *60*, 719–745.

Strully, K. (2009). Racial-ethnic disparities in health and the labor market: Losing and leaving jobs. *Social Science & Medicine*, *69*, 768–776.

Worden, W. (1982). *Grief counseling and grief therapy*. London: Tavistock.

Chapter 7

PTSD, Trauma, and Community Disasters

_____ 1. The symptoms of PTSD and acute stress disorder are the same, except for the duration.

_____ 2. The first stage of community disaster is the heroic phase.

_____ 3. Hypervigilance is common in people suffering from PTSD.

_____ 4. Most precipitating events that lead to a crisis state lead to PTSD.

_____ 5. An example of a man-made disaster was the 9/11 attacks in 2001.

_____ 6. Katrina was an example of a natural disaster.

_____ 7. Compassion fatigue occurs when an emergency worker fails to truly care about clients.

_____ 8. One sign of burnout is being emotionally energized.

_____ 9. Crisis workers may be prone to secondary traumatization.

_____ 10. Personal threat is usually the basis for PTSD.

Posttraumatic Stress Disorder (PTSD)

Posttraumatic stress disorder (PTSD) is a broad category that applies to people who have been severely traumatized at one or more times in their lives; at present, they are not functioning effectively because they have not integrated the trauma and laid it to rest. The cause is exposure to a situation perceived to be threatening to oneself or one's loved ones.

The American Psychiatric Association's *Diagnostic and Statistical Manual of Mental Disorders*, Fourth Edition, Text Revision (DSM-IV-TR) (2000) describes PTSD as being induced after an exposure to a traumatic event in which a person experienced actual or threat of death or serious injury or threat to physical integrity of self or others. Symptoms of PTSD include:

- Intense fear and feelings of helplessness
- Recurrent and intrusive recollections, flashbacks, and dreams of the event
- Physiological reactivity when exposed to cues that symbolize the event
- Avoidance of stimuli associated with the event
- Numbing of feelings
- Inability to recall aspects of the event
- Feelings of detachment
- Pessimism about the future
- Sleep difficulties
- Anger and irritability
- Difficulty concentrating
- Hypervigilance and exaggerated startle response

Gabbard (2000) suggests that "the most common precipitating event reported among persons with PTSD was the sudden, unexpected death of a loved one" (p. 252). He discusses the idea that trauma victims alternate between denying the event and compulsively repeating it through flashbacks or nightmares. This is the mind's attempt to process and organize overwhelming stimuli. He further proposes that most people do not develop PTSD even when faced with horrifying trauma, so there must be certain predisposing factors such as genetic makeup, childhood trauma, personality characteristics, compromised support system, and perceptions that locus of control is external rather than internal. The reader is reminded of what was presented in Chapter 1 regarding factors that determine whether someone goes into a crisis, such as material factors, personal factors, and social factors, which supports Gabbard's ideas. This oscillation between memory intrusion and memory failure seen in PTSD suggests that intervention should address both of these aspects of the syndrome.

When the symptoms mentioned have lasted for less than one month, the DSM IV (2000) defines the condition as acute stress disorder. It is logical that when a person seeks help for this type of trauma within a month of the precipitating event, the crisis counseling might be a bit less challenging. When a person experiences PTSD symptoms for more than one month, the symptoms tend to become a habit, and the person learns to survive by using defense mechanisms such as **dissociation** and repression. So, as crisis workers, we prefer to work with someone as soon as possible after a trauma to prevent this type of pattern from developing. It might reduce the amount of time the person needs to participate in professional counseling and prevent them from being a crisis-prone person in the future as discussed in Chapter 1.

There are several different categories of experiences that typically cause PTSD or acute stress disorder. They include being in combat or in a war zone, suffering personal or family victimization, living through a natural disaster, or experiencing a man-made disaster. In addition to physical and sexual assault, the following types of trauma may lead to PTSD:

- Witnessing a loved one being murdered
- Witnessing or being part of a gruesome car accident
- Being kidnapped or being the parent of a child who is abducted
- Having personal property vandalized (e.g., tires slashed)
- Having one's home burglarized
- Being robbed at gunpoint

PTSD for survivors of these types of trauma may be severe or mild, depending on the perceived level of threat. They often suffer from feelings of paranoia, **hypervigilance**, and powerlessness. They are usually angry and fearful. Each situation creates different emotional experiences for the survivors and different cognitions associated with the trauma. However, survivors of all these experiences tend to have the symptoms of PTSD. A crisis worker is bound to come into contact with clients who did not deal with traumas immediately after they experienced them, and so have most likely been living in some state of PTSD for some time. An event in the present often triggers a memory of the trauma, or the person's functioning may diminish to the point that he or she can't deal with society any longer. Thus, the person seeks the help of a mental health worker. Some victims exist in a chronic crisis state, never really functioning at all. They often go from one therapist to another, or from hospital to jail to clinic looking for coping skills to deal with their current problems. Unfortunately, many cannot be effective in the present until they deal with their past traumas.

Effects on Young Children

Children may be prone to exhibit certain behaviors after exposure to a trauma. These symptoms are similar to those seen in abused children. The following behaviors are common in young children after a critical incident:

- Returning to earlier behavior, such as thumb sucking or bed wetting
- Clinging to parents
- Being reluctant to go to bed
- Having nightmares
- Having fantasies that the disaster never happened
- Crying and screaming
- Withdrawing and becoming immobile
- Refusing to attend school
- Having problems at school and being unable to concentrate (American Red Cross, 2001)

Military Service

Due to the current and upcoming drawdowns in Iraq and Afghanistan, PTSD as related to military-related crises must be dealt with in detail. Chapter 8 is devoted to discussing the many issues facing veterans and their families.

Personal and Family Victimization

Sadly, we live in a society where people are frequently victimized by others who intend to kill, harm, intimidate, or all three. The prevalence of child abuse, spousal abuse, and sexual assault is so high that Chapters 9 and 10 are devoted to these topics. In fact, according to **EMDR (Eye Movement Desensitization and Reprocessing)** experts, Shapiro and Forrest (1997, p. 132), sexual abuse survivors constitute the largest number of PTSD victims.

Many perpetrators of this type of victimization know their victims personally. This adds to the emotional trauma for the victims in ways that "impersonal" traumas such as an earthquake might not. Trust becomes a big issue for people who are attacked by someone they know. Of course some people are victims of other forms of assault by strangers during muggings, robberies, and car accidents. These experiences can potentially cause the victim to suffer from PTSD. Even the significant others of victims may suffer from **secondary PTSD** or **secondary traumatization** as well.

The remainder of this chapter will focus on trauma that affects an entire community such as man-made disasters and natural disasters. Trauma response and critical incident debriefing will be discussed and the reader will notice how the origins of crisis intervention created by Caplan and Lindemann have remained intact over the past 70 years with a few modifications.

Natural Disasters

Natural disasters include landslides, floods, fires, earthquakes, hurricanes, and other storm conditions that wreak havoc on humans. The most recent example was the devastating Hurricane Sandy which caused billions of dollars worth of damage primarily in the New Jersey area. As a result of the mismanagement of Hurricane Katrina of 2005, which nearly destroyed the city of New Orleans and caused billions of dollars worth of damage in several states bordering the Gulf of Mexico, the federal government seemed to provide services more rapidly and effectively to the victims of Sandy. During the days following the flooding caused by Katrina, a large area of New Orleans left thousands of people homeless and without food, water, and electricity for several days, until rescue workers arrived to help evacuate those stranded. Although the victims of Sandy certainly suffered much of these same inconveniences, the response was deemed quicker and the perception that the federal administration was prepared to offer resources was vital in helping victims deal with this disaster emotionally. In comparison, the victims of Katrina frequently held the perception that the federal government was not offering services rapidly and didn't seem to care. These perceptions made a difference between survivors of Sandy and survivors of Katrina. As with any trauma, certain factors determined how severe the consequences of this flooding were to particular individuals. Various concepts presented in previous chapters will be linked with the Katrina crisis.

Material Resources   As was discussed in Chapter 1, individuals with access to material resources such as personal transportation, savings accounts, and home-owner's insurance were undoubtedly able to manage this crisis more easily than those without them. To start, people who owned cars were able to evacuate New Orleans prior to the hurricane and subsequent flood. Additionally, those who had home-owner's insurance and money in savings accounts were better able to start over once the acute crisis phase was over and rebuilding began.

Perception of the Precipitating Event Leads to Emotional Distress   As a result of the delay in rescuing many of those stranded in the flood, who had to cling to rooftops for several days, and also the delay in providing food and water for survivors, many survivors and other concerned citizens formed ideas about the reasons for the delays. Many people blamed government officials at all levels for failure to act quickly. This blame led to feelings of rage. When one explores the cognitive tree further, one sees that the blame was fueled by beliefs that racism and classism were reasons for the delays. Because most of the people who needed immediate assistance were poor African Americans, many believed that the failure to rescue and provide was due to the lack of importance given to this subgroup in American culture. This cognition, of course, led to much emotional distress, primarily anger.

Crisis as Danger and Opportunity   As in many other community disasters, people in the United States and around the world responded to Hurricane Katrina with charity and activism. Of course, this disaster has strong elements of danger. People died, homes and businesses were lost, and the historic city of New Orleans was all but destroyed. However, opportunity also arose during this crisis. Americans and people from other countries were enlightened about the disparity that exists between the poor and the upper classes. The disaster provided an opportunity for people to show their humanity, pitch in and help, and engage in dialogue about how to ensure that a similar situation does not occur again.

The catastrophic tsunami that occurred on the coasts of Indochina and other countries in 2004 is another example of the devastation caused by natural disasters. Throughout time, many people have been traumatized by the powerful destruction of earthquakes, blizzards, storms, and floods. These types of disasters make people feel helpless. They may even become angry with God.

Four Phases of Community Disasters

When a disaster hits, communities tend to go through certain phases to overcome the psychological and physical consequences of the disaster. The **four phases** that have been observed and described are: (1) heroic, (2) honeymoon, (3) disillusionment, and (4) reconstruction. The Mental Health Center of North Iowa, Inc. (retrieved 6/8/2005) provides information about these phases. The first stage is the heroic phase. This usually occurs during and immediately after the disaster. Emotions are strong and direct. People find themselves being called upon for and responding to demands for heroic action to save their own and others' lives and property. Altruism is prominent, and people expend much energy in helping others to survive and recover. People have a lot of energy and motivation to help. Everyone pitches in to help people that they might not ordinarily have assisted. The second stage is the honeymoon phase, which lasts from one week to six months after the disaster. There is a strong sense of having shared with others a dangerous, catastrophic experience and having lived through it. Survivors clean out mud and debris from their homes and yards, anticipating that a considerable amount of help will soon be given to them to solve their problems. Community groups that are set up to meet specific needs caused by the disaster are important resources during this period. The third stage is the disillusionment phase. When the "honeymoon high" wears off, people realize that life isn't a "bowl of cherries." They realize that people have returned to their normal states of greed, jealousy, and selfishness. The "utopia" they had envisioned doesn't materialize. Strong feelings of disappointment, anger, resentment, and bitterness may arise if promised aid is delayed or never arrives. Outside agencies may leave the affected region, and some community groups may weaken or may not adapt to the changing situation. There is a gradual loss of the feeling of "shared community" as survivors concentrate on rebuilding their lives and solving their own individual problems. The final stage is the reconstruction phase, in which survivors realize that they will need to rebuild their homes, businesses, and lives largely by themselves, and gradually assume the responsibility for doing so. This phase might last for several years following the disaster. Community support groups are essential during this phase as well.

The National Center for Posttraumatic Stress Disorder (retrieved 6/8/2005) refers to these phases as the impact phase, immediate postdisaster phase, recoil and rescue phase, and recovery phase.

Man-made Disasters

Recall from Chapter 1 that crisis work began when a man-made disaster, the Coconut Grove fire, occurred. Many disasters of this magnitude or worse have occurred since the fire. Sometimes they are accidental, as when a plane crashes; others are perpetrated on purpose and with malicious intent.

Boston Bombing in 2013   Most readers will recall the Boston Marathon terrorist bombing that took place on April 15, 2013. Bostonians have longed referred to their famous marathon as taking place on Patriot's Day. What a shock to have that wonderful afternoon ruined by two men who decided they had a right to kill and maim people due to religious and political reasons. Although there have been other terrorist attacks worldwide, the United States hadn't experienced one since the horrific attacks that took place on a day most of us refer to as 9/11. Not only are the injured individuals affected by

---

Box 7.1   A True Story Related to the Attacks on 9/11

A powerful story related to the World Trade Center attacks was told to the author by a former student. He had become a sheriff at a local law enforcement agency. After he completed his master's degree in psychology, he was asked to fly to New York and help out. He didn't know exactly what he would be doing, but he was ready to do anything. When he arrived, he went right up to the emergency workers, firefighters, and police, who were heaving heavy cement pieces from Ground Zero, searching for bodies. They were sweating, breathing heavily, and crying. He started helping them, until one of the workers told him to stop. The student said, "But I'm here to help." The worker looked at him and with tears in his eyes said, "This is our job. Your job is to take care of us. There are over 600 people in that building over there who need someone to talk to, share their feelings with, and we hope you can do this." The student walked over to the building and was met by hundreds of people who had been working day and night, survivors of the attacks, and people who had lost loved ones in the attacks. At this point, he certainly felt needed. He was able to use the ABC model that he had just learned to help these people begin to put their lives back together.

---

the bombings, but also the many who were watching the marathon. They witnessed horrific injuries, especially to very young children. Several marathon runners even completed the finish line and ran straight to the hospital to donate blood. This is indicative of that heroic phase referred to earlier.

World Trade Center and Pentagon Attacks   Another devastating man-made disaster was the terrorist-hijacked airplane crashes into the New York World Trade Center and the U.S. Pentagon on September 11, 2001. These traumas led to the death of over 5,000 people, the highest disaster-related death toll in U.S. history. Most of us can still remember how the entire country proceeded through the different phases already discussed. The pictures of men and women working day and night to remove debris from the areas affected by the attacks are etched in our minds. This behavior helped increase feelings of power in all of us. At least something could be done. Unfortunately, this tragedy did not end with the plane crashes but continued with the introduction by terrorists of the anthrax virus into the U.S. Postal System. In 2005, terrorists left bombs in backpacks in the London transit system, reminding us that the threat continues. In Box 7.1, the author shares a true story based on a conversation she had with a sheriff within one week of 9/11/2001.

Gun Violence and Shootings

Campus Lockdown 2012   On December 12, 2012, the author was teaching her class at California State University, Fullerton at 4:00 P.M. At 4:10, the classroom speaker system announced that everyone who was inside was to remain sheltered and those outside were to evacuate immediately. Class continued as usual. At 4:30, another announcement went out that told us that we would be on lockdown until further notice because there was a suspect at large on campus who was armed and dangerous. The author, who will now be referred to in the first person (I), proceeded to lock classroom doors. Students began to show signs of panic, anxiety, and being generally upset. One of the students offered his assistance because he works as a security guard. I enlisted him to help me make sure doors were secured and he escorted several women to the restroom while maintaining vigilance in the hall. We had a pregnant student and a diabetic, who both needed food, so I went upstairs to seek food which I received from faculty who were all locked in their offices. There were students outside in the hall asking what they should do since their instructor didn't make it to campus. I invited them into our room so they could be locked in and safe. We were able to gain information about what was going on through text messages and phone calls from campus police as well as from our friends and family who were watching the events on television. At that point, I knew I needed to gain as much information as possible to proceed realistically and calmly. I was able to boot up the classroom computer and found a live feed from a local news channel. We now for the first time were able to see the events occurring outside our building. When we saw the SWAT team and a multitude of police officers with heavy armor, we knew it was serious. Some students wanted to leave and I suggested that it might not be safe if there was an armed person running around who had already shot a clerk while committing a robbery. I asked them if they wanted to risk being taken hostage and strongly but calmly assured them that we were being protected by the police who were stationed outside our building. It would only be a matter of time until the police would enter our building to conduct a thorough search to ensure that all of us would leave campus safely and uninjured, which is exactly what happened, albeit four hours later.

The worst part of this trauma for me was being locked in and losing my freedom. I was angry and felt powerless. Some students became highly anxious due to claustrophobia and fears of being assaulted. Fortunately for me and them, I happened to be experienced at trauma response situations and have dealt with earthquake and fire traumas and bank robberies in the past. I had students do some deep breathing, talked about the reality of the situation, managed things slowly and broke things down into manageable bits. Students were encouraged to express their feelings and I sought help from others. I attempted to provide them with optimism and hope about the outcome and I kept them functioning as normally as possible. I encouraged them to use the time to study for finals that were coming up next week. In conclusion, I used all of Caplan's seven characteristics of effective coping people (see Chapter 1) to keep the situation under control.

Did we develop PTSD? Although neither I nor any student I know of had all the symptoms of PTSD, there were some aspects that did occur. For example, we were all exhausted and wanted to sleep or couldn't sleep. I'm writing this two days after the event and many of us simply do not want to talk about it at all. It seems as though my friends, family, and students and faculty who weren't here want to keep talking about it and I want to forget about it, period! This is my mind's way of coping. I even thought that writing about it would help me slowly integrate it. Two days later, I still think about it, but now I am mostly angry at the suspects for invading our lives. Sadly, a much worse trauma has occurred while I am writing this story. Today December 14, 2012, 20 children and six adults were killed by a gunman at Sandy Hook Elementary School in Newtown, Connecticut. Hearing about this school shooting has triggered anxiety and sadness in me, but I am still numb from the other night and now will need more time to integrate these events that make me and others feel so powerless.

Sadly, those deaths are not the only ones our nation has experienced even in the past 10 years. On April 16, 2007, 32 people were murdered in a mass shooting at Virginia Tech University. These types of horrible shootings are unexpected and reduce the feeling of safety and normalcy among students, faculty, and college staff. A popular documentary created by noted filmmaker Michael Moore, *Bowling for Columbine*, rigorously deals with yet another mass shooting by two high school students at Columbine High School in Colorado. Many of these surviving students have described symptoms of PTSD and mental health challenges due to this tragedy.

Of course there have been many other shootings nationwide and throughout history. Some people believe that gun violence is just a natural outcome of the freedoms we enjoy such as Second Amendment rights to bear arms and that the real solution is not gun control but doing a better job in preventing and identifying the types of mental disorders that lead to these types of shootings.

Unfortunately, elementary schools and high schools have had to develop training programs for teachers and administrators to deal with shooting and invasions because they have become so prevalent in the past 20 years. During the year 2009–2010 there were seven deaths by shootings and one by a fight at schools nationwide, resulting in 11 deaths. Total nondeath shooting incidents at schools during that same period was 33 (National School Safety and Security Services, Inc., 2012).

In the aftermath of the Sandy Hook shootings and on the anniversary of the Virginia Tech shootings, various groups have lobbied for Congress to take action to reduce gun violence (Schmidt, 2013). Disappointingly for many, even requiring universal background checks prior to purchasing a gun was not enacted by Congress, so it may once again fall into the hands of mental health professionals and other social helpers to deal with survivors and potential perpetrators of this type of tragedy.

Interventions

When disasters happen, they affect not only those directly involved but others who suddenly feel that their security is threatened. Communities throughout the United States responded to the recent traumatic events by providing much-needed support.

Examples of community support included relief funds for families of the victims, generous donations to the Red Cross, and crisis response units established in a variety of locales such as elementary schools and even public parks. The crisis intervention was aimed at helping children and adults deal with beliefs that the community is no longer a safe place. Shock that something like this could happen to "me and my family" was a common response by many. Crisis workers needed to help people think differently about the situation, showing the secondary victims through education and empowerment statements that they could cope with this situation.

To function during an emergency situation, people must put their feelings and normal human reactions aside. This state of denial allows individuals to act in order to survive. If this initial shock did not exist, people would be so overwhelmed with feelings that they could not function at all. After the emergency is stabilized, those involved can come to terms at an appropriate pace with what has happened. This process is referred to as a *delayed reaction* and is the basis for PTSD.

The tendency is for individuals who have been traumatized to seek resolution at some point in some way. This resolution takes a variety of forms and may occur at conscious as well as unconscious levels. For example, nightmares that replay the event are common in PTSD. It is as if the unconscious mind is trying to help the person bring closure to the trauma by creating stress at night so the person will be motivated to deal with the trauma in a wakeful, conscious state.

Once individuals have allowed the trauma to surface, floods of feelings are aroused. Professional help is then needed to channel those feelings into productive avenues for growth. As with all crisis situations, people need to see that some new meaning can be ascribed to even the most devastating trauma. Victor Frankl's work on **logotherapy** or *meaning therapy* is a good example; it shows how he used his trauma as a Nazi concentration camp survivor to create growth in himself as a person. Despite the catastrophic nature of his experience, he found a way to see meaning in it. This ability no doubt helped him survive psychologically.

If people do not receive help after a trauma, the posttraumatic symptoms get worse over time, and the individuals learn to adjust to life in a less functional way. Such people will have less psychic energy available for dealing with daily stresses, because they are using their energy to continue to deny the feelings associated with the trauma. These people will most likely have difficulty in interpersonal relationships, which require feelings if they are to be at all satisfying.

Critical Incident and Debriefing

As a result of the extent of man-made and natural disasters, mental health professionals have developed special programs and training that focus on helping people and communities overcome the effects of traumas or critical incidents. (All of the traumas discussed so far in this chapter are examples of critical incidents.) Some mental health professionals refer to this process as *trauma response* or **disaster mental health** (Ladrech, 2004). Special training programs are available for workers wanting to help victims of disasters through the Red Cross and other responding organizations such as the International Medical Corps. Disaster mental health is a crisis intervention method that "stabilizes, supports and normalizes people in an effort to strengthen their coping abilities, and hopefully, prevent long-term damage such as PTSD, substance abuse, depression, and family and relationship problems. It is not meant to be treatment." (p. 21).

There are a few special considerations to keep in mind when dealing with people who have experienced a critical incident. The Los Angeles County Department of Mental Health (2001) has listed common signs and signals of a stress reaction to a traumatic event. Most of these symptoms correspond to those listed in the earlier definition of PTSD. This information is useful for crisis workers so that they may educate victims of trauma about the normalcy of such symptoms. Knowing that these symptoms are typical may relieve victims who thought they were going "crazy."

Physical signs include fatigue, nausea, muscle tremors, twitches, chest pain, difficulty breathing, elevated blood pressure, rapid heart rate, thirst, visual difficulties, vomiting, grinding of teeth, weakness, dizziness, profuse sweating, chills, shock symptoms, and fainting. Typical emotional and behavioral signs of critical incident stress include anxiety, guilt, grief, panic, fear, uncertainty, loss of emotional control, depression, irritability, apprehension, change in activity, change in speech patterns, withdrawal, outbursts, suspiciousness, loss or increase of appetite, alcohol consumption, antisocial acts, pacing, hyperalertness, and startle reflex.

There may also be cognitive symptoms such as blaming, confusion, poor attention, poor decisions, poor concentration, memory problems, increased or decreased awareness of surroundings, poor abstract thinking, loss of time, place, or person, nightmares, and intrusive images. Counselors should assess whether these symptoms are due to a serious mental disorder such as schizophrenia or part of the PTSD.

The American Red Cross (2001) suggests that these initial symptoms may change over time and have observed certain responses occurring in the weeks and months following a critical incident. Sometimes, a person may not connect these symptoms to the trauma because of the time that has elapsed between the symptoms and the incident. Crying for no apparent reason; apathy and depression; frustration and feelings of powerlessness; increased effects of allergies, colds, and flu; moodiness; disappointment with, and rejection of, outside help; isolation; guilt about not being able to prevent the disaster; and domestic violence are common delayed responses. Table 7.1 provides a summary of the causes and symptoms of PTSD.

TABLE 7.1 Summary of PTSD Causes and Symptoms

Posttraumatic Stress Disorder (PTSD)	
Causes	Real or perceived threat or harm to oneself or close loved ones
Symptoms	Recurring nightmares, reexperiencing the event, hypervigilance, anxiety, sleeplessness, numbness, dissociation
Precipitating events	Loved one is murdered or dies in an accident, assault; rape; war; bombings
Types of PTSD	
Acute stress disorder	Symptoms of PTSD lasting only one month
Delayed PTSD	When situation is not dealt with, person uses defenses to cope, so symptoms subside until something triggers an acute reaction

Burnout and Secondary Posttraumatic Stress Disorder

People who regularly work with individuals in crisis situations may be prone to develop symptoms of burnout, or what can be referred to as secondary posttraumatic stress disorder (secondary PTSD).

Burnout has been studied by many and has been seen in a variety of workers throughout the nation. Crisis workers should be informed about the possible symptoms and causes of burnout to be able to identify this state in themselves.

Definitions of Burnout

Maslach and Jackson (1986) have proposed three dimensions of burnout. Often the reactions of workers to chronic stress are lack of personal accomplishment, emotional exhaustion, as well as depersonalization and deindividuation of clients. Burnout can be thought of as a "syndrome of physical and emotional exhaustion involving the development of negative self-concept, negative job attitudes, and a loss of concern and feelings for clients" (Pines & Maslach, 1978, p. 224). When these reactions occur, individuals in the helping professions who are particularly susceptible to burnout may develop negative and cynical attitudes and feelings toward clients and may not be as supportive as needed (Vettor & Kosinski, 2000, p. 1).

Symptoms of Burnout

Researchers have described a variety of physical and emotional symptoms indicative of burnout. In the 1980s, hundreds of workers at an aircraft manufacturing facility developed symptoms of burnout that were referred to as *aerospace syndrome*. Most suffered from dizziness, nausea, headaches, fatigue, palpitations, shortness of breath, and cognitive impairment. Three-fourths of them also showed symptoms of major depression and panic disorder (Sparks et al., 1990).

Other common symptoms of burnout include psychosomatic illness, social withdrawal, substance abuse, and deterioration of family and social relationships (Freudenberger, 1975; Maslach & Jackson, 1986).

Causes of Burnout

Negative emotional and behavioral reactions on the job occur in many professions. Human service workers may be more prone to burnout as a result of conflicts between an idealistic "professional mystique" and the harsh realities of working in human services (Leiter, 1991). In addition, human services workers may find it emotionally taxing when clients resent them, when they must work with consumers with limited capabilities to help themselves, when they must deal with tedious bureaucratic exercises daily, and when they receive little positive feedback from authority figures (Gomez & Michaelis, 1995). Lack of company support, poor relations among staff, lack of competence, and a perception that success is unlikely on the job are other general causes of burnout (Clarke, 2000).

In helping professions in which the professionals such as emergency medical technicians (EMTs) must deal with intense emotional arousal, depersonalization is used to minimize this arousal. Burnout may be seen as a coping strategy to ensure that performance is not affected in these crisis situations. Burnout may also occur as part of a tendency for helping professionals to evaluate themselves negatively when assessing their work with patients (Vettor & Kosinski, 2000). EMTs may be more susceptible to burnout because they are faced with human tragedies such as an injury, mutilation, and death on a daily basis. Services are often delivered in a hostile world of darkness, poor weather conditions, difficult terrain, and unpredictable dangers (Vettor & Kosinski, 2000). The technicians are at risk for developing secondary PTSD from exposure to critical incidents.

Negative emotional and behavioral reactions have also been observed in professionals who are not considered to be in the helping professions but who deal with crisis situations. Aerospace syndrome was determined to be caused by several psychosocial aspects in the workplace. Fear of chemicals, labeling of aerospace syndrome, fear of AIDS, mass hysteria crisis building, work intensity, mental strain, increased production pressure, tense labor-management relations, inadequate attention to safety, and reinforcement of fear by media and coworkers were all found to be causes of high work-stress burnout among aerospace workers (Vettor & Kosinski, 2000). The mass hysteria was so extreme that only 14 of the hundreds of workers observed showed no symptoms!

Several conditions may help prevent burnout and increase positive emotional reactions among workers. Kruger, Bernstein, and Botman (1995) suggest that having fun with team members, work discussions, peer cohesion, and social support, in which assistance is directed toward helping the worker cope with stressful circumstances, combine to reduce symptoms of burnout.

Human services workers who spend more time in direct contact with consumers and less time processing paperwork had higher scores on personal accomplishment assessments (Gomez & Michaelis, 1995). Reduced feelings of personal accomplishment have been associated with burnout, so it appears that one way to reduce burnout would be to spend more time with clients. However, because paperwork is often required in human services occupations, management would be wise to ensure that workers have enough client contact, as this seems to buffer workers against the worst effects of stress and is a valuable source of reward among staff. Other factors that may reduce burnout include workers feeling that they have some control over their time at work, some control over their workload, and an ability to organize their own work. Recognition of quality of care is also helpful in reducing burnout, as is clarity over one's role at work.

Secondary Traumatic Stress

A particular type of burnout might be thought of as secondary trauma stress or compassion fatigue (Collins & Long, 2003) and is sometimes referred to as *secondary traumatic stress disorder* (Figley, 1995). Too much exposure to serious illness or crisis states might create feelings of depression and learned helplessness in a helper. Demanding case loads and long hours might precipitate these feelings. When a crisis worker deals with trauma daily, he or she might experience vicarious stress or trauma (Bride, 2004), that is, absorbing the trauma from the victims that they help. Figley (1995) suggests that this vulnerability is a natural consequence that results from listening to others speak about traumatizing events, and that the level of distress experienced by the mental health worker depends on the characteristics of the helper and of the client population.

Study of Community Crisis Workers as Related to Secondary PTSD and Burnout

Sixty-seven community workers were surveyed in 2001 by the author with the assistance of several of her students who collected data by personally distributing questionnaires to various community workers experiencing frequent work with crisis situations. These workers responded to questions regarding their emotional and behavioral reactions to working with people in crisis. Emergency-room physicians and nurses, ambulance drivers, mental health workers, rape crisis counselors, firefighters, and police were included. The types of crisis situations they commonly work with were also identified.

Of the 67 workers surveyed, 21 identified themselves as counselors or therapists, 12 as police officers, 3 as physicians, 11 as nurses, 5 as emergency response workers, 7 as firefighters, and 8 as "other."

TABLE 7.2 Types of Crises Dealt with by Occupation

Types of Situation	Counselor	Police	MD	Nurse	EMT	Firefighter	Other
	N = 21	N = 12	N = 3	N = 11	N = 5	N = 7	N = 8
Medical	4	12	3	11	4	3	0
Sexual assault	12	7	1	8	3	5	6
Spousal abuse	17	8	2	7	2	6	7
Child abuse	19	7	1	7	2	6	4
Robbery/burglary	1	3	0	7	1	5	1
Physical assault	14	7	2	10	4	6	5
Significant other of a murder victim	1	3	0	4	1	5	0
Natural disaster	1	2	0	7	3	4	0
Victim of shooting spree	1	3	1	7	3	3	0
Substance abuse	6	11	3	9	3	5	3
STD/AIDS	5	6	2	9	2	3	1
Teen runaway pregnancy	16	4	2	2	1	4	6
Disability	5	9	2	8	3	2	2
Illness	8	11	3	9	4	2	2

© Cengage Learning

Table 7.2 shows the types of crises dealt with according to occupation.

The participants were asked several questions about their reactions to working with people in crisis. When asked if they felt anxiety when a client reports being suicidal, 23 (34%) of the crisis workers said yes. Only 12 (17%) reported being depressed after working with a person in crisis. However, when asked if there had ever been times when the worker was unable to stop thinking about clients in crisis, 41 (64%) said yes. These problems do not seem to prevent workers from going to work, as only 1 percent of all counselors said they had missed work as a result of working with people in crisis. There was little increase in drug or alcohol use reported as a result of working with crises. Only five people stated that their use increased. This low number does not mean that the workers do not feel stress. In response to the question about feeling powerless after working with people in crisis, 23 (34%) answered that they did. This same percentage stated that they felt grouchy or agitated after dealing with people in crisis.

One common response of workers who deal with crises seems to be anger at the system. Thirty (45%) stated feeling angry at the system when working with someone in crisis. It is no wonder then that 35 (52%) of the workers stated that they think of quitting their job one to five times a month.

As to what these workers do when feeling emotionally stressed after working with people in crisis, the vast majority (80%) stated they talk with coworkers. Only 13 (19%) stated that they seek professional mental health services when feeling emotionally stressed.

The results of this study and previously discussed studies indicate that workers have many emotional, psychological, and behavioral reactions to stressful working conditions. In the case of crisis workers, many of the symptoms reported in this study are similar to the types of symptoms found in people going through a crisis. Symptoms of posttraumatic stress disorder included the inability to stop thinking about the client in crisis, agitation, irritability, anxiety, depression, and thoughts of wanting to quit the job. Because these symptoms are a result of working with people going through a crisis and not the result of the workers' own personal crises, it can be thought of as **secondary PTSD** *or* **secondary traumatization**.

The fact that these symptoms were reported to exist by so many of the surveyed crisis workers indicates a need for a strategy to reduce these symptoms. As was shown in many of the studies presented earlier, as well as in the responses of this current study, maintaining ongoing communication with coworkers is essential in managing the symptoms. It is hoped that this will allow crisis workers to stay on the job at peak effectiveness.

A recent case (November, 2009) of extreme burnout and secondary traumatization occurred when a military psychiatrist shot and killed over 10 people at Fort Hood. Officials who investigated this situation were trying to determine whether he committed these killings due to religious or terrorist reasons or as a result of listening to soldiers describe their experiences in Iraq and Afghanistan, with the possibility that he too would soon be deployed to Iraq.

Debriefing Process

The debriefing process after a critical incident follows the same process as the ABC model of crisis intervention and uses Caplan's model regarding characteristics of people coping effectively (see Chapter 1). According to both the American Red Cross (2001) and the Los Angeles County Department of Mental Health (2001), coping with stressful situations begins with listening and empathizing. Both groups further suggest that traumatized persons need someone to spend time with them. Support and reassurance about safety is critical, as is respecting the need to grieve losses. Support statements that tell the person you're sorry the event occurred are better than statements such as, "You're lucky it wasn't worse." It is also helpful to encourage the traumatized person to talk to others about the trauma and accept help from others. Providing information about special assistance for victims of the traumatic event is vital. Crisis interventionists should also help people to be tolerant of irritability in others and redefine priorities and focus energy on those priorities.

This is similar to Caplan's suggestions about pacing oneself and breaking tasks down into manageable bits.

Traumatized people are typically encouraged to function where possible and maintain healthy eating habits and sleep patterns. Actively seeking information about the trauma is encouraged as well. Crisis workers might share with trauma survivors about the multitude of support groups available in their community. Talking with others who have experienced the same trauma is helpful.

Other Therapeutic Approaches Commonly Used to Treat PTSD

According to the National Center for Posttraumatic Stress Disorder (2005), the first phase of treatment with PTSD survivors and their families includes educating them about how people get PTSD, how it affects survivors and their loved ones, and other problems that are commonly associated with PTSD symptoms. It is helpful to inform people that PTSD is a medically recognized anxiety disorder that occurs in normal individuals under extremely stressful conditions. Another aspect of this first phase of treatment is exposure to the event via imagery, as this allows survivors to reexperience the event in a safe, controlled environment as they examine their reactions and beliefs about it. It is also necessary to have clients examine and resolve strong feelings such as anger, shame, or guilt, which are common in survivors of trauma.

Cognitive-behavioral techniques such as teaching clients how to engage in deep breathing and relaxation exercises, manage anger, prepare for future stress reactions, handle future trauma, and communicate and relate effectively with people are useful.

A relatively new treatment approach for traumatic memories, eye movement desensitization and reprocessing (EMDR), involves elements of exposure therapy and cognitive-behavioral therapy. The theory and research are still evolving for this form of treatment, but there is some evidence that it may facilitate the accessing and processing of traumatic material (Shapiro, 2002). For clients who do not respond to brief crisis intervention, trained EMDR therapists are an invaluable resource in overcoming PTSD.

Group therapy is also a good resource. Trauma survivors can share traumatic material within an atmosphere of safety, cohesion, and empathy provided by other survivors. By sharing their feelings of shame, fear, anger, and self-condemnation, survivors are enabled to resolve many issues related to their trauma.

Medication may be necessary for some trauma survivors. It can reduce the anxiety, depression, and insomnia often experienced. It is useful for relieving symptoms so that the survivor is able to participate in psychological treatment. Box 7.2 provides cases to assist in role playing situations that led to PTSD.

Box 7.2   Cases to Role-Play

Practice the ABC model with the following cases.

Case 1 An 11-year-old boy saw his grandfather killed in a car accident while they were vacationing in Mexico. He cannot concentrate in school and refuses to go anywhere in a car.

Precipitating event: Witnessed grandfather killed in car accident.

Cognitions: He should have been the one killed. Why did this happen to his grandfather, did he do something wrong? I'm going to die in a car the next time I go somewhere. Life is not safe.

Emotional distress: Afraid, sad, guilty. Worried about the future, hyperalert, can't stop thinking about it, feels numb sometimes.

Impairments in functioning: Cannot concentrate in school, has nightmares, can't sleep or eat, doesn't want to leave the house.

Low risk suicide: Ideation, no plan.

Validation statements: Give support and validation statements about how traumatic this experience was.

Reframe: Your love for your grandfather is obvious by the extent of your suffering. I'm sure he loved you equally and wouldn't want your life to end just because his did.

Empowerment: It is difficult to accept that we don't have control over how others drive but we can control certain things. For example, being aware of our surroundings more, slowing down.

Education: You have many symptoms of PTSD. (Explain what PTSD is and how to overcome it.) It will slow but you can feel better. Car accidents happen, but most are not fatal. Coping strategies: EMDR, support grief group, relaxation training, play therapy.

Case 2 A 40-year-old college professor went to the parking lot after work and found that three tires on her car were flat. They had been slashed by a knife. She is paranoid, thinks someone is out to get her, and constantly worries about her car being vandalized again. She is hypervigilant and notices every minute change in her environment. She is not able to have fun anymore.

Precipitating event: Tires slashed.

Cognitions: Someone is out to get her. Someone is following her and wants to kill her.

Emotional distress: Afraid, guarded, numb, has nightmares.

Impairments in functioning: Poor concentration at work, can't sleep, afraid to park her car.

Nonsuicidal.

Educate about PTSD.

Give support statements about how scary this situation would be.

Empower by pointing out that by not enjoying life, she lets the perpetrator continue to victimize her.

Hint: Reframe the paranoia as having been appropriate for a brief time, but now her fears are working against her, not for her.

Coping strategies: Talk to police about typical consequences and results of situations like this, encourage her to keep a journal, use EMDR, brief counseling, advise about safety strategies while walking to parking lot.

Case 3 A 33-year-old city worker was squatting on one knee, fixing a fire hydrant, when a man held a knife to his throat and told him to hand over his wallet. Since then, he has not been able to work, cannot sleep, and will not let his children go out at night.

Precipitating event: Held at knife point.

(Continued)

> ## Box 7.2   Cases to Role-Play (Continued)
>
> *Cognitions:* He is not safe to be out alone working. He is weak for not fighting. He is going to get fired.
> *Emotional distress:* Afraid, guilty.
> *Impairment in functioning:* Can't leave house, can't work, no interest in his wife or friends.
>
> Nonsuicidal.
>
> Validate his fears as normal.
>
> Educate about PTSD.
>
> Empower him by focusing on what he can do now to be safe.
>
> Reframe his avoidance of work as giving the perpetrator continuous power. Going to work gives the client back power.
>
> *Coping strategies:* Use EMDR and cognitive counseling, encourage him to keep a journal.
>
> **Case 4** An eight-year-old boy was brought in by his parents after a magnitude 6.6 earthquake occurred in his town. He is anxious all the time and won't play. He perseverates about the earthquake and says he has nightmares all the time.
> *Precipitating event:* Earthquake.
> *Cognitions:* A bigger earthquake will happen and destroy our home and kill us. What will I do if my parents die?
> *Emotional distress:* Afraid, panic attacks, numb, has nightmares.
> *Impairment in functioning:* He can't concentrate in school. He doesn't want to play with friends.
>
> Educate about earthquakes and offer earthquake preparedness information.
>
> Validate his concerns but put into context.
>
> Empower him by letting him know what he can do to ensure safety if another earthquake happens.
>
> *Coping strategies:* Talk with scientist or teacher, talk to other kids.

© Cengage Learning

Chapter Review

PTSD is a common syndrome that develops when people experience a life threatening trauma. People suffering from PTSD often oscillate between reexperiencing the trauma and numbing themselves to the trauma, and they also show a variety of anxiety symptoms. Crisis intervention may be done at an individual level or at a community level when the trauma is a community disaster. Critical incident debriefing and trauma response are often provided when groups of people experience the same trauma such as natural disasters or man-made disasters. Many people consider the treatment of PTSD to be most effective if it occurs soon after the trauma, and crisis intervention is very effective.

Answers to Pre-Chapter Quiz

1. T   2. T   3. T   4. F   5. T   6. T   7. F   8. F   9. T   10. T

Key Terms for Study

burnout: A state that may occur when dealing with crises that affects a worker's emotional, mental, and physical well-being negatively.

disaster mental health: A specialty field of mental health treatment in which counselors are trained how to respond with people after they have experienced some form of community disaster. Often referred to as *trauma response*.

dissociation: A defense mechanism that assists people who have experienced trauma to continue to function. They split off from the terror and fear of the event and push their feelings into their subconscious.

EMDR (eye movement desensitization and reprocessing): A type of treatment for PTSD that combines cognitive, behavioral, and exposure therapies.

four phases (of community disaster): Conceptualization that communities experience certain stages during and after a serious disaster: heroic phase, honeymoon phase, disillusionment phase, and reconstruction phase.

hypervigilance: A state of preparedness and anxiety that often occurs after someone has been personally attacked.

logotherapy: A form of psychotherapy created by Victor Frankl in which clients are encouraged to actively explore meaning in their lives and behave in ways to work toward a more meaningful existence. Often, the focus is on finding meaning in crises.

PTSD (posttraumatic stress disorder): Condition that occurs when people have been severely traumatized and are not functioning effectively. They demonstrate a variety of anxiety and depressive symptoms.

Secondary PTSD or Secondary Traumatization: Condition that can develops when either working with someone suffering from PTSD or being involved in a close relationship with someone with PTSD, that is, a person who has not been personally traumatized experiences symptoms similar to PTSD.

References

American Psychiatric Association. (2000). *Diagnostic and statistical manual of mental disorders, fourth edition, text revision* (DSM-IV-TR). Washington, DC: Author.

American Red Cross. (2001). *Emotional health issues for victims*. Retrieved from www.trauma-pages.com/notalone.htm

Bride, B. E. (2004). The impact of providing psychosocial services to traumatized populations. *Stress, Trauma, and Crisis, 7,* 29–46.

Clarke, J. D. (2000). Burned down to the wick? *Black Enterprise,* 31.

Collins, S., & Long, A. (2003). *Working with the psychological effects of trauma: Consequences for mental health-care workers-A literature reveiw.* Journal of Psychiatric and Mental Health Nursing, 10, 417–424.

Figley, C. R. (1995). Compassion fatigue as a secondary traumatic stress disorder: An overview. In C. R. Figley (Ed.), *Compassion fatigue: Coping with secondary traumatic stress disorder in those who treat the traumatized* (pp. 1–20). New York: Brunner/Mazel.

Freudenberger, H. J. (1975). The staff burnout syndrome in alternative institutions. *Psychotherapy: Theory, Research and Practice, 12,* 73–82.

Gabbard, G. O. (2000). *Psychodynamic psychiatry in clinical practice* (3rd ed.). Washington, DC: American Psychiatric Press Inc.

Gomez, J. S., & Michaelis, R. C. (1995). An assessment of burnout in human service providers. *Journal of Rehabilitation, 61,* 23.

Kruger, L. J., Bernstein, G., & Botman, H. (1995). The relationship between team friendships and burnout among residential counselors. *Journal of Social Psychology, 135,* 191.

Ladrech, J. (2004). Serving on CAMFT's trauma response network. *The Therapist, 16*(6), 20–21.

Leiter, M. (1991). The dream denied: Professional burnout and the constraints of human service organizations. *Canadian Psychology, 32,* 547–558.

Los Angeles County Department of Mental Health. (2001). *Critical incident stress information sheet.* Retrieved from www.trauma-pages.com/cisinfo.htm

Maslach, C., & Jackson, S. E. (1986). *Maslach burnout inventory: Manual* (2nd ed.). Palo Alto, CA: Consulting Psychologists Press.

Mental Health Center of North Iowa, Inc. (2005). *Background phases of disaster.* Author. Retrieved June 8, 2005, from http://www.mhconi.org/Topic-disasterBkgrd.htm

National Center for Posttraumatic Stress Disorder. (2005). *Phases of traumatic stress reactions in a disaster.* Author. Retrieved June 8, 2005, from http://www.ncptsd.va.gov/facts/disaster/fs-phases-disaster.html?rintable=yes

National Center for Posttraumatic Stress Disorder. (2005). *Treatment for PTSD.* White River Junction, VT: National Center for Posttraumatic Stress Disorder, VA Medical Center. Retrieved from http://www.ncptsd.org/facts/treatment/fs_treatment.html

National School Safety and Security Services. (2012). *School-related deaths, school shooting, & school violence incidents.* Retrieved December 14, 2012, from http://www.schoolsecurity.org/trends/school_violence09-10.html

Pines, A., & Maslach, C. (1978). Characteristics of staff burnout in mental health settings. *Hospital and Community Psychiatry, 29,* 223–233.

Schmidt, M. (2013). On anniversary of Va. Tech shooting, bipartisan gun-control compromise reaches senate. *Richmond Times-Dispatch.* Retrieved February 2, 2013, from http://www.timesdispatch.com/news/state-regional/government-politics/on-anniversary-of-v

Shapiro, F. (2002). EMDR twelve years after its introduction: Past and future research. *Journal of Clinical Psychology, 58,* 1–22.

Shapiro, F., & Forrest, M. S. (1997). *EMDR.* New York: Basic Books.

Sparks, P. J., Simon, G. E., Katon, W. J., Altman, L. C., Ayars, G. H., & Johnson, R. L. (1990). An outbreak of illness among aerospace workers. *Western Journal of Medicine, 153,* 28.

Vettor, S. M., & Kosinski, F. A., Jr. (2000). Work-stress burnout in emergency medical technicians and the use of early recollections. *Journal of Employment Counseling, 37,* 216.

Chapter

8

Veteran's Issues

_____ 1. OIF stands for Operation Iraqi Freedom.

_____ 2. OEF stands for Operation Enemy Fighting.

_____ 3. PTSD is associated with anger.

_____ 4. It is common for a veteran with PTSD to misuse alcohol.

_____ 5. Most family members of veterans never experience any mental health issues.

_____ 6. Suicide is rare among OIF veterans.

_____ 7. It is a myth that war veterans suffer from PTSD.

_____ 8. Veterans are better off suppressing their feelings and staying strong as instructed by their commanding officer once they return home.

_____ 9. TBI stands for Trauma-Based Intervention.

_____ 10. College-enrolled veterans seem to be immune to PTSD.

Serving in the Military: An Historical View

Counselors first became aware of PTSD when they were dealing with war veterans, especially those of the Vietnam War. Often, they were 19-year-old boys who were sent across the world lacking the coping skills to deal with seeing their buddies blown up and small children killed. Vietnam veterans' symptoms have included reexperiencing the sounds of war, suffering from nightmares, and being unable to manage interpersonal relationships effectively. Support groups were set up to allow these veterans an opportunity to discuss their traumas and to find ways to integrate their war experiences into present-day functioning.

The veterans of World War II had similar responses to their combat experiences. Anyone who exhibited signs of trauma was said to have "shell shock." Unfortunately, World War II veterans did not seek or receive mental health treatment when they returned home in the same way that veterans of the Vietnam War and veterans of more recent wars have done. They were encouraged to "buck up" and "be a man." While it is true that veterans of the Iraq and Afghanistan wars have also been told to be strong and deal with "it" on their own, many have rejected these ideas and have sought treatment despite being told they don't really need it. Recent films such as *Saving Private Ryan* have put a realistic perspective on the extent of the trauma experienced by the men serving in World War II. It is easy to forget that they suffered because, unlike their Vietnam veteran counterparts, World War II veterans received a hero's welcome when they returned home. World War II was a popular war, and most Americans were supportive of the efforts of the military.

When soldiers are engaged in combat and see the trauma of war, some do experience acute stress disorder. They are often treated by doctors and given time to recuperate. However, the military trains soldiers to numb themselves to war trauma so that they may engage in warfare effectively. This allows them to deal with combat as it is happening. It is when they return home that many combat and support military personnel show signs of PTSD. The disorder has been delayed, almost, by training. Once soldiers return home, many have difficulty adjusting to civilian life. They report being preoccupied with the troops that are still fighting. They often feel guilty for leaving the other soldiers and think they should return to help fight.

The recent war fought to free Kuwait in the early 1990s, often referred to as the Persian Gulf War, has also left emotional scars on combat veterans. Some refer to the PTSD experienced by soldiers who fought to free Kuwait in the 1990s as Persian Gulf syndrome. I have personally worked with such a veteran who still experiences flashbacks and hypervigilance. In fact, his children cannot have balloons at their birthday parties because when he hears a balloon burst, he feels the same panic he felt when he was being fired upon in Kuwait.

Introduction to the Population of OIF and OEF Veterans

OIF is the acronym for Operation Iraqi Freedom and **OEF** refers to Operation Enduring Freedom. These are the names of the military operations that began in 2001 after the terrorist attacks on the World Trade Center. Those serving in OEF are stationed in Afghanistan or supporting this front and those serving in OIF are stationed in Iraq or supporting that front. While many of the troops have been drawn down from both fronts, there are still military personnel serving in both locations.

Statistics

Over 2.04 million service members have been **deployed** to Afghanistan or Iraq since October 2001 (VHA Office of Public Health, 2010). Approximately 15 to 20 percent of combat troops have symptoms of anxiety or depression disorders (MHAT, 2008; Miliken, Auchterlonie & Hoge, 2007 and Tanielian & Jaycox, 2008). Disorder risk increases to 35.5 percent at six months **post-deployment** (Miliken et al., 2007). It is these returning veterans that crisis workers will encounter.

Military Culture

Crisis workers must keep in mind the military's culturally based worldview of the returning veterans. Most enlisted persons and officers in the armed forces are indoctrinated to believe that mental health problems are a source of weakness leading the service member to perceive counseling for emotional issues as weak. Military culture values honor, courage, loyalty, integrity, and commitment, leading to high ethical standards but may hamper mental health utilization (Coll, Weiss, & Metal, 2013). Additionally, military culture tends to promote a warrior mentality in the service member. Hoge (2010) has developed an approach to counseling veterans that doesn't require the veteran to give up being a warrior, but instead can learn to dial up or down the warrior response depending on the situation. LANDNAV is the acronym for his model which includes: Life survival skills (understanding how the body responds to stress and combat), Attend (paying attention to and modulating their psychological, emotional, and cognitive and physiological reactions), Narrate (narrating war stories), Deal (learning positive coping skills), Navigate (veteran's family learn how to navigate veteran health care and service systems), Acceptance (learning to reach a point of acceptance in their lives regarding their losses and experiences), and Vision, Voice, Village, and Victory (celebrating what is good in their lives and having hope).

Warriors of these conflicts frequently engaged in killing enemy combatants and civilians. Some of the returning veterans who will seek help have experienced the stages of killing another human being and counselors should keep these stages in mind as an aid in understanding and educating. Grossman (1995) describes five stages of killing as consisting of concern, killing, exhilaration, remorse, and finally rationalization and acceptance. When a veterans presents to a crisis worker trying to accept the killing, knowing that these stages are typical, may provide some relief and normalize their experience.

Issues Particular to These Veterans

New kinds of casualties have been observed in these wars; in particular there have been less deaths compared to other wars due to new advances in body armor, armored vehicles, and sophisticated lifesaving techniques. By 2009, more soldiers died from suicide, drugs and alcohol than by hands of the enemy (U.S. Army, 2010). These veterans have also been treated differently by the Veteran's Administration and by the combat units than other veterans as well. For example in 2009, the army was giving 225,000 soldiers some form of behavioral health care and almost half of them were on mood-stabilizing prescription drugs and 10 percent had been prescribed narcotic painkillers like **OxyContin**, leading to widespread abuse (Philipps, 2010).

Another interesting aspect of these wars is the prevalence of invisible wounds such as PTSD, depression, and **traumatic brain injury** (Tanielian & Jaycox, 2008). Each of these will be discussed later. Referring to these disorders as **combat stress injuries** might help the veteran destigmatize their experience and encourage seeking help. Counselors can reframe their symptoms as occupational hazards and just as much an injury as if they were struck by a bullet. According to Shay (2009), injury is more culturally acceptable and less of a barrier to receiving help than is a mental disorder.

Invisible Wounds

PTSD

Since this disorder has been discussed in Chapter 7, suffice it to say that the veterans of these wars are suffering from PTSD. It has been estimated that the rates of PTSD for OIF and OEF veterans is 12.5 percent. Multiple deployments may increase the likelihood of suffering from PTSD (Yarvis & Schiess, 2008). Many veterans seek help because they frequently reexperience trauma from the war and it affects their personal relationships.

Depression and Suicide

Along with the symptoms of PTSD discussed previously, depression, anger, and substance misuse are highly associated with the PTSD experienced by the OIF and OEF veterans.

Depression is another **invisible wound**. An estimated 9.3 percent of veterans experienced at least one major depressive episode in 2007, leading to impairment in functioning (National Survey on Drug Use and Health, 2008). Veterans suffering from major depression often show symptoms such as sleep problems, feelings of guilt, worthlessness, hopelessness, regret, loss of energy and interest in life, and concentration deficits, appetite disorder, psychomotor retardation or agitation, and suicidal thoughts.

In 2007, the Veterans Crisis Line answered more than 500,000 calls and made more than 18,000 life-saving rescues. In 2009, this anonymous online chat center helped more than 28,000 people. These centers are staffed with professionals specializing in crisis intervention and mental health techniques (Department of Veterans Affairs, 2011). As of 2007, veterans were committing suicide at a rate that far exceeds the nonveteran population (Hampton, 2007). There were 108 confirmed suicides committed among young enlisted, unmarried white males who used firearms primarily (U.S. Department of Defense Task Force on Mental Health, 2007). Suicide among veterans is on the increase and is a public health problem. Tarabay (2010) reports that more soldiers are dying from suicide than are killed in combat. In 2009, 245 died of suicide and as of May 2010, there were already 163.

Anger Issues

Symptoms of PTSD have been found to be associated with anger, hostility, and aggression among OIF and OEF veterans (Jakupcak et al., 2007) and Teten et al. (2010) found that impulsive aggression was overrepresented among veterans with PTSD and premeditated aggression was found more in veterans without PTSD. Elbogen et al. (2010) suggest that anger management interventions should focus on risk factors related to aggression in veterans such as their background involving violence and aggression, firing weapons in combat, and long deployments.

Treatment of PTSD

According to Simpson (2012), common aspects of best practices for PTSD include education and normalization, challenging thoughts and beliefs, and the use of supportive communities and self-care. Clearly, these strategies are built into the ABC Model of Crisis Intervention. The Department of Veterans Affairs suggests the use of many cognitive and behavioral techniques such as cognitive-processing therapy, prolonged-exposure therapy, eye movement desensitization and reprocessing, stress inoculation training, family and group therapy. One of the newest approaches in working with the PTSD of our returning veterans is **Virtual Reality Exposure**. The Virtual Iraq application and the Virtual Afghanistan scenario are two virtual programs designed to represent relevant contexts for Virtual Reality Exposure which was developed at the University of Southern California in 2005 (Rizzo, Reger, Gahm, Difede & Rothbaum, 2009). By exposing the veteran with PTSD to these scenarios, it is hoped that he or she will be desensitized to the anxiety-evoking aspect of combat such as when a person with a phobia become desensitized to an anxiety-evoking stimuli upon repeated exposure to it. These are excellent coping strategies for a crisis worker to offer or use as referrals.

Alcohol Misuse

In addition to PTSD being related to anger issues, PTSD has been found to be associated with high rates of alcohol-use disorders, which might help explain some decrease in overall functional health for those with PTSD (Jacobsen, Southwick & Kosten, 2001; Rheingold, Acierno, & Resnick, 2004). McDevitt-Murphy et al. (2010) found in their study of OIF and OEF veterans that indeed, PTSD symptoms were positively associated with alcohol problem severity and negatively associated with functional health.

Burnett-Zeigler et al. (2011) sampled 585 members of the National Guard and found that 36 percent of those sampled met the criteria for alcohol misuse. While 31 percent did receive some form of mental health treatment, only 2.5 percent received specific substance abuse treatment largely because they feared it would appear in their records. This stigma of receiving adequate treatment is an aspect of working with veterans that counselors must keep in mind. It is quite realistic for these service members to be concerned about appearing weak as the military culture strongly encourages a "be strong at all costs" mentality. However, since it is known that alcohol and substance abuse are related to physical health, it is vital that we guide this population into proper treatment. Since mental health carries a stronger negative stigma than impaired physical health, a crisis worker might reframe the need for specific substance abuse treatment as being necessary for physical health rather than suggesting it is a mental health disorder.

Unfortunately, alcohol misuse has also been found to be a precipitating factor for suicidality and aggression (Jakupcak et al., 2007; Lemaire & Graham, 2011; Taft, Street, Marshall, Dowdall, & Riggs, 2007), making it even more important for counselors to be aware of tendencies for alcohol misuse among this population and be tuned into its relationship to depression, anger, and self-destructive behaviors.

It has been proposed that integrated treatments are effective for the treatment of PTSD and alcohol misuse. Counselors should keep in mind that the veterans' traumatic events happened while deployed to combat, outside their typical social environment. Not only do these veterans need to adapt to their absence from society while deployed, but must also attempt to reconnect with family and other social support networks (McDevitt-Murphy, 2011). The use of stress inoculation training in which clients learn to develop cognitive and behavioral skills to cope with the distress of PTSD may help these veterans not feel the need to turn to alcohol to cope (Marlatt & Gordon, 1985). By learning new coping skills, the individual will not need to use alcohol as a maladaptive coping response to the stress of PTSD. In addition to cognitive and behavioral-oriented approaches, involving significant others in PTSD treatment may help. Social support is often necessary to successfully cope with PTSD. Behavioral couples' therapy for alcohol dependence resulted in higher rates of abstinence, fewer alcohol-related problems, greater relationship satisfaction, and lower divorce rates than individual treatment (O'Farrell & Fals-Stewart, 2003). Crisis counselors can refer clients to marital counselors or provide it themselves for increased treatment effectiveness.

Traumatic Brain Injury

The final invisible wound is TBI (Traumatic Brain Injury). Explosive munitions have caused 75 percent of all U.S. casualties from these wars. The use of IEDs (improvised explosive devices) car bombs, rocket-propelled grenades, mortars, and rockets are common causes of someone suffering a TBI (Institute of Medicine Committee on Gulf War and Health, 2008). Symptoms of TBI include decreased levels of consciousness, amnesia and other neurological irregularities (Tanielian & Jaycox, 2008). This type of injury is particularly challenging for veterans enrolled in college as it can cause impairments in thinking, judgment, attention span, and concentration. College personnel are encouraged to provide support to veterans suffering from TBI, and encourage the use of any special accommodations that will increase the likelihood of the veteran's success in college. Tips for interacting with veterans with TBI include reduced verbiage, shorter sessions, reminders of appointments, written list of steps to take, redirecting client to current topic, keeping a calm and steady voice and trying not to overattend to emotional displays (Struchen, Clark, & Rubin, 2013).

Issues Facing the Families of Veterans

Not only do the military service members exposed to high operational stress experience higher rates of PTSD, substance abuse, depression, but combat stress may lead to **secondary traumatization** of spouses and children and interfere with effective parenting. Children might experience emotional or behavioral difficulties during deployments and during reintegration upon postdeployment. Data distributed by the Iraq and Afghanistan Veterans of America (2011) suggests that in families of military personnel, 36.6 percent suffer from a mental health disorder. Up to one-third of children aged 5 to 12 have a high likelihood of developing psychosocial problems, and have lower achievement test scores among children of parents deployed longer than 19 months. There is also a higher rate of domestic violence than in civilian families, higher rates of unemployment, as well as higher financial debt.

As a result of the effects on the family, researchers have developed a variety of interventions that have been effective for family members. Once such program is FOCUS (Families Overcoming Under Stress) developed at UCLA and Harvard Medical School (Lester et al., 2011). This is a family centered resiliency training program in which education and effective coping skills are offered in an effort to improve adjustment, stress management, and problem solving. It allows for developing a shared family narrative which opens up family communication and understanding, emotional regulation, management of trauma and loss reminders, goal setting, support, enhanced family cohesion, and increased social support. As the crisis worker moves into the "C" section of the ABC Model, keeping these aspects of intervention in mind will increase effectiveness when working with veterans and their families. This fits nicely with the "B" section in which education and validation are encouraged as well.

Many have focused on the resiliency of the children of military service members. It has been suggested that smaller challenges such as frequent residential moves and school transitions might actual bolster their ability to adapt to other stressors such as parental deployment (Rutter, 1993). Mmari,

Bradshaw, Sudhinaraset, & Blum (2010), explored this idea and found that the biggest stressor for children was frequent moves and the lack of social connectedness to others. They found that living on a base enhanced social connections among military families. Also, children coped in much the same manner as the remaining parent was coping when another parent was deployed. Based on these results, social connectedness is another area in which crisis counselors should focus when completing the "C" section with children and spouses of military service members.

Issues Facing College Enrolled Veterans

When working with veterans who are seeking college degrees, crisis counselors might keep in mind some of the special challenges they face and how these might precipitate a crisis. Lighthall, (2012) offers her ten principles for working with students veterans. When crisis workers deal with student veterans, they should consider that the veterans are highly diverse, they do not see themselves as victims, they often feel alone on campus, they may be unaware of their own mild traumatic brain injuries, they don't need to hear things like, "The wars were a waste of human life," or "You volunteered, why are you struggling?" or "Did you kill anyone?" Female veterans often suffer in silence more profoundly, and many often want to go back to the war zone. Counselors might help reframe combat trauma as an injury, not mental illness. They need understanding, compassion, and respect, and should be thought of as a great untapped human resource.

A 2008–2009 Research Study of OIF and OEF Veterans and PTSD

There have been numerous studies attempting to understand the mental health issues of the veterans returning from Operation Iraqi Freedom (OIF) and Operation Enduring Freedom (OEF). In 2008 and 2009, the author (Kristi Kanel) conducted a research project to study the symptoms of PTSD and depression that the college-enrolled veterans of the Iraq and Afghanistan wars experienced while in combat and after returning home. Additionally, these veterans were asked about interventions that they believed to be helpful to them in overcoming their mental and emotional problems. Of the 300 veterans enrolled at a Southern California University, 39 participated in the survey. Table 8.1 provides the demographic information about the participants.

Table 8.2 provides the data related to the frequency of reported symptoms of PTSD that the veterans had experienced after their combat time.

Data was tabulated to determine if participants met the DSM's diagnostic criteria for PTSD or acute stress disorder. The DSM states that a certain number of symptoms from each category must exist for this diagnosis: at least one symptom from Category I; at least three symptoms from Category II; and at least two symptoms from Category III. Additionally, the duration must be for

TABLE 8.1 Demographic Information for the PTSD and Depression Survey Participants

PTSD and Depression Survey Participants (number = 39)		
	Frequency	**Percentage**
Gender		
Male	39	100
Female	0	
Marital status		
Married	9	23
Single	26	67
Separated	0	
Widowed	0	
Divorced	4	10
Cohabitating	0	
Age		
18–20	0	
21–24	6	15
25–30	24	62
31–35	4	10
36–40	2	5
Over 40 under 65	1	3
Served in Iraq?		
Yes	33	85
No	6	15
Served in Afghanistan?		
Yes	7	18
No	32	82
How long in Iraq?		
Less than 1 year	13	33
1 year	14	36
1.5 years	3	8
2 years	3	8
2.5 years	0	
3 years	0	

(Continued)

TABLE 8.1 Demographic Information for the PTSD and Depression Survey
Participants (*Continued*)

PTSD and Depression Survey Participants (number = 39)		
	Frequency	Percentage
3.5 years	0	
4 years	0	
4.5 years or more	0	
How long in Afghanistan?		
Less than 1 year	5	13
1 year	2	5
1.5 years	0	
2 years	0	
2.5 years	0	
3 years	0	
3.5 years	0	
4 years	0	
4.5 years or more	0	
Location of residence		
Military base	6	15
Own home	4	10
Rent home	4	10
Rent apartment	11	28
With relatives	9	23
Still officially in the military?		
Yes	14	36
No	21	54
If yes, how long do you plan to stay active?		
Less than 1 year	2	5
1–5 years	4	10
6–10 years	2	5
11–15 years	0	
16–20 years	3	8
21–30 years	3	8
More than 30 years	0	

(*Continued*)

TABLE 8.1 Demographic Information for the PTSD and Depression Survey
Participants (*Continued*)

PTSD and Depression Survey Participants (number = 39)		
	Frequency	Percentage
Are you enrolled in college?		
Yes	35	90
No	0	
Major		
Undeclared	1	
Business	7	
English	2	
International Security and Conflict Resolution	1	
Civil Engineering	1	
Kinesiology	2	
Psychology	3	
Communications	1	
Human Services	2	
Anthropology	1	
History	1	
Art	1	
Accounting	1	
Criminal Justice	3	
Nurse Anesthesia	1	
Human Resources	1	
Biology	1	
Sociology	1	
Software Engineering	2	

(Note: Some items may not show 39 responses because some participants didn't respond to all items.)

© Cengage Learning

more than one month, and there must be impairment in functioning. If these
symptoms occur for less than one month, the appropriate diagnosis is acute
stress disorder. Based on these criteria, 21 percent of participants qualified for
a diagnosis of PTSD, and 49 percent met the criteria for acute stress disorder.
As shown in these tables, a high percentage of participants met the criteria for
many of the categories, and 77 percent reported they experienced one of the

TABLE 8.2 Frequency of Responses to PTSD Questionnaire

Question	Frequency	Percentage
Symptoms experienced since returning from combat (PTSD)		
Recurrent recollections of event	12*	31
Recurrent dreams of event	7	18
Reliving the experience	5	13
Intense psychological distress at exposure to cues that symbolize the event	6	15
Physiological reactivity on exposure to cues that symbolize the event	10	26
None	19	48
Efforts to avoid thought, feelings, or conversation associated with the event	13	33
Efforts to avoid activities, places or people that arouse recollections of the event	7	18
Inability to recall an important aspect of the event	5	13
Diminished interest or participation in activities	9	23
Feeling detached or estranged from others	16*	41
Restricted range of feelings	14	36
Sense of not having a normal future	13	33
None	13	33
Difficulty falling or staying asleep	14	36
Irritability or outbursts of anger	18*	46
Difficulty concentrating	12	31
Hypervigilance	8	21
Exaggerated startle response	5	13
None	12	31
Occurred for more than one month?		
Yes	21*	54
No	9	23
Impairment in social, occupational, academic, or other areas of functioning?		
Yes	13	33
No	21*	54

*Totals don't always add up to the number of participants (i.e., 39) because some individuals did not respond to certain items, and some responded to more than one item in a given category.

TABLE 8.3   Frequency of Responses for Those Who Met Criteria for PTSD Diagnosis According to the DSM IV

PTSD	Frequency of Yes Responses		Frequency of No Responses	
Category I	16	41%	23	59%
Category II	24	62%	15	38%
Category III	24	62%	15	38%
Category IV	21	54%	9	23%
Category V	13	33%	21	54%
Met criteria for all categories	8	21%	31	79%

© Cengage Learning

TABLE 8.4   Frequency of Responses for Those Who Met Criteria for Acute Stress Disorder

Acute Stress Disorder	Frequency of Yes Responses		Frequency of No Responses	
Category I	30	77%	9	23%
Category II	23	59%	16	41%
Category III	22	56%	17	44%
Met criteria for all categories	19	49%	20	51%

© Cengage Learning

symptoms related to reliving the traumatic event. Table 8.3 shows how many of these veterans would meet the DSM criteria for a diagnosis of PTSD, and Table 8.4 shows how many would receive the diagnosis for acute stress disorder.

The symptoms of depression most frequently reported were, "depressed mood most of the day, fatigue or loss of energy nearly every day, and insomnia or hypersomnia" with 50 percent, 45 percent, and 50 percent reporting these symptoms, respectively. To meet the DSM criteria for major depression, at least five symptoms must be reported. Twenty-seven percent of respondents answered "yes" to at least five symptoms. Table 8.5 presents the data related to symptoms of Depression.

In addition to tabulating frequency of responses for each group independently, correlational statistics were analyzed to determine any relationship between certain demographic variables and responses to both PTSD and depressive symptoms.

Two demographic variables were significantly correlated to items on either questionnaire. Marital status was related to whether symptoms lasted more than one month, whether the participant had seen a counselor, and whether the participant experienced a depressed mood, feelings of worthlessness and guilt, and low self-esteem. It is clear that being single is related to more "yes" responses on those particular survey items. The amount of time served was found to be related to experiencing a depressed mood and suicidal thoughts, in that those serving for one year were more likely to respond "yes" to these two items.

To understand help-seeking behaviors and the types of things participants found helpful in overcoming their symptoms, more questions were asked. Thirty-one percent of participants said they had seen a counselor, and the most commonly reported factor that was said to be helpful was "having someone just listen." A few subjects stated that the following were helpful: expressing how helpless they felt, being in a relationship, being able to talk honestly and face the truth, reassurance, and allowing themselves to explain what they were thinking and going through. A few participants said the following were least helpful: watching the president talk about the troops, reliving the experience, group counseling, and having to explain themselves. Only five percent admitted taking psychiatric medication, which they reported as either an antidepressant or a sleep aid.

TABLE 8.5 Responses to Depression Questionnaire

Question (all began with "Have you experienced any of the following symptoms since returning from combat?")	Depression Group (number = 22)	
	Frequency	Percentage
Depressed mood most of the day (feel sad or empty)		
Yes	11*	50
No	11	50
Diminished interest or pleasure in all or almost all activities most of the day for at least two weeks		
Yes	9	41
No	12	55
Significant weight loss or decrease or increase in appetite nearly every day		
Yes	7	32
No	14	64
Insomnia or hypersomnia		
Yes	11*	50
No	11	50
Agitation or physical slowing down		
Yes	8	36
No	13	59
Fatigue or loss of energy nearly everyday		
Yes	10*	45
No	12	55

(Continued)

TABLE 8.5   Responses to Depression Questionnaire (*Continued*)

Question (all began with "Have you experienced any of the following symptoms since returning from combat?")	Depression Group (number = 22)	
	Frequency	Percentage
Feelings of worthlessness or excessive guilt nearly every day		
Yes	6	27
No	15	68
Diminished ability to think or concentrate or indecisiveness nearly every day		
Yes	8	36
No	13	59
Recurrent thoughts of death, suicidal ideation without a plan or suicide attempt		
Yes	4	18
No	17	77
Low self-esteem		
Yes	6	27
No	15	68
Feelings of hopelessness		
Yes	9	41
No	12	55

Meet DSM IV Criteria for Major Depression	Frequency of Yes for at Least 5 symptoms		Frequency of No for at Least 5 symptoms	
	6	27%	16	73

© Cengage Learning

Of the 59 percent of subjects who had not seen a counselor, 26 percent said at least one of the following helped them overcome negative experiences: dealing with it, driving on, family, living life without much thought of it, getting involved with a veterans group, family planning, moving life in a forward direction, having a buddy or mate, ignoring negative feelings, having a spouse, and reading the Bible.

From these results, it is clear that this nonclinical sample of Iraq and Afghanistan war veterans have experienced many symptoms indicative of both PTSD and depression. Despite the fact they experienced these symptoms, only 31 percent sought the services of a counselor. This may be due to the military training that teaches soldiers to "deal with it" and "be strong" which were indicated by those who hadn't seen a counselor. It is also likely due to marital status. Being single was significantly correlated with seeing a counselor. Out of the 31 percent who saw a counselor, 20.5 percent of them were single. Perhaps the married veterans were able to overcome symptoms and problems with the support of their spouses, therefore perceiving it unnecessary to see a professional counselor. Interestingly, even though this was not a clinical sample, 21 percent met the criteria for a formal diagnosis of PTSD, 15 percent met the criteria for major depression, and 49 percent met the criteria for acute stress disorder. The fact that only two participants were taking medication indicates that they may be lacking appropriate intervention. Clearly, these veterans have many symptoms, and this must not be ignored by mental health practitioners or physicians.

General Interventions

Veteran's Administration (VA)   There has been an increase in the utilization of military social workers both in uniform and those who work contractually on bases, for the VA and other federal departments such as Homeland Security, as well as in community agencies. They engage in direct practice such as psychotherapy, case management, counseling, family psychoeducation, and advocacy. Social workers also work in developing community-level programs, policies, and procedures. With the increasing biopsychosocial problems of the current returning veterans, practicing mental health workers need knowledge of biological issues such as TBI, psychological issues such as PTSD, and depression and social issues that exist for the veterans in their families, at work, and at school (Rubin, 2013).

Vets Centers   More and more communities are creating centers in neighborhoods. Many of these centers look like homes or small offices rather than the sometimes-overwhelming appearance of the huge bureaucratic VA buildings. They employ veterans trained as mental health counselors as well as civilians interested in working with this population. They offer individual, family, and group counseling.

Department of Social Services: Advocacy and Rights   In many communities across the nation, County and State Social Service Agencies have created services specific for veterans to ensure they utilize the services to which they are entitled, including medical care, mental health care, and financial care.

Acceptance and Commitment Therapy (ACT)   Many mental health clinicians would agree that cognitive-oriented counseling is effective for PTSD and depression. One such approach is Acceptance and Commitment Therapy. This "third wave" cognitive-behavioral therapy uses experiential acceptance and value-directed strategies to increase psychological flexibility while pursuing personal values. It consists of six processes: acceptance, cognitive defusion, being in the present moment, self as context, values and committed action (Hayes, Luoma, Bond, Masuda & Lillis, 2006). Much of this approach can be viewed as similar to the ABC Model with its focus on cognitions and committed action.

Sand Tray   McCabe (2012) has recently started implementing Sand Tray Therapy with veterans. She describes this type of therapy as an expressive and projective mode of psychotherapy involving the unfolding and processing of intra- and interpersonal issues through the use of items as a nonverbal medium of communication. She believes this model is great for veterans who may be unable to express their trauma from combat verbally. The theory behind this model is that during trauma, the nervous system becomes dysregulated and the use of a sand tray with boundaries allows for a contained space to deal with emotions with leads to regulation of the nervous system. Healing occurs as the client's disorganized nervous system finds regulation from the organization of the story pieces while in the presence of a therapist who is resonating with a calm and contained repose.

EMDR   One of the newer approaches to working with trauma victims is EMDR (eye movement desensitization and reprocessing). Most communities have certified **EMDR** therapists who have had considerable success in helping a variety of individuals suffering from trauma-based disorders such as combat and sexual assault victims. EMDR therapy targets all of the information related to the trauma, allowing the cognitive elements and emotional elements to be reprocessed. Often, the end result is increased feelings of control and power. Part of the treatment includes facilitating the emotional adoption of positive self-beliefs, such as, "I am now in control," or "I now have choices" (Shapiro & Forrest, 1997).

Box 8.1 provides cases to use for role plays using the ABC Model.

Box 8.1   Cases to Role-Play

Case 1: A 30 year old veteran comes to counseling with his wife. He had served in Iraq in the Army for one year, and was deployed to Afghanistan for nine months. He has been home for the past six months and things at home have become increasingly challenging for him. Last week, he and his wife took their five-year-old daughter and two-year-old son to a restaurant. The two-year-old needed changing so the wife went to the restroom and left the husband with the daughter. The daughter began to whine, screaming that she wanted to go with the mother. As they all went to the car, the screaming escalated culminating in the daughter kicking the father. While in the car, he turned around and barked an order to her. He feels guilty and like he's a horrible father. He doesn't want to be like his father, who was fairly violent when the client was a child. His therapist at Kaiser stopped seeing him because his insurance benefits ran out. He still suffers from flashbacks, nightmares, depression, and hypervigilance.

Precipitating event: Daughter screaming and kicking him last week.

Cognitions: He's a horrible father, he should be more patient, he should be able to manage the kids better. He must be crazy because he sometimes can't control his anger.

Emotional distress: Sadness, guilt, frustration, anxiety.

Impairment in functioning: Withdrawn from kids and friends, sad at work, can't concentrate at work, afraid wife is mad at him.

(Continued)

Box 8.1   Cases to Role-Play (Continued)

Suicidal ideation: Yes, he has had thoughts a few times a week since returning home. He would consider shooting himself, has a gun, but won't do it because his wife and kids need him. He knows he needs help. He wants to be a good "Dad" and be normal.

Alcohol misuse: He does drink at night while wife is putting kids down for sleep. No drugs.

Validation: It is challenging to manage a five-year-old and a two-year-old. They require a lot of attention. It is common for returning veterans to experience anger for seemingly normal situations.

Education: It does seem like you have the symptoms of PTSD which is the number one combat stress injury seen from these wars. Unfortunately, PTSD, depression and anger are occupational hazards for many soldiers. Impulsive anger is strongly associated with PTSD, especially since you experienced violence when you were a child. Your daughter is most likely experiencing secondary traumatization which often occurs in family members of our service members.

Empowerment: Right now, it may seem you are out of control of your anger and your parenting, but by talking about it openly, you can gain control because we can set up a plan of action. Acceptance of your combat injuries can allow you the power over them.

Reframe: While the military might encourage you to be strong and may say that any symptoms of emotional problems makes you weak, please consider that that line of thinking really only works while in combat. In civilian life, allowing oneself to experience painful feelings leads to emotional strength. Pushing it down, continues the problem. You had the strength to fight in war and had to deal with traumatic situations. Now that you are home, you can use that same strength to manage your feelings.

Coping: Vet Center for him, possibly marital therapy, focus on activities in which all can create a memory of being a military family and feel pride in that together. Obtain written no-suicide contract. Explain to wife about secondary traumatization.

Case 2: A 24-year-old male veteran is attending college after having served in Iraq for 18 months. He has TBI and feels uncomfortable in class. He finds his fellow students to be irritating when they don't take their studies seriously. He has a hard time sitting in class and paying attention. No one knows he is a veteran in his classes. He has gone to the campus veteran's center and only feels comfortable when he is there. He has to leave class periodically and is afraid his professors will be upset with him.

Precipitating event: He left one of his classes during an exam last week because he couldn't concentrate and had a panic attack.

Cognitions: I'm too stupid to be in college. No one likes me. I don't fit in. I can't graduate. I didn't do enough in combat.

Emotional distress: Sad, irritated, afraid.

Impairment in functioning: Isolating himself, not going to classes, not sleeping

Suicidal ideation: Yes, frequently since returning from war. No attempts or plan. Just gets thoughts of being dead, especially when he thinks about several soldiers that died in front of him. He wonders why he didn't die, wishes he did rather than have TBI.

Substance Abuse: None.

Validation: TBI is challenging because its invisible many don't understand its impact on you. After being in a war zone, it is so hard to join back in with civilian life. It must be strange to be around people your age who are immature when you are so mature.

Education: TBI is as much a combat injury as losing a limb or being shot. Additionally, it sounds like you also have two other injuries, PTSD and depression. As with most occupational wounds, they take time to heal so that you can work again. Fortunately, our campus has an excellent veterans

(Continued)

Box 8.1   Cases to Role-Play (Continued)

center and disabled student service center. You are entitled to these services which are designed to make sure you graduate because you do have injuries from war.

Reframe: While you might think you don't fit in, in fact, you are probably one of the most outstanding students. Veterans tend to take studies more seriously and therefore will be more successful. Your experiences with leadership and other skills from combat duty make you a valuable asset to the community.

Empowerment: Understandably, TBI often feels like you are not in control of all of your brain power. However, with guidance and patience, you can learn tricks to deal with this injury much the same way veterans who lose a limb learn to deal with that injury.

Coping: Encourage him to see a counselor at the campus veteran's center, use the DSS, and perhaps start talking about his experiences in Iraq.

© Cengage Learning

Chapter Review

With the coming drawdown of the Iraqi and Afghanistan military personnel, crisis workers will no doubt see more and more veterans in a variety of clinical settings. Many will be suffering from invisible wounds such as PTSD, depression, and TBI. Counselors are encouraged to think of these as combat stress injuries rather than disorders to help reduce stigma. It is vital to keep in mind military culture views that encourage service members to be strong and that they may perceive seeking help as weakness.

Answers to Pre-Chapter Quiz

1. T   2. F   3. T   4. T   5. F   6. F   7. F   8. F   9. F   10. F

Key Terms for Study

combat stress injuries: This is a phrase that refers to various psychological challenges that veterans experience due to military service such as depression, posttraumatic stress disorder, and traumatic brain injury.

deployment (deployed): When a military service member is called to go to a base throughout the world and serve either in combat or in a support role.

EMDR: Eye Movement Desensitization and Reprocessing: This technique was created for individuals who have suffered a traumatic event. It is a combination of cognitive and behavioral techniques.

invisible wounds: These are common in OIF and OEF veterans. Whereas in previous wars, most veterans returned with physical wounds, these new veterans are returning with high prevalence of PTSD, depression and TBI which aren't also visible to the average person.

OEF: Operation Enduring Freedom was the name given to the war in Afghanistan that began after the 9/11 terrorist attacks on the World Trade Center.

OIF: Operation Iraqi Freedom was the name given to the war fought in Iraq that began in 2003.

OxyContin: A pain-killer drug often prescribed to war veterans. It is also used on the streets as an illicit drug.

postdeployment: When a veteran returns home from service.

secondary traumatization: When family members begin to experience some of the same symptoms of PTSD as the returning service member.

TBI: Traumatic Brain Injury: Prevalent among the OIF and OEF veterans and occurs when there is exposure to explosions. It leads to poor concentration and other disorganization in brain functioning.

Virtual Reality Exposure: A new approach to working with the PTSD suffered by the returning veterans. They observe a video of scenarios that replicate their experience in Iraq or Afghanistan and while doing so, a therapist guides them in changing cognitions and emotional responses to events.

References

Burnett-Zeigler, I., Ilgen, M., Valenstein, M., Zivin, K., Gorman, L., Blow, A., et al. (2011). Prevalence and correlates of alcohol misuse among returning Afghanistan and Iraq veterans. *Addictive Behaviors, 36*(8), 801–806.

Coll, J. E., Weiss, E. L., and Metal, M. (2013). Found in Handbook of Military Social Work, Eds. rubin, A., Weiss, E L., and Coll, J. E. New Jersey: John Wiley and Sons, Inc.

Department of Veterans Affairs. (2011). *Suicide prevention.* Washington, DC: Author. Retrieved from http://www.mentalhealth.va.gov/suicide_prevention/index.asp

Elbogen, E. B., Wagner, H. R., Fuller, S. R., Calhoun, P. S., & Kinneer, P.; Mid-Atlantic Mental Illness Research, Education, and Clinical Center Workgroup, Beckham, JC. (2010). Correlates of anger and hostility in Iraq and Afghanistan war veterans. *American Journal of Psychiatry, 167*(9), 1051–1057.

Grossman, D. A. (1995). *On killing: The psychological cost of learning to kill in war and society.* Boston: Little, Brown.

Hampton, E. (2007). Research, law address veteran's suicide. *Journal of the American Medical Association, 298*(23), 27–32.

Hayes, S. C., Luoma, J. B., Bond, F. W., Masuda, A., & Lillis, J. (2006). Acceptance and commitment therapy: Model processes and outcomes. *Behaviour Research and Therapy, 44,* 1–25.

Hoge, C. W. (2010). *Once a warrior always a warrior.* Guilford, CT: Globe Pequot Press.

Iraq and Afghanistan Veterans of America. (2011). *Unsung heroes: Military families after ten years of war.* Retrieved from www.Media.iava.org/reports/unsungheroes_quickfacts.pdf

Jacobsen, L. K., Southwick, S. M., & Kosten, T. R. (2001). Substance use disorders in patients with posttraumatic stress disorder: A review of the literature. *American Journal of Psychiatry, 158,* 1184–1190.

Jakupcak, M., Conybeare, D., Phelps, L., Hunt, S., Holmes, H. A., Felker, B., et al. (2007). Anger, hostility, and aggression among Iraq and Afghanistan war veterans reporting PTSD and subthreshold PTSD. *Journal of Traumatic Stress, 20*(6), 945–954.

Lemaire, C. M., & Graham, D. P. (2011). Factors associated with suicidal ideation in OEF/OIF veterans. *Journal of Affective Disorders, 130,* 231–238.

Lester, P., Mogil, C., Saltzman, W., Woodward, K., Nash, W., Leskin, G., et al. (2011). Families overcoming under stress: Implementing family-centered prevention for military families facing wartime deployments and combat operational stress. *Military Medicine, 176,* 19–25.

Lighthall, A. (2012). Ten things you should know about today's student veteran. *Thought and Action: The NEA Higher Journal,* 81–90.

Marlatt, G. A., & Gordon, J. R. (1985). *Relapse prevention: Maintenance strategies in the treatment of addictive behaviors.* New York: Guilford Press.

McCabe, S. (2012, November 6). *Sandtray therapy.* Presentation given at California State University, Fullerton.

McDevitt-Murphy, M. E. (2011). Significant other enhanced cognitive-behavioral therapy for PTSD and alcohol misuse in OEF/OIF veterans. Professional Psychology: Research and Practice, 42, 1, 40–46.

McDevitt-Murphy, M. E., Williams, J. L., Bracken, K. L., Fields, J. A., Monahan, C. J., & Murphy, J. G. (2010). PTSD symptoms, hazardous drinking, and health functioning among U.S. OEF and OIF veterans presenting to primary care. *Journal of Traumatic Stress, 23*(1), 108–111.

The Mental Health Advisory Team V. (2008). *MHAT (Mental Health Advisory Team) V. Operation Iraqi Freedom 06-08: Iraq. Operation enduring freedom 8: Afghanistan.* Retrieved from http://www.armymedicine.army.mil/reports/mhat/mhat_v/mhat-v.cfm

Miliken, C. S., Auchterlonie, J. L., & Hoge, C. W. (2007). Longitudinal assessment of mental health problems among active and reserve component soldiers returning from the Iraq war. *Journal of the American Medical Association, 298,* 2141–2148.

Mmari, K. N., Bradshaw, C. P., Sudhinaraset, M., & Blum, R. (2010). Exploring the role of social connectedness among military youth: Perceptions from youth, parents, and school personnel. *Child, Youth, Care Forum, 39,* 351–366.

National Survey on Drug Use and Health. (2008, November 6). Major depressive episode and treatment for depression among veterans aged 21–39. Retrieved from http://www.samhsa.gov/2k8/veteransDepressed/veteransDepressed.html.

O'Farrell, T., & Fals-Stewart, W. (2003). Alcohol abuse. *Journal of Marital and Family Therapy, 29*, 121–146.

Philipps, D. (2010). *Lethal warriors: When the new band of brothers came home.* New York, NY: Palgrave Macmillan.

Rheingold, A. A., Acierno, R., & Resnick, H. S. (2004). Trauma, post-traumatic stress disorder, and health risk behaviors. In P. P. Schnurr & B. L. Green (Eds.), *Trauma and health: Physical health consequences of exposure to extreme stress* (pp. 217–312). San Francisco: Jossey-Bass.

Rizzo, A. A., Reger, G., Gahm, G., Difede, J., & Rothbaum, B. O. (2009). Virtual reality exposure therapy for combat related PTSD. In P. Shiromani, T. Keane, & J. LedDoux (Eds.), *Post-traumatic stress disorder: Basic science and clinical practice* (pp. 375–399). New York, NY: Humana Press.

Rutter, M. (1993). Resilience: Some conceptual considerations. Journal of Adolescent Health Care, 14, 626–631.

Shapiro, F., & Forrest, M. S. (1997). *EMDR.* New York: Basic Books.

Shay, J. (2009). The trials of homecoming: Odysseus returns from Iraq/Afghanistan. *Smith College Studies in Social Work, 79*, 286–298.

Simpson, P. (2012). Reclaiming hope: Understanding, treatment, and resources for clients with PTSD and the clinicians who serve them. *The Therapist, 24*(6), 12–16.

Struchen, M. A., Clark, A. N., & Rubin, A. (2013). TBI and social work practice. In A. Rubin, E. Weiss, & J. Coll (Eds.), *Handbook of military social work* (Chapter 11, pp. 179–190). Hoboken, NJ: John Wiley & Sons.

Taft, C. T., Street, A. E., Marshall, A. D., Dowdall, D. J., & Riggs, D. S. (2007). Posttraumatic stress disorder, anger, and partner abuse among Vietnam combat veterans. *Journal of Family Psychology, 21*, 270–277.

Tanielian, T., & Jaycox, L. (Eds.). (2008). *Invisible wounds of war: Psychological and cognitive injuries, their consequences, and services to assist recovery.* Santa Monica, CA: RAND Corporation.

Tarabay, J. (2010). *Suicide rivals the battlefield in toll on U. S. Military.* Retrieved from http://www.npr.org/templates/story/story.php?toryld=127 860466

Teten, A. L., Miller, L. A., Stanford, M. S., Petersen, N. J., Bailey, S. D., Collins, R. L., et al. (2010). Characterizing aggression and its association to anger and hostility among male veterans with post- traumatic stress disorder. *Military Medicine, 175*(6), 405–410.

U.S. Army. (2010). *Army health promotion, risk reduction, suicide prevention report 2010.* Retrieved from http://usarmy.vo.llnwd.net/e1/HPRRSP/HP -RR-SPReport2010_v00.pdf

U.S. Department of Defense Task Force on Mental Health. (2007). *An achievable vision: Report of the department of defense task force on mental health*. Falls Church, VA: Defense Health Board.

VHA Office of Public Health and Environmental Hazards. (2010). *Analysis of VHA health care utilization among Operation Enduring Freedom (OEF) and Operation Iraqi Freedom (OIF) Veterans, cumulative from 1st quarter FY 2002 through 4th quarter FY 2009*. Retrieved from http://www.acatoday.org/ppt/4th QtrFY09OEF_OIF_HCU.ppt

Yarvis, J. S., & Schiess, L. (2008). Subthreshold PTSD as a predictor of depression, alcohol use, and health problems in soldiers. *Journal of Workplace Behavioral Health*, 23(4), 395–424.

Chapter 9

Sexual Assault and Rape

_____ 1. Most rapes occur by someone the victim knows.

_____ 2. MST stands for Military Sexual Trauma.

_____ 3. Rape victims usually have an unconscious wish to be overtaken by a man.

_____ 4. Crisis counselors should report any rape that a client tells them about to the police.

_____ 5. Less than five percent of women in the military report being sexually assaulted.

_____ 6. Rape Trauma Syndrome is a myth.

_____ 7. Rape survivors do well in support groups.

_____ 8. PTSD can exist in women who are survivors of MST.

_____ 9. Rape is usually about power and control and humiliation.

_____ 10. Stranger rape is more common than date rape.

In this chapter, issues facing survivors of sexual assault will be discussed. After discussing general principles, there will follow a section specific to **military sexual trauma.**

Rape is the common term used when discussing sexual assault. It is a frequent form of assault in our society. Some of the clients who seek crisis intervention might have just recently been raped. Others will have been raped many years ago but have been motivated to come for help by a recent triggering event. For example, watching the Tyson trial brought out the anger of a 69-year-old woman who had been raped by her fiancée 40 years earlier (Heller, 1992). Victims of rape often go through similar stages called **rape trauma syndrome** (another type of PTSD). This syndrome is recognized in California courts as a condition that occurs following a rape. The crisis worker must help the rape victim proceed through these stages, which will be discussed later.

Like so many other common topics, rape has generated its own set of myths. Wesley (1989), a rape crisis counselor with the Orange County Sexual Assault Network, discussed a variety of myths and corresponding facts about rape. Crisis workers are encouraged to know the difference between fact and myth so that they may be better prepared to present a more realistic picture about sexual assault to victimized clients. Some of these myths are:

1. *Myth:* Rape is rare and will never happen to me.
   Fact: A rape takes place every six minutes. The FBI estimates that 1 in 4 women and 1 in 10 men will be sexually assaulted in their lifetime. Most rapes are not even reported.
2. *Myth:* Rape is about sexual desire.
   Fact: Sex has little to do with it. Sex becomes the weapon, the vehicle to accomplish the desired end result, which is to overwhelm, overpower, embarrass, and humiliate another person. Also, looking at typical rape victims shows clearly that this crime is not about sex: Ninety percent of disabled women will be raped. Children and the elderly are also at high risk of being raped because of their vulnerability. An attacker can easily overpower these victims.
3. *Myth:* Only strangers commit rape. Forced sex among acquaintances is not rape.
   Fact: In 60–80 percent of rapes, the victim and the assailant know each other. In addition, for women 15 to 25 years of age, 70 percent of the assaults are date rape. The woman is vulnerable at these ages because she is starting to have sexual feelings, set limits, and pursue intimate relationships.
4. *Myth:* Rapists are psychotic or sick men.
   Fact: Less than five percent of convicted rapists are clinically diagnosed as psychotic. The media present these cases to the public because of the bizarre nature of the rapes, but the rapist can be anyone.
5. *Myth:* Women who get raped are asking for it.
   Fact: Women who try to look attractive and sexy are asking for attention, approval, and acceptance—not victimization. Babies in diapers and fully clothed grandmothers being raped are evidence that rape is not caused by sexy clothes.
6. *Myth:* He can't help it; once he's turned on, he can't stop.
   Fact: Could he stop if his mother walked in? Humans can control their sexual behaviors. (Adapted from Wesley, 1989)

What Is Rape?

Rape is a sexual act against one's will; it is sexual violence. It might be intercourse, oral sex, anal sex, or penetration with any foreign object. Rape is a felony that carries a sentence of 1 to 16 years for each count. Most rapists don't go to prison because most rapes aren't reported. About 95 percent of rapists are men. Almost none of the men who are raped report it because of the perceived homosexual aspect of male-to-male rape. This is unfortunate because male rape victims underuse crisis services, leaving a population of men who will be struggling emotionally with feelings of humiliation and loss of masculinity. In a 1995 survey (U.S. Bureau of the Census, 1998), 1 out of 6 women and 1 out of 33 men has experienced an attempted or completed rape as a child or adult. Specifically, 14,903,156 women, and 1,947,708 men reported having been raped at some time in their life (Tjaden & Thoennes, 1998).

Rape Trauma Syndrome

Rape victims often experience three identifiable stages after the assault; together, these stages comprise the rape trauma syndrome. This is the type of PTSD often seen in rape survivors. A crisis worker is well advised to understand these stages so as to better empathize with the client at any given point in the crisis.

> **Stage 1:** *Immediate Crisis Reaction* During this acute phase, which lasts from two to six weeks, the victim experiences emotional pain, specific physical pain, and general soreness. As with PTSD, sleep disturbances are common.
>
> The person often feels vulnerable when asleep or is fearful of nightmares.
>
> Eating disturbances will also be seen, evidenced by nausea and loss of appetite. Emotional reactions encompass hysteria, fear, anxiety, humiliation, shame, embarrassment, guilt, anger, and an acute sense of vulnerability. How the victim copes has a lot to do with her previous coping style.
>
> **Stage 2:** *Reorganization* As the initial feelings start to subside, victims realize they may get through it. They may tell themselves they need to get back to normal and can't keep dwelling on the attack. This type of thinking leads to a state of denial whereby the experience is minimized or blocked altogether.
>
> If victims don't get professional help, they may stay stuck in this phase. They may be able to function somewhat, but it will be at a lower level than before the rape. Mood swings, depression, psychosomatic illnesses, substance abuse, phobias, failed relationships, sexual dysfunctions, suicide attempts, and revictimization may be part of this phase. The crisis worker is likely to encounter victims who have been stuck in this phase for several years because they just can no longer function.
>
> As discussed in Chapter 1, it is easier to work with victims who are in Stage 1 because they haven't invested energy in denial yet. The longer they wait, the longer the intervention will have to be.
>
> **Stage 3:** *Reintegration* In reintegration, clients move from being victims to being survivors. With proper crisis intervention, they can emerge as stronger, more assertive persons, more aware of themselves and with increased self-esteem. After all, they have survived an extremely traumatic experience—evidence of their strength (Wesley, 1989).

Interventions with a Rape Victim

Much of the material about how to work with rape victims originally came from literature produced by the Orange County Sexual Assault Network (OCSAN). What follows is an integration of that agency's treatment approach to sexual assault with the ABC model presented in this book.

If rape victims contact a crisis worker immediately after the rape, they are likely to be confused about what steps to take. They may feel guilty and not consider themselves a victim who has the right to medical attention and police assistance (Heller, 1992). A counselor can help survivors decide what to do by providing information and resources. Overall, an **empowerment model** is suggested with this population. It encompasses the steps described next.

The Empowerment Model with Sexual Assault Survivors

A: *Achieving Contact* During the first five minutes or so, survivors are probably sizing up the crisis worker and thinking, "Can this counselor handle what I've got to say?" It is important for the helper to be calm, clear, and trustworthy and somehow convey the message, "I'm not going to be shocked."

During this early contact, counselors should reassure and validate clients for seeking help. Asking questions to get a clear picture of what happened helps to get the interview moving and calms clients. At this point, it isn't important to attain a full graphic picture of every detail. Reflecting, paraphrasing, and asking open-ended questions are excellent strategies for this stage.

Assessing for symptoms is also important in case a client needs help from a physician. Sometimes a client will be severely depressed and needs medication to function at even a minimum level.

B: *Boiling Down the Problem to Basics* At this point, it is appropriate to identify how clients are feeling now, keeping them in the present. To understand what makes the rape a crisis for them, a good question is this: "What is the hardest part for you?" The answer gives the counselor a place to begin, a focus for reframing, educating, empowering, and supporting the client. The following statements are models of the types you might find helpful at this time.

Supportive Statements: Every rape victim needs to be believed and the experience legitimized. People rarely make up stories about being raped. Statements like the following will help to restore the victim's dignity and reduce his or her sense of embarrassment:

"It must have been frightening."

"It wasn't your fault; you didn't ask for this to happen and you deserve to be taken care of and treated with dignity and respect."

"It's difficult to scream when you're frightened."

"Sure, you were hitchhiking, but not in order to get raped."

Educational Statements: Clients can benefit from learning about rape trauma syndrome. This information helps normalize their experience so they don't think they're reacting unnaturally. Clients also benefit from knowing that rape is not about sex but about power. The rapist just happened to use sexual behavior as the weapon of assault.

Empowering Statements: Constantly help clients focus on being in control of their decisions:

"You weren't in control during the assault, but now you are in control." "You've already chosen to seek help from me." "Let's look at some other options so you have more choices."

Reframing: The crisis worker can offer a different way of interpreting victims' behavior while being raped. She can help clients see that in no way should they consider themselves stupid for not resisting the rapist.

"It sounds as though you were very wise to keep still and quiet rather than risk further injury by fighting."

C: *Coping* By exploring the ways clients have coped with other crisis situations, you can activate their strengths and further empower them. Encourage them to think of other ways to cope. Perhaps they can use their current support systems and reach out to such new systems as support groups.

After clients have presented all the ways of coping they can think of, the crisis worker can suggest other resources and brainstorm additional ways. The worker might recommend reading certain literature, taking a self-defense course, or calling a hotline; she might also offer to accompany the client to the police station or doctor's office. As long as the client makes the decision, many options are possible for the crisis worker.

Date and Acquaintance Rape

Date rape refers to a situation in which a woman voluntarily goes out with a man and may even engage in some form of sexual conduct but at some point is overpowered by the man. It brings up some especially difficult issues because the woman is confused. At a certain point, she wanted to be with this person. However, when the situation gets out of control, she often doesn't know what to do. Women are most often date raped between 16 and 24 years of age. The peak rate of victimization occurs in the 16- to 19-year-old age group, with the next highest rate in the 20- to 24-year-old age group (Koss, 1992). About 90 percent of college women surveyed report that their attacker was a boyfriend, ex-boyfriend, friend, acquaintance, or coworker. Nearly 13 percent of the women surveyed reported being the victim of date rape, and 35 percent the victim of attempted rape while on a date (Fisher, Cullen, & Turner, 2000).

Steiner (1994), a former clinical supervisor at Mariposa Women's Center in Orange, California, offers some valuable thoughts on how to educate and support women who are survivors of date rape or any woman at risk of date rape (see Box 9.1).

> **Box 9.1   Things to Keep in Mind When Helping Survivors of Date Rape**
>
> - First, you can't predict how [you] will react in a threatening situation. Nor can you blame yourself for not reacting differently. Too much of a survivor's recovery is spent trying to redo what has already happened. We all can change only our future, not our past.
> - Don't be afraid to be seen as rude or paranoid. If he gives you a hard time or humiliates you because you don't want to go into his room, or to his apartment, or for a drive, he is exhibiting a behavior common to date rapists—no respect for your feelings.
> - Go ahead, wreck his stereo or anything else you can reach if he doesn't stop when you say no. When it's all over, he'll have a hard time saying, "You know you wanted it, and no one would believe you anyway" if his room is in a shambles. If somehow you were wrong about him, a new stereo is a lot cheaper than a year of recovery from rape.
> - When you don't report it, and you don't tell your close friends, you increase the damage inflicted by the rape by isolating and blaming yourself. If your friends don't react the way you had hoped, don't blame yourself. Remember that what happened to you is bad, and they are afraid to believe it could happen to them. They need help facing it.
> - Everybody needs help recovering from traumatic events. Ask for what you need from friends, family, rape support centers, and others trained to help.
> - People do recover from rape, and they are never the same. They can be stronger, more compassionate to others, and more respectful of themselves.

Military Sexual Assault

The issues facing victims or survivors of military sexual assault are in many ways similar to acquaintance rape because the victim almost always knows the perpetrator. However, there are many special considerations to keep in mind when working with victims of sexual assault that took place while serving in the military. On October 5, 2005, the Sexual Assault Prevention and Response Office (SAPRO) at the Department of Defense created the first agency to monitor and report on sexual assault cases that take place in the military. The goal was to eliminate sexual assaults that take place in the military (Department of Defense, 2005). The Department of Defense counted about 2,700 victims of sexual assault in 2011, but due to underreporting, it estimates that there were far more, maybe 19,000. The reporting of sexual assault has grown steadily since 2007, from 2,223 in 2007 to 2,723 in 2011 (Kitfield, 2012). Many women describe horrific sexual assault experiences such as being drugged and raped during basic training, to being fired for being raped. Others who report being sexually assaulted in the military are diagnosed with a personality disorder for failing to adjust adequately to being raped.

One of the unique aspects of the OIF and OEF wars was the fact that women veterans will make up nearly 10 percent of total veteran user population at the VA (Veteran's Administration) by the year 2010. Women occupy more than 80 percent of all military occupational specialties and 90 percent of careers in the military (Pierce, 2006). Currently, women comprise 15 percent of the total active force and it is expected that this figure will increase (Moore & Kennedy, 2011). Though they don't serve in direct combat, they do serve in combat support roles. Schading (2007) points out that one of the reasons for not allowing women to serve in active fighting is because of the possibility of romance and rape inherent as they are weaker. Unfortunately, because the military has not had a zero tolerance of inappropriate sexual behavior, some of this is a reality. Not necessarily because the woman is physically weaker, but because the rapist is in a position of power. Not only do woman have to struggle with stereotypes if they serve in the military, they must also deal with isolation and few role models and mentors (Moore & Kennedy, 2011).

Military sexual trauma (MST) can be defined as sexual violence occurring while serving in the military and occurs to both men and women, but the prevalence is much higher in the case of women. Women often do not report MST due to fears of revenge, scorn, and negative work repercussions (Pierce, 2006). Katz, Bloor, Cojucar, and Draper (2007) found that in their sample of 18 women who had served in OIF or OEF, 56 percent reported military sexual assault. All ten of these assaulted women were sexually harassed (experiencing sexually inappropriate, degrading, or suggestive comments), 6 of the 10 reported unwanted physical advances, and 3 of the 10 reported being raped. They also found that the women who experienced military sexual trauma reported significantly greater difficulties with readjustment and were rated by clinicians as having more severe symptoms of PTSD compared to those who were not sexual traumatized. These women are at higher risk for developing PTSD than those who were physically injured or who witnessed others being injured.

Intervention for MST Intervening with this population is still in the early stages since these women are just returning from service and have only begun to open up to mental health workers about their abuse. As with any sexually assaulted individual, a female veteran who has been sexually assaulted needs a sense of community support. Cognitive therapy will be useful in helping her change her thoughts about the assault. Crisis counselors can help her reduce feelings of guilt, shame, and weakness by letting her know the assault is unacceptable and was not her fault. She must understand that the perpetrator is the rapist and his motivation was to gain control over her and make her feel humiliated. She can reduce his control over her by holding her head up high and proving to herself she has done nothing wrong, Also, by talking with others, she can feel reassured that she was assaulted. She may need to learn about date and acquaintance rape to better understand what coercion and lack of consent really means. For many years, allowing women to serve with men in the military was opposed because of the increased risk of sexual assaults. It is probable that by having men and women live in close quarters for long periods of time, date rape risk is increased. However, this does not in any way justify or excuse any sexual assault. The rape survivor must always be assured that her lack of consent makes it rape. EMDR might also be useful. Counselors should also be aware of advocacy groups and current laws regarding military sexual assault and encourage her to utilize all of the services available.

Crisis workers must also keep in mind that she may also be suffering from PTSD due to war-related experiences and so may be depressed, suicidal, angry, or use drugs in addition to MST. Intervention will include a multifaceted approach.

Box 9.2 provides cases to role-play using the ABC Model.

Box 9.2   Cases to Role-Play

Case 1 A young woman who has recently been raped by an old friend comes to counseling. She went to a party and had a few drinks. The friend walked her to her car and then forced her into the car and raped her. She has told no one. Her biggest problem is that this friend works for the same company she does.

Precipitating event: She was raped last weekend by a friend from work.

Cognitions: I might have been asking for it because I was flirting with him. I shouldn't have had so many drinks. Everyone will know we had sex. I am responsible, I should have fought him off.

Emotional distress: Afraid, angry, guilty.

Impairments in functioning: She hasn't gone to work. She isn't talking to girlfriends. She's just lying around the house.

Suicidal thoughts: None

Substance misuse: None

Validation: That sounds very scary. You must have felt out of control. It would be uncomfortable to see him at work.

Education: Rape is not the fault of the victim. It is the fault of the rapist. Flirting doesn't cause rape. His need to control you and humiliate you caused him to rape you. This type of rape, acquaintance rape, is very common for your age group.

Empowerment: The way for you to gain power is to continue functioning in as many areas as possible. By missing work, you communicate to him that he did humiliate and intimidate you. You gain power back by going to work. You have done nothing wrong, he has.

Reframe: He committed a felony and he should be the one worried and afraid of you. Those feelings of guilt you have belong to him. He is guilty of a felony.

Coping: Offer her support group, discuss whether she wants to press charges, or get a medical examination. Also, there are many books to read.

Case 2 A 32-year-old male was raped by two men. He is feeling a great deal of shame because he thinks he's the only male this has ever happened to. He is also very angry because he was unable to do anything to stop the rape. One of the men had a gun. He is afraid no one will believe his story. He feels that he might just end it all now because his life won't be worth living after this.

Precipitating event: He was raped a few weeks ago.

Cognitions: Life is not worth living. No one will believe him. This never happens to men. It was my fault. I might turn gay now that a man has had sex with me.

Emotional distress: Angry, afraid, ashamed.

Impairments in functioning: He can't concentrate at work. He can't talk to wife.

Suicidal thoughts: Yes. Ideation, plan (shoot self), no gun available. Won't do it because he loves his wife and needs to take care of her financially.

Substance misuse: Yes, he has been drinking a lot more.

Validation: It is very scary to be assaulted. Your anger is warranted, you were attacked. You were violated.

Education: A violent felony was committed on you. You were assaulted and it is just that they used their genitals to assault you, but it doesn't mean you are now gay. This was not a consensual act but instead a crime committed against you. Men are raped in our society, but they often don't report it. There are even support groups for male survivors of rape.

Empowerment: Because they had a gun, you really had no choice about being assaulted, but now you have a choice. You can press charges, get medical help, go to support groups, and focus on strengthening yourself by talking about it and not feeling the need to hide from something that you have no reason to feel ashamed of.

Reframe: You didn't actually have sex with the men. They violently committed a felony against you.

(Continued)

> ### Box 9.2   Cases to Role-Play (Continued)
>
> Coping: Support groups, books, talk to police and doctor, continue in individual therapy and then marital therapy.
>
> **Case 3** A female veteran has just returned from Iraq. While going to brush her teeth one night while in Iraq, she was attacked by a fellow soldier and raped. She screamed and no one came to help her. She reported it to her commanding officer and he said he would speak to the other soldier. Nothing was ever said about this incidence. She is afraid to follow up and afraid to go to the VA and talk about it. She had a nightmare about the rape last week.
>
> Precipitating event: Nightmare about the rape last week.
>
> Cognitions: The military won't do anything about this. I wasn't strong enough to handle it on my own, so I am weak. Other women have been able to cope with this better than me. It's my fault for joining the military.
>
> Emotional distress: Angry and scared.
>
> Impairments in functioning: Can't concentrate at college, can't sleep or eat.
>
> Suicidal thoughts: Yes, no plan or means.
>
> Substance misuse: Yes, she drinks wine every night to get to sleep.
>
> Validation: That sounds scary to be attacked in the night while brushing teeth. It is challenging to proceed in these cases and it's understandable that you would be wary about the military helping you.
>
> Education: While the military may not be perfect, they have implemented SAPRO for cases like yours. They are attempting to help in rape cases like yours. It really isn't about you being strong enough to handle it, you were caught off guard, and never expected someone you work with to violate you. There are about 29% of women in the military who report sexual assault. Joining the military doesn't mean you should have to deal with being raped. It is against the law.
>
> *Coping:* Refer to support group, sand tray therapy, EMDR and the SAPRO.

Chapter Review

Rape and sexual assault are prevalent in society and in the military. Generally speaking, the perpetrator is seeking to have control and power over the victim and humiliate her or him. Offering empowerment is the best approach for rape victims. The goal is to move the victim from role of victim to that of survivor. Support groups work well as do cognitive behavioral approaches.

Answers to Pre-Chapter Quiz

1. T   2. T   3. F   4. F   5. F   6. F   7. T   8. T   9. T   10. F

Key Terms for Study

date rape: When a rape occurs between someone that the victims knows as a friend or acquaintance. This is the most common type of rape and is difficult to prosecute.

empowerment model: This approach is encouraged when working with rape victims. The focus is on the victim gaining a sense of control and moving from "victim" to "survivor."

military sexual trauma (MST): When a service member is raped or in another way sexually harassed or assaulted while serving.

rape trauma syndrome: This is a three-stage process that many rape victims experience and includes the following: (1) the initial stage just after the assault when she is in shock and is highly emotionally charged, (2) the reorganization stage in which defense mechanisms are employed such as denial, repression, and dissociation, and (3) the reintegration stage in which the victim becomes aware of her feelings and thoughts about the rape and is able to integrate the rape into her identity and life.

References

Department of Defense 6495.01. (2005). *Sexual assault prevention and response program.* Washington, DC.

Fisher, G. S., Cullen, F. T., & Turner, M. G. (2000). *The sexual victimization of college women.* Washington, DC: U.S. Department of Justice, National Institute of Justice.

Heller, M. (1992). *Sexual assault.* Presentation at California State University, Fullerton, CA.

Katz, L. S., Bloor, L. E., Cojucar, G., & Draper, T. (2007). Women who served in Iraq seeking mental health services: Relationships between military sexual trauma, symptoms and readjustment. *Psychological Services,* 4(4), 239–249.

Kitfield, J. (2012, September 18). The enemy within. *National Journal.* Retrieved from http://www.nationaljournal.com/magazine/the-military-s-rape-problem-20120913

Koss, M. (1992). Rape on campus: Facts and measure. *Planning for Higher Education,* 20(3), 21–28.

Moore, B. A., & Kennedy, D. H. (2011). *Wheels down: Adjusting to life after deployment.* Washington, DC: APA Lifetools.

Pierce, P. E. (2006). The role of women in the military. In T. W. Britt, A. B. Adler, & C. A. Castro (Eds.), *Military life: The psychology of serving in peace and combat* (pp. 97–118). Westport, CT: Greenwood.

Schading, B. (2007). *A civilian's guide to the U.S. Military: A comprehensive reference to the customs, language and structure of the armed forces.* Cincinnati, OH: Writer's Digest Books.

Steiner, L. (1994). *Date rape.* Presentation at California State University, Fullerton, CA.

Tjaden, P., & Thoennes, N. (1998). *Prevalence, incidence, and consequences of violence against women: Findings from the national violence against women survey*. Washington, DC: National Institute of Justice, Centers for Disease Control and Prevention: Research in Brief.

U.S. Bureau of the Census. (1998). *Statistical abstract of the United States*. Washington, DC: Author.

Wesley, J. (1989). *Rape*. Presentation at California State University, Fullerton, CA.

Crises of Personal Victimization: Child Abuse, Elder Abuse, and Intimate Partner Abuse

_____ 1. Child abuse rates are less than 100,000 a year in the United States.

_____ 2. Spousal abuse only exists when couples are poor.

_____ 3. The main reason a battered wife stays with her batterer is fear.

_____ 4. Counselors are mandated to report suspected cases of child sexual abuse.

_____ 5. Financial abuse is a prevalent form of elderly abuse.

_____ 6. Child abuse accommodation syndrome includes secrecy.

_____ 7. Battered woman's syndrome is very rare amongst wives who are battered for more than 10 years.

_____ 8. Honeymoon is the first stage in the battering cycle.

_____ 9. Elderly abuse must be reported by crisis workers.

_____ 10. Perpetrators of abuse often have very high self-esteem.

As was discussed in Chapter 7, personal threat can be a cause of post-traumatic stress disorder (PTSD). This chapter deals with three very prevalent forms of personal threat that continue to occur in the United States and worldwide. The survivors of these forms of victimization frequently suffer from the delayed type of PTSD because they are prevented from or inhibited in seeking professional help while the victimization is occurring. Unlike the victims of a natural disaster or a bombing, these victims are sometimes not believed and are blamed for the assaults against them. This leads to feelings of shame, guilt, and suppression of the victimization. Additionally, because these forms of victimization are often committed by family members and acquaintances, victims and their families have real reasons not to report the assault; namely, that they may be dependent on the perpetrator for survival. Lastly, and unfortunately, even when these forms of victimization are reported, the judicial system does not always provide justice for the victim, though judicial decisions in favor of victims have become much more common over the past 20 years.

Child Abuse

Child abuse may come to a crisis worker's attention in several ways. In each case, the person's feelings of shame, fear, guilt, and anger exist and need to be identified, so he or she can begin to understand the family or individual dynamics that led to the abuse. Once the person understands why and how the abuse occurred, there is hope that he or she can overcome the emotional trauma created by the abuse.

Prevalence

The National Center on Child Abuse Prevention Research (2005), a program of the National Committee to Prevent Child Abuse, estimates that in 2002 there were 1.8 million referrals alleging child abuse or neglect accepted by state and local child protective services agencies for investigation or assessment. These referrals included more than three million children of which, approximately 896,000 children were determined to be victims of child abuse or neglect by the child protective services agencies. By 2010, there were 3.3 million child abuse reports filed nationwide (Report on the Conditions of Children in Orange County, 2012). This increase does not necessarily indicate that there was more abuse, but perhaps society has increased its awareness of abuse thereby leading to more reports. In 2007, The National Child Abuse and Neglect Data System reported approximately 1,760 child fatalities caused by an injury resulting from abuse or neglect. The number and rate of fatalities have been increasing over the past five years. This might be attributed to improved data collection and reporting (Child Welfare Information Gateway, 2010). Box 10.1 provides some facts about child abuse.

Of course, not all reported cases of child abuse are **substantiated** (proven to be abuse according to state law). The discrepancy between reported cases and cases considered actual cases of child abuse by the judicial system could be the result of a variety of factors, such as false reporting, inaccurate reporting, or lack of evidence; also, children sometimes change their minds about reporting the abuse. Counselors are advised to be aware of the emotional ramifications of

---

Box 10.1   Child Abuse Facts

- More than half of child fatalities due to maltreatment are not recorded on death certificates.
- Ninety percent of child sexual abuse victims know the perpetrator in some way and 68% are abused by family members.
- Child abuse occurs at every socioeconomic level, across ethnic and cultural lines, within all religions, and at all levels of education.
- Thirty-one percent of women in prison in the U.S. were abused as children.
- Over 60% of people in drug rehabilitation centers report being abused or neglected as a child.
- About 30% of abused and neglected children will later abuse their own children.
- About 80% of 21-year-olds that were abused as children meet the criteria for at least one psychological disorder.
- The estimated annual cost resulting from child abuse and neglect in the United States for 2007 was $104 billion!

Source: National Child Abuse Statistics, 2010.

---

child abuse reports, whether substantiated or not. Even a false report could be a signal that a family is in crisis. The crisis worker can use the feelings and perceptions associated with both false and substantiated reports as a way to identify unmet needs and other problems in a family unit.

Sometimes the crisis interventionist will be called on to work with a child, the child's parents, or the entire family when a child is being abused by the parents. The abuse may or may not be the presenting problem. At times, a social worker will refer the family for counseling after a teacher or doctor reports the case to the district's child protective services agency. In other cases, the crisis counselor may discover abuse to exist in a family that came in for other reasons. When this occurs, the crisis worker is mandated by law to report the case to the state's child protective services agency.

Types of Child Abuse

Child abuse can be categorized into four types. Physical abuse occurs when damage to tissues or bones is inflicted on a minor by other than accidental means. Whenever parental discipline causes marks on a child, it is typically considered abuse. Sexual abuse occurs when an adult or individual several years older than the minor engages in any sexual contact with the minor. This can include intercourse, oral sex, anal sex, exhibition, fondling, or kissing. When a family member sexually abuses the minor, the contact is considered incest and is reported to child protective services. When the sexual abuse is perpetrated by someone other than a family member, the offender is usually dealt with by law enforcement. General neglect occurs when parents fail to provide for the minor's basic needs, such as food, shelter, clothing, and proper medical care. Society and the law expect a child to be properly supervised, fed, and protected from bad weather by clothing and housing. Emotional abuse is the hardest to prove, but probably the most prevalent type of abuse. In this type, a minor is repeatedly criticized and demeaned, receives no love or nurturance, and is not allowed to develop a sense of self.

How to Detect Child Abuse and Neglect

There are many clues for identifying child abuse and neglect. One sign alone may not necessarily indicate abuse, but if a number of signs are present, it is prudent to consider the possibility of abuse. Box 10.2 presents some signs that a child might currently being abused or has been abused.

A counselor might suspect abuse or neglect when a child exhibits several of the behaviors listed in Box 10.2. These behaviors might be observed directly by the crisis worker or may be shared with the counselor by someone else who has seen these behaviors in the child.

In addition to observing signs in the child, a counselor may have the opportunity to observe parental behaviors and attitudes about the child. These often provide information to a counselor about a parent being abusive with a child. Box 10.3 presents some possible indicators that parents are being abusive.

The San Francisco Child Abuse Council (1979) has identified specific indicators of physical abuse to watch for: bruises on an infant; bruises on the posterior side of a child's body; bruises in unusual patterns (belt buckle, loop from wire); human bite marks; clustered bruises; bruises in various stages of healing; burns from cigarettes or ropes; dry burns; lacerations of the lip, eyes, gum tissues, or genitals; possible fractures; absence of hair; bleeding beneath the scalp.

Prevalence of Child Sexual Abuse

Approximately 15–25 percent of women and 5–15 percent of men were sexually abused when they were children. Most sexual abuse offenders are acquainted with their victims: approximately 30 percent are relatives of the child, most

---

Box 10.2   Signs That a Child Is Being Abused or Has Been Abused

- Is habitually away from school and constantly late; arrives at school very early and leaves very late because the child does not want to go home
- Is compliant, shy, withdrawn, passive, and uncommunicative
- Is nervous, hyperactive, aggressive, disruptive, or destructive
- Has an unexplained injury, a patch of hair missing, a burn, a limp, or bruises
- Has an inordinate number of "explained" injuries, such as bruises on arms and legs over a period of time
- Has an injury that is not adequately explained
- Complains about numerous beatings
- Complains about the mother's boyfriend doing things when the mother is not at home
- Goes to the bathroom with difficulty
- Is inadequately dressed for inclement weather, for example, is wearing only a sweater in winter for outerwear
- Wears a long-sleeved top or shirt during the summer months to cover bruises on the arms
- Has clothing that is soiled, tattered, or too small
- Is dirty and smells, has bad teeth, hair that is falling out, or has lice
- Is thin, emaciated, and constantly tired, showing evidence of malnutrition and dehydration
- Is unusually fearful of other children and adults
- Has been given inappropriate food, drink, or drugs

Box 10.3   Signs That a Parent Is Being Abusive

- Shows little concern for his or her child's problems
- Takes an unusual amount of time to seek health care for the child
- Does not adequately explain an injury the child has suffered
- Gives different explanations for the same injury
- Continues to complain about irrelevant problems unrelated to the injury
- Suggests that the cause of the injury can be attributed to a third party
- Is reluctant to share information about the child
- Responds inappropriately to the seriousness of a problem
- Is using alcohol or drugs
- Has no friends, neighbors, or relatives to turn to in crises
- Is a very strict disciplinarian
- Was abused, neglected, or deprived as a child
- Has taken the child to different doctors, clinics, or hospitals for past injuries (doctor shopping)
- Is unusually antagonistic and hostile when talking about the child's health problems

Source: Orange County Social Services Agency, 1982.

often brothers, fathers, uncles or cousins; about 60 percent are other acquaintances such as friends of the family, babysitters, or neighbors; strangers are the offenders in approximately 10 percent of child sexual abuse cases. Most child sexual abuse is committed by men. Studies show that women commit 14–40 percent of offenses reported against boys and 6 percent of offenses reported against girls (Gorey & Leslie, 1997). Most offenders who abuse prepubescent children are pedophiles (individuals who are only sexually attracted to children). Sexual abuse has several specific indicators.

When a child displays any of the four presumptive behaviors indicating child sexual abuse presented next, it is assumed that he or she has been sexually abused. Of course, it is not up to a crisis worker to make that determination, but these behaviors are enough to warrant a child abuse report to child protective services because they create suspicion. Suspicion is all that is required for a mandated reporter to follow through with a report. The four presumptive behaviors indicating child sexual abuse are:

1. Direct reports from children. False reports from young children are relatively rare; concealment is much more the rule. Adolescents may occasionally express authority conflicts through distorted or exaggerated complaints, but each such complaint should be sensitively and confidentially evaluated.
2. Pregnancy. Rule out premature but peer-appropriate sexual activity.
3. Preadolescent venereal disease.
4. Genital bruises or other injuries. Remember that most sexual abuse is seductive rather than coercive and that the approach to small children may be nongenital. The presence or absence of a hymen is nonspecific to sexual abuse.

In addition to these presumptive behaviors, there are a variety of other signs that a child may be or may have been sexually abused. If there are enough of these behaviors observed or described by the child or another in that child's life, a crisis worker may be suspicious of abuse and therefore required to make a report to child protective services. Some other possible Indicators of child sexual abuse are:

1. Precocious sexual interest or preoccupation.
2. Indiscreet masturbatory activity.
3. Vaginal discharge; more often masturbatory or foreign body than abusive.
4. Apparent pain in sitting or walking. Be alert for evasive or illogical explanations. Encourage physical examinations.
5. Social withdrawal and isolation.
6. Fear and distrust of authorities.
7. Identification with authorities. Too-willing acquiescence to adult demands may represent a conditioned response to parental intrusion.
8. Distorted body image; shame, sense of ugliness, disfigurement.
9. Depression.
10. Underachievement, distraction, daydreaming.
11. Low self-esteem, self-deprecation, self-punishment, passiveness.
12. Normal, peer-appropriate behavior. Children may show no signs and carefully avoid risk of detection. (Orange County Social Services Agency, 1982)

Infant Whiplash Syndrome

In the past couple of decades, a potentially life threatening injury to children has been identified and described: **infant whiplash syndrome**, or **shaken baby syndrome**. It is a serious injury, and the results can be devastating.

Most of the time, infant whiplash syndrome occurs when adults become frustrated and angry with a child and shake the child. Most people are not aware how seriously this can hurt a child. Children have received whiplash injuries at other times also, such as at play and in car accidents. Such an injury can be sustained when anxious adults try to wake a child who is unconscious after a fall or a convulsion.

Young infants have very weak neck muscles and only gradually develop the strength to control their heavy heads. If they are shaken, their heads wobble rapidly back and forth. The result can be somewhat like the whiplash injury an adult suffers in a car accident. Usually, however, the injury to the infant is much more severe. The back-and-forth vigorous movement of the head may cause damage to the spinal cord in the neck and bleeding in and on the surface of the brain. It is very important that parents and other adults know about this kind of injury and never shake an infant or child for any reason.

Association of Child Abuse with Posttraumatic Stress Disorder

If child abuse is not detected and brought to the attention of mental health workers, the abused individual often develops symptoms of PTSD following the abuse, symptoms that often continue into adulthood. The trauma of being abused often affects a person's functioning in work and personal relationships. Often, adults who were sexually abused as children (**AMACS**, or **adults molested as children**) may unwittingly repeat the abuse with their own children or perpetuate abuse on themselves. Suicide and substance abuse are commonly associated with these individuals as well. As children, denying the abuse helped in their daily survival, but as adults, denial often works against their surviving daily stress.

Many children who are repeatedly abused develop a condition referred to as **child abuse accommodation syndrome.** In order not to feel the emotional torment of being abused, neglected, and sexually abused, the child protects himself or herself by accepting the abuse and not fighting it. Abuse can continue for many years before it gets reported. Sometimes it is never reported, and victims die with the secret of having been a victim of abuse. When it does get reported, it is often by accident. The family is not ready psychologically to handle the disclosure and everyone goes into a crisis state. Table 10.1 describes the child abuse accommodation syndrome and the defenses used to maintain an abusive relationship.

Providing crisis intervention for abused children and their families is key in reducing the extent of damage done. If intervention comes early, many children will not have to suffer from delayed PTSD as adults, and the abused children and their parents, siblings, and other relatives have the chance of salvaging some form of satisfying relationship.

Reporting Child Abuse

Mandated reporting of child abuse nationwide began after passage of the Child Abuse Prevention and Treatment Act in 1974. This federal legislation required every state to adopt specific procedures for identifying, treating, and preventing child abuse and to report the efficiency of these procedures to the federal Department of Health, Education, and Welfare.

Currently, all 50 states have **mandated reporting laws**, although the person required to report differs from state to state. Professionals who are involved

TABLE 10.1   Child Abuse Accommodation Syndrome

Abuse	Child is physically, sexually, emotionally abused or neglected
Secrecy	The perpetrator asks or demands that the child not tell anyone
Accommodation	The child does not fight the abuse or demand to be treated better
Disclosure	The abuse somehow is mentioned to someone, often by accident
Suppression	The child recants his or her story of abuse, may be told to do so by the perpetrator

All family members use defenses: dissociation, repressions, denial, minimization, externalization with children, such as teachers, nurses, doctors, counselors, and day-care workers, have become increasingly important in the detection and treatment of child abuse (Tower, 1996, pp. 13–14). Any professional who works with children must be knowledgeable about the mandated reporting laws in his or her state.

In most states, when a crisis worker suspects that abuse is occurring or has occurred, the worker must call the local child abuse registry or other welfare or law enforcement agency and report the information to a peace officer or social worker. Next, the worker usually submits a written report. Once the abuse is reported to the **child protective services agency**, a social worker becomes responsible for investigating the case. Most reports are unsubstantiated; that is they do not meet the criteria of abuse specified by law. Others result in referral for crisis intervention. The goal is to remove the risk from the child rather than remove the child from the risk. When child abuse is reported, parents often enter into a major crisis state and need intervention to get through the ensuing social services investigations, the judicial system process, and the reality of having a child taken out of the home. Most people are not prepared to deal with these things and need support and education to cope with them and continue functioning. When a report is false, the crisis state is even worse, and these parents are often in extreme distress. Many have tremendous fear that their child will automatically be taken away when a report of suspected abuse is made, so the crisis worker can help by educating the parents on the probabilities of this not happening. While their child might temporarily be removed from the home, approximately 75 percent of families are reunited within 12 months nationwide (Report on the Conditions of Children in Orange County, 2012). As a sign that the child protective services agencies are effective in helping families, nationwide data indicates that only about 10 percent of families have further reports of child abuse following involvement with child protective services.

When the child has been abused by someone other than a family member, the police are to be notified. In most states, this type of abuse becomes a criminal case, and children are usually not taken from the home unless it is determined that the parents cannot protect the child.

Interventions with an Abused Child

When a crisis worker suspects that a child may be a victim of abuse, the worker must first, as gently as possible, confirm the abuse, and second, treat the problem. An abused child is not likely to come right out and confess being abused, because the child has been taught not to tell. Box 10.4 presents a variety of reasons that a child might not tell others that he or she is being abuse.

Crisis workers should provide abused children with a very safe atmosphere and assure them that they will be protected by the counselor and other helpers who will be contacted. A helpful reframe is to point out that the child's parents just need guidance or help so they can learn better ways to discipline the child.

If a young child is being sexually abused, the counselor can point out that, "Daddy or Grandpa, or Uncle, etc. has a problem and needs professional help from a doctor to stop what he (or she) is doing." Another effective comment is

---

Box 10.4   Reasons Why an Abused Child Might Not Tell Anyone of the Abuse

1. The child is physically, financially, or emotionally dependent on the abuser.
2. The abuser has threatened the child's safety or that of another family member.
3. The child blames himself or herself for what happened.
4. The child has been taught that the good are rewarded and the bad are punished and therefore assumes responsibility for the assault.
5. The child fears that no one will believe him or her, either because the abuser is a known and trusted adult or because the child has no proof.
6. The child has been given the message that sexual issues are never discussed.
7. The child does not have words to explain what happened, and adults in the child's environment are not sensitive to what the child means.
8. The child totally blocks the incident from his or her memory because of the trauma of the assault.

Source: Colao and Hosansky (1983).

---

to tell the child that "many other children go through this, and when the helpers get involved, usually things start getting better." If the crisis worker believes that the parents, when they have the child alone, will coax him or her to deny the abuse, the worker should call the child protective services agency and detain the child if possible. However, if the worker is going to continue working with the family, it is often helpful to reframe the reporting so it appears to be *for* rather than *against* the parents. To prevent outrage from parents, it is a good idea to have every client sign a form before treatment outlining the limits of confidentiality and mandatory reporting requirements. This can be used when informing them of a report.

Reframing for the abusing parents or for the spouse of a perpetrator can also help reduce defensiveness. A counselor can point out to the parents that they should be glad someone cares enough about their child to take the time and energy to protect him or her, even if the abuse doesn't really exist.

Educating the parent about the system is also very helpful. By explaining that the social services agency does not want to take their child if there is any other way to resolve the crisis, parents may feel less distress. If, however, the parents are guilty of severe abuse, they may remain hostile. In these cases, it is better to lose a client and get protection for the child.

Reporting child abuse to the state protective agency can be reframed as opening a way the family can gain access to resources and services they might not otherwise get. Saying, "I need all the help I can get in serving you" might help reduce their defensiveness.

In cases of neglect, it is fairly easy to convince parents that the social services agency is there to teach or provide resources. In incest and severe physical abuse cases, parents are often more resistant, and they need classes, group therapy, and marital and individual counseling. Sometimes, these **perpetrators** may go to jail, which leads to different issues for the children, **nonperpetrating parent**, and incarcerated parent. Children may feel guilt; the nonperpetrating parent may suffer financially; and the incarcerated parent will experience loneliness. Counselors may need to deal with any or all of these various problems.

Play Therapy   Abused children, especially very young, preverbal children who don't often respond to verbal therapy, respond well to play therapy. Their concrete rather than abstract mental capacities prevent them from benefiting from insight-oriented verbal therapy. In play, they can work out their feelings symbolically and unconsciously. Coloring, painting, molding clay, telling stories, and playing with dolls can help clear up nightmares, acting-out behaviors, and withdrawal behaviors. If the abuse was reported early enough, three to seven sessions of play therapy for a young child (age four to ten years) may be all that is needed, providing that parents are supportive and the risk of further abuse is eliminated. Crisis workers should refer children to therapists with expertise in play therapy when it seems appropriate. Although crisis workers may not be trained to provide play therapy, they may be able to explain the purpose and process of play therapy to a child or parents and encourage participation in it.

Family Therapy   Sometimes, children need to confront their parents so the children can hear an apology and acknowledgment of responsibility. These sessions can also be used to set up contracts between parents and children. An abused child may feel less afraid to be around a perpetrating parent if he or she is assured that the parent has a nonabusive plan of action that the parent will follow during times of stress or just daily life, which has been and will be monitored by a third party (the therapist).

The Battering Parent

Counselors can work more easily with abusive parents if they have some idea of why the parents behave as they do. The Orange County Social Services Agency (1982) has developed an outline (adapted, to follow), that attempts to explain the battering parent. Remembering this information may be helpful for crisis workers trying to empathize with batterers, who often repulse them.

Battering parents often share certain characteristics. They were often violently or abusively treated physically or emotionally, or both, as children. They had insufficient food. They often lived with dirt and disease. As children, they suffered repeated fractures, burns, abrasions, and bruises. They commonly experienced overwhelming verbal onslaughts. They knew sexual abuse by molestation, incest, or aberrant sexual acting out. They engaged in little two-way communication. They tend to repeat the same behavior with their children.

As children, they developed a deep loss of self worth and experienced intense, pervasive demands and criticism from their parents. They were convinced that regardless of what they did, it was not enough, not right, at the wrong time, or a source of irritation or disgrace to the parents. They never had the opportunity to work out their anger toward, and forgiveness of, the parents. These people tend to perpetuate those feelings into adulthood and are often lonely and friendless, whether living an active or a lonely life.

When confronted with suspicions of battery, some parents display these behaviors:

- They show little concern, guilt, or remorse for the child's battered condition.
- They are fearful or angry about being asked for an explanation of the child's injuries.
- They make evasive or contradictory statements about the circumstances of the mistreatment, whether emotional or physical battery.
- They place blame on the child for any injuries.
- They criticize the child and say little that is positive about him or her.
- They see the worker's interest in the child's injuries or problems as an assault on themselves and their abilities.
- They refuse to participate in treatment.
- They cooperate out of fear for themselves rather than concern for the child, while they try to conceal as much as possible.
- They don't touch or look at the child.
- They have unrealistic expectations of the child's capabilities and behavior, disregard for, and minimization of, the child's needs, and no perception of how a child can feel.
- They show overwhelming feelings of the child's worthlessness as well as their own worthlessness.
- They express guilt over, or expectation of, another failure, or both.

The family unit of which the battering parent is a part often has these characteristics:

- There is little communication and understanding among family members.
- The family unit is vulnerable to any and all stresses or ill winds.
- The family generally fails in problem solving.
- The family uses the child as a scapegoat for pent-up frustrations resulting from personal and marital conflicts.
- Parents demonstrate their frustrations by child abuse that is only rarely premeditated (Orange County Social Services, 1982).

The crisis worker can reframe therapy to these people as an opportunity to correct their own behavior and do better for their children than their parents or others did for them. Providing parenting information and skills will be a part of crisis interventions. Many parents will for the first time be educated on how to talk rather than yell; restrict rather than hit; and understand rather than discipline. Learning new skills will empower them to be more effective parents and be more successful in getting their children to do what they want them to do.

They will learn how to have a social relationship rather than a functional parent-object relationship. Giving them specific alternative behaviors to use when stressed with a child is helpful. Box 10.5 offers some suggestions for battering parents when they feel like they might abuse their child.

Box 10.5   Suggestions for Battering Parents to Prevent Abusing a Child

1. Call a friend or neighbor.
2. Put the child in a safe place and leave the room for a few minutes.
3. Take ten deep breaths and ten more.
4. Do something for yourself, such as play your favorite music, make a cup of tea or coffee, exercise, take a shower, read a magazine or book.
5. Change your activity into productive energy, such as shaking a rug, doing dishes or laundry, scrubbing a floor, beating a pan or pillow, or throwing away unwanted trash.
6. Sit down, close your eyes, think of a pleasant place in your memory. Do not move for several minutes.

Interventions for Adults Who Were Sexually Abused as Children

As mentioned earlier, many adults molested as children seek crisis intervention. Sexual abuse is often repressed so well by children that it may not be detected even by skilled clinicians. When sexual abuse started in early childhood, continued for years, and was accompanied by physical abuse, ritual abuse, or emotional abuse, the surviving child or adult may need long-term therapy. Crisis workers may be needed to provide short-term counseling for these people to help them through the crisis of remembering and having to deal with their parents, knowing what they now know. This moment often has an emergency quality to it, and the counselor must watch for suicide closely. Once the initial crisis state has begun to subside, the client may choose to continue in long-term therapy.

Other molestation survivors can respond well to participating in support groups and reading books designed for them. Crisis workers are encouraged to become familiar with books about the topic and refer them to clients.

Intervention for Perpetrators of Sexual Abuse

Perpetrators of sexual abuse need a different intervention plan than battering parents. Typically, sexual abuse perpetrators abdicate their responsibility for themselves, feel victimized by the family, and lash out all at once. Perpetrators must take full responsibility for their actions and work to reclaim the parts of themselves that they have disowned (Caffaro, 1992). A male perpetrator often views his child as a substitute wife, caretaker, and sexual partner; these demands require far more emotional energy than a child has.

Although controlling the sexually abusive behavior may be the initial goal of crisis intervention, at some point the offender will have to focus on the origins of his problem. According to Caffaro (1992), sexually abusive behavior by a father stems from his relationship with his own father. This relationship can be characterized as one of physical abuse, neglect, rejection, and abandonment. Because his largely absent father frequently did not display tender emotions toward him, the perpetrating father must learn to develop empathy in himself. Belonging to a men's group can be helpful. The members can serve as substitute fathers and can mirror the man's growing sense of self as well as demonstrate how to bond appropriately with others.

The crisis worker would do well to help this father express feelings of shame, fear, anger, and guilt in an accepting climate. Then, groups need to be created that focus on this man's early childhood relationships with his father and his need to express his feelings and develop his sense of self. Although women sometimes sexually abuse children, it is more common for men to do so.

Elder Abuse

According to the California Department of Justice's Bureau of Medi-Cal Fraud & Elder Abuse and Crime & Violence Prevention Center (2002), the three most prevalent areas of elder abuse include physical and emotional abuse, financial abuse, and abuse in long-term facilities. Most states collect data on these types of abuse and have mandatory reporting laws.

Physical abuse includes physical assault, sexual assault, unreasonable physical constraint, prolonged deprivation of food and water, and inappropriate use of a physical or chemical restraint or psychotropic medication. Neglect of the elderly includes the same behaviors observed in neglect of children. It occurs when caretakers fail to assist in personal hygiene, provide clothing and shelter, provide medical care, protect from health and safety hazards, prevent malnutrition or dehydration, or allow the elderly person (or child) to engage in self-neglect. As with children, emotional abuse includes verbal assaults, threats or intimidation, subjecting an individual to fear, isolation or serious emotional distress, withholding emotional support, and confinement. Financial abuse is also prevalent with the elderly. It occurs when anyone engages in the theft or embezzlement of money or other property from an elder. Americans lose an estimated $40 billion each year due to the fraudulent sales of goods and services over the telephone. Approximately 56 percent of those who are called by telemarketers are age 50 or older. Identity theft and predatory lending are other forms of financial abuse of the elderly that counselors should be aware of, and report, if suspected (California Department of Justice's Bureau of Medi-Cal Fraud & Elder Abuse and Crime & Violence Prevention Center, 2002).

The crisis worker needs to understand why some caretakers abuse the elderly. Crisis intervention may focus not only on helping the victim, but also on helping the abuser, who is probably a caregiver.

Stress in the caregiver is often a cause of abuse. Dealing with elderly people who are mentally impaired is frustrating, especially for caregivers without proper equipment or skills. If this is the case, the crisis counselor may refer the caregiver to a support group, offer education about mental impairments, or help the caregiver find low-cost medical equipment. Respite care may be very useful for some caregivers. It gives them a break, allowing them to have a vacation from caregiving while a paid caregiver comes to the residence and cares for the elderly person.

In some facilities, the elderly can be kept for the entire day. The crisis counselor often helps the caregiver work through guilt feelings caused by the sense of abandoning the elderly relative. A useful reframe is to suggest that without getting a break, the caretaker is abandoning the elder in other ways, such as emotionally. A really loving husband, wife, or child would take a break in order to be refreshed and offer appropriate caregiving.

Remember that caregivers have other life stressors to deal with, and they may be taking out their frustrations on the elder because the elder is an easy target. If this is the case, the crisis worker can help caregivers cope better with life problems; these issues should be addressed as part of crisis counseling.

In cases of physical abuse, some suggest that the cycle-of-violence theory holds, in that the children of the elderly parents were abused by them when they were children. They then act out their anger on the dependent elder parent because the use of violence has become a normal way to resolve conflict in their family. The crisis worker must help adult child caregivers address their own past history of child abuse to stop the cycle.

In some cases, the abuser has personal problems, such as substance abuse, financial problems, emotional disorders, or other addictions. Adult children with such problems are dependent on their elderly parents to support them and provide a home for them. This situation increases the likelihood of conflict and abuse. Many states provide training for caregivers; some hospitals have support groups for caregivers; and the state's adult protective agency may offer support services for caregivers. The crisis worker needs to be aware of what is available in the community.

Interventions with Abused Elderly People

Dealing with elder abuse is a multifaceted process. It includes interventions by physicians, social workers, nurses, psychiatrists, psychologists, and other professionals and paraprofessionals, all working together to protect and heal the damage done to the elderly person. The crisis worker must be knowledgeable about community support groups for abused elders and the array of supportive and protective services that are available.

Public guardianship programs, financial planning, and transportation are just a few of the services available to help the elderly be more autonomous and be taken care of by people who are closely monitored. Mental health providers can also use an empowerment model with the elderly, teaching them assertiveness skills and self-advocacy. The crisis worker can encourage the elder abuse victim to join with others in educating the public and elders about the prevalence of the problem so he or she won't feel shame and guilt in coming forward with reports of abuse.

As with all forms of abuse, crisis counseling must be supportive as the person speaks, always validating the shame and pain of abuse but always later focusing on the survival aspect that allows the person to move forward.

Family counseling may be an option, especially if the abuser and the abused will continue living together after the abuse has been reported. This counseling may focus on airing and resolving resentments, improving communication, and defining roles and expectations.

Intimate Partner Abuse/Domestic Violence

A Historical Perspective

Many feminists have examined the beginnings of abuse of women by their husbands and boyfriends in an attempt to understand this social problem. As part of a grassroots movement in the 1970s, women began to propose an alternative causality model for wife battering to that offered by traditional psychiatric theories. Battering became viewed as a social illness rather than the result of a man's or woman's individual psychopathology. Women, according to these pioneer feminists, have always been portrayed as subservient in the media and have been trained to be so by parents and men alike since ancient times.

As far back as 750 B.C., laws were written that sanctioned wife abuse, making a woman property and the husband responsible for her. A "rule-of-thumb law" existed until 1864 stating that a man was allowed to beat his wife so long as the stick he used was no wider than a thumb (Fenoglio, 1989).

In 1974, the first battered women's shelter was created in Minnesota. Since that time, about 700 such shelters have been established throughout the United States. This is not enough, but at least it is a start. Feminists are now proposing that more emphasis be placed on making the man leave the home, as he's the one with the problem, rather than sending the wife and children out to a shelter for safety (Woods, 1992).

Women in Western industrialized nations are more fortunate than those in certain South American countries, where wife battering is legally sanctioned. One example is the case of a Brazilian man who was acquitted of murdering his wife by using the defense of machismo. The blow to his honor from having to live with the fact that she had committed adultery was more than a man should have to bear, according to the rules of this male-dominated society.

Although it is against the law to batter one's spouse, it is sometimes difficult to press charges and secure justice even in severe cases of spousal abuse. In 1989, police officers in some states were given the right to press charges if they observed spousal abuse, even if the battered spouse did not press charges. This change of attitude came about in part because of recent acknowledgment of the **battered woman syndrome** (a type of PTSD), which often inhibits the battered partner from pressing charges. In 1994, a new bill was passed in California requiring health practitioners who are employed in a health-care facility, clinic, or doctor's office and who have knowledge of a woman being battered by a partner to report this behavior to a law enforcement officer. The reason for external control is the relatively new idea that a battered woman cannot adequately make the decision to get out of the dangerous situation if she suffers from battered woman syndrome. An additional bill was also passed in California that requires applicants for several professional licenses to show that they have completed course work in spousal abuse. Since the terrorist bombing on September 11, 2001, what formerly had been referred to as a "terrorist threat" (a batterer threatening to kill his partner) was instead referred to as a "criminal threat" (Arambarri, 2005). Although a criminal threat does not physically harm a victim, it is a form of emotional abuse and often prevents a victim from leaving a batterer.

The murder of Nicole Brown-Simpson in June 1994 alerted the entire nation about the reality of spousal abuse. The famous O. J. Simpson trial may have precipitated the abundance of spousal abuse movies, talk-show topics, and legislative proposals that came in the mid-1990s. A major change prompted by the Simpson case has been a focus on providing counseling services for the batterer. The obvious flaws in the judicial system have been looked at, and instead of simply ignoring a batterer's behavior, as in years past, funding is now available to help prevent repeat battering by requiring that the batterer go to diversion groups. In years past, people held many misconceptions about what occurs in a violent relationship. Some of these myths about spousal abuse are:

1. *Myth:* Battering happens only to minorities and in lower socioeconomic families.
   Fact: Domestic violence occurs among all races and in all socioeconomic backgrounds.
2. *Myth:* Women are masochistic and achieve unconscious satisfaction in being beaten.
   Fact: This antiquated concept has not been accepted for many years. If women liked being beaten, they wouldn't suffer from battered woman's syndrome, depression, and PTSD.
3. *Myth:* The battered woman has a dependent personality disorder.
   Fact: Not all battered woman demonstrate dependency traits. Many are self-sufficient and highly capable of self-care and autonomy. The batterer is often dependent on the partner.
4. *Myth:* Battering is caused by alcohol and drug abuse.
   Fact: Although substance abuse is correlated to violence, it is not always involved in domestic violence. There are many causes for battering.
5. *Myth:* Batterers are mentally ill.
   Fact: Although batterers certainly have anger and control issues, they do not necessarily meet the criteria for mental illness. (Woods, 1992)

Cultural Factors and Universal Factors Related to Intimate Partner Abuse

Universal Factors   Men asserting power over women is a historical reality. Since the beginning of human civilization, men have been responsible for the survival of the family unit in large part because of their larger size and superior strength. There may have been a built-in mechanism to ensure aggressivity and survival. It is possible that women learned to be patient and tolerate the man's needs and behaviors in order to ensure she and the children would survive. It was not uncommon for men to raid neighboring tribes and forcibly take women back to live with them with the intent of impregnating them, probably an inherent instinct to propagate the species of *Homo sapiens*. It is likely that a man controlled his mate to ensure she would take care of his children. This history of men asserting dominance over women is probably a universal reality in most cultural groups.

While these traditions were universal for many centuries, in today's world, brute strength is not as vital for survival. Men and women are more equal in terms of keeping the family unit alive. It is possible that men haven't caught up to women evolutionarily speaking, hence the high rates of domestic violence throughout all cultures worldwide.

Cultural Considerations

Latinos   Isolation may be a particular problem for Latinas who do not speak English and are unacculturated to mainstream values. These victims of domestic violence often feel disconnected from medical care providers, and recent immigrants may feel threatened to call the police for fear of deportation. The unacculturated Latina might be unaware of resources available such as shelters and may experience a deeper stigma associated with problems in the family making it difficult to tell others of her abuse. Economic abuse may be a related problem for some unacculturated immigrant Latinas who lack economic self-sufficiency due to poor English, poor employment history, and lack of skills or education. Other issues particular to Latinas may include the Latina tradition of machismo in which males are allowed to assert male privilege over females. Some Latinas might find it hard to discern which behaviors by the man are abusive, and which are signs of normal machismo. Familismo might intensify the Latina's desire to maintain the family unity at all costs (Volpp & Main, 1995; Sorenson, 1996).

African Americans   The abused African American woman might, like the Latina, also feel isolated from the outside community due to not wanting to betray her own community and further societal feelings of racism. She may also feel mistrust of the legal system and health care providers due to past experiences of racism. As with many women, African American women may not have economic self-sufficiency and feel unable to leave a violent situation. Lastly, some African American women who are subject to emotional and physical abuse by a male partner may feel they need to support African American males and not expose them to any more stressors from a racist society (Thompson & Maslow, 2000; White, 1994; Campbell, 1993).

Asian Americans   As with other women, the Asian American woman often feels isolated from outside communities. Her reluctance to discuss family violence may be due to the fear of bringing shame on her family and ostracism from her own community. She may also have language and other cultural differences, be unaware of basic civil rights afforded them in the United States, and lack resources that are linguistically and culturally appropriate, especially if she is the only surviving refugee of her family. In Asian cultures there also tends to be a norm that encourages gender inequality which is often very visible and pronounced. Men are often seen as superior to make important decisions, and a woman does not usually disagree with her spouse in public (Huisman, 1996; Richie, 1988).

While it seems true that these cultural groups seem to have built-in norms that encourage domestic violence, this does not mean we must support these norms. Counselors can always proceed with the knowledge that domestic violence is a crime and punishable in the United States. The goal is to understand and not judge, and still help both the victims and the perpetrators understand that their lives can be more satisfying without violence. For these ethnic groups, crisis workers can aid both victims and perpetrators in finding ways to fulfill the need for power and control through education, discussion of cultural norms and why those norms may not be viable within mainstream culture. Helping clients understand the etic and emic of any crisis is often very helpful. We just focused on domestic violence, but the model may be useful for other struggles they may present.

Prevalence of Intimate Partner Abuse

Physical assault against both women and men is astonishingly common in our country. In a survey conducted in 1995 and 1996 (Tjaden & Thoennes, 1998), 8,000 women and men were asked about their experiences of being assaulted in their lifetime. The results indicated a very high prevalence of physical violence in our society. Fifty-two percent of the women and 66 percent of the men stated they had been physically assaulted in their lifetime. The type of assaults ranged from being pushed, grabbed, or shoved; having hair pulled; being slapped, hit, kicked, bitten, choked, hit with an object, or threatened with a gun or knife; or having a gun or knife used on them. Although it may be true that men are assaulted more than women throughout their life, violence against women by a spouse or partner is more prevalent than it is for men. In fact, 25 percent of surveyed women, compared with 8 percent of men, stated that they had been raped or assaulted by a current or former spouse or partner.

It is widely accepted that violence against women is primarily partner violence, with 76 percent of the women reporting that a rape or physical assault was perpetrated by a current or former husband or partner, compared with 18 percent of the men. Additionally, women are significantly more likely than men to be injured during an assault.

Stalking is another form of violence against men and women. The victim feels high levels of fear at the thought of the former spouse or lover following and perhaps inflicting injury on her or him. About eight percent of the surveyed women and two percent of the men said they had been stalked during their lifetime. It is estimated that 1 million women and 371,000 men are stalked annually in the United States.

Violence against women by a significant other is so prevalent in our country that many websites have been created to disseminate information about this topic. The National Women's Health Information Center through the Office on Women's Health in the U.S. Department of Health and Human

> **Box 10.6   Facts About Domestic Violence**
>
> - Domestic violence is the leading cause of injury for American women ages 15 to 44 years.
> - An estimated 1.1–4 million women are victims of partner abuse per year.
> - One in four women will be assaulted by a domestic partner in her lifetime.
> - Nearly one-third of women report being physically abused by a husband or boyfriend.
> - Thirty percent of female murder victims have been killed by their intimate partners.
>
> *Source:* The National Women's Health Information Center through the Office on Women's Health in the U.S. Department of Health and Human Services, 2000.

Services (2000) offers a variety of services for Internet users. Its purpose is to increase awareness of the problem, sponsor research, and provide information about facts and statistics regarding violence against women. It defines domestic violence (intimate partner violence) as acts of violence against women within the context of family or intimate relationships that include physical abuse, psychological abuse, sexual assault, emotional abuse, isolation, and economic abuse. Box 10.6 presents pertinent facts about domestic violence.

Although battering of a male partner by a woman occurs, this is not discussed in this chapter. (Examine the current literature on abuse of males by their female partners to learn more about this phenomenon.) About 90–95 percent of partner-abuse cases are male to female battering. It is these cases that will be the focus of this section. Additionally, partner violence occurs in gay and lesbian couples. The reader is encouraged to refer to literature about this specific type of intimate partner violence.

How Are Children Affected?

Each year an estimated 3.3 million children are exposed to violence by seeing a family member abuse their mother or female caretaker (American Psychological Association, 1996, p. 11). Children are more likely to be abused themselves in homes where partner abuse occurs (U.S. Department of Justice, 1993). Although not all men who abuse women also abuse children, about 40–60 percent of men who abuse women also abuse children (American Psychological Association, 1996, p. 80). Sadly, when children are killed during a domestic dispute, 90 percent are under the age of 10, and 56 percent are under the age of 2 (Florida Governor's Task Force on Domestic and Sexual Violence, 1997, p. 51).

Why Do Women Stay?

You can probably make a few guesses why a woman would stay with a man who verbally, emotionally, physically, or sexually abuses her. Each woman being abused stays for her own reasons. Crisis counselors explore those reasons with the woman and help her understand that while she may be enduring the abuse for good reason, there is help available so that she doesn't have to continue living with the abuse. Review Box 10.7 to understand some reasons why a woman might stay in an abusive relationship.

Box 10.7   Reasons a Woman Might Stay in an Abusive Relationship

- She is afraid that he'll kill her, the pets, her children, her family. He often threatens to do this.
- Her religious beliefs forbid her leaving (till death do us part).
- She is influenced by the profamily society (stay together at all costs).
- She is economically dependent on the man. He often has forced her to quit school or her job, or never allowed her to work or know about their finances.
- She has no resources (no place to go, no transportation, no money).
- The children need a father.
- She gets no support from her family; many of these women are told to stick it out.
- She hopes he'll change because she loves him when he's not abusive.
- She believes him when he says it is her fault he beats her.
- She sees no other options.
- She feels insecure and unable to take care of herself (psychological dependence).

The Battering Cycle

Spousal abuse can be understood as a recurrent three-phase pattern. According to Woods (1992), the **battering cycle** usually starts out in the honeymoon phase, proceeds through the tension building phase, moves onto the explosive stage, and returns to another honeymoon phase. At some point, over many years, the second honeymoon stage disappears and the relationship is based on a tension-explosion cycle. Table 10.2 describes this cycle.

TABLE 10.2   The Battering Cycle

Stage	Woman	Man	Dynamics
Honeymoon Phase	Feels special, love, dependent	Jealous, overpossessive, love, dependency	Lack of mutuality, lack of healthy intimacy
Tension-Building Phase	Walks on eggshells, tries to prevent violence	Minor incidents, criticizing, yelling, blaming, may still feel in control of himself, tension is strong	Woman believes it's her fault that he's upset. Both may see that there is a problem. Window of opportunity for preventing next stage through intervention by counselor.
Explosive Phase	If she survives, often has bruises and broken bones, may end up in a hospital. Focus on survival versus escape.	Out of control, may terrorize wife for hours, break things, hit, spit, push, choke, burn, tie up, rape, or kick her.	Violence gets worse over time, sometimes police are called. Window of opportunity exists for woman before denial sets in.
Honeymoon Stage Again	In shock, vulnerable to accepting apologies and flowers, hopes it won't happen again.	Apologizes, swears it'll never happen again, encourages her to go shopping, throw a party, treats her well for a while.	False resolution based on denial and minimization, life goes on. Tension reoccurs and the cycle continues. Honeymoon is the first stage to end until eventually, it consists of just tension-explosion.

Battered Woman Syndrome

After this pattern has been experienced for more than a couple of cycles, the woman often develops battered woman syndrome. This is a type of PTSD that needs to be addressed and treated by the crisis counselor. The three components of battered woman syndrome are:

1. **PTSD Symptoms:** Because of the traumatic effects of victimization by violence, various symptoms develop, as this violence is outside the range of normal human experience. The woman may reexperience the trauma in dreams, avoid stimuli associated with the trauma, avoid feelings, and experience a numbing of general responsiveness. She may be detached, experience loss of interest, show increased arousal and anxiety, and have difficulty sleeping.

2. **Learned Helplessness:** A state of learned helplessness develops after she attempts to leave or get help and meets with no success because of system failure or other factors. She defends against this frustration by learning to survive rather than by escaping the battering.

3. **Self-Destructive Coping Responses to Violence:** Because she may perceive that her only choice is to stay (she may fear getting killed or have no place to go), she often uses drugs and alcohol to escape or may attempt suicide; at least, electing to die would be her choice (Fenoglio, 1989).

After determining that a client is a battered woman, a counselor can attempt to understand the phenomenological view of the woman without judging her. It may be helpful for you to have an idea of some of the beliefs these women have based on previous cases of counselors working at battered women's centers and shelters. Woods (1992) says that many of these women were brought up to take care of men and believe it is their role to nurture their partner when he's hurt.

Also, the woman may have been convinced by books, the media, or other mental health professionals that she is a codependent and is the sick one for deciding to stay. Rather than acknowledging that women in our society are socialized to be dependent, she may be judging herself and calling herself weak for staying.

Other women may not even be aware they are in an abusive relationship, and you may have to ease the client into accepting this idea and giving up denial. When a counselor begins to suspect that a client may be in an abusive relationship, it may be appropriate to explore various behaviors she has experienced with her partner. The next list presents various behaviors, feelings, and dynamics that are typical in relationships when a woman is being battered and abused. Crisis counselors may use this information to guide their questions with a woman to ascertain whether she is being abused. These behaviors may also be used to educate the woman about typical patterns experienced by other women going through what she has been going through which might serve the purpose of validating and normalizing her experiences. If she has experienced many or most of these patterns, she is most likely in a battering relationship and educating her about the cycle of abuse and battered woman's syndrome may also be helpful. When trying to help someone identify whether she is in an abusive relationship, counselors should inquire about the patterns presented in Box 10.8.

Box 10.8   Typical Patterns Seen in Abusive Relationships

The partner has:

- Ignored her feelings
- Ridiculed or insulted women as a group
- Ridiculed or insulted her most valued beliefs, religion, race, heritage, or class
- Withheld approval, appreciation, or affection as punishment
- Continually criticized her, called her names, shouted at her
- Humiliated her in private or public
- Refused to socialize with her
- Kept her from working, controlled her money, made all decisions
- Refused to work or share money
- Took car keys or money away from her
- Regularly threatened to leave or told her to leave
- Threatened to hurt her or her family
- Punished or deprived the children when angry at her
- Threatened to kidnap the children if she left
- Abused, tortured, or killed pets to hurt her
- Harassed her about affairs he imagined she was having
- Manipulated her with lies and contradictions
- Destroyed furniture, punched holes in walls, broke appliances
- Wielded a gun in a threatening way
- Thoughts or questions that the woman may have had:
- Does she often doubt her judgment or wonder if she is crazy?
- Is she often afraid of her partner and does she express her opinion less and less freely?
- Has she developed fears of other people and does she tend to see others less often?
- Does she spend a lot of time watching for her partner's bad, and not-so-bad, moods before bringing up a subject?
- Does she ask her partner's permission to spend money, take classes, or socialize with friends?
- Is she frightened of her partner's temper?
- Is she often compliant because she is afraid to hurt her partner's feelings or is afraid of her partner's anger?
- Does she have the urge to rescue her partner when, or because, her partner is troubled?
- Does she find herself apologizing to herself or to others for her partner's behavior when she is treated badly?
- Has she been hit, kicked, shoved, or had things thrown at her by her partner when he was jealous or angry?
- Does she make decisions about activities and friends according to what her partner wants or how her partner will react?
- Does she drink or use drugs?

Source: Southern California Coalition on Battered Women, 1989.

Intervening with Battered Women

The purpose of intervention with a battered woman is to encourage her to act for her own well-being and safety. The five goals of intervention with a battered woman are:

1. Let her know help is available.
2. Give her specific information about resources.
3. Document the battering with accurate medical records.
4. Acknowledge her experiences in a supportive manner.
5. Respect her right to make her own decisions.

While you are helping her identify the battering and her perspective, you will also be offering her your knowledge of battering and reframing some of her ideas. In addition, the crisis worker will offer empowering and supportive comments as well as suggest resources such as books, shelters, or groups.

Education Woods (1992) believes it is also important to give the woman various facts about battering presented at the beginning of this section. This will help her see she is not alone. She needs to be told as well that the violence usually increases in intensity and frequency and that her batterer needs professional help if he is ever to change.

Reframes Woods (1992), like most feminists working in the battered women's movement, believes that someone needs to tell the woman that the batterer has the problem and nothing she can do will prevent the next battering episode. This goes against the woman's belief that if she only had dinner ready, had the kids quiet, made the bed, and so on, he wouldn't get upset. Pointing out to her that he is sick and needs help from a professional may be accepted by her.

Another reframe has to do with her belief that she is weak for staying and for using drugs and alcohol. The crisis worker might reframe these behaviors as evidence of strength. Her behavior can be equated to that of a prisoner-of-war who learns how to get what he or she needs to survive. Her weakness is now strength. This new perspective can often turn her perspective around, so she starts to believe that she has strength to take new action with the crisis worker's support.

Cusick (1992) also agrees that the "therapist must show the client that she has orchestrated her own survival and has the skills to continue to do so" (p. 48).

Empowerment and Support The last thing the battered woman needs is for someone else to make decisions for her about what she should do. The crisis worker may find it very stressful *not* to make decisions, because often the battered woman client will choose to stay with her batterer and be abused again. Crisis workers must pay attention to their own frustrations and feelings of helplessness with this population. It is easy for a counselor to fall prey to secondary PTSD while working with clients who have been assaulted repeatedly.

Remember to consult with other counselors when you become aware of these feelings.

Typically, a battered woman has had every decision made for her by the batterer, so the best thing the counselor can do is provide her with choices and support them. The counselor can give her names, phone numbers, and suggestions. The woman's main concern will often be, "How am I going to be safe?" The counselor may let her know she is most at risk when she leaves her batterer but that if she wishes, a plan can be made that will ensure her safety.

Helping her explore her own resources, such as family, friends, or church associates, is a good idea before you offer your own ideas. Battered women's shelters are usually free and should be used as a last resort. They are not like resort hotels, and a considerable amount of freedom is lost in a shelter. However, if there is nowhere else to go or no funds, the shelter is a great resource.

Following is an outline presented by Judy Bambas, volunteer coordinator at the Women's Transitional Living Center, on how to provide effective support for a battered woman:

1. Let her know you believe her.
   "Many women have been beaten by their partners."
   "I'm glad you've told me about the abuse."
2. Let her express her feelings. She has a right to be angry, scared, and so on. This may be the first time she is feeling safe enough to express anger over the abuse.
   "You seem very afraid of your partner."
   "You seem nervous talking about being abused."
   "You seem very angry about being abused."
3. Express your concern for her safety and the safety of her children. She may deny that abuse occurs or deny the level of danger to herself or her children.
   "This injury shows you are in great danger. You have a right to be safe."
   "Your safety is important. I'm very concerned about you and your children."
4. Let her know that help is available. Keep information at hand to share with her about help lines, shelters, counseling, and other resources. Ask her if she wants to report the abuse to the police. Explain slowly and carefully the choices available to her. She may need time and a safe place before she makes any decisions.
   "I have information that can help you."
   "There are many people in the community who can help you."
5. Reinforce the idea that nobody deserves to be beaten. She tends to believe some of the myths about domestic violence even though they may contradict her own reality. Remind her that she is not the cause of the beatings.
   "No one deserves to be hit."
   "You aren't the reason he hits you."

6. Realize that she may be embarrassed and humiliated about the abuse. She may worry that those who have offered to help in the past (e.g., family and friends) will be too burned out to help this time. Support her desire for help now. "You may feel embarrassed, but there are many women who have told me they are abused."

7. Be aware of the effects of isolation and control through fear. The woman may be physically or socially isolated, or both, due to location, language, intimidation, economic dependence, and other factors. Remind her that she is not alone. Connecting with others, through services such as support groups, can help break the isolation that battered women experience. Support her efforts to reach out to others. "You are not alone. Others can help and understand. I have information that may help you."

8. Assure her that you will not betray her trust. "What you share with me is confidential. My concern is for your safety."

9. Document the battering with specific information in her medical record. Her medical records may be used as evidence if she decides to press charges against the batterer. Be specific in description and sites of injuries. If the patient says that abuse is the source of the injuries, note, "Patient stated …," then continue the statement with who injured whom with what. If the patient refers to an instrument or weapon used by the abuser, note that in her record. If the injuries are inconsistent with the patient's explanation, make a note of it. If you suspect battering but the patient denies it, note "suspected abuse" in her record. Your notes may help identify her as battered on a future visit.

10. Remember that she may have other problems that demand immediate intervention. She may lack food or housing or be unable to care for her children or herself. Make appropriate referrals. If she is staying in a hospital, she may fear that the batterer will visit her. She may want her location to be kept confidential. "It seems you have a concern about housing. I have information about other resources."

The Batterer

Is there ever hope for a batterer? Can he be cured? Can marriage counseling help? The answers to these questions are tricky because they depend on the man and his motivation. According to Woods (1992), there is only a one percent success rate for batterer treatment programs. Despite this very low estimate, some studies do show that court-ordered counseling may help.

A 1990 outcome study compared 120 court-referred abusers with a group of 101 nonreferred abusers. Results indicated that 75 percent of court-referred men who attended court-sponsored counseling reduced their recidivism rate. Another 1990 study found that after counseling, abusive men had not committed violent acts for one year. Based on these studies, the Family Service Center of the Marine Corps in San Diego established a model program to combat domestic violence (Barnett & La Violette, 1993, pp. 126–127).

Other studies have suggested that short-term (6–12 weeks) psychoeducational batterer-intervention programs have helped some batterers to stop physical violence in the short term but were inadequate in stopping abuse over time. Some of the batterers even became more sophisticated in their psychological abuse and intimidation after attending such programs (American Psychological Association, 1996, p. 85).

More and more battered women's shelters are including batterers' programs in their facilities. Many more therapists are offering groups for this population, who really need the help. Judges are mandating counseling instead of jail time when a man is charged and convicted of battering his partner, a trend that demonstrates a greater focus on the man's part in the problem.

Arambarri (2005) suggests that these groups should focus more on power and control rather than anger management. Many times these batterers are referred to anger management groups led by therapists who are not specifically trained in domestic violence. She believes that unless the power and control issues are dealt with, the batterer may not be dealing with the real problem.

The alternative to counseling and jail may be a restraining order, by which the man is prohibited from physical proximity to the woman. However, recent statistics indicate that more than two-thirds of the restraining orders obtained by women against intimates who raped or stalked them were violated, and approximately one-half of the orders obtained by women against intimates who physically assaulted them were violated (U.S. Department of Justice, 2000). Although protection orders are a good idea, they aren't sufficient in preventing further violence. It would seem then that counseling is still an essential aspect of domestic violence prevention.

A Phenomenological View of the Batterer

It is possible that crisis workers will on occasion interview a batterer. This man may or may not see himself as a batterer, may or may not have chosen to seek help, and may or may not be amenable to intervention, depending on his personal and social resources. If a man somehow lands in a counselor's office (perhaps brought in by his partner or for a seemingly unrelated issue) and the crisis worker begins to suspect that battering may be an issue in the home, there are various factors that can aid the counselor and the client in recognizing that he is an abusive partner. Counselors are encouraged to proceed slowly and carefully when questioning these men in order to lessen resistance to intervention and to reduce denial when possible. Below is a list of characteristics typical of battering partners that counselors may consider asking about when ascertaining whether the suspected partner is abusive. The counselor might ask the person being abused if many of these qualities exist in the suspected abusive partner. Once the woman or the man sees how many of these qualities exist, they may be able to see the reality of the abusive relationship. Some of the personal characteristics of batterers are:

- They are very jealous.
- They sulk silently when upset.
- They have an explosive temper.

> Emotional distress
>
> Impairments in functioning
>
> Suicidal ideation
>
> Validation statements
>
> Educational statements
>
> Empowerment statements
>
> Reframes
>
> Coping strategies

Box 10.9   Cases to Role-Play

Case 1 A 14-year-old girl comes to this clinic because her mother believes something is wrong; her daughter's grades have been going downhill, and she does not like the people her daughter hangs around with at school. The girl's father has been having a sexual relationship with her since she was seven years old. She does not want to tell anyone because he threatened to throw her out of the house if she told. Her mother appears to be happy with him.

Case 2 A 47-year-old man, who is an elder at his church, comes to counseling. He runs his own business, which is very successful. He lives in a high-class neighborhood and everyone believes he is an ideal citizen and parent. He is raising three children on his own because his wife died two years ago. He has come in because for the last year he's been taking out his frustrations on his oldest child, who is nine years old. He has broken the boy's arms twice and has hit him with a board on several occasions. He realizes he needs help.

Case 3 A woman brings her family in because she and her spouse were reported for child neglect. She tells the interviewer that she is very upset by the false statement. She is a very religious person, and her children are very well taken care of. They eat at specific times and are not allowed to snack. During the interview, the children are going through the wastepaper baskets looking for food. The mother tells you that they missed breakfast this morning and will have to miss another meal because good children do not miss meals.

Case 4 A very upset 25-year-old woman comes to you. Her husband has threatened to kill her four-year-old son. Her son is not the child of her husband. Last night her husband was drinking, and her son was bothering him. He hit the boy and gave him a black eye. It is the first time he has hit her son. Usually, he takes his frustrations out on her. She tells you not to tell anyone because she is afraid of what her husband would do if he found out that he had been reported.

Case 5 A 27-year-old nurse comes to you. She is working to put her husband through medical school. She is complaining about being unassertive. She sits uneasily in the chair. When she moves, she sometimes grimaces in pain. She loves her husband and wants to please him but does not think she can. Due to her lack of sexual responsiveness, he sometimes gets extremely angry and does things.

Case 6 A 65-year-old woman comes to you. She lives in a retirement trailer village with her husband, who is a retired salesman. She comes to the session crying. Her mouth is cut and her right eye is swollen and bruised. She expresses anger and hatred toward all men. Her husband beat her last night because there was too much grease on his plate. She wants to leave but is afraid. He has threatened to kill her if she tries to leave.

Chapter Review

Abuse of children, the elderly, and of intimate partners is prevalent in most societies. Children and elderly are considered vulnerable and therefore laws have been enacted that mandate counselors to report suspected physical, sexual, and general neglect abuse of these clients to various protective service agencies. Working with the victims and the perpetrators is challenging because the abuse is often done by family members. Spousal abuse is universal across all cultures and requires knowledge about the battering cycle and battered woman's syndrome.

Answers to Pre-Chapter Quiz

1. F   2. F   3. T   4. T   5. T   6. T   7. F   8. T   9. T   10. F

Key Terms for Study

AMACS (adults molested as children): Adults who often manifest PTSD because of the unresolved emotional residue of childhood sexual abuse. Support groups for this population are increasing.

battered woman syndrome: A form of PTSD frequently manifested by women who are continually beaten by their domestic partners. Often, the woman develops a sense of helplessness and hopelessness. She does not consider leaving her abuser; rather, she focuses on surviving the abuse. She is often in a daze.

battering cycle: The events leading to, through, and away from domestic violence. The cycle begins in the honeymoon period, when both partners are in love and feel happy. The tension builds and eventually an explosion happens, either verbally or physically. After the explosion, the batterer feels relieved and seeks forgiveness, and the honeymoon begins again. Eventually, the honeymoon period goes away, and the couple oscillates between tension and violence.

child abuse accommodation syndrome: A protective condition in which an abused child maintains secrecy about the abuse, permits it to reoccur, and, even if the abuse is accidentally disclosed, tries to suppress it.

child protective services agency: A county or state agency established to protect children from abuse by investigating reports of child abuse and intervening when necessary.

infant whiplash syndrome/shaken baby syndrome: A very serious form of child abuse that results when a baby is shaken. The shaking causes the brain to roll around in the skull cavity. This abuse can lead to brain damage or death.

mandated reporting laws: Laws requiring professionals such as counselors, teachers, and medical personnel who work with children to report any suspicions of child abuse to either a child protective services agency or a law enforcement agency. Exactly who is required by law to report and the procedures for reporting vary from state to state.

nonperpetrating parent: This refers to the parent who has not actually abused the child directly. This parent may or may not know of the abuse and may or may not try to stop it.

perpetrator: This refers to a person who abuses someone either physically or sexually.

substantiated: This is the legal term used to indicate that a child abuse claim has been investigated by officials and found to fit the legal criteria for abuse.

References

American Psychological Association. (1996). *Violence and the family: Report of the American psychological association presidential task force on violence and the family* (p. 85). Washington, DC: Author.

Arambarri, P. (2005). *Domestic violence 101.* Presentation given at the 7th Annual Conference on Domestic Violence and Victim Advocacy: Through the Lens of Culture. Fullerton, CA: Western State University College of Law.

Barnett, O. W., & La Violette, A. D. (1993). *It could happen to anyone: Why battered women stay.* Newbury Park, CA: Sage.

Caffaro, J. V. (1992). A room full of fathers. *California Therapist, 4*(2), 37–44.

California Department of Justice's Bureau of Med-Cal Fraud & Elder Abuse and Crime & Violence Prevention Center in conjunction with AARP. (2002). *A citizen's guide to preventing & reporting elder abuse.* Author.

Campbell, D. W. (1993). Nursing care of African-American battered women: Afrocentric perspectives. *AWHONN's Clinical Issues, 4*(3), 407–415.

Child Welfare Information Gateway. (2010). *Child abuse and neglect fatalities: Statistics and interventions.* Retrieved January 13, 2010, from http://www.childwelfare.gov/pubs/factsheets/fatality.cfm

Colao, F., & Hosansky, T. (1983). *Your child should know.* Handout from M. Wash of the California Department of Social Services at California State University, Fullerton, CA.

Report on the Conditions of Children in Orange County (2012). Orangewood Children's Foundation & the Center for Community Collaboration. Orange, CA: Author. CSUF at (657)278-5681 or hhd.fullerton.edu/ccc/ and Orangewood Children's Foundation at (714)704-8777.

Cusick, M. (1992). When your client has been battered. *California Therapist, 4*(4), 47–49.

Fenoglio, P. (1989). *Battered women and their treatment at the woman's transitional living center.* Presentation at California State University, Fullerton, CA.

Florida Governor's Task Force on Domestic and Sexual Violence. (1997). *Florida mortality review project* (p. 45). Table 11.

Gorey, K. M., & Leslie, D. R. (1997). The prevalence of child sexual abuse: Integrative review adjustment for potential response and measurement biases. *Child Abuse & Neglect (Elsevier Science Ltd.)*, 21(4), 391–398.

Huisman, K. A. (1996). Wife battering in Asian American communities: Identifying the service needs of an overlooked segment of the U. S. Population. *Violence against Women*, 2(3), 260–283.

Kugler, D. (1992). An opposing view on partner abuse. *California Therapist*, 41, 43–45.

National Center on Child Abuse Prevention. (2005). *Statistics on child abuse during 2002*. Washington, DC: U.S. Department of Health and Human Services. Retrieved from http://nccanch.acf.hhs.gov/pubs/statsinfo/nis3.cfm

National Child Abuse Statistics. (2010). Retrieved on January 13, 2010, from http://www.childhelp.org/resources/learning-center/statistics

National Women's Health Information Center. (2000). *Violence against women. Office on women's health: U.S. Department of health and human services*. Retrieved November 5, 2001, from www.4woman.gov /violence/index.htm

Orange County Social Services Agency. (1982). *Battering parent syndrome: Handout #7*. Santa Ana, CA: Author.

Richie, B. E. (1988). *Understanding family violence within U.S. Refugee communities: A training manual*. Washington, DC: Refugee Women in Development, Inc.

Segel-Evans, K. (1991, July–August). The dangers of traditional family therapy when intervening in domestic violence. *California Therapist*, 45–48.

Sorenson, S. B. (1996). Violence against women: Examining ethnic differences and commonalties. *Evaluation Review*, 20(3), 123.

Southern California Coalition on Battered Women. (1989). *Am I in a battering relationship?* Santa Monica, CA: Author.

Tjaden, P., & Thoennes, N. (1998). *Prevalence, incidence, and consequences of violence against women: Findings from the national violence against women survey*. Washington, DC: National Institute of Justice, Centers for Disease Control and Prevention: Research in Brief.

Thompson, M. P., & Maslow, N. J. (2000). Partner violence, social support, and distress among inner-city African American women. *American Journal of Community Psychology*, 28(1), 127–143.

Tower, C. C. (1996). *Child abuse and neglect* (3rd ed.). Boston: Allyn & Bacon.

U.S. Department of Justice. (2000). *National violence against women survey*. Washington, DC: Author.

U.S. Department of Justice, Bureau of Justice Assistance. (1993). *Family violence: Interventions for the justice system.* Washington, DC: Author.

Volpp, L., & Main, L. (1995). *Working with battered immigrant women: A handbook to make services accessible.* San Francisco, CA: Family Violence Prevention Fund.

White, E. C. (1994). *Chain, chain, change: For black women in abusive relationships.* Seattle, WA: Seal Press.

Woods, K. (1992). *Domestic violence fact sheet.* Presentation at California State University, Fullerton, CA.

Crises Related to Substance Abuse

_____ 1. Marijuana is no longer a problem because it is legal.

_____ 2. The fastest growing drug problem is the nonmedical use of prescription pills.

_____ 3. LSD and crystal methamphetamine are the same type of drug.

_____ 4. The misuse and abuse of alcohol remains the number one problem in the field of substance and alcohol abuse.

_____ 5. A codependent often focuses on controlling the drug abuse of a significant other.

_____ 6. Withdrawing from heroin is always lethal.

_____ 7. Crack is a form of cocaine.

_____ 8. 12-step groups are considered obsolete for treating substance abuse.

_____ 9. AA groups are run by highly specialized professionals who have studied the physiological effects of drugs.

_____ 10. Ecstasy is considered a safe drug.

The media, celebrities, and politicians have been campaigning against drug abuse since the War on Drugs began under the Nixon Administration in the late 1960s and early 1970s. This War on Drugs escalated with the "Just Say No" and "Red Ribbon Week" campaigns of Nancy Reagan during the 1980s. Although drug use has been accepted by certain individuals in our society since narcotics such as morphine and cocaine

were first introduced in the late 1880s, it has never really been socially acceptable to be a drug addict. The counterculture of the 1960s and 1970s set forth slogans such as "tune in," "trip out," "experience," "turn on," and "try it, you'll like it," and for many disgruntled youth drug use was "in." However, although many people use and misuse drugs (illicit and legal) as we proceed into the twenty-first century, drug abuse is no longer respected in the way it was during those counterculture years. That is not to say that there is zero tolerance for drug use in our nation. Over the past decade several states have legalized recreational marijuana use or have decriminalized its use. Alcohol remains legal and the most widely misused drug, and the abuse of prescription drugs, in particular painkillers, is rampant.

Drug Use Statistics in the Twenty-First Century for the United States

In 2007, 38,371 people died of drug-induced causes, up from 19,128 in 1999.

There is a drug-induced death every 15 minutes which exceeds death from injuries to firearms, suicides, and other homicides.

In 2007, one in eight weekend nighttime drivers tested positive for illicit drugs.

In 2009, 10.5 million Americans reported driving under the influence of an illicit drug.

Annual averages for 2002–2007 indicate that more than 8.3 million youths lived with a parent who was dependent on alcohol or an illicit drug.

In 2009, 23.5 million people needed treatment for an alcohol or drug problem.

In 2008, there were approximately two million visits to emergency departments related to drug misuse (Brohl & Ledford, 2012).

What Is Substance Abuse?

Essentially, substance abuse deals with the use, and in some cases, dependence on most street drugs, prescribed medications, and alcohol. Formal psychiatric diagnostic labels found in the *Diagnostic and Statistical Manual of Mental Disorders* (DSM) do not use the terms *alcoholic* and *drug addict*, but instead refer to individuals commonly called these labels as suffering from either substance or alcohol dependence or substance or alcohol abuse. The DSM-IV defines **alcohol abuse** as repeated use despite recurrent adverse consequences and **alcohol dependence** as alcohol abuse combined with **tolerance**, withdrawal, and an uncontrollable drive to drink (American Psychological Association, 1996). The National Council on Alcoholism and Drug Dependence and American Society of Addiction Medicine define alcoholism as a chronic disease characterized by impaired control over drinking, preoccupation with the drug alcohol, use of alcohol despite adverse consequences and distortions in thinking (Morse & Flavin, 1992). The DSM-IV categorizes addiction into three stages: preoccupation/anticipation, binge/intoxication, and withdrawal/negative affect (1994).

Types of Drug Abuse Crises

When dealing with substance abuse problems, the crisis worker can be most effective when the person is truly in crisis. A crisis condition is needed to confront clients successfully about the negative impact the drug is having on their functioning. Until a drug abuser truly feels the consequences of the drug or alcohol abuse, there is very little motivation to seek help. Sometimes these consequences are referred to as **bottoming out**. Crisis counselors must identify what specific consequences the person is suffering from due to the drug or alcohol use and eventually help the person see the connection between the abuse and effects on his or her life. Often, a drug or alcohol abuser seeks counseling because a loved one has threatened to leave if help is not sought. Other times, a person may suffer from a medical condition related to the abuse. Sometimes, a legal situation arises that precipitates seeking help, and finally, at times the abuser becomes psychologically overwhelmed by the negative effects of a drug and becomes suicidal or paranoid.

Family Crises

At some point, the spouses, children, or parents of a drug or alcohol abuser decide they simply will not continue to tolerate the abuser's behaviors and use. They frequently will put pressure on the user to get help. Formal Interventions may be sought. This procedure was brought to light in the television show, Intervention, in which a professional counselor guides family and friends in confronting the user with love. An addict may decide to seek help when confronted with the idea that he or she may lose his or her family and friends.

Medical Crises

Medical problems are most severe when alcohol or barbiturates are the substance of abuse. Seizures, heart attacks, strokes, and liver failure are some of the common reasons for hospitalization. For someone who is physiologically dependent on either of these two categories of drugs, medical detoxification is necessary because life-threatening complications can occur when a person tries to withdraw from the drug.

Despite the many stereotypes about heroin withdrawal, the medical risk is actually not serious. To the heroin addict, however, coming off the drug feels like a crisis of enormous proportions. For several days, the addict experiences flu-like symptoms that often prompt a visit to an emergency room. Although heroin addicts in withdrawal may feel as though they are dying, they are seldom in danger. Most medical facilities encourage abrupt and complete (cold turkey) withdrawal. Some outpatient clinics provide an alternative to heroin called methadone. These clinics allow the addict to withdraw from heroin slowly under the supervision of medical professionals while taking the substitute, methadone.

Medical crises also occur with abuse of stimulants, such as cocaine, crack, or crystal meth (methamphetamine). Some users have seizures or heart attacks and require emergency medical treatment. These events can be life threatening, but they can also pave the way for clients to confront the addiction and do something about it.

At times, drug users take more than one drug, such as ecstasy, alcohol, and marijuana, and have negative reactions. They may pass out or get ill and need to be taken to a hospital. Adolescents are particularly at risk for this type of medical emergency because they do not often think before they take drugs, especially at "rave" parties and other social gatherings.

Legal Crises

Another reason that substance abusers and their families may seek crisis intervention is because of an arrest or some type of court-ordered mandatory counseling. In a 2009 study of arrestees in 10 major areas across the country, drug use among the arrestee population is much higher than in the general population. Among the areas surveyed, arrestees testing positive for illicit drugs ranged from 56–82 percent with marijuana being most common, followed by cocaine, opiates, and methamphetamine (Brohl & Ledford, 2012). During 2007, there were 109,444 juveniles arrested for drug abuse violations. These statistics indicate that there will be a substantial amount of individuals and families dealing with legal issues as a result of drug use. Often, counselors are needed to help these families navigate the criminal justice system, and counseling may even be an alternative to serving time in jail. The media is filled with cases of celebrities being offered drug rehab rather than doing time in jail. Many mental health counselors specialize in working with alcohol and drug abuse issues and various states have certifications for these professionals.

A common arrest for alcohol abusers is drunk driving or public drunkenness. Most states require not only a fine but also counseling and participation in **Alcoholics Anonymous** as part of the sentence for these crimes.

In addition to being arrested for being under the influence of alcohol or drugs, a person may be arrested for drug possession or sale of drugs. Because of overcrowding in jails and prisons, many diversion programs have been established to provide rehabilitation in lieu of incarceration in traditional correctional facilities. These programs almost always include counseling and education. Diversion programs are especially common for juveniles who are caught with drugs at school. They often lead to increased family involvement as well as cessation of abuse by the teenager.

At times, a state's child protective services agency may discover that parents are substance abusers, and the workers will remove the children from the home. The agency may require the parents to enter counseling as a condition of having their children returned to them. The premise for this condition is that having one's children taken away should be a motivator for parents to stop the substance abuse; unfortunately, the desired result is not always obtained.

Substance abuse is often related to domestic violence against a spouse, so similarly, a person convicted of domestic violence may be required to enter substance abuse treatment as part of his or her sentence.

Psychological Crises

Many people seek crisis counseling because of intense anxiety and depression associated with both the use of certain drugs and the sensation of "coming down" after the drug effects wear off. Most of the drugs in the "speed" category create feelings of paranoia when too much is ingested or during the phase following a major binge. People who snort cocaine, smoke crack cocaine, snort or inject crystal meth, or take Ritalin experience a sense of unreality and often have delusions that they are being followed or are in danger. In addition, a profound depression often follows several days of using and can precipitate suicide attempts or ideation.

Lysergic acid diethylamide (LSD) has long been associated with "bad trips," or adverse reactions to its ingestion. The affected person may be **pseudopsychotic** and delusional to the point of not being in control of his or her mind. People in this state need to have someone with them constantly to talk them through these **derealized** and **depersonalized** feelings. They need to be continually told that all the bizarre sensations they are experiencing are a result of the LSD and that in 8–12 hours, the trip will end.

Lastly, many people who abuse alcohol and drugs suffer from ongoing depression. Over 50 percent of suicides are related to alcohol or drug dependence with about 25 percent of alcoholics committing suicide. In adolescents, the figure may be up to 70 percent (Miller, Mahler, & Gold, 1991).

Alcohol: The Most Common Drug of Abuse

The term "alcoholism" was first used in 1849 by the European physician Magnus Huss to describe the systematic adverse effects of alcohol. In the United States, the use of the word "alcoholism" was popularized when Alcoholics Anonymous (AA) was founded in 1935. The "Big Book" used by AA describes alcoholism as an illness involving a physical allergy to alcohol and a mental obsession (Anonymous, 1939).

Although much media attention lately has focused on the use of speed and heroin, alcohol remains the number one most abused substance (Gabbard, 2001). Alcoholism affects the alcoholic's entire family, job performance, and health. It is extremely costly to the nation. Groups such as MADD (Mothers Against Drunk Driving) have lobbied for stricter drunk-driving laws in an effort to reduce alcohol consumption and the resulting deaths caused by drunk drivers. Other efforts to minimize alcohol use include an increase in sales taxes on alcohol products and the reduction of alcohol consumption by characters on television programs. In addition, many television movies and soap operas have been portraying realistic alcoholic dynamics in both teens and adults.

Unfortunately, alcohol, like drugs, is big business; corporations and underworld drug lords are not likely to encourage consumers to stop using. However, certain television commercials have been promoting responsible drinking.

The Alcoholic

The person with an alcohol problem may be called an alcoholic, *problem drinker*, or *alcohol abuser*. Many people working in the field of chemical dependency see alcoholism as a disease in which alcohol abuse covers up other underlying problems. Feelings such as shame, guilt, disgust, remorse, anger, and fear are denied by the alcoholic and anesthetized by alcohol consumption.

When alcoholics stop drinking they may exhibit symptoms of the *dry alcoholic* as they struggle with the emotions that used to be covered up by the effects of alcohol. Family members often complain about newly sober alcoholics because they often behave worse than when they were drinking. This phenomenon underscores the necessity of intervention on the part of the entire family while the alcoholic is recovering.

Family involvement is one aspect of alcoholism that makes it different from other types of diseases. Another aspect is that alcoholics can control their own disease and accept full responsibility for the consequences of their actions. This assumption is one of the basic tenets of AA. However, AA's 12-step program suggests that alcoholics participate in the program and accept the support of a sponsor as part of assuming responsibility and controlling the disease.

Although alcohol dependence probably has some genetic and biological components about 50–60 percent genetically determined, (Dick & Bierut, 2006), it is largely a psychological disorder in the beginning stages. In other words, a person experiences emotional problems, or was socialized in an alcoholic home, and turns to a substance (alcohol) to deal with life stresses. Once used, alcohol helps the person cope with stress by denying and minimizing his or her feelings. Addicts seem to have strong dependency needs and anger issues. Crisis workers need to be aware of these shame issues and build an environment of safety in which the client may express these emotions and still feel accepted by the counselor. Denial is strong in these types of clients because most of them who come in for counseling are still capable of functioning on the job; therefore, they do not see themselves as addicts.

Intervention

Treatment approaches for an alcoholic range from education about the disease of alcoholism to psychodynamic characterological analysis, family therapy, behavior modification, and detoxification. The most popular approach is involvement in AA. Since AA (like all **12-step programs**) is not costly for the client, it is by far the most practical treatment approach on a long-term basis that most would agree is necessary for an addict.

Before the long-term approaches in treating alcohol or other drug abuse are explored, some general techniques and suggestions need to be examined for dealing with the crisis state. Once the crisis is identified and the ABC model is applied, the client can be referred to the most appropriate setting. Following is a list of actions for the worker in a crisis situation:

- If the client is under the influence of alcohol or other drug, ask questions that will let you know what he or she took and when it was ingested. Do not try to conduct any type of therapy if the person is intoxicated.
- Safety comes first—your safety, that is. Also, do not let an intoxicated client leave your office in a car. You may be held responsible should the client be involved in a car accident.
- Try not to be alone in a building or office with an addict or alcoholic, especially one who is under the influence of the drug.
- If the client is not currently intoxicated, find out when the client last used drugs and what types of substances were used. Remember, polysubstance (the use of more than one drug) abuse is very common.
- Check for lethal combinations.
- Find out pertinent medical information, including prescribed medications and illnesses.
- Inquire about possible genetic predispositions by asking whether any family members are drug or alcohol abusers.
- Get a picture of what the person's abuse is like: When does the client typically use alcohol or other drug? With whom? Under stress?
- Get as much information as possible about the client's functioning level and relationships.
- Find out what in the person's life might be falling apart now.
- Find out why he or she keeps using alcohol or the drug.
- Once enough information has been gathered, begin to confront the client on how the alcohol or drug use is tied into his or her overall problems.
- Deal with the crisis presented.
- Never minimize the crisis or the abuse level.
- Deal with the family when possible.
- Encourage a crisis in the family when possible in order to disrupt the status quo. As we learned in Chapter 1, too little anxiety creates a state of inertia leaving the family very little motivation to change.
- Keep the focus on behavior that is a result of the abuse rather than focusing on the drinking or drug use itself. (Author's note: This is vital for crisis intervention to succeed.)

Prior to intervention, some counselors may prefer to conduct screenings to ascertain the level of substance abuse or dependence. The following list provides a variety of screening tools that assist counselors in assessing risk and identification of substance abuse.

1. The CAGE questionnaire: (a) Have you ever felt you needed to Cut down on your drinking? (b) Have people Annoyed you by criticizing your drinking? (c) Have you ever felt Guilty about drinking? (d) Have you ever

felt you needed a drink first thing in the morning (Eye-opener) to steady your nerves or get rid of a hangover? (Ewing, 1984).

2. The Alcohol Dependence Data Questionnaire: It helps distinguish a diagnosis of alcohol dependence from one of heavy alcohol use.
3. The Michigan Alcohol Screening Test: widely used by courts to determine appropriate sentencing especially by drunk drivers.
4. The Alcohol Use Disorders Identification Test: has been validated in six countries and is used internationally.
5. The Paddington Alcohol Test: designed to screen for alcohol-related problems amongst those attending Accident and Emergency departments.

Alcoholics Anonymous (AA)   Alcoholics Anonymous was created in 1935 by Bill Wilson, an alcoholic New York stockbroker, with the help of Robert Holbrook Smith. AA is a mutual self-help group that follows a holistic philosophy. During a meeting, members focus on a person's physical, psychological, emotional, and spiritual aspects. Members are able to explore such issues as how they feel about themselves, their jobs, their families, and other interpersonal relationships and issues dealing with self-image and self-esteem.

There are also purely educational meetings that attempt to break through denial and other defense mechanisms as well as provide information. Many people convicted of drunk driving are ordered by the court to attend these types of meetings, evidence of the respect society holds for the AA program. Box 11.1 presents the 12 steps of AA.

Lancer (2004) shares her view of the 12-step process from a Jungian perspective. She says that recovering from an alcohol or drug abuse problem is a process. The addict or abuser uses the 12 steps to work through the process. The steps are not necessarily linear, however. The process may be circular, that is, working through one step may affect the work a client has done in a

---

Box 11.1   The 12 Steps of AA

1. We admitted we were powerless against alcohol, and that our lives had become unmanageable.
2. Came to believe that a Power greater than ourselves could restore us to sanity.
3. Made a decision to turn our will and our lives over to the care of God, as we understood Him.
4. Made a searching and fearless moral inventory of ourselves.
5. Admitted to God, to ourselves, and to another human being the exact nature of our wrongs.
6. Were entirely ready to have God remove all these defects of character.
7. Humbly asked Him to remove our shortcomings.
8. Made a list of all persons we had harmed and became willing to make amends to all of them.
9. Made direct amends to such people wherever possible, except when to do so would injure them or others.
10. Continued to take personal inventory, and when we were wrong, promptly admitted it.
11. Sought, through prayer and meditation, to improve our conscious contact with God, as we understood Him, praying only for knowledge of His will for us and the power to carry that out.
12. Having had a spiritual awakening as the result of these steps, we tried to carry this message to alcoholics and to practice these principles in all our affairs.

previous step, work that the client thought was sufficient. In general, addicts deal with each of the following situations during their recovery process:

1. Facing the problem
2. Surrender
3. Self-awareness
4. Inventory: building self-esteem
5. Self-acceptance and transformation
6. Compassion for others
7. Tools for daily growth

Twelve-Step Facilitation (TSF)   Although 12-step groups are not facilitated by mental health clinicians, counselors and crisis workers may play a large part in facilitating the involvement of addicts with appropriate 12-step groups. This model of crisis intervention consists of a brief, structured, manual-driven approach to facilitating early recovery from alcohol and drug abuse and addiction. It is intended to be implemented on an individual basis in 12 to 15 sessions and is based on the principles of AA. The goal of TSF is to help clients accept the fact that they need to abstain from alcohol and drug use and surrender to the fact that they are helpless to control their behavior and therefore need to participate in a 12-step fellowship in order to remain sober (Nowinski, 2000).

Family Therapy   Another treatment model for alcoholism is to bring the family together and give the alcoholic a choice: either go into treatment or move out of the family home. The idea is that if the family system changes, the alcoholic can no longer live comfortably in it. To change requires much effort from codependent family members, who are used to, and comfortable with, enabling behaviors (discussed later in the chapter).

Once the alcoholic is in treatment, family sessions can be conducted to explore new patterns of living for all family members. Sometimes, when the alcoholic sobers up, marriages end because the alcoholic decides he or she no longer wants the partner, for Being intoxicated is often the only way the alcoholic could tolerate the spouse. Box 11.2 provides an example of how a family is affected by an alcoholic.

Medical Approaches   One of the most important aspects to consider in assessing the needs of a substance abuser is whether he or she needs medical intervention. Providing medical care is particularly vital when the abuser is physically addicted to alcohol, barbiturates, tranquilizers, or heroin. There are many types of withdrawal symptoms with each of these drugs, some of which are life threatening.

Detoxification usually takes 2–30 days, during which the person is in a hospital and provided with medical attention. People undergoing withdrawal are given various alternative drugs, such as minor tranquilizers, to ease them through this very difficult time. These drugs must be given in some cases to prevent seizures and convulsions.

Box 11.2   Example of a Family in Which Alcoholism Kept the Family Together

An attractive, articulate, successful 44-year-old woman came to therapy very much in crisis because her husband, whom she described as an alcoholic, had become verbally abusive to her children (his stepchildren) and she couldn't cope with this behavior. She believed that if only he would stop drinking, everything would be all right.

The husband had been drinking since they met, however, so there had never been any relationship based on sobriety. After a few individual sessions, she and the children confronted him and told him to stop drinking or they were moving out.

The husband stopped drinking for about one month. During this time, marital sessions were conducted in which the husband decided that he didn't want to be a part of this family emotionally. The wife found this unacceptable, so they decided to divorce.

Heroin addicts can more readily be detoxified abruptly (cold turkey) than other abusers, though this is not popular among this population of addicts. At times, they might receive a mild tranquilizer or begin a methadone program as a substitute for the heroin addiction.

Once the drug is out of the person's system safely, other psychological and social methods of intervention can be instituted. During the hospital stay, clients participate in many groups and activities, such as occupational therapy, recreational therapy, assertion training, educational classes, and groups for building self-esteem. Often, an individual therapist will be assigned to provide psychological counseling as well. A psychiatrist may also be part of the team approach and may prescribe such medications as antidepressants or lithium.

Some hospitals that have alcohol or drug rehabilitation programs have designed partial hospitalization programs or day-treatment programs. These offer the same groups and activities as inpatient facilities, but the client lives at home and goes to work during the day, attending the groups daily. This type of program has been widely accepted as more cost effective than residential treatment and is probably the way of the future. These hospitals offer a variety of therapies ranging from behavioral methods to social methods.

Behavior Modification Approaches   A number of behavior modification approaches are used with drug abusers. Two of them are discussed next.

Aversion Therapy   **Aversive conditioning** is based on Pavlov's classical conditioning model, which pairs noxious stimuli with the alcohol (or drugs). Schick Shadel started this treatment in 1935. Its popularity has lessened in recent years because its effects are not long lasting. After patients have been detoxified physiologically with the aid of antidepressants or mild tranquilizers, they are ready for this "throw-up" therapy. On an empty stomach, they drink two large glasses of salt water and take Emetine, a drug that makes them nauseated. A bottle of their favorite liquor is then placed in front of them. First they sniff it, then gargle and swallow it. They immediately vomit. This is repeated several times.

The next day, patients are given the "butterfly," a combination drink that smells like beer and continues the nausea. The third day, they are given a truth serum, sodium pentothal, and are asked if they want their favorite drink. If they say no, they are asked if they would like another kind of drink. If they say yes, the aversion process is repeated with that type of alcohol.

This same process is used for cocaine addicts with a substance that looks, tastes, and smells like cocaine. Treatment usually takes 10 days and costs about $11,000. After 30 days and 60 days, the patient returns for two-day follow ups.

Synanon   Charles E. Dederich, a former alcoholic, developed a confrontational style of group therapy in 1958. He started **Synanon**, a self-help therapeutic community based in a Venice, California, storefront and run by recovering addicts.

The basic goal of Synanon is to have drug abusers undergo a complete change in lifestyle; this includes abstaining from the drug, breaking patterns of criminal activity and learning job skills, developing self-reliance, and cultivating personal honesty. Counselors help residents confront their behavioral problems, mainly in group therapy sessions. A resident usually singles out another resident and confronts that person with an issue. The discussion goes from there.

Although Synanon emphasizes rejection of life outside the community during the program, reentry into society is a major goal (Orange County Register, 1990, p. M3).

Most communities have a few of these recovery, residential, or halfway houses, though the need far outweighs the availability. The Synanon approach is not practiced in its pure form in most homes, but the idea of change in social life is still a prominent component. Phoenix House is a popular example of one of these residential treatment facilities.

Biopsychosocial Model   Probably a more common type of residential program is a community in which the medical, psychological, and social aspects are treated. Gerry House West in Santa Ana, California, is an example of a successful home. Francis (1998) explains the philosophy of this one-year residential facility, where drug addicts live while they undergo structured treatment.

One of the beliefs of the staff is that drug use starts in adolescence as experimentation and rebellion. As the user continues into adulthood, the reason for the rebellion gets lost but the user still acts like an adolescent with many narcissistic thought patterns. The narcissism necessitates providing a lot of attention to these addicts, who need to feel special. Much of the therapy is cognitive based; the addict is forced to examine the many unrealistic thought patterns that lead to negative feelings and behaviors. Box 11.3 presents some typical irrational thoughts.

The treatment model progresses from complete containment and restriction to integration into the community. Much of the focus is on skill building and relapse prevention. A "trigger chart" has been developed to help clients look at their cognitive distortions and the ways in which those distortions lead to inappropriate behaviors.

Box 11.3   Irrational Thoughts Often Experienced by Drug Users

- Catastrophizing: The "Chicken Little" complex (i.e., everything is going to turn out badly).
- Personalizing: The tendency not to look for facts but instead think that everything is about me.
- Mind reading: "I know what they are thinking about me."
- Fallacy of fairness: "I've done what I'm supposed to do. Why aren't good things happening to me?"
- Always or never: Approaching life in absolutes.

Crisis intervention is a large part of the treatment. Effective crisis intervention begins with a containment and time-out so that clients may focus on their thoughts. The counselor then provides active listening so clients can feel heard and empowered. This approach, by the way, is exactly the way in which parents are often encouraged to communicate with an "acting-out" adolescent.

Brief Intervention for Alcohol Problems   Some clients may not need to be hospitalized or live in a residential facility. They may be able to control their drinking and function adequately by participating in a few sessions with a health professional who does not specialize in addiction treatment. This brief intervention therapy is most often used with clients who are not alcohol dependent; the goal may be moderate drinking rather than total abstinence. These clients may be abusing alcohol and may be at risk for developing alcohol-related problems. Miller and Sanchez (1993) proposed six elements summarized by the acronym FRAMES for this type of intervention. The crisis worker may offer feedback of personal risk, focus on the responsibility of the patient to change, give advice to change, offer a menu of ways to reduce drinking, create an empathetic counseling style, and encourage patients to believe in their own self-efficacy to make changes. Research has shown that brief intervention for alcohol problems is more effective than no intervention and often as effective as more extensive intervention (Bien, Miller, & Tonigan, 1993; Fleming, Barry, Manwell, Johnson, & London, 1997), so if clients refuse to go to a 12-step group or other forms of treatment, this type of approach may be effective.

The Codependent

In the past two decades, many books have been written dealing with the psychological and behavioral dynamics of the spouses and children of alcoholics and drug abusers. A **codependent** is an individual who is closely involved with the person who is dependent on alcohol or drugs and engages in behaviors that enable the alcohol or substance abuse or feels the need to control it, or both. The codependent experiences many of the same emotions as the substance abuser—guilt, resentment, fear, shame, and low self-esteem. The hallmark of a codependent, or **enabler**, is the need to be in control, whereby they do not allow users the dignity of living their own life as they choose. Instead, codependents' lives center around the activities of the users. They usually try to control the addicts' use of drugs or alcohol and spend a lot of time worrying about whether users are getting into trouble because of their addiction.

Davis (1982) has designed an outline that describes various enabling behaviors of the codependent. These are defense mechanisms that maintain the alcoholic family system in its disease form and are found in Box 11.4.

Adult Children of Alcoholics   Adult children of alcoholics are often codependents and enablers, who have been socialized in an alcoholic home. In this environment they learned about finances, relationships, jobs, isolation, and self-esteem. Adult children often develop problems in these areas because they did not learn realistic coping mechanisms for dealing with life's stresses. Instead, they learned to use denial in dealing with their feelings.

Treatment for the Codependent   Whereas about 40 percent of substance abusers seek mental health treatment because of outside pressure, a much larger percentage of the significant others of abusers seek counseling voluntarily. These people are often in a crisis state and feel nervous and depressed because they cannot control the drinking or substance abuse of their spouse, parent, or child.

As with all people involved in alcoholism, the crisis worker provides an atmosphere of warmth and safety, for these people have little trust in the world. Many have had to grow up early because of parental irresponsibility. They believe that they should be able to handle everything on their own because they have always had to do so.

Box 11.4   Defense Mechanisms of the Alcoholic Family

1. Denying: "He's not an alcoholic or other drug addict." As a result:
   a. expecting him to be rational
   b. expecting him to control his drinking
   c. accepting blame
2. Drinking with the alcoholic or using with the addict.
3. Justifying the use by agreeing with the rationalization of the alcoholic or addict (e.g., "Her job puts her under so much pressure.")
4. Keeping feelings inside.
5. Avoiding problems: keeping the peace, believing lack of conflict makes a good marriage.
6. Minimizing: "It's not so bad. Things will get better when ...."
7. Protecting the image of the alcoholic or user; protecting the alcoholic or user from pain or the codependent from pain.
8. Avoiding reality by numbing feelings with tranquilizers, food, or work.
9. Blaming: criticizing, lecturing.
10. Taking over responsibilities.
11. Feeling superior: treating the alcoholic or addict like a child.
12. Controlling: "Let's skip the office party this year."
13. Enduring: "This too shall pass."
14. Waiting: "God will take care of it."

Education works well with this population. Most are willing to read books that describe their personality patterns and needs. Also, educating them about substance abuse is helpful.

Reframing can be useful as well. Codependents often perceive themselves as being helpful to the user. It is easy to reframe this thinking by suggesting that their help is actually perpetuating the abuse. Rather than treating the user like a mature responsible adult, the codependent has taken away the user's dignity and respect.

Codependent people may present as though they are in full control. However, it is easy to show them how controlled they are by their significant other. The crisis worker can empower these people by releasing them from the responsibility of "fixing" the abuser. They must be shown that they need to develop their own life in a way that doesn't revolve around the addict if they are to regain self-control. Box 11.5 offers some ideas to help empower enablers and codependents.

Box 11.5   Ideas to Empower Enablers and Codependents

- Don't regard this as a family disgrace. Recovery from alcoholism can come about as in any illness.
- Don't nag, preach to, or lecture the alcoholic. Chances are he has already told himself everything you can tell him. He will take just so much and shut out the rest. You may only increase his need to lie or force him to make promises he cannot possibly keep.
- Guard against the "holier than thou" or martyr-like attitude. It is possible to create this impression without saying a word. An alcoholic's sensitivity is such that he judges other people's attitudes toward him more by small things than spoken words.
- Don't use the "if you loved me" appeal. Because the alcoholic's drinking is compulsive and cannot be controlled by willpower, this approach only increases guilt.
- Avoid any threat unless you think it through carefully and definitely intend to carry it out. There may be times, of course, when a specific action is necessary to protect the children. Idle threats only make the alcoholic feel you don't mean what you say.
- Don't hide the liquor or dispose of it. Usually this only pushes the alcoholic into a state of depression. In the end, he will simply find new ways of getting more liquor.
- Don't let the alcoholic persuade you to drink with him on the grounds that it will make him drink less. It rarely does. Besides, when you condone his drinking, he puts off doing something to get help.
- Don't be jealous of the method of recovery the alcoholic chooses. The tendency is to think that love of home and family is enough incentive for seeking recovery. Frequently the motivation of regaining self-respect is more compelling for the alcoholic when he turns to other people for help in staying sober. You wouldn't be jealous of the doctor if someone needed medical care, would you?
- Don't expect an immediate 100% recovery. In any illness there is a period of convalescence. There may be relapses and times of tension and resentment.
- Don't try to protect the recovering alcoholic from drinking situations. It is one of the quickest ways to push him into a relapse. He must learn on his own to say "no" gracefully. If you warn people against serving him a drink, you stir up old feelings of resentment and inadequacy. (Davis, 1982, pp. 1–2)

12-Step Groups You may also recommend groups to codependent clients. Several have been created on the model of Alcoholics Anonymous and use the 12-step, peer, and mutual self-help pattern. Al-Anon, Co-Dependents Anonymous (CO-DA), and Adult Children of Alcoholics (ACA) have been created for the spouses, relatives, and children of alcohol abusers. Their purpose is to help these individuals cope with their feelings and unproductive behaviors associated with trying to control and change the alcoholic. At these mutual support, self-help meetings, the members receive support for nonenabling behaviors, and their feelings of isolation are reduced. Because these 12-step groups are free, widely available, and effective, crisis workers should have knowledge about the ones in their community.

Illicit Drug Misuse

The next sections briefly examine other substance abuse issues. Most of the information about alcoholism also applies to these issues. The following sections should provide enough information about specific issues, however, that you will not be totally naïve when you come into contact with drug abusers. Most people realize that substance abuse is a serious national problem.

Speed: Cocaine, Crack, and Crystal Meth

Health Communications, Inc., has developed pamphlets that describe cocaine and other drugs. They are updated regularly and can be ordered from the organization at this address: Health Communications, Inc., 2119-A Hollywood Boulevard, Hollywood, FL 33020.

Cocaine is a central nervous system stimulant possessing both anesthetic and vasoconstricting properties. It produces a combination of amphetamine-like energy with the numbing (anesthetic) effect of some narcotics. It has been misclassified by the Drug Enforcement Administration for years as a narcotic. In recent years, cocaine use has increased rapidly, most notably in the educated middle-class population. In the year 2000, there were an estimated 1.2 million cocaine users and 265,000 crack users in the United States (U.S. Department of Health and Human Services, 2000). According to the 2008 National Survey on Drug Use and Health, close to 36.8 million Americans had tried cocaine at least once in their lifetime. Approximately 5.3 million had used cocaine in 2008 and 1.9 million had used cocaine in the past month (Substance Abuse and Mental Health Services Administration, 2009).

Cocaine is derived from the coca bush. The leaves are 1–4 inches in length and are harvested three times a year. The leaves are reduced to coca paste by the use of petroleum solvents, and the result of this manufacturing process is a white powder. Cocaine is rarely available in its pure form. Common additives are lactose, procaine, lidocaine, benzocaine, tetracaine, and amphetamines. The amphetamine enhances the high-energy effect and the other additives produce the anesthetic effect.

The most common way of using cocaine is by sniffing or snorting it up the nose. One popular technique is to form lines of cocaine on a mirror and sniff it through a straw or rolled-up dollar bill. The drug takes effect within three minutes after snorting. A riskier technique—shooting—is to dissolve the cocaine in water and inject it by needle; the drug takes effect in about 20 seconds. Shooting puts impurities into the blood, and shared needles can spread infectious diseases, including hepatitis and AIDS. The fastest way to get cocaine to the brain is by smoking it in a freebase form such as crack or rock. This creates a very intense high in less than 10 seconds. Smoking cocaine can cause addiction in weeks (StayWell Company, 1998, p. 5).

After ingesting low doses of cocaine, users usually experience a short-lived (20–30 minute) sense of exhilaration and euphoria. They tend to talk a lot and feel energetic and self-confident, but the exhilaration is very short-lived. After the initial euphoria, psychological depression, nervousness, irritability, loss of temperature sensations, and muscle tightening or spasms may occur. To prevent these coming-down effects, users must use the drug every 20 minutes or so.

Another form of cocaine is crack cocaine, that is, cocaine in smokeable (freebase) form. People have been smoking freebase for some time. Before crack was developed, however, they had to convert cocaine into freebase with highly flammable chemicals that only users were foolish enough to risk handling. You may remember the comedian Richard Pryor, who nearly died from burns caused by converting cocaine to freebase.

Now, there is a relatively safer way to convert cocaine into freebase. Ammonia or baking soda and water are used. The result is crack, so-called because of the crackling sound it makes when smoked. The crack looks like shavings or chips scraped from a bar of soap and is packaged in small plastic vials that sell for $10 to $20 each. Crack may be smoked through the stem of a specially designed glass pipe or sprinkled on tobacco or marijuana and smoked.

When smoked, crack triggers an explosive release of neurotransmitters in the brain and depletes the brain's supply of these natural substances, producing an intense craving for more stimulation. The user takes more and more crack to appease a craving that can never be satisfied.

Initially, the user will experience euphoria and excitement, but soon avoidance of coming down becomes the reason for using the drug. Crack is almost instantly addictive. As the addiction takes hold, the user experiences memory problems, insomnia, fatigue, depression, paranoia, irritability, loss of sexual drive, suicidal ideation and at times suicide attempts, and violent behavior.

Soon, crack becomes the most important thing in the user's life and overpowers other needs such as eating, sex, family life, personal health, and career. In addition to these effects, physical dangers are associated with crack use. About 64 percent of users report chest congestion, 40 percent have a chronic cough, and 7 percent say they have suffered brain seizures with loss of consciousness. Many others report chronic hoarseness; they produce black phlegm when they cough or suffer persistent bronchitis (National Council on Alcoholism of Orange County, 1986). According to the 2008 National Survey on Drug Use and Health, approximately 8.4 million people reported trying crack cocaine at least once during their lifetimes. Close to 1.1 million reported using crack in 2008, and 359,000 used in the past month (National Institute on Drug Use, 2008).

Another illegal drug in the speed family is crystal methamphetamine, or "meth." Its popularity reflects its low cost and its strong potency. In the 2008 National Survey on Drug Use and Health, 12.6 million individuals reported using methamphetamine at least once during their lifetimes; close to 850,000 reported using in 2008 and 314,000 reported using crystal meth in the past month (Substance Abuse and Mental Health Services Administration, 2009). This type of speed is a stimulant that is snorted, injected, or smoked as "ice." It can cause paranoia, weight loss, and disturbed sleep.

Crystal meth is highly addictive; the heavy addict often needs hospitalization to detoxify as well as participation in a 12-step program. The psychodynamics and treatment are similar to those for cocaine addicts and abusers. One major difference between speed and cocaine is that speed lasts longer. Unfortunately, long-term use often leads to paranoia, violence, and serial arrests or psychological crises. Methamphetamine is dangerous and can cause physical harm to the brain, heart, and general health. Users often binge for several days before taking a break from using it, a practice that takes a heavy toll on the body.

Effects of Cocaine and Speed on the Family

When cocaine or speed controls someone in the family, life for that family can't be normal. Dependence on these drugs makes the user behave in hurtful ways to family members. The drug occupies most of the user's time, money, and attention. The family often suffers from the following emotions:

- *Suspicion and insecurity:* This leads to frequent conflicts over drug use. Money and time become a focus of the family member's insecurities.
- *Resentment and disappointment:* Family members must often make unreasonable compromises. As a result of the user's focus on drugs, the family feels deprived because the joys of normal family living are sacrificed to the chemical dependency.
- *Isolation and hurt:* The user often withdraws from participation in the family. Often children and spouses feel they cause this isolation.
- *Fear and guilt:* The family often fears the consequences for the addict as well as for the family, often blaming itself for the addict's behaviors. (Staywell Company, 1998, pp. 10–11)

In order to help family members cope with the user's behaviors, the crisis worker can teach members how to stop enabling the user and how to properly intervene and help the addict get professional treatment. Once the family understands that it cannot fix the addict, it is free to return to healthy living.

Marijuana

People rarely seek crisis intervention for marijuana abuse; nonetheless, crisis workers should be familiar with it. Marijuana, or "pot," is widely used and may impair a person's functioning and coping while the person is in a crisis.

Also, rather than use sober coping strategies, many people use marijuana to deal with stress. Because it has been legalized in some states either for recreational use or medicinal use, our society may be moving toward more acceptance of marijuana use. Just as it would be difficult to convince someone that no one should drink a beer or a glass of wine, it is becoming increasingly difficult to convince young adults and adolescents of the horrors of marijuana use. However, it is still illegal in most states and at the federal level. Many employers give drug tests to either secure employment or retain employment. If someone shows up positive for marijuana on these tests, they may be subject to losing their job. This could create a crisis.

Marijuana is the most commonly used illegal drug. According to the National Survey on Drug Use and Health, in 2008 approximately 104 million Americans had tried marijuana at least once in their lifetime, which is about 41 percent of the U.S. population that is 12 years and older. Close to 28.5 million reported using marijuana in 2008 and 16.7 million used in the past month (Substance Abuse and Mental Health Services Administration, 2009).

Marijuana is the unprocessed dried leaves, flowers, stems, and seeds of the *Cannabis sativa* plant. Delta-9-tetrahydrocannabinol (THC) is thought to be the primary psychoactive or mind-altering compound in this plant. The drug is usually rolled with cigarette papers into a joint or reefer and smoked like a cigarette or in a pipe or "bong." Hashish is the solidified resin of the *Cannabis sativa* plant (Zimbardo, 1992, p. 129). It is usually smoked in a pipe as a brownish chunk and is many times stronger than marijuana. Marijuana and hashish may also be baked and eaten in brownies.

The common street names of marijuana are pot, weed, reefer, smoke, hooch, and dope. Its effects depend on the potency of the particular plant, experience of the user, and user's expectations. Some marijuana users describe an emotional state of increased sensory awareness to music, touch, light, and social interaction. Other users experience anxiety, fear, and withdrawal from social interaction because of drug-induced paranoia.

When marijuana use interferes with performance and safety on the job or creates problems at school, the pot user may be required to seek some form of help to quit using. Signs of marijuana dependence are hard to spot, but the following are some of the signs that may indicate chronic pot use:

- Absenteeism
- Erratic performance
- Errors in judgment
- Lack of fitness for duty
- Risk to coworkers
- Frequent accidents

Other psychological and social risks often associated with marijuana use include missed milestones such as graduation (the stoned person is in a "cloud" emotionally), emotional immaturity (feeling most comfortable in superficial relationships), and **amotivational syndrome** (lacking initiative) (Krames Communications, 1995, p. 6).

Signs that a student is using marijuana in school may include:

- Giving in to peer pressure
- Impaired short-term memory
- Low energy
- Low achievement (pp. 10–13)

Pot Smokers Anonymous or Narcotics Anonymous may be helpful for marijuana users. Individuals who use marijuana typically need to develop a social network of nonusing people with whom they can have fun and interact socially. Denial is a large part of the marijuana smoker's perception of his or her problem. This person minimizes the extent of use or the idea that it is a problem. The crisis interventionist may want to help the smoker explore what life is like when he or she is sober. Also, remember that the marijuana grown today is unusually potent compared with that grown even 10 years ago.

LSD (lysergic acid diethylamide)

LSD is also known as acid. It is taken orally in tablet form or licked off paper. A crisis worker may treat someone on a "bad trip" that has extreme panic associated with it. Many emergency room doctors and nurses as well as mental health workers have had to talk someone through a crisis state set off by LSD. According to the National Survey on Drug Use and Health, in 2008 approximately 36 million Americans reported lifetime use, 3.7 million reported using in the past year, and 1.1 million reported using in the past month (Substance Abuse and Mental Health Services Administration, 2009).

LSD distorts the person's sensory perception and sense of self. He or she may resemble a psychotic person because of having hallucinations and delusions. The effect usually lasts 10–12 hours, and the person needs comfort and reassurance that the feelings are due to the acid.

LSD has made a major comeback in the 1990s and into this century, perhaps because teenagers are trying to imitate the perceived excitement of teenagers in the 1960s. This drug can precipitate a psychotic reaction in otherwise normal teens, but it is less prevalent than other drugs.

Ecstasy (3,4-methylenedioxymethamphetamine, or MDMA) is another hallucinogen that has grown in popularity since the 1990s for adolescents and young adults. The 2008 National Survey on Drug Use and Health showed that approximately 12.9 million Americans have tried ecstasy in their lifetime, about 5.2 percent of the total population 12 years and older. The estimated number of past year users in 2008 was 2.1 million and close to 555,000 used the drug in the past month (Substance Abuse and Mental Health Services Administration, 2009). It was first synthesized by German chemists in 1912. It was considered for use as an appetite suppressant but was rejected because of its side effects (Harvard Mental Health Letter, 2001). Its effects are unpredictable and include extreme states of altered consciousness. It is often combined with other drugs and alcohol, leaving the young user in a vulnerable state. Ecstasy affects the body like a stimulant. Other effects have been reported, also, such as strong feelings of intimacy, which often lead to intimate revelations or personal decisions that are later regretted.

Many adolescents use LSD and ecstasy to imitate the perceived excitement of teenagers in the 1960s. These drugs are frequently associated with underground "rave parties," the locations of which are unknown to parents and authorities. The music is loud, and teens and young adults engage in wild dancing.

Heroin

Approximately 130,000 Americans used heroin in 2000 (U.S. Department of Health and Human Services). This drug is usually injected and is highly addictive. A person withdrawing from heroin often experiences flulike symptoms and may do anything to get a "**fix**" of the drug. Methadone is often prescribed in oral-liquid form to help addicts withdraw from heroin; and sometimes an addict may be talked through an abrupt (cold turkey) **withdrawal**.

Unfortunately, quitting permanently is very difficult because heroin covers up all pain and stress. When sober addicts must deal with normal life stresses, they are not prepared to cope; starting to use again is a strong temptation. Residential halfway-house programs are somewhat effective for heroin addicts, but as with all substance abusers, heroin users must make a complete lifestyle change to be cured.

Users usually start by snorting, then move into mainlining (injecting the drug directly into a vein). After three or four days, the physical craving is so strong that they feel they have no choice but to use the drug. At this point, they are using the drug to keep from getting sick. The term "kicking the habit" is derived from the miniconvulsions users often go through when withdrawing; they want to avoid this trauma at all costs (Turning Point, 1994).

As a result of the high rate of return to heroin use and because the user's life is completely wrapped up in how to get the next drug fix, this addiction needs a great deal of attention. Knowledge of how to work with this population is beneficial for crisis workers. Some mental health and medical health practitioners avoid working with heroin addicts because the addicts are so difficult, but the impact on the community (e.g., crime, AIDS, welfare) is significant and needs to be addressed. In conclusion, a crisis worker can only point the way and offer information about resources to substance abusers. The addict must do the rest. Give yourself a break and don't accept responsibility for substance-abuse clients.

Nonmedical Use or Abuse of Prescription Drugs

The abuse of prescription drugs is the fastest growing drug problem and account for the second most commonly abused category of drugs. These types of drugs include pain relievers, OxyContin, tranquilizers, stimulants, and sedatives. According to the 2008 National Survey on Drug Use and Health, 52 million Americans reported nonmedical use of prescription drugs at some point in their lifetimes, which is about 20 percent of the population over age 12.

TABLE 11.1 Drugs of Abuse and Their Effects

Drug	Method of Use	Effects
Alcohol	Drink	Depressant; euphoria, blackouts, slowed reaction time
Marijuana	Smoke	Euphoria, slowed reaction time, munchies (a strong craving to eat sweets and other junk food), amotivation syndrome
Cocaine	Snort	Upper; high, accelerated thoughts
Crack	Smoke	Increased activity, racing heart
Crystal meth	Snort	Paranoia, agitation
Heroin	Snort, inject	Depressant; euphoria, nodding out; highly addictive
Ecstasy	Take pill	Euphoria, opening of the mind, increased focus on feelings
LSD	Absorb into system by placing on tongue or swallowing a pill	Hallucinations, increased sensory stimulation

© Cengage Learning

Close to 6.2 million reported current use. Unfortunately, this data shows that 2.5 million persons used these drugs nonmedically for the first time in 2008 which averages out to about 7,000 new users per day! (Substance Abuse and Mental Health Services Administration, 2009).

Since many of these drugs cause physical dependence, treatment usually includes physician involvement to aid in detoxification. Crisis counselors often serve to help in the psychological aspect of the addiction by giving support, empowerment, and education.

Table 11.1 summarizes the various drugs of abuse and their effects.

Chapter Review

Substance abuse crises include issues that arise due to use of alcohol (the number one abused drug), illicit street drugs, and prescription drugs. An individual using these drugs may seek crisis counseling due to a legal, medical, psychological, or spiritual crisis. The precipitating event and the consequences of the substance abuse must be identified, and the person must face the reality of these facts and relate them to the substance abuse. Family members involved with substance abusers often participate in the abuse and show typical signs of enabling and are often referred to as codependents. They need intervention as well. Substance abuse has long been considered a family problem. Twelve step groups such as Alcohol Anonymous have been established for all and are considered effective treatment in the long run. Crisis workers are encouraged to facilitate substance abusers into working with these 12-step groups.

As you role-play the cases presented in Box 11.7, use the outline in Box 11.6 to assist you in proceeding through the ABC model. It encompasses the multitude of assessment needs, therapeutic interactions, and referral options.

Box 11.6   Drug and Alcohol Issues Assessment Tool

1. Assess the crisis
   a. What brought the person in?
   b. What triggered the crisis?
   c. Was it a medical issue?
   d. Was there a legal issue?
   e. Is there a significant other involved?
   f. Is the person suicidal?
2. Assess the impact of drug or alcohol use
   a. Assess typical use
      (1) How long has the abuse gone on?
      (2) How much?
      (3) When and where?
      (4) What is being used?
      (5) Remember, abusers tend to be in denial. Stay nonjudgmental!
   b. Identify how the abuse is related to the crisis
      (1) Help client experience how his or her distress is related to abuse.
      (2) Help client to see past problems related to abuse.
   c. Educate about abuse
      (1) Abusers and addicts are powerless over drugs and alcohol.
      (2) Although the substance used to be a friend, it is now working against the user.
      (3) Stay objective and supportive.
      (4) Don't confront denial. Educate about denial and relapse.
   d. Empowerment
      (1) Point out choices.
      (2) Help client see how new decisions can be made.
      (3) Show client how each experience can be a learning opportunity.
      (4) Relapse can even be a learning opportunity.
   e. Reframe when possible
      (1) Help client think differently about behaviors.
      (2) Perhaps abuse of drugs and alcohol is a form of self-medication.
      (3) If so, then what is being medicated?
      (4) Does the client show signs of insecurity, depression, fear of rejection?
      (5) This crisis may be the opportunity to get counseling for other issues.
3. Treatment options
   a. Goal of crisis management is to get client to continue with further treatment.
   b. Treatment ranges from 12-step programs to inpatient detoxification and rehabilitation programs.

Box 11.7   Cases to Role-Play

Case 1 A 54-year-old woman comes to you. She is chronically depressed but is still able to work and is not suicidal. Her husband has been drinking beer for as long as they have been married, and she tries to control his drinking.

Precipitating event: Husband fell down at a party this past weekend because he was so drunk.

Cognitions: People are going to think badly of me. I should have prevented it from happening. He is never going to stop drinking. I am such a fool.

Emotional distress: Embarrassment, anger.

Impairments in functioning: Too embarrassed to socialize or see family, stopped going to the gym. Overeating and oversleeping.

Educational statements: People who live with alcoholics often try to control their drinking. The term used for this is called *codependency* and it has been studied. Counseling is useful in learning ways not to enable your drinker.

Reframe: Although you think you are helping him by focusing on his behavior, you are really showing disrespect for him and taking away his dignity, which probably makes him feel the need to drink more. Why should you be embarrassed? He is the one who fell down drunk, not you.

Validation statement: I can understand how hard it must be to have to be the only responsible person in the family. It is embarrassing for your loved one to make a scene in front of others.

Empowering statement: Although you cannot control his drinking, you can control whether you focus on him or on your own needs in life. You are not responsible for his behaviors.

Coping: Referral to Al-Anon or Co-dependents Anonymous. Go to the gym. Refuse to buy his alcohol. Don't attend any functions with him where he will drink. Recommend marital therapy and perhaps a 12-step facilitation for husband.

Case 2 A 17-year-old boy is sent to you because his parents found crystal meth in his bathroom. He tells you this was the only time he's used meth.

Precipitating event: Parents found meth.

Cognitions: They're making a big deal out of nothing. I'm not a drug addict. I don't need counseling. It's only meth. Everyone has done it.

Emotional distress: Angry.

Impairments in functioning: Not doing well in school. Missing classes. Not doing homework. May not graduate. Can't get along with parents. Doesn't hang out with friends he knew in childhood. Doesn't eat dinner with parents.

Nonsuicidal.

Validation statement: It's understandable that you don't want to be here in counseling. Because you believe everyone does meth, I can see why you don't think it's a big deal.

Education statement: Meth is a very dangerous drug. It is made up of many toxic chemicals and your parents are correct in being concerned. It often leads to addiction, it is illegal, and based on your behavior at school and at home, it looks like it may be leading to problems in your life. While you say you have never used the drug previously, you do show many of the signs of continuous meth use such as not performing in school, changing friends and not getting along with your parents.

Empowerment: Since you are still a minor, your parents do have power over your life. You can control whether you have to keep coming to counseling by whether you are willing to be honest and focus on your behaviors.

(Continued)

Box 11.7   Cases to Role-Play (Continued)

Reframe: You may think your parents aren't being good parents by dragging you in here against your will, but what kind of parents would they be if they didn't consider all of the signs of serious drug use you have shown them.

Coping: 12-step facilitation with teens. Family counseling.

Case 3 A 28-year-old woman and her husband come to you because of financial difficulty. The wife has spent more than $30,000 over the past year on her cocaine habit.

Precipitating event: Husband found out that they are $30,000 in debt due to her cocaine use.

Cognitions: Wife: I need cocaine to help me do housework. He works and makes enough money. He always has dinner ready and a clean house. Husband: Maybe I'm making a big deal out of things. She does have a lot to do at home.

Emotional distress: Wife: Angry. Husband: Sad and confused, afraid.

Impairments in functioning: No intimate times together. He has to work overtime to keep up with bills. She has no hobbies or interests or friends and neither does he.

No suicidal issues.

Validation statements: It must be shocking to discover that your wife has been so dependent on cocaine. It is probably difficult for you (wife) to be caught after all this time.

Education: Spending this kind of money is a big deal. Cocaine is not cheap and does affect you both in many ways. One of the effects of cocaine is feeling happy, energized, and productive. This can be a problem because that puts you two in a different emotional space from each other. Also, coming down from cocaine no doubt leads you to feel depressed, paranoid, and unable to communicate. It is clearly affecting your marriage.

Reframe: (To husband): You may think you are being kind by not setting strong boundaries; however, you are enabling your wife to continue to use which is not very kind. This is a serious problem, not a fun little activity.

Empowerment: (To husband): You cannot control whether she uses. However, you can control where you put your money and not letting her get a hold of it all. (To wife): At this point, cocaine probably controls you. It would not be unusual if all that you can think about is using cocaine. You really need help in gaining control over your life.

Coping: Wife: Recommend 12-step facilitation at Cocaine Anonymous. Husband: Refer to Co-dependents Anonymous. Recommend marital therapy.

Answers to Pre-Chapter Quiz

1. F   2. T   3. F   4. T   5. T   6. F   7. T   8. F   9. F   10. F

Key Terms for Study

alcohol abuse: A formal term used in the DSM-IV that refers to drinking that leads to impairment in functioning in one or more areas. This person abusing alcohol may also be drinking for psychological comfort.

Alcoholic's Anonymous: The original 12-step group founded in 1935 in which members focus on putting their belief for recovery from alcoholism in a higher power and the support of the group.

alcohol dependence: A term from the DSM-IV referring to a condition where a person is physically addicted to alcohol and would suffer withdrawal symptoms if he or she were to quit drinking.

amotivational syndrome: A term used to describe a chronic marijuana smoker's lack of initiative and drive.

aversive conditioning: A behavioral approach to help drug addicts and alcoholics quit by pairing the substance with a noxious stimulus such as emetine, electric shock, or dirty water. Formerly used frequently at Schick centers.

bottoming out: A term used when an addict's use has caused so many consequences in his life that he can barely function.

codependent: Significant other involved with a substance abuser and the controlling and helping behaviors associated with this family member or friend.

depersonalized: This often occurs during a trip on LSD or when someone is coming down from crystal methamphetamine. The individual no longer perceives himself as the person he used to be or feels no sense of being a person.

derealized: This can occur while coming down or tripping on LSD. The user does not perceive reality as stable or consistent with the usual way reality has been viewed.

detoxification: Cleaning a person's system of a drug. When a person is physically dependent on a substance, it usually takes 3–5 days for the substance to be flushed out of the body. Detoxification often needs to occur in a hospital setting under the care of a physician.

enabler: The nonusing member in a family who encourages or helps the substance abuser continue to use.

fix: A slang term for the dose or unit of consumption of a drug addict. Most commonly associated with heroin addicts.

pseudopsychotic: A condition when someone is either using LSD or coming down from a meth or cocaine binge. He or she may become delusional and not experience himself or herself or the world in a normal way.

Synanon: A type of treatment for addicts that relies on confrontation and a strong social support network to change the user's lifestyle.

tolerance: Resistance to a drug. After prolonged use of drugs or alcohol, the body builds up resistance to them. More and more of the substance must be used for its effects to be felt.

12-step programs: Considered the most effective model in treating substance abusers. These programs are based on the Alcoholics Anonymous model, which acknowledges that users need to seek out and trust a higher power in order to overcome their lifelong problem with a substance.

withdrawal: Symptoms experienced when a user stops taking a drug. The user experiences various physical and psychological symptoms such as nausea, depression, paranoia, convulsions, and anxiety.

References

American Psychiatric Association. (2000). *Diagnostic and statistical manual of mental disorders, fourth edition, text revision* (DSM-IV-TR). Washington, DC: Author.

American Psychological Association. (1996). *Violence and the family: Report of the American psychological association presidential task force on violence and the family* (p. 85). Washington, DC: Author.

Anonymous: the first 100 members of AA (1939, 2001). New York City: Alcoholics Anonymous World Services.

Bien, T. H., Miller, W. R., & Tonigan, J. S. (1993). Brief interventions for alcohol problems: A review. *Addiction, 88*(3), 315–336.

Brohl, K., & Ledford, R. (2012). Consequences of illicit drug use in America. In *Continuing education for California social workers and marriage and family therapists*. Ormond Beach, FL: Elite Continuing Education. 1-866-653-2119.

Davis, H. (1982). *Enabling behaviors*. Unpublished paper from Recovery Services/Family Recovery Services St. Joseph Hospital, Orange, CA.

Dick, D. M., & Bierut, L. J. (2006). The genetics of alcohol dependence. *Current Psychiatry Reports, 8*(2), 151–157.

Ewing, J. A. (1984). Detecting alcoholism. The CAGE questionnaire. *JAMA: The Journal of the American Medical Association, 252*(14), 1905–1907.

Fleming, M. G., Barry, K. L., Manwell, L. B., Johnson, K., & London, R. (1997). Brief physician advice for problem alcohol drinkers: A randomized trial in community based primary care practices. *Journal of the American Medical Association, 277*(13), 1039–1045.

Francis, K. (1998). *Substance abuse treatment at Gerry House West*. Presentation at California State University, Fullerton, CA.

Gabbard, G. O. (2001). *Treatments of psychiatric disorders* (3rd ed.). Washington, DC: American Psychiatric Association.

Krames Communications. (1995). *Marijuana: Are the highs worth the isolation?* San Bruno, CA: Author.

Lancer, D. (2004). Recovery in the twelve steps. *The Therapist, 16*(6), 68–71.

MDMA. (2001). *Harvard Mental Health Letter, 18*(1), 5.

Miller, N. S., Mahler, J. C., & Gold, M. S. (1991). Suicide risk associated with drug and alcohol dependence. *Journal of addictive diseases, 10*(3), 49–61.

Miller, W. R., & Sanchez, V. C. (1993). Motivating young adults for treatment and lifestyle change. In G.Howard (Ed.), *Issues in alcohol use and misuse in young adults* (pp. 55–82). South Bend, IN: University of Notre Dame Press.

Morse, R. M., & Flavin, D. K. (1992). The definition of alcoholism. The joint committee of the National Council on Alcoholism and Drug Dependence and the American Society of Addiction Medicine to Study the Definition and Criteria for the Diagnosis of Alcoholism. *JAMA: The Journal of the American Medical Association, 268*(8), 1012–1014.

National Council on Alcoholism of Orange County. (1986). *Facts on crack.* Santa Ana, CA: Author.

National Institute on Drug Abuse. (2008). *Info facts: Crack and cocaine.*

Nephew, T. M., Williams, G. D., Stinson, F. S., Nguyen, K., & Dufour, M. C. (2000). *Surveillance report #55: Apparent per capita alcohol consumption: National, state and regional trends, 1970-98.* Rockville, MD: National Institute on Alcohol Abuse and Alcoholism, Division of Biometry and Epidemiology.

Nowinski, J. (2000). *Twelve-step facilitation.* Bethesda, MD: National Institute on Drug Abuse, National Institutes of Health, U.S. Department of Health and Human Services.

StayWell Company. (1998). *Cocaine in the family: Is everyone's strings being pulled?* San Bruno, CA: Author.

Substance Abuse and Mental Health Services Administration. (2009). *Results from the 2008 National Survey of Drug Use and Health: National Findings.* Retrieved September 2009, from http://oas.samhsa.gov/nsduh/2k8nsduh/2k8Results.cfm

Turning point. (1994). Channel 7 news program. Los Angeles

U.S. Department of Health and Human Services: Office of Applied Studies. (2000). *Substance abuse statistics.* Retrieved November 5, 2001, from www.samsha.gov/oas/oasftp.cfm

VandenBos, G. R. (Ed.). (2007). *APA dictionary of psychology.* Washington, DC: American Psychological Association.

What are the treatments? (1990, September 20). *Orange County Register,* p. M3.

Zimbardo, P. G. (1992). *Psychology and life* (3rd ed.). New York: HarperCollins.

Chapter 12

Crises Related to Serious Illness and Disabilities

_____ 1. The AIDS antibody test tells whether a person will develop AIDS.

_____ 2. It is possible to be infected with HIV without having a sexual encounter.

_____ 3. Palliative care focuses on curing life-threatening diseases.

_____ 4. Crisis workers often serve as part of a multidisciplinary team when dealing with Alzheimer's patients.

_____ 5. The biopsychosocial model is becoming irrelevant in the field of crisis management.

_____ 6. The term "mentally retarded" is not used as commonly as it was in the past.

_____ 7. About five percent of the elderly suffer from a disability.

_____ 8. Optimistic support groups are discouraged for people suffering from disabilities and life-threatening illnesses.

_____ 9. The ADA stands for AIDS treatment Distribution Association.

_____ 10. People with mental disabilities can benefit from psychological counseling.

Palliative Care

This term is often used in the medical field when discussing serious illnesses and disabilities. It usually refers to medical care or treatment that concentrates on reducing the severity of symptoms rather than striving to reverse the progression of the disease itself or provide a cure. The goal is generally to prevent and relieve suffering and improve quality of life. Sometimes, **palliative care** moves into **hospice** care which typically refers to palliative care for those at the end of life. In any case, palliative care is used to improve the quality of life for patients and their families associated with life-threatening illnesses and the treatments that go along with these illnesses. It is used for disorders related to cancer, renal disease, chronic heart failure, pulmonary problems, and progressive neurological conditions as well as less life-threatening disorders such as disabilities, schizophrenia, and AIDS.

While medical doctors provide the medical component of palliative care, counselors, social workers, and other human service professionals often take the lead in reducing the psychological distress of a person's total suffering (Strang, Strang, Hultborn, & Arner, 2004). An interdisciplinary team is vital, because when people exhibit physiological symptoms related to serious illness or disability, there are often psychological, social, or spiritual symptoms as well. Crisis workers play a vital part in helping individuals diagnosed with serious illness reduce their fears about the future, loss of independence, worries about their family, and feeling like a burden.

The Biopsychosocial Model

In dealing with serious illness and disabilities, counselors are encouraged to approach their clients from the biopsychosocial model in which biological, psychological (thoughts, emotions, and behaviors), and social factors are assessed and considered when offering interventions. Health is best understood in terms of a combination of biological, psychological, and social factors rather than in purely biological terms (Santrock, 2007). This means that crisis workers will no doubt be part of a multidisciplinary team when dealing with clients suffering from the types of problems discussed in this chapter. Physicians focus on the biological aspects and counselors and social workers focus on the psychological and social aspects.

It is widely acknowledged that the workings of the body can affect the mind, and that the workings of the mind can affect the body (Halligan & Aylward, 2006). Most of the diseases referred to in which the biopsychosocial model is relevant tend to be behaviorally moderated illnesses with high-risk factors such as Type 2 diabetes in which obesity and physical inactivity play a role (Bruns & Disorbio, 2006; Wild, Roglic, Green, Sicree, & King, 2004).

One of the roles of counselors and crisis workers is to engage clients to change behaviors that impair optimal functioning. We definitely have an important place on the biopsychosocial team in terms of dealing with a variety of physical illnesses.

Many of the issues and dynamics found in Chapter 6 on loss will be useful in dealing with crises related to life-threatening illnesses and disabilities because loss is usually a central issue when someone becomes ill or disabled. For example, in May 2013, I (the author), broke my leg and lost the ability to drive which necessitated several lifestyle adjustments. If I didn't have the material, personal and social resources to aid me during this temporary disability, I might have suffered from a crisis. Fortunately for me, I did have these resources and was able to continue to create the fifth edition of this text.

However, there are also many issues and facts relating specifically to various serious illnesses and disabilities with which crisis workers may wish to be familiar. If a counselor is working with someone who is terminally ill, death and dying interventions are applicable. However, if one is working with a symptom-free client (temporarily not suffering but still has the underlying illness such as HIV), or someone with a disability, the interventions will be different.

Serious Illnesses

At one period in history (during the 1970s and 1980s) being infected with HIV was considered a death sentence, just as in the past having cancer or heart disease was usually associated with imminent death. Due to modern science and medical innovations, cancer, AIDS, and heart disease are no longer automatic death sentences. All of these illnesses can be managed with great success if the patient adheres to medical advice. Trained counselors are often needed to assist certain patients in following the doctor's orders and modifying their lifestyles. For example, someone with diabetes who continues to eat sugar and fats is at a higher risk of death than someone who eats appropriately and takes medication daily. A family member may bring that uncooperative diabetic to a counselor to try to motivate him to reduce this risk. We will now take a look at a few specific illnesses and how crisis workers and counselors might intervene to reduce risk and increase the longevity and quality of life for the patient.

AIDS and HIV

Before beginning the discussion on AIDS and HIV, a few terms and acronyms will be defined. **AIDS** is an acronym that stands for **acquired immunodeficiency syndrome** and may occur when someone becomes infected with the **HIV (human immunodeficiency virus)**. **ARC** was an acronym used when people first became infected with HIV. It stands for **AIDS-related complex** and is a state of illness between being HIV positive but asymptomatic and developing full-blown AIDS.

AIDS and HIV were discovered to exist in the late 1970s. Over the past 40 years, there have been many advances in the diagnosis and treatment for AIDS which has shown a steady decline over the past 20 years due to enhanced medications that manage the progression of the illness. Someone infected with HIV can live many years as long as they take their medication and practice safe and healthy lifestyles. Instead of thinking that someone is dying of AIDS, we can now think that the person is living with HIV. Box 12.1 provides an outline of the history of HIV/AIDS worldwide and in the United States.

Box 12.1   The History of HIV/AIDS

1977–1978	First cases of AIDS probably occur in the United States, Haiti, and Africa.
1979	Aggressive Kaposi's sarcoma and rare infections first seen in Europe and Africa.
1981	Kaposi's sarcoma and rare infections first reported in homosexual men in the United States; link with sexual transmission suspected.
1982	U.S. Centers for Disease Control and Prevention (CDC) establishes AIDS case definition; formal surveillance starts in United States and Europe. First educational efforts started in United States by local homosexual groups. AIDS linked to blood transfusions, intravenous (IV) drug use, and congenital infection.
1983	2,500 AIDS cases reported in United States. HIV identified in France and United States.
1984	First studies indicate AIDS is common among heterosexuals in Africa.
1985	Enzyme-linked immunosorbent assay (ELISA) blood test developed to detect HIV antibodies. United States begins screening donated blood. HIV is isolated in brain cells and cerebrospinal fluid. First controlled clinical trials of anti-HIV drugs begin in United States.
1986	Estimated 5–10 million people infected with HIV worldwide. World Health Assembly recommends global strategy for AIDS control. Some estimates indicate 1–3 million people infected in the United States. Estimate is reduced by Reagan administration. Several governments start national communication programs.
1987	National Education Association (NEA) publishes "The Facts about AIDS" and joins Health Information Network. Education programs begin to expand; so does the number of AIDS cases.
1988	The Names Project creates the AIDS Memorial Quilt, which helps publicize the epidemic.
1989	Over 100,000 AIDS cases in United States.
1990	International AIDS conference held in San Francisco. Many new treatments and potential vaccines discussed. Federal Drug Administration (FDA) loosens regulations to allow AIDS patients to have access to experimental medication.
1996	Discovery of "triple whammy" doses of (1) the original antiretroviral drugs, such as AZT; (2) the nonnucleoside reverse transcriptase inhibitors, such as nevirapine; and (3) the newest class of drugs, protease inhibitors, such as invirase. The combination is expected to increase life expectancy of HIV-positive patients by suppressing the development of resistance to a drug type and producing a rapid and sustained drop in viral load. (Association for Continuing Education, 1997, p. 115)
1996	U.S. AIDS deaths = 39,200
1997	U.S. AIDS cases (reported) = 58,493 cases
1999	U.S. AIDS cases = 41,900 (42% gay men, 33% heterosexuals, and 25% IV drug users). (Centers for Disease Control and Prevention, 2003)

(Continued)

Box 12.1   The History of HIV/AIDS (Continued)

2003	U.S. AIDS cases = 43,171 (31,614 males, 11,498 females, 59 children under age 13). Estimated number of deaths of persons with AIDS in the United States = 18,017.
2007	Estimated deaths of adults and children from AIDS in the United States = 14,110.
2007	Persons living with AIDS in the United States = 455,636. (CDC, 2008)
2011	Of 49,273 persons in the United States diagnosed with HIV, 38,825 were adults. About 50,000 HIV cases are diagnosed each year. Two-thirds are gay and bisexual men.
2013	There were a cumulative 1,155,792 cases of AIDS in the U.S. (CDC, 2013).

In terms of ethnicity, blacks account for 51 percent of the cases, whites 29 percent, Latinos 18 percent and others 3 percent. The most prevalent age group is 40–49 at 27 percent, with the ages 30–39 making up 26 percent of the cases, and the age group 20–29 making up 25 percent of the cases (U.S. Centers for Disease Control, 2008). In females, the largest percent of those diagnosed with HIV/AIDS was due to high-risk heterosexual contact (83%) with 16 percent becoming infected through **intravenous (IV) drug use**. In just males, male-to-male sexual contact made up 71 percent of the cases, high-risk heterosexual contact made up 14 percent of the cases and injection drug use made up 10 percent of the cases (U.S. Centers for Disease Control, 2008). Currently, Latino men make up 79 percent of new HIV cases. The cultural inhibition of condom use makes Latinos three times more likely to become HIV positive. Certainly counselors and social workers should keep this in mind when working with this population.

What Is AIDS?

AIDS is the disease that develops when the HIV invades the body and disrupts the immune system so that it cannot ward off deadly infections such as cancer or pneumonia. AIDS is a life-threatening disease that sooner or later kills almost everyone who has it. In the past, most people died within six months to two years after being diagnosed with AIDS. Today, medications that fight **opportunistic infections** prolong life for people with AIDS. As a result of advancements in antiviral medications, many people infected with HIV live for 10–20 years without developing AIDS.

Patients infected with HIV begin to develop different signs and symptoms as the infection progresses. Following are some of the symptoms that indicate that infection has begun to destroy the immune system. This information was provided by the Centers for Disease Control and Prevention (2002).

Fever

Fatigue

Diarrhea

Skin rashes

Night sweats

Loss of appetite

Swollen lymph glands

Significant weight loss

White spots in the mouth or vaginal discharge

Memory or movement problems

As the virus continues to destroy the immune system, infections not normally seen in people with healthy immune systems may occur. These infections, which are referred to as opportunistic infections, include invasive cervical cancer, Kaposi's sarcoma, lymphoma, pneumonia, and tuberculosis. When one of the opportunistic infections is diagnosed, the person is typically said to have AIDS instead of being HIV positive.

Misconceptions About AIDS

Misconceptions about AIDS are numerous and widespread. The following information should help dispel the most common misconceptions.

Misconception 1: AIDS can be spread by kissing. Research suggests that saliva from healthy individuals actually inactivates the AIDS virus. Although HIV can be isolated from saliva, the concentration of the virus is so low that the likelihood of someone becoming infected from kissing is very remote.

Misconception 2: AIDS can be spread by touching. HIV is present in sweat and tears; however, its concentration in these fluids is extremely low. Studies of health-care workers who are in close contact with AIDS patients have shown that the risk of infection through patient contact is remote (less than 1%). For persons coming into casual contact (e.g., hugging and shaking hands), the risk of HIV transmission is nonexistent.

Misconception 3: AIDS can be spread by sharing eating utensils. The HIV concentration in saliva is too low to cause infection and, also, saliva inactivates the virus.

Misconception 4: A person can contract AIDS by being near someone with it. This is more a psychological response than a physical threat. People are generally repulsed by disease, especially a disease that is known to be infectious and is poorly understood. It is important to remember that HIV is not transmitted through the air, as is influenza or cold viruses. HIV is spread solely through the exchange of bodily fluids, primarily semen and blood.

Modes of Transmission

As important as it is to dispel misconceptions about the ways HIV can be spread, it is equally important to know how the disease is transmitted. The five common modes of transmission are these:

1. Person-to-person transmission through sexual behavior that involves the exchange of body fluids such as vaginal fluid and sperm.

2. Use of HIV-contaminated injection equipment by more than one person (e.g., needles for injecting heroin, tattoo needles) involving the exchange of blood.
3. Mother-to-infant transmission during pregnancy, labor, and delivery or breast-feeding.
4. Transfusion of infected blood or blood products (Association for Continuing Education, 1977, pp. 21–22).
5. Contact with infected feces that enters the bloodstream.

HIV may also be spread in other ways, but such instances are much less common. One may contract HIV infection by kissing an infected person if both people have open sores in the mouth. Also, health-care workers and police officers may become infected by inadvertent punctures from HIV-contaminated needles.

Progression of HIV Infection to AIDS

The development of AIDS can be thought of as a five-stage process:

1. *Acute infection:* The virus enters the body and replicates itself.
2. The second stage may take one of two forms:
    a. *Acute symptomatic illness (primary HIV infection):* Within the first 2–4 weeks, some people experience fever, weakness, sore throat, skin rashes, and lethargy. This stage can last 1–2 weeks.
    b. *Immune reaction against HIV:* The body begins to produce antibodies to fight infection. Within two months after infection, typical HIV-testing procedures can detect the virus. For 95 percent of those infected, antibodies can be detected within six months.
3. *Asymptomatic HIV infection:* The HIV-infected person shows no symptoms for 6 months to 15 years or longer, depending on medical treatment.
4. *Chronic or symptomatic infection:* This stage was previously called AIDS-related complex (ARC) because it was believed that full-blown AIDS would be seen after these symptoms occurred. Medical interventions have delayed the onset of AIDS in the last 10 years. Symptoms include fever, fatigue, diarrhea, skin rashes, thrush, and bacterial, fungal, and parasitic infections.
5. *AIDS:* The person develops one or more of the 26 AIDS-defining opportunistic infections or has a T-helper cell count below 200 cells in conjunction with HIV infection, or T-helper cells that register less than 14 percent of total lymphocytes. (Association for Continuing Education, 1997, pp. 10–14)

AIDS Testing

Current tests for signs that HIV is in one's blood stream include having a mouth swab specimen analyzed, having urine analyzed, and having a blood sample analyzed.

Treatment

To date, there is no curative treatment for AIDS. There is no vaccine available, despite many years of research. Many AIDS patients and HIV-positive patients take a variety of medications, the most popular being zidovudine (AZT), the original medication for AIDS patients. The use of three different types of medications, often called "the triple whammy" can affect the virus so significantly that it does not show up on a blood test in some people. The purpose of these medications is to block the deterioration of the immune system. Box 12.2 outlines how the HIV infection develops and how the triple whammy medications attempt to block it.

Although there is no cure for AIDS or HIV, crisis workers and counselors can help society by understanding how those infected and not infected can reduce the risk of spreading the virus. Box 12.3 gives ideas of how to reduce the risk of infecting others that counselors can share with clients who may be at risk of spreading or being infected by HIV.

Box 12.2   The Process of HIV Infection

Stage 1: *Binding.* On entering the bloodstream, HIV binds to a receptor on the surface of an appropriate host cell. The only cells it targets are those that display a surface molecule called CD4 (T4). T-helper cells carry the CD4 surface marker. When HIV randomly encounters a T-helper cell, the proteins on its envelope bind to CD4 receptors on the cell.

Stage 2: *Uncoating.* HIV is then internalized by the host cell. The virus enters the cell by means of the same CD4 surface molecule to which it was originally bound. Once inside the cell, HIV sheds its protective coating, or envelope. Shedding, or uncoating, exposes the genetic material (RNA) at the core of the HIV.

Stage 3: *Reverse transcription.* HIV transcribes its RNA into DNA, a process accomplished by means of a viral enzyme called reverse transcriptase. (At this stage, the reverse transcriptase inhibitor drugs, such as AZT and 3TC, can be effective.)

Stage 4: *Integration.* The retroviral DNA (the virus's DNA) is incorporated into the genetic material (DNA) of the host cell. Incorporation is achieved by means of a viral enzyme called integrase. The integrated retroviral DNA can remain as a latent infection in the host cell's genetic material for a variable period of time. (The drugs known as integrase inhibitors can stop this process.)

Stage 5: *Transcription.* Either immediately or when activated, the integrated retroviral DNA (provirus) works inside the host cell, using the cell's metabolic machinery to transcribe viral messenger RNA. Once transcribed, viral RNA can serve to produce more copies of HIV.

Stage 6: *Protein synthesis.* Viral RNA makes structural proteins in the production of new viral RNA and envelope proteins.

Stage 7: *Assembly.* New viruses are assembled. The new viral RNA is incorporated as the core of newly produced envelope proteins. A viral enzyme called protease is necessary for the assembly of new viruses. (Drugs called protease inhibitors block this stage.)

Stage 8: *Budding.* Assembled viruses (viral copies) eventually "bud," are released from the host cell, and infect other appropriate cells.

Box 12.3   Reducing the Risk of Infecting Others with HIV

- Reduce the number of sexual partners, preferably to one.
- Practice safe sex, and have all sexual partners tested.
- Use condoms.
- Use fondling, mutual masturbation, and other safe sexual practices for gratification.
- Clean up accidental spillage of body fluids, especially blood and semen but also feces and vomitus. Fortunately, the AIDS virus is destroyed easily by alcohol, hydrogen peroxide, and bleach.
- Do not pass or receive body fluids, especially blood and semen.
- Avoid poppers and other drugs that can cloud thinking and reduce self-control.
- Avoid intravenous or other injectable drugs.
- Follow the rules of ordinary, good personal hygiene. Give special attention to bathing before and after sex and keeping the mouth, teeth, and tongue clean.
- Avoid sharing personal items, especially those that may be contaminated by a small amount of blood, such as razors and toothbrushes.

Social Aspects

Despite increased knowledge and education about the AIDS virus, a stigma continues to be attached to people with AIDS. The stigma comes not only from the public but from professional health-care workers as well. Much of the negative reaction toward AIDS patients stems from negative attitudes toward homosexuality and IV drug users. The generally accepted view is that the spread of AIDS started with gay men and heroin addicts. Many consider the lifestyles of these two groups to be wrong, and extremists believe those afflicted are getting what they deserve because they are being punished by God. As a result of these views, many AIDS patients have been isolated from family and friends who stay away because of fear and self-righteousness. Being a social outcast only worsens the trauma of AIDS.

Just as the general population discriminates against gays and IV drug users because of their perceived immorality, many professionals also discriminate against these patients, patients who frequently don't comply with traditional medical model treatment plans. Some HIV-positive IV drug users suffer from personality problems that do not respond to education and counseling. Since many people are disdainful of heroin addicts, it is not uncommon for addicts to be deprived of needed treatment. According to Slader (1992), the HIV-infected IV drug user often feels entitled to use drugs and manipulates people relentlessly to get a fix. He asserts that many continue to share needles despite treatment and education. They behave as if they do not care about their health because the "high" they get from the drug is all-important to them. Treatment of IV drug users infected with HIV must be different from the treatment of others.

Individuals diagnosed with AIDS as well as the precursor symptoms often suffer as much psychologically from the diagnosis as they do physically; therefore, psychological counseling is very appropriate for this population. With proper counseling, patients may be able to reduce their feelings of stress and depression, enabling them to enjoy a better quality of life. Counseling can also help clients address issues of death and dying and the denial, anger, and frustration associated with these events. Isolation often compounds these emotions and is reinforced by the withdrawal of family and friends once the AIDS diagnosis becomes known. Counseling must also focus on the psychosocial issues brought on by the stigma associated with the disease, homophobia, and loss of friends, work, housing, insurance, and other essentials of life (Baker, 1991, p. 66).

Type of Clients Who May Seek Crisis Intervention Related to HIV/AIDS

One group of clients an intervention worker might see is also the largest: the **worried well**. Many of these individuals experience sexual guilt caused by fear of AIDS. They are often anxious about their own mortality and their children's future. They are ambivalent about being tested for HIV. While waiting for their test results, they often experience fear arising from their past sexual behaviors. An example of this type of crisis might be a man married with children and seemingly heterosexual who had engaged in several male-to-male sexual acts and is worried about being infected and what disclosure would mean to his family. As a reframe, the crisis worker might say, "This can be an opportunity to bring out past lies, which may help open up relationships and enhance communication."

Issues of suicide for this type of client must be taken seriously. For example, a bisexual man may believe suicide would be preferable to telling his wife and children that he has engaged in risky behaviors such as oral or anal sex with a gay man. He may believe suicide would spare his family embarrassment.

The crisis worker can reframe this issue by pointing out the burden his family would feel if they lost him suddenly to suicide. After all, his wife can choose to leave him or stay with him. Is it really his right to make that choice for her?

A second type of client is one who is pondering whether to be tested for the virus. Issues of denial may be present, a sense that "it could never happen to me." Some people may suspect they are infected but may have irrational thoughts such as, "If I find out, I may really die." Also, moral issues may cause the person to think, "If I don't get tested, I don't have any responsibility to tell any sexual partners." Other people cope by using a form of denial in which they just assume they are positive and restrict their sexual behaviors. If they don't get medical help, however, they put themselves at risk. Therefore, denial can be dangerous for others as well as for the possibly infected person.

A crisis worker can explain how the test detects the virus and how knowing whether one is infected can prevent exposing others to the virus. Several reframes will also be useful. The worker can point out that even if the client tests positive, at least the client can use the knowledge to prolong life through nutrition, medications, and physical wellness. This is a common experience for people who have had near-death experiences. Another reframe could ask,

"Wouldn't it help you to know you aren't positive? At least then you can carry on with life rather than be paralyzed with fear from day to day." Encourage the client to talk to others who have been tested to gain support and encouragement for completing this step.

A third group who come to the crisis interventionist's attention is made up of clients who are dealing with an HIV-positive test result. Many issues must be explored during the time following the news of the result. Denial of the potentially life-threatening nature of HIV can be honored for a while because an HIV-positive test result is not a death sentence. The client's energies will be best spent in attending optimistic support groups, complying with medications, and learning to engage in healthy behaviors that lead to good health and low risk for infecting others. Discussion of Kübler-Ross's stages may be more helpful when a client becomes terminally ill, which may not happen for many years.

Once persons are infected, they may believe that they have lost a world of free and unencumbered sexual activity and any opportunity for childbearing. They may experience feelings of ostracism from family and friends. In the beginning, there may be a ceaseless vigil for symptoms; this is a waste of the person's valuable time and energy. Listening while the client expresses his or her pain and despair is helpful to the client.

Two struggles often experienced by individuals diagnosed with AIDS or as HIV positive are disclosing the condition to partners and changing sexual practices. Denying the impact of a positive result—that it can lead to AIDS—can be useful in the beginning as the client works on these struggles and the impact of the infection on his or her relationships. Some clients may struggle with losing their partner if they disclose the positive test result. The counselor will need to support both partners as they express fear, pain, anger, and sadness. When clients choose not to tell a partner, counselors must struggle with their own responsibility to let the partner know. Workers should encourage clients to explore both positive and negative reactions to disclosure.

Changing one's sexual practices is a completely private issue for most people. Sensitivity to cultural and family traditions is vital because resistance to safer sex can often be understood better in these contexts. Some uninfected partners may feel guilty, so they will have unprotected sex to risk becoming infected as a form of punishment. Others may become suicidal at the thought of losing their infected partner to AIDS. In some marital situations, the woman may feel a need to protect her husband's masculinity by not requiring him to wear a condom.

Support groups that focus on optimism and education are an excellent resource for HIV-positive clients. Here, clients can share common concerns and offer one another practical problem-solving advice that may not be well received from a well-meaning counselor who is not HIV positive. All of the struggles of the HIV-positive client are delicate and difficult to talk about openly. These issues need to be addressed by crisis workers in a non-judgmental manner. This is not easy for workers. Workers must stop and ask themselves how they are feeling at various points.

A fourth group that will need the help of a crisis worker is made up of those who start to develop symptoms (usually of precursor illnesses). These clients commonly feel dirty and contaminated. Fears of physical deterioration often lead to thoughts such as, "I just want to die because I know sooner or later ARC will turn into AIDS." Such clients may not allow themselves to get close to others because of their extreme fear of an imminent and painful death.

The counselor can help by working to restore a sense of hope. Typical clients have the attitude that AIDS equals death. The counselor can begin to reframe the condition as a catalyst for a more meaningful life, in which clients can learn to appreciate more fully what they have. Rather than creating distance from others, disclosure can rekindle relationships and create closeness.

Educational comments pointing out that family members are probably curious but afraid to ask about the diagnosis may encourage clients to open up to those who live with them. Once disclosures are made and the client has adjusted to changed sexual behavior, the person's crisis state will stabilize. Medical issues, of course, will continue to appear, as will death and dying issues once opportunistic diseases begin.

Interventions

Since the scientific community began to do research on AIDS and HIV, the professional literature has been addressing the counseling of those afflicted. Education and support seem to be the prevalent modes of counseling for all levels of infected persons, from asymptomatic persons to patients with chronic pneumonia (Price, Omizo, & Hammett, 1986; Slader, 1992). In his residential treatment house for (HIV-positive) IV drug users, Slader focuses on teaching clients the skills to help them live a healthy life. The focus for this particular population is mainly on preventing spread of the virus. Eliminating needle sharing is the most effective prevention. Some would say that treatment should focus on complete sobriety; but stopping heroin use quickly is extremely difficult, so treatment may have to be more realistic. Many infected IV drug users need to be told that they will die more quickly if they continue to use drugs because drug use damages an already-deficient immune system. Pointing out that sharing needles could cause infections with other diseases, which deplete the immune system further, is an example of a useful educational comment. Support groups that deal with feelings and groups such as Narcotics Anonymous can also be helpful with this population.

A counselor may want to reassure clients that their status is guarded by confidentiality ethics, though disclosure to partners will most likely be recommended by the physician. Counselors can also point out that HIV infection does not equal having AIDS. The HIV-infected person is encouraged to avoid infecting others and to stay in good physical condition rather than focus on preparing for full-blown AIDS.

For those already ill with AIDS, support groups are recommended. Participation will create a sense of family and reduce feelings of isolation. For the counselor, this is a time to model efforts to initiate and develop rapport with AIDS clients. These contacts will help reduce clients' feelings of dirtiness. Since brokering appropriate services is a vital part of any crisis intervention, knowledge of AIDS service centers in the area is helpful for crisis workers and their clients.

Table 12.1 provides a concise summary of the major issues related to AIDS and HIV and intervention strategies.

TABLE 12.1   HIV and AIDS-Related Issues and Interventions

HIV	AIDS
Human immunodeficiency virus	*Acquired immunodeficiency syndrome*
Contracted through: Sperm Blood Mother's milk Feces Vaginal fluid	**When diagnosed?** Opportunistic infection T-cell count below 200
Progression: 1. 1–2 weeks after infection, person may have cold-like symptoms, feel run down 2. For six months to one year the virus may be dormant with no symptoms 3. Within six months to one year, the person may test HIV positive; antigens show up in a blood test	**Progression:** 1. Without medication, new opportunistic infections occur 2. Needs antiviral and antibacterial medications
Crisis issues: 1. Death sentence 2. Fear of disclosure 3. Fear of lifestyle changes 4. Medication cooperation (denial) 5. Suicide as only way out	**Crisis issues:** 1. Death and dying issues 2. Medical care 3. Financial issues 4. Disability issues 5. Caretaker issues 6. Suicide issues
Intervention strategies: 1. Education 2. Suicide prevention 3. Optimistic groups 4. Medication 5. Honor the denial 6. Family therapy 7. Encourage safer sex 8. Encourage healthy lifestyle	**Intervention strategies:** 1. Grief therapy 2. Case management 3. Suicide watch 4. Medical intervention issues 5. Support groups 6. Hospice

Before concluding this section, it is vital to point out that there are many other sexually transmitted diseases (STDs) that are more common than HIV infection. Counselors have the obligation and privilege to educate people about risky behaviors that may increase the likelihood of other infections. According to the 2003 surveillance report by the Centers for Disease Control and Prevention, chlamydial infection is the most commonly reported infectious disease in the United States. In 2003, 877,478 chlamydial infections were reported to the Centers for Disease Control. Because this disease is probably underreported, the actual number is probably 2.8 million new cases each year. Cases of gonorrhea are at an all-time low number, but it is still the second most commonly reported infectious disease in the United States, with 335,104 cases reported in 2003. Syphilis has increased among men who have sex with men and has decreased in other populations; about 7,177 cases were reported in the United States between 2002 and 2003.

Other STDs such as herpes, genital warts, trichomoniasis, and bacterial vaginosis also compel people to use precautions when engaging in sexual activity. Crisis workers may come across clients who are in crisis because they are suffering from one or more of these infections. Many of the issues discussed in the section on HIV and AIDS apply, such as disclosure, safe sex, medication management, and prevention of further infection.

Alzheimer's Disease

An estimated five million Americans are afflicted with Alzheimer's disease (Alzheimer's Association, 2013). An estimated one in three seniors dies of Alzheimer's disease. The average length of time between the onset of symptoms and the diagnosis is 2.8 years. This disease is expected to increase to 11.3–16 million cases in American by 2050 (Brohl & Ledford, 2012).

A national survey conducted in 1993 indicated that about 19 million Americans say they have a family member with the disease, and 37 million know someone with it. It is the fourth leading cause of death among American adults. Ten percent of those over age 65, and almost half of those over age 85 have the disease (Alzheimer's Association of Orange County, 1998). These statistics tell us that we need to be aware of the problem and its effects on the significant others of the patient. Age seems to be the major cause of this disease although there may be other genetic risk factors. The number of people with the disease doubles every five years beyond age 65 (Brohl & Ledford, 2012).

What Is Alzheimer's Disease?

Alzheimer's disease is a progressive degenerative disease that attacks the brain, causing impaired memory, thinking, and behavior. Symptoms include a gradual loss of memory, declining ability to perform routine tasks, disorientation, impaired judgment, and personality change. There are also difficulties in learning and loss of language skills. The disease eventually renders its victims totally incapable of caring for themselves.

There are three stages to this disease. In the early stage one will experience memory loss but the person can compensate for this and function independently. Motor skills are still intact. In the middle-stage the person experiences a decline in cognitive abilities such as memory and self-care. There are personality changes and confusion and the person is more and more dependent on caregivers. The person may have trouble communicating and recognizing family members or friends, may wander, have delusions and hallucinations, and can be cared for at home or in an institutional setting. In the late stage there is complete deterioration of the personality and loss of control over bodily functions. The person is completely dependent on others for daily living. (Brohl & Ledford, 2012).

Effects on the Caretaker

It is caretakers who often use crisis intervention services because of the emotional drain Alzheimer's patients put on them. Although there is no cure for the disease, caretakers can be supported and referred to groups to vent their frustrations and ambivalent feelings. The crisis worker should be knowledgeable about available services for these families. Alzheimer's disease is particularly difficult because of the pervasive impairments it brings in cognitive, emotional, and physical functioning. Patients are often depressed, paranoid, incontinent, and psychotic. It is very sad for people to see a spouse or parent deteriorate to the point where he or she does not recognize his or her own children. Caretakers need empathy along with education about the disorder. Box 12.4 provides some signs that a caregiver may need intervention.

When a crisis worker comes into contact with the caretaker of an Alzheimer's patient, he or she might consider the following to aid in his or her relief offered by the Alzheimer's Association in Box 12.5.

Of course the ideas presented in Box 12.5 will be useful for caretakers of many illnesses and disabilities.

Box 12.4   Signs That a Caregiver May Need Intervention

1. *Denial* about the disease and its effect on the person who has been diagnosed.
2. *Anger* at the person with Alzheimer's disease or others; that there is no effective treatment or cure; and that people don't understand what's going on.
3. *Social withdrawal* from friends and activities that once brought pleasure.
4. *Anxiety* about facing another day and what the future holds.
5. *Depression* beginning to break the caregiver's spirit and affecting the ability to cope.
6. *Exhaustion* making it nearly impossible to complete necessary daily tasks.
7. *Sleeplessness* resulting from a never-ending list of concerns.
8. *Irritability* leading to moodiness and triggering negative responses and reactions.
9. *Lack of concentration* making it difficult to perform familiar tasks.
10. *Health problems* beginning to take their toll, both mentally and physically.

Source: Alzheimer's Association of Orange County, 1998.

Box 12.5   Ways to Reduce Caretaker Stress

1. *Get a diagnosis as early as possible:* Once caretakers know what they are dealing with, they are better able to manage the present and plan for the future.
2. *Know what resources are available:* Adult day care, in-home assistance, and visiting nurses are some of the community services that can help. The local Alzheimer's Association chapter is a good place to start.
3. *Become an educated caregiver:* Care techniques and suggestions can help one to better understand and cope with the many challenging behaviors and personality changes that often accompany Alzheimer's disease.
4. *Educate about getting help:* Trying to manage everything on one's own can be exhausting. Encourage the caretaker to ask for the support of family, friends, and community resources. Support groups and help lines are good sources of comfort and reassurance.
5. *Talk about taking care of oneself:* Caretakers should pay attention to their own needs and attend to their diet, exercise, and sleep. They should use respite services that allow time for shopping, a movie, and other recreational activities.
6. *Suggest ways to manage stress levels:* Stress can cause physical problems and changes in behaviors. Caretakers should use healthy relaxation techniques and perhaps consult a physician.
7. *Help the person to accept changes as they occur:* People with Alzheimer's disease change and so do their needs. An investigation of available care options should make transitions easier.
8. *Talk about legal and financial planning:* Planning now will alleviate stress later. The caregiver can consult an attorney and discuss issues related to durable power of attorney, living wills and trusts, future medical care, housing, and other key considerations.
9. *Be realistic:* Neither the caretaker nor the Alzheimer's patient can control many of the circumstances and behaviors that occur. Caretakers should give themselves permission to grieve for the losses experienced but should also focus on the positive moments as they occur and enjoy good memories.
10. *Talk about giving oneself credit, not guilt:* Occasionally, one may lose patience with oneself. Caretakers should remember that they are doing the best possible. Patients need the caretakers and would thank them if possible. Be proud.

Source: Alzheimer's Disease and Related Disorders Association, Inc., 1995.

Issues Related to Disabilities

(This section was written by John Doyle, Ph.D., Associate Professor of Human Services at California State University, Fullerton with minor edits from the author.)

When compared with the general population, persons with disabilities are more prone to crises, and as such deserve particular attention from a crisis intervention perspective. Box 12.6 shows three examples of how disabled individuals might need the assistance of a crisis worker.

A Brief History of Disabilities

Disability, a broad concept, is physical or mental impairment that substantially prevents or restricts the ordinary course of human development and accomplishments. Disabilities are often present from birth but can develop at

---

Box 12.6   Examples of Persons with Disabilities Who May Be Prone to Crisis States

Example: Jack, a disabled police officer in his mid-30s, has been forced to resign his position because of a diagnosis of bipolar affective disorder. Like many with this condition, even when he takes his medications as prescribed, it is difficult for him to maintain his emotional equilibrium, to the point where he requires psychiatric hospitalization about twice a year. He is also alcohol dependent, which he controls by rigorous participation in the Alcoholics Anonymous 12-step program. With the benefit of vocational rehabilitation services, Jack has been relatively successful in maintaining part-time employment.

Example: Victor, a retired teacher in his mid-60s, has been enjoying his leisure years in a wide array of activities, including travel. Suddenly and unexpectedly, his vision has deteriorated; the cause is an eye condition that is progressive and irreversible. He is no longer allowed to drive, which is a severe blow to his sense of independence. But for both him and his family, the psychological impact of his disability has proved to be the more difficult adjustment.

Example: Debbie, age 39, has a diagnosis of mild to moderate cerebral palsy and is profoundly deaf. She has always resided with her mother, who has provided her with the necessary support to live a relatively normal and independent life. Debbie has an awkward gait, which gives the impression that she is intoxicated. This appearance has led to frequent arrests by the police as she walks to and from her place of part-time employment. Her hearing impairment limits her communication skills, further complicating her ability to communicate with the police and others. Her mother, now elderly and in deteriorating health, has been Debbie's lifetime advocate and care provider.

---

any time in the life cycle. They include such clearly recognizable conditions as blindness, deafness, mental retardation, and mental illness, but also conditions that are less obvious, such as learning disabilities, AIDS, heart disease, and cancer. Depending on the severity of the impairment, the functional level of the person is impaired to a lesser or greater degree. Some people have more than one disability or struggle with both physical and mental impairments. The level of impairment dictates the degree of support needed; not only is the disabled person challenged but so are his or her family members, caregivers, and society at large.

Throughout human history, society has frequently greeted disabled people with stigma, prejudice, mistreatment, discrimination, social isolation, inferior status, and inferior services. Changing the culture of disability is an ongoing challenge. Until relatively recent times, mentally retarded people were officially referred to as idiots, feeble-minded people, imbeciles, or morons. These terms, now obsolete in professional and clinical settings, survive in everyday language as powerful derogatory epithets. It is often easier to find agreement on terms that should not be used than on terms that are suitable to use. The term *mentally retarded* has negative connotations and is being replaced in some settings by the term **developmentally disabled** or *mentally challenged*. However, the terms *disability* and *disabled* are often seen to connote weakness, dependence, abnormality, and inferiority.

Even when people have the best of intentions, they often view persons with disabilities unrealistically. Disabled people may view themselves unrealistically. On the one hand, the disability can be overestimated to a point where the individual is sentimentalized and unnecessarily relegated to a position of overdependence. On the other hand, the disability can be underestimated to the point where the person and his or her family experience endless failure and emotional frustration. Achieving a realistic balance in which the functional strengths of the individual define him or her rather than the disability can be difficult; however, achieving that balance is important in preventing crises.

The Disabled Population and the ADA

Depending on the definition applied, the number of disabled individuals in American society varies. The legal journey defining persons with disabilities and articulating their rights reached a high point when Congress passed the **Americans with Disabilities Act (ADA) of 1990**, which broadly challenges discrimination against disabled people. The ADA went into effect in July 1992. It defines a person with a disability as having a physical or mental impairment that substantially limits one or more major life activities; has a record of such an impairment; or is regarded as having such an impairment. The intent of the legislation is to make society more accessible to people with disabilities, but its implementation continues to be a major challenge. According to Census 2000, 48.9 percent of people who were five years old and over living in housing units had a disability, which is approximately 19.2 percent of the disabled population in the United States (Stern, 2001). Congress recognizes the historical and present tendency of society to discriminate against disabled people, and mandates remedies in such areas as employment, housing, public accommodations, education, transportation, communication, recreation, institutionalization, health services, voting rights, and access to public services. It also prohibits coercion of, or retaliation against, people with disabilities or those who advocate for rights for the disabled.

Not only are people with disabilities discriminated against, but they are frequently abused. Women with disabilities are more likely to experience abuse by a greater number of perpetrators and for longer periods than non-disabled women (Young, Nosek, Howland, Chanpong, & Rintala, 1997). Unfortunately, many people with disabling conditions are especially vulnerable to victimization because of their real or perceived inability to fight or flee, notify others, or testify in court. Despite the advocacy of ADA workers, crime victims with disabilities are less likely than those without disabilities to reap the benefits of the criminal justice system. The reason is that crimes against disabled victims go unreported because of victims' mobility or communication barriers, social or physical isolation, or normal feelings of shame and self-blame, or because the perpetrator of the crime is the victim's caretaker (U.S. Department of Justice, 2001).

Once the ADA was passed, one could say that people with disabilities entered **mainstream** society. However, their challenges continue. The main controversy concerns the cost of changes for accommodating disabled people in both the public and private sectors of society. According to Title II of the ADA, discrimination of any kind on the basis of disability is prohibited. Community agencies, including the police force, firefighting force, state legislature, city councils, state courts, public schools, public recreation departments, and departments of motor vehicle licensing, must allow people with disabilities to participate fully in all of their services, programs, and activities. An example of the effect of the ADA on the police force can be seen in the Police Executive Research Forum, which provides a detailed training curriculum and model policy for responding to people with mental illness, developmental disabilities, and speech and hearing impairments.

Vulnerable Subgroups Within the Disabled Population

As a result of the ADA, many people with disabilities can now live more as part of mainstream society. For instance, wheelchair-accessible buildings allow many with physical disabilities to enjoy social and vocational independence. However, some subgroups within the disabled population are particularly prone to crises, and there is no simple way to offset their vulnerability. The most vulnerable groups are fragile elderly people, mentally ill people, and developmentally disabled people.

Disabled Elderly People

Elderly people are not automatically disabled. However, there is a greater risk of disability as a person ages. In 1994 and 1995, 52.5 percent of people over 65 years of age reported having at least one disability, and 33 percent reported having at least one severe disability. Over six million, or 21 percent, had difficulty in carrying out activities of daily living. As people grow older, there is a corresponding increase in disabilities. Walker (1994) argues that prevention of disabilities in older adults is a shared responsibility, involving the elderly individual, health-care providers, and society at large. Individual choice is not sufficient; rather, there is a need for a broad social commitment to the promotion of health. However, diseases are significant risk factors for disability in elderly people, and age itself is a risk factor for those over 85 years of age. Hogan, Ebly, and Fung (1999) examined cognitively intact community-resident seniors and found that age alone accounts for the fact that twice as many in the 85-plus age group are physically disabled compared with the 65- to 84-year-old age group. Hence, disease prevention will not necessarily impede disability in older seniors. Compared with the 65- to 80-year-old population, those over 80 are twice as likely to have difficulty with such activities as bathing, dressing, eating, preparing meals, shopping, managing money, and taking medication.

It is clear from the literature that intervention for elderly people with disabilities must be holistic in nature, involving a network of community resources. In a study of the characteristics of older adults with intellectual disabilities who required crisis intervention, Davidson and colleagues (1995) concluded that intellectually disabled adults require comprehensive age-span community mental health and behavioral supports. The severity of the behavioral crises decreases over the life cycle, but the need for intervention remains constant. The need for intervention is not limited to elderly persons with a disability. Altman, Cooper, and Cunningham (1999) described the struggles of a family with a disabled elder. Families experience an increased number of emotional, financial, and health crises. Graham (1989) points out that as these diseases and disabilities progress, day-care placement may be necessary; even with day care, the stress level does not necessarily decrease for family caregivers. Frail elderly people are the most vulnerable to neglect and abuse by caregivers, both professionals and family members.

Alecxih (2001) reports that by 2050 the number of elderly people requiring institutional care will likely more than double, from 5 million to 11 million. The elderly population will be more diverse, so the long-term care workforce will have to be more culturally competent. Human-service workers generally will need more training in dealing with the problems of an aging population (Rosen & Zlotnik, 2001).

Mentally Disabled People

Although it is more difficult to define and measure mental disabilities, the debilitating nature of emotional and psychological problems is quite clear. Under the ADA, a mental impairment includes any "mental or psychological disorder, such as...emotional or mental illness." Among the examples cited are "major depression, bipolar disorder, anxiety disorders (which include panic disorder, obsessive disorder, and PTSD), schizophrenia, and personality disorders." Comer (1995) gives the following statistics on mental illness in the United States: 13 percent have significant anxiety disorders; 6 percent have serious depression; 5 percent have debilitating personality disorders; 1 percent has schizophrenia; 1 percent has Alzheimer's disease; and 10 percent are suffering from drug and alcohol difficulties.

With the introduction of the major tranquilizer medications in the 1950s, psychotic behaviors could be controlled, and the treatment of people with serious mental illnesses changed significantly. Before this new treatment mode, those with serious mental illness were confined to psychiatric hospitals, which were locked facilities. The major tranquilizers made deinstitutionalization possible. Treatment is now community based; and hospitalizations, especially long-term stays, are avoided as much as possible. Further goals of deinstitutionalization are the promotion of the rights and independence of mentally ill people and a more cost-effective delivery of services. The National Institute of Mental Health indicates that the number of institutionalized mental health patients decreased from a high of 559,000 in 1955 to 69,000 in 1995.

As discussed in Chapter 1, the Community Mental Health Act of 1963 set goals for the provision of community-based services for the mentally disabled. These services include inpatient care for seriously ill patients, with the goal of returning them to the community as soon as possible; outpatient clinics for ongoing care; partial hospitalization, where patients can go home at night and on weekends; 24-hour crisis centers; and consultation, education, and information services for those who regularly interact with these disabled people in the community. Unfortunately, the provision of these community-based services has lagged, making deinstitutionalization, at best, a measured success. Although the major tranquilizers work well for seriously mentally ill people when they are in the hospital setting and help them return to the community, individuals who do not have the support of friends, are unemployed, or do not have access to ongoing mental-health services are destined for failure in community-based living. Some observers feel that the deinstitutionalization policy for the mentally ill has been a dismal failure. Others see it as a success in that it promotes civil liberties for those with serious mental illness. Johnson (1990) points out that with certain supports in place, such as housing, outreach by human service workers, independent living skills support, and occasional hospitalizations for stabilization of their condition, community-based placement is appropriate. Without the necessary supports, seriously mentally ill people in the community are in a permanent state of crisis. Unfortunately, people in the community often see these people as a public nuisance who should be controlled by the criminal justice system; this is an inappropriate and highly unfair assessment.

It can be argued that institutionalization in the absence of proper community support is more humane for seriously mentally ill people because they do not fall victim to homelessness, hunger, abuse, or the criminal justice system and because, with their limited coping skills, they avoid living in a permanent state of crisis. It is also clear that because of the number of community support services needed to help some of these people, community placement is not necessarily less costly than institutionalization.

Developmentally Disabled People

The developmentally disabled population includes those with mental retardation, cerebral palsy, epilepsy, autism, and other neurological disorders. In particular, mentally retarded people have been unnecessarily institutionalized and subject to involuntary sterilization. The deinstitutionalization movement of the 1970s reflected a concern for the civil rights of the developmentally disabled; today, very few are institutionalized. The guiding principle is that they have the right to develop as fully as they can and live as normally and independently as possible. Most now live more independently with their families or in group homes. The movement of developmentally disabled people into the community means that crises that once occurred behind the walls of state institutions now are seen in every community. There is an ongoing need to meet this inevitable problem. Community-based living places more demands on the limited coping skills of the developmentally disabled, making them even more prone to crises.

Like the general population, more developmentally disabled people are living to be elderly. Advances in medicine have helped these people, just as they have helped nondisabled people. The longer life span means that developmentally disabled people need more extensive and complex interventions over the life cycle. For the first time in history, these people are outliving their parents (Ansello, 1988). Estimates of the number of elderly developmentally disabled people vary from at least 4 in every 1,000 older persons (Janicki, 1991) to as many as 1 in every 100 older persons (Ansello & Eustis, 1992). To prevent or delay institutionalization, strengthen independence, and enhance daily functioning of the older population with developmental disabilities, a new emphasis on service needs must emerge. Collaboration is critical between service providers and family caregivers in serving the needs of the developmentally disabled elderly.

Coogle, Ansello, Wood, and Cotter, (1995) argue for resource sharing and collaboration among the providers for the developmentally disabled and other human service networks, and also for a managed approach to intervention in order to avoid costly duplication of services. They further argue for education of the public and community leaders about those with lifelong disabilities and their families; increased funding for supportive housing and independent living centers; advocacy for older adults with developmental disabilities and their families so they can secure community-based long-term care; respite care and income support; and an increase in federal and state resources for continued community living. Zola (1988) believes that the aged and disabled populations should be served together because of their similar conditions, the technical and medical requirements of their care, and the full implications of the home-care revolution. The traditional approach of dividing them into two opposing entities is a form of unnecessary segregation.

Crisis Intervention Strategies for Persons with Disabilities

Effective intervention for people with disabilities requires detailed knowledge of this population, information on their civil and legal rights, a willingness to advocate for those rights, and comprehensive knowledge of available sources of support and intervention.

Crises do not occur in a vacuum. For disabled people, crises often occur because helpers do not have adequate knowledge and understanding of a particular disability and fail to establish the necessary support systems. For instance, a high-functioning autistic person who works in a predictable environment with structured supervision can be extremely productive and successful. However, because such an individual typically has great difficulty with social and environmental transitions, any change in work routine or personnel can provoke a major crisis. To decrease the likelihood of such a crisis requires not only the maintenance of a predictable work routine but also ongoing education for other employees and the management staff on how to successfully interact with this individual. This requires a considerable commitment on the part of all concerned. Depending on the disability and circumstances, similar preventive strategies need to be employed.

Case management is one of the most important developments in human services in the past half century. Schneider (1988) emphasizes the importance of case management as an intervention strategy. It is consumer centered; embraces the elements of screening, assessment, specific goals, interdisciplinary and interagency cooperation, and measurable outcomes; and is subject to monitoring and evaluation. Case management is a proactive, positive way of intervening with regularity with the chronically disabled, a way of anticipating situations before they become full-blown crises.

Effective crisis intervention and prevention are rooted in a system of comprehensive collaboration. Knowledge of available services and the ways in which they can be accessed is essential. For example, the 1975 federal Education for All Handicapped Children Act (Public Law 94-142), updated in 1997 as the Individuals with Disabilities Education Act (IDEA), is just one of many federal programs for the disabled. It mandates free, appropriate, individualized public education for handicapped children—those with learning handicaps, developmental disabilities, orthopedic conditions, and mental illness. Local school districts play a major role in the lives of disabled children from the time they are three years of age until they reach 22 years of age, so an important intervention is assisting the disabled and their families in using this resource.

People who are not disabled, even human-service workers, react differently to disabled people. Some common reactions are fear, repulsion, anxiety about loss and dependence, embarrassment, and avoidance of social contact. Working with disabled people may be perceived as less prestigious than working with other types of people. Legislation mandating full inclusion of the disabled population is one thing; implementation of the legislation is another. Both physical and psychological obstacles to inclusion remain, including the cost of services, competing interests, and discrimination, as well as the self-limiting roles of disabled people themselves. This population requires meaningful intervention and attention, not stigmatization or sentimentalization. Box 12.7 provides a few cases to role-play using the ABC Model.

Box 12.7   Cases to Role-Play

Case 1 A 30-year-old man comes to you after finding out that he is infected with the HIV. He found out at the public health department. He is married but does not have children yet. He thinks he contracted the disease from a prostitute. His wife does not know.

Precipitating event: Tested positive for HIV.

Cognitions: My wife will leave me. I should just kill myself because I'm worthless and horrible. I can't tell my wife because she'll be devastated. I'm going to die and I deserve to die.

Emotional distress: Afraid, sad, and worried.

Impairments in functioning: He cannot talk to his wife. He cannot concentrate at work. He has no social contact.

Suicide assessment: He has ideation, plan, means (middle risk).

Validation: This is very challenging and difficult. It is scary to be infected and also to deal with the reaction of your wife.

Education: HIV positive does not mean you will die. There are many treatments now that prolong life. If you start with medications now you can learn to live a healthy lifestyle and prolong your life.

Reframe: You are concerned about your wife. She may be hurt and angry that you cheated on her, but she would be even more devastated should you kill yourself. Many people learn to live HIV positive rather than think about dying of AIDS.

Empowerment: True, you cannot undo your behavior in the past and undo being HIV positive. However, you can change your behaviors now and use this very challenging situation to grow and take control of your life. You cannot control if your wife chooses to leave, but you can control how you live from here on out.

(Continued)

Box 12.7 Cases to Role-Play (Continued)

Coping: After thorough suicide assessment, have him sign a no-suicide contract, give you his pills, bring wife in and let her know he is suicidal, increase visits to three times weekly. Encourage him to go to a support group, marital therapy, follow medication prescriptions, practice safe sex, and live a healthy lifestyle.

Case 2 A man is in a wheelchair because his legs were paralyzed in a surfboard accident a year ago. He comes to you because he is lonely. Last weekend at a party he talked with a woman that he had met once before, prior to his accident. He wants to date her but is afraid she will not want to date him because of his disability.

Precipitating event: Met a girl at a party whom he likes.

Cognitions: She will never date me. No one will ever want me, I'm crippled and useless. I'm repulsive and could never please a woman.

Emotional distress: Sad.

Impairments in functioning: He has stopped socializing. He can't sleep or eat.

Suicidal risk: He has some ideation, but no plan or means (low risk).

Validation: True, being in a wheelchair has many drawbacks and some people will reject you and it is understandable to feel hurt and sad by that.

Education: Not all people are turned off by people in wheelchairs. Some people care more about a person's character; maybe that would be the type of person you would want to meet.

Empowerment: While you don't have control about being in a wheelchair, you have control about how you approach others. By focusing on what you can do, you can create a persona of optimism and confidence which is much more attractive to others.

Reframe: Even if the woman doesn't want to date you, she may want to be your friend and would that be so bad? If she is not the type who would be interested in who you are, maybe she isn't the right one for you anyways.

Coping: Encourage him to join a support group for people in wheelchairs, keep a journal, practice assertive friendship, and not think about dating right away.

Case 6 A couple in their fifties come to you because they are tired, feel guilty, and are very stressed out. They have been taking care of the wife's father, age 78 years, who started showing symptoms of Alzheimer's disease two years ago. Just recently, they have been invited by the husband's company to go on a cruise to the Mediterranean, all expenses paid, but do not have anyone to take care of the father while they are gone.

Precipitating event: Being invited on a cruise.

Cognitions: We would be horrible people if we go, we should stay home and take care of our father. He won't be able to make it without us. We don't deserve such happiness when he is suffering so. There is no one else to take care of him.

Emotional distress: Sad, angry, guilty.

Impairments in functioning: Marital squabbling. Neither of them can concentrate at work. They have no social life.

No suicidal issues.

Validation: Feelings of guilt and sadness are normal for caretakers of Alzheimer's patients.

Education: Being a caretaker is very challenging. Caretakers must take care of themselves in order to continue to care for others. There are respite care programs through the Alzheimer's Association.

Reframe: If you don't start taking care of yourself, you may not be able to continue to care for your father.

Empowerment: You are powerless over the disease but not over how you take care of him. You can control the quality of your life even if you cannot control the quality of his life.

Coping: Alzheimer's Association has respite care programs. There are support groups for you to attend and material to read.

Chapter Review ——————————————————

Crisis workers may be called upon to work with individuals with a serious illness or a disability to aid in adjusting psychologically and socially to the illness. Oftentimes, caretakers also seek the help of crisis counselors to obtain help in dealing with stress and frustration and loss.

Answers to Pre-Chapter Quiz ——————————

1. F   2. T   3. F   4. T   5. F   6. T   7. F   8. F   9. F   10. T

Key Terms for Study ——————————————

AIDS (acquired immunodeficiency syndrome): Disease caused by HIV infection either when an opportunistic infection has invaded the body or when the T-cell count is very low.

American with Disabilities Act of 1990 (ADA): The intent of this legislation is to make society more accessible to people with disabilities. It defines disabilities and challenges the discrimination associated with disabilities.

ARC (AIDS-related complex): A term seldom used today. It originally referred to patients who had symptoms such as night sweats, thrush, and lesions but had not yet caught an opportunistic infection. It is a state between dormant HIV infection and full-blown AIDS.

case management: An effective approach to working with individuals and families in which a disability is a factor. It includes such elements as screening, assessment, setting goals, interagency and interdisciplinary cooperation.

developmentally disabled: Neurological disorders such as mental retardation, cerebral palsy, epilepsy, and autism.

disability: Physical or mental impairment that substantially prevents or restricts the ordinary course of human development and accomplishments.

HIV (human immunodeficiency virus): The virus that usually leads to AIDS. It depletes the body of T-cells, which fight off bacteria and viral infections.

Hospice: This type of program is offered to terminally ill patients. The focus is on providing comfort while someone is dying rather than offering curative interventions.

intravenous (IV) drug use: Use of syringes by people to inject themselves with an illicit drug such as heroin. Such people who share needles have a high risk of spreading HIV because the virus is directly transmitted into the bloodstream.

mainstream: People with disabilities who function in society with as much independence as possible both socially and vocationally.

Opportunistic infections: When someone is infected with HIV, the body is susceptible to developing a variety of bacterial and viral infections that only occur when the immune system is compromised.

palliative care: Focusing on providing relief from symptoms rather than on curing the disease.

worried well: This group of individuals have engaged in risky sexual behaviors and often seek testing for HIV regularly due to concerns of being infected even though they show no symptoms of HIV infection.

References

Alecxih, L. (2001). The impact of sociodemographic change on the future of long-term care. *Generations (Spring)*: 7–11.

Altman, B. M., Cooper, P. F., & Cunningham, P. J. (1999). The case of disability in the family: Impact on health care utilization and expenditures for nondisabled members. *Milbank Quarterly, 77*(1), 39–75.

Alzheimer's Association (2013). Statistics about Alzheimer's Disease. http://www.alz.org/alzheimers_disease_facts_and_figures.asp?gclid=clc1zkr10 lgcfqnyqgodcx4avw Retrieved 7/27/2013

Alzheimer's Association of Orange County. (1998). *Alzheimer's disease fact sheet*. Author.

Alzheimer's Disease and Related Disorders Association, Inc. (1995). *Caregiver stress: Signs to watch for … steps to take*. Author.

Ansello, E. F. (1988). The intersecting of aging and disabilities. *Educational Gerontology, 14*(5), 351–363.

Ansello, E. F., & Eustis, N. N. (1992, Winter). A common stake? Investigating the emerging "intersection" of aging and disabilities. *Generations, 16*, 5–8.

Association for Continuing Education. (1997). Phone: 1-800-777-6839.

Baker, C. (1991). An AIDS diagnosis: Psychological devastation!. *California Therapist, 3*(5), 66–67.

Brohl, K., & Ledford, R. (2012). Alzheimer's diagnostic basics for mental health professionals. In *Continuing education for California social workers and marriage and family therapists*. Ormond Beach, FL: Elite Continuing Education.

Bruns, D., & Disorbio, J. M. (2006). Chronic pain and biopsychosocial disorders. *Practical Pain Management, 6*(2), 2.

Centers for Disease Control (CDC). (2013). *HIV/AIDS statistic overview*. Retrieved May 21, 2013, from www.cdc.gov/hiv/statistics/basics/

Centers for Disease Control and Prevention. (2002). Guidelines for preventing opportunistic infections among HIV-infected persons: Recommendations of the U.S. Public Health Service and the Infectious Diseases Society of America. *MMWR, 51*, RR-8.

Centers for Disease Control and Prevention. (2003). *STD surveillance 2003*. Author.

Centers for Disease Control and Prevention. (2008). *HIV/AIDS in the United States*. Retrieved February 4, 2010, from http://www.cdc.gov/hiv/resources/factsheets/us.htm

Comer, R. J. (1995). *Abnormal psychology* (2nd ed.). New York: Freeman.

Coogle, C., Ansello, E. F., Wood, J. B., & Cotter, J. J. (1995, September 3). Partners II: Serving older persons with developmental disabilities: Obstacles and inducements to collaboration among agencies. *Journal of Applied Gerontology, 14*, 275–288.

Davidson, P., Cain, N. N., Sloane-Reeves, J., Giesow, V., Quijano, L., Van Heyningen, J., et al. (1995). Crisis intervention for community-based persons with developmental disabilities and behavioral and psychiatric disorders. *Mental Retardation, 33*, 21–30.

Graham, R. (1989). Adult day care: How families of the dementia patient respond. *Journal of Gerontological Nursing, 15*(3), 27.

Halligan, P. W., & Aylward, M. (Eds.). (2006). *The power of belief: Psychosocial influence on illness, disability and medicine*. United Kingdom: Oxford University Press.

Hogan, D., Ebly, E. M., & Fung, T. S. (1999). Disease, disability, and age in cognitively intact seniors: Results from the Canadian study of health and aging. *Journal of Gerontology: Medical Sciences, 54A*(2), 77–82.

Janicki, M. P. (1991). *Building the future: Planning and community development in aging and developmental disabilities*. Albany, NY: New York State Office of Mental Retardation and Developmental Disabilities.

Johnson, A. B. (1990). *Out of bedlam: The truth about deinstitutionalization*. New York: Basic Books.

Price, R. E., Omizo, M. M., & Hammett, V. L. (1986, October). Counseling clients with AIDS. *Journal of Counseling and Development, 65*, 96–97.

Rosen, A., & Zlotnik, L. Z. (2001). Social work's response to the growing older population. *Generations* (spring), 69–71.

Santrock, J. W. (2007). *A topical approach to human life-span development* (3rd ed.). St. Louis, MO: McGraw-Hill.

Schneider, B. (1988). Care planning: The core of case management. *Generations, 12*(5), 16–18.

Slader, S. (1992). *HIV/IV drug users*. Presentation at California State University, Fullerton, CA.

Stern, S. M. (2001). Poverty and health statistics branch of the U. S. Census bureau, *HHES division*. Washington, DC.

Strang, P., Strang, S., Hultborn, R., & Arner, S. (2004). Existential pain-an entity, a provocation, or a challenge? *Journal of Pain Symptom Management, 27*(3), 241–250.

U.S. Department of Justice, Office for Victims of Crime Bulletin. (2001). *Working with victims of crimes with disabilities*. Washington, DC: Author.

Walker, S. (1994). Health promotion and prevention of disease and disability among older adults: Who is responsible? *Preventive Healthcare and Health Promotion for Older Adults (spring)*, 45–50.

Wild, S., Roglic, G., Green, A., Sicree, R., & King, H. (2004). Global prevalence of diabetes: Estimates for the year 2000 and projections for 2030. *Diabetes Care, 27*, 1047–1053.

Young, M. E., Nosek, M. S., Howland, C. A., Chanpong, G., & Rintala, D. H. (1997). Prevalence of abuse of women with physical disabilities. *Archives of Physical Medicine and Rehabilitation, 78*, 534–538.

Zola, I. K. (1988). Aging and disability: Toward unifying an agenda. *Educational Gerontology, 14*(5), 365–367.

Name Index

A

Abbey-Hines, J., 84
Acierno, R., 180
Aguilera, D. C., 85
Alecxih, L., 289
Allen, M., 83
Altman, B. M., 289
Ansello, E. F., 290, 291
Arambarri, P., 225, 235
Archer, R. P., 19, 114
Arner, S., 271
Arredondo, P., 36
Auchterlonie, J. L., 178
Aylward, M., 271

B

Baker, C., 279
Baker, R., 100
Barnett, O. W., 234
Barry, K. L., 254
Beck, A. T., 2, 19, 85
Beigel, A., 16
Bell, T., 143
Berchick, E. R., 147
Berkman, L. F., 147
Bernstein, G., 166
Bevilacqua, J., 14, 15
Bien, T. H., 254
Bierut, L. J., 248
Bisconer, S. W., 86
Bloor, L. E., 205
Blum, R., 182–183
Bond, F. W., 191
Borduin, C. M., 19, 114

Borges, G., 84
Botman, H., 166
Bowen, M., 115
Bowlby, J., 135
Bradley, E. H., 146
Bradshaw, C. P., 182–183
Brenner, C., 18
Bride, B. E., 167
Briere, J., 96
Brohl, K., 96, 120, 121, 244, 246, 283, 284
Brown, T. R., 84
Bruns, D., 271
Buckner, F., 33
Bugental, J. F. T., 18
Burnett-Zeigler, I., 181

C

Caffaro, J. V., 221
Callanan, P., 31, 32, 34
Campbell, D. W., 226
Caplan, G., 2, 4, 5, 13, 14, 16, 49, 57, 67, 71, 136
Caplan, R., 16
Carney, J. V., 84
Catalano, R., 146
Chanpong, G., 287
Clark, A. N., 182
Clarke, J. D., 166
Clark, J., 97
Cojucar, G., 205
Colao, F., 218
Cole, C., 90, 92, 99, 100
Collins, S., 167

Coll, J. E., 178
Comer, R. J., 289
Conterio, K., 97
Coogle, C., 291
Cooper, P. F., 289
Cooper, R., 120
Corey, G., 31, 32, 34, 49
Corey, M. S., 31, 32, 34
Cormier, L. S., 20, 52
Cormier, W. H., 20, 52
Corsini, R. J., 19
Cotter, J. J., 291
Cremens, M. C., 97
Cullen, F. T., 203
Cunningham, P. J., 289
Currier, G., 83
Cusick, M., 232
Cutler, D., 14, 15

D

Darche, M. A., 96
Darwin, C., 135
Davidson-Nielson, M., 135
Davidson, P., 288
Davis, H., 255, 256
Dick, D. M., 248
DiClemente, R. J., 96
Difede, J., 180
Disorbio, J. M., 271
Dooley, D., 146
Dowdall, D. J., 181
Draper, T., 205
Dreikurs, R., 49

E

Ebly, E. M., 288
Elbogen, E. B., 180
Ellis, A., 2, 19
Erbaugh, J., 85
Erikson, E., 110, 113
Eustis, N. N., 291
Ewing, J. A., 250
Eyman, J. R., 86

F

Fals-Stewart, W., 181
Farberow, N. L., 83–84
Fenoglio, P., 224, 230
Figley, C. R., 167

Firestone, M., 33
Fisher, G. S., 203
Flavin, D. K., 245
Flavin, P., 84
Fleming, M. G., 254
Forrest, M. S., 157, 192
Francis, K., 253
Freudenberger, H. J., 166
Freud, S, 135
Fung, T. S., 288
Furman, D. M., 28–29

G

Gabbard, G. O., 7, 155, 247
Gahm, G., 180
Gallo, T., 146
Gallo, W. T., 147
Garfield, S. L., 20
Gershkovich, A., 95
Gil, E., 96
Gilliland, B. E., 2, 10
Giordano, J., 39, 40
Gluckstern, N. B., 52, 53, 58
Goldman, S., 95
Gold, M. S., 247
Gomez, J. S., 166, 167
Gontz, A. S., 147
Gordon, J. R., 181
Gorey, K. M., 214
Graham, D. P., 181
Graham, R., 289
Green, A., 271
Gross, D. M., 86
Grossman, D. A., 178
Gueulette, C. M., 84

H

Halligan, P. W., 271
Hammett, V. L., 281
Hampton, E., 179
Hartley, D., 96
Hayes, S. C., 191
Heath, N., 96
Heidemeier, H., 147
Heilig, S. M., 84
Heller, M., 199, 202
Henslin, E., 97
Hesley, J. W., 73

Hogan, D., 288
Hoge, C. W., 178
Hollander, E., 96
Hong, G. K., 41
Hosansky, T., 218
Howland, C. A., 287
Huisman, K. A., 227
Hultborn, R., 271

I

Ivey, A. E., 52, 53, 58
Ivey, M. B., 52, 53, 58

J

Jackson, S. E., 165, 166
Jacobsen, L. K., 180
Jacobs, J., 122
Jakupcak, M., 180, 181
James, R. K., 2, 10
Janicki, M. P., 290
Janosik, E. H., 3, 5, 10
Jaycox, L., 178, 179, 182
Jobes, D. A., 86
Johnson, A. B., 290
Johnson, K., 254
Johnston, J. R., 144
Johnston, M., 86
Jones, W., 20, 49

K

Kanani, K., 36
Kashiwagi, S., 42
Kasl, S. V., 146, 147
Katz, L. S., 205
Kendler, K. S., 125
Kennedy, D. H., 204, 205
Kennon, M., 123
Kessler, C. Jr., 84
King, H., 271
Kirsch, I., 11
Kitfield, J., 204
Kosinski, F. A., Jr., 165, 166
Koss, M., 203
Kosten, T. R., 180
Kramer, J., 84
Kruger, L. J., 166
Kübler-Ross, E., 134, 135, 136
Kugler, D., 237

L

Lader, W., 97
Ladrech, J., 164
Lancer, D., 250
La Violette, A. D., 234
Ledford, R., 96, 120, 121, 244, 246, 283, 284
Leick, N., 135
Leiter, M., 166
Lemaire, C. M., 181
Lembeck, P., 120
Lenell, M., 30
Leonard, C. S., 83
Leslie, D. R., 214
Lester, P., 182
Liebowitz, M. R., 40
Lighthall, A., 183
Lillis, J., 191
Lindemann, E., 12, 49
Litman, R. E., 83, 84
Lloyd, E. E., 96
London, R., 254
Long, A., 167
Lopez, S. R., 37, 38
Ludt, N., 140, 141, 142
Luoma, J. B., 191

M

Mahler, J. C., 247
Main, L., 226
Manwell, L. B., 254
Maralani, V., 147
Marlatt, G. A., 181
Marshall, A. D., 181
Maslach, C., 165, 166
Maslow, H . A., 8
Maslow, N. J, 226
Masuda, A., 191
McCabe, S., 192
McDevitt-Murphy, M. E., 180, 181
McFarland, B., 14, 15
McGoldrick, M., 39, 40
Meichenbaum, D., 19
Mendelson, M., 85
Metal, M., 178
Michaelis, R. C., 166, 167
Miliken, C. S., 178
Miller, N. S., 247
Miller, W. R., 254

Minuchin, S., 115, 128
Mmari, K. N., 182–183
Mock, J., 85
Moline, M., 49
Moore, B. A., 204, 205
Moore, L. F., 29
Morse, R. M., 245
Mulley, A. G., 97

N

Nauert, R., 120
Nelson, C., 86
Nock, M. K., 95, 96
Nosek, M. S., 287
Nowinski, J., 251

O

O'Farrell, T., 181
Omizo, M. M., 281
Oquendo, M. A., 40

P

Peake, T. H., 19, 114
Pearce, J. K., 39, 40
Philipps, D., 179
Piasecki, M., 97, 98
Pierce, P. E., 204, 205
Pines, A., 165
Ponton, L. E., 96
Price, R. E., 281
Prinstein, M. J., 95, 96
Pryor, R., 258
Purington, A., 95

R

Radcliff, B., 84
Regehr, C., 36
Reger, G., 180
Resnick, H. S., 180
Rheingold, A. A., 180
Richie, B. E., 227
Riggs, D. S., 181
Rintala, D. H., 287
Rizzo, A. A., 180
Roberts, A. R., 5
Rogers, C., 19
Rogers, J. R., 84
Roglic, G., 271

Rosen, A., 289
Ross, C. E., 147
Ross, S., 96
Rothbaum, B. O., 180
Rubin, A., 182
Russell, G., 125
Rutter, M., 182

S

Saltzman, A., 28–29
Sanchez, V. C., 254
Santrock, J. W., 271
Schading, B., 204
Schechter, D. S., 40
Schiess, L., 179
Schmidt, M., 162
Schneider, B., 291
Schwartz, J. H., 97
Segel-Evans, K., 237
Shadel, S., 252
Shaffer, D., 86
Shapiro, F., 157, 170, 192
Shneidman, E. S., 83, 84
Shrivastava, A., 86
Sicree, R., 271
Siegel, M., 146
Simeon, D., 96
Simpson, C., 122
Simpson, P., 180
Singer, E., 31
Slader, S., 278, 281
Slaikeu, K. A., 5, 9, 10, 13
Smith, R. H., 250
Sorenson, S. B., 226
Southwick, S. M., 180
Sparks, P. J., 166
Steadman, H. J., 88
Steiner, L., 87, 92, 93, 95, 203
Stern, S. M., 287
Stern, T. F., 97
Strang, P., 271
Strang, S., 271
Street, A. E., 181
Struchen, M. A., 182
Strully, K., 147
Sudhinaraset, M., 182–183
Sullivan, H. S., 49, 50
Swearer, S., 120
Szasz, T., 94–95

T

Taft, C. T., 181
Tanielian, T., 178, 179, 182
Tarabay, J., 180
Teten, A. L., 180
Thienhaus, O. J., 97, 98
Thoennes, N., 201, 227
Thompson, M. P., 226
Tjaden, P., 201, 227
Tonigan, J. S., 254
Tower, C. C., 217
Treasure, J., 125
Trzepacz, P. T., 100
Turner, M. G., 203

V

Veague, H. B., 97
Vettor, S. M., 165, 166
Volpp, L., 226

W

Walker, S., 288
Walsh, B. W., 97
Walters, E. E., 84, 125
Ward, C. H., 85
Wedding, D., 19

Weiss, E. L., 178
Weisser, R. J. Jr., 20, 52
Werth, J. L. Jr., 84
Wesley, J., 200, 201
White, E. C., 226
Whitlock, J., 95
Wild, S., 271
Wold, C. I., 84
Wood, J. B., 291
Woods, K., 222, 225, 229, 230, 232, 234, 236
Worden, W., 136
Wu, C., 147
Wyman, S., 89, 91

Y

Yager, C., 39
Yang, A., 43
Yarvis, J. S., 179
Young, M. E., 287
Yufit, R. I., 86

Z

Zager, G., 124
Zimbardo, P. G., 260
Zlotnik, L. Z., 289
Zola, I. K., 291

Subject Index

A

ABC model of crisis intervention, 20–21,
  48–79
  attending behavior in, 52–53
  clarification in, 55–56
  commitment and follow-up in, 73–74
  coping behavior in, 69–74
  developing and maintaining rapport,
    50–59
  emotional distress and functioning
    level identification in, 64
  ethical checks in, 65–66
  overview of, 49–50
  paraphrasing in, 56
  precipitating events, identifying, 62–63
  precipitating events, recognizing
    meaning of in, 63–64
  problem identification in, 59–69
  questioning in, 53–55
  reflection of feelings in, 56–58
  as related to Alderian counseling, 49–50
  sample script, 74–79
  substance abuse issues check in, 66
  summarization in, 58–59
  therapeutic interaction and, 66–69
abuse issues, 65
acceptance and commitment therapy
  (ACT), 191–192
acceptance, as stage in death and dying,
  134
acquaintance rape, 203, 214
ACT. See acceptance and commitment
  therapy (ACT)
acute stress disorder
  in veterans, 156

Adlerian counseling, 49
adolescence. See teenagers
Adult Children of Alcoholics (ACA), 255,
  257
adults molested as children (AMACS),
  216
  intervention strategies for, 221–222
aerospace syndrome, 165
African American families, 40–41
  intimate partner abuse, 226
  racism, 41
  religion, 41
AIDS (acquired immunodeficiency
    syndrome), 272–283
  client types, crisis intervention,
    279–281
  defined, 272, 274–275
  drug abuse and, 258, 262
  drug use and, 274
  history of, 273–274
  intervention strategies, 281–283
  misconceptions about, 275
  overview of, 272–274
  progression of HIV infection to, 276
  social aspects, 278–279
  testing, 276
  treatment for, 277–278
  triple whammy treatment for, 277
AIDS-related complex (ARC), 272
Al-Anon, 71, 72, 257
alcohol abuse, 247–257
  alcoholic, 248
  codependent, 254–257
  intervention strategies, 248–254
alcohol dependence, 244

Alcohol Dependence Data Questionnaire, 250
alcoholic, 248
Alcoholics Anonymous (AA), 71, 72, 246, 247, 250–251, 257
alcoholism, 244–245, 247
  defense mechanisms observed in, 232
alcohol misuse, 180–181
Alcohol Use Disorders Identification Test, 250
Alzheimer's Association, 284, 285
Alzheimer's disease, 66, 100, 283–285
  defined, 283–284
  effects on caretaker, 284–285
AMACS. *See* adults molested as children (AMACS)
American Psychiatric Association, 155
American Society of Addiction Medicine, 244
Americans with Disabilities Act (ADA) of 1990, 287
amotivational syndrome, 260
anger
  as stage in death and dying, 134
  veteran's issues, 180
anorexia nervosa, 125
anxiety
  curvilinear model of, 10–11
  as motivator for change, 10–11
ARC. *See* AIDS-related complex (ARC)
Asian American culture, 41–42
  communication process in, 42
  shame and obligation in, 41–42
Asian American families
  Asian American culture, 41–42
  family structure, 41
  intimate partner abuse, 226–227
assertiveness training, 73
ataque de nervios (los nervios), 40
attending behavior, 52–53
attention deficit disorder with hyperactivity (ADHD), 66
autonomy, 119
aversive conditioning, 252
AZT (zidovudine), 277

B

Bambas, Judy, 233
barbiturates, 245, 251
bargaining, as stage in death and dying, 134

battered woman syndrome, 224, 230–231
  battering cycle, 229
  intervention strategies for battered women, 232–234
batterer, 234–235
  interventions with, 236–238
  phenomenological view of, 235–236
battering cycle, 229
battering parent, 219–220
battering spouse, 224–226
  intervention strategies for, 236–238
  phenomenological view of, 235–236
Beck Depression Inventory, 85
behavioral problem-solving model, 19
bereavement, 135
bibliotherapy, 73
biopsychosocial model
  for serious illness and disabilities, 271–272
  for substance abuse, 253–254
bipolar disorder, 66
bisexual, 42. *See also* lesbians, gays, bisexuals, and transgenders (LGBT)
blended families, 145–146
body language, 53
Boston bombing in 2013, 159–160
bottoming out, 245
Bowlby, John, 135
brief therapy, 19–20
bulimia nervosa, 125
bullying, 120–121
  definition, 120
  intervention strategies, 120–121
  statistics, 120
  working with families and bully, 121
  working with families and victims, 121
burnout, 165–170
  causes of, 166–167
  community crisis workers, 167–169
  debriefing process, 169–170
  definitions of, 165
  secondary traumatic stress, 167
  symptoms of, 165–166

C

CAGE questionnaire, 249–250
calibration, 114
Campus Lockdown 2012, gun violence and shootings, 160–162

Cannabis sativa, 260
Caplan, Gerald, 2, 4, 13, 16, 49, 71
caretakers, 284–285
Carpenter, Karen, 125
case management, 291
Catholicism, 39
child abuse, 211–222
    battering parent, 219–221
    identifying, 213
    intervention strategies, 217–219
    neglect and, 213
    posttraumatic stress disorder and,
        215–216
    prevalence of, 211–212, 213–215
    reporting, 65–66, 216–217
    sexual abuse of, 213–215
    types of, 212
child abuse accommodation syndrome,
    216
Child Abuse Prevention and Treatment
    Act, 216
Child Abuse Reporting Act, 34
child protective services agency, 217
children
    adult children of alcoholics, 255
    blended families and, 145–146
    divorce and, 144–145
    effects of trauma on, 156
    intimate partner violence and domestic
        violence, 224
    losing a child, 141–143
    sexual abuse of, 213–215
client's rights, 36
close-ended question, 53–55
closet gay, 43
cocaine, 257–259
    effects on family, 259
Cocaine Anonymous, 71
Coconut Grove fire, 12
codependent, 254–257
    adult children of alcoholics, 255
    treatment for, 255–256
    twelve-step programs, 257
Co-Dependents Anonymous (Co-DA),
    71, 257
cognition tree, 61
cognitive approaches, 9
cognitive-behavioral theories, 19
cognitive key, 9
combat stress injuries, 179

coming out, 43
commitment and follow-up, 73–74
community agencies and resources,
    71–72
community disasters, four phases of,
    158–159
Community Mental Health Act of 1963,
    14–17, 289
competence, 35
confidentiality, 32–36
coping behavior
    characteristics of, 13–14
    client's own attempts at coping, 70
    development of new, 70
    presenting alternative, 70–71
coping methods, 2, 12
counseling
    principles and procedures in crises of
        loss, 151
counteraction, 114
countertransference, 31–32
County and State Social Service Agencies,
    191
crack cocaine, 257–259
crises
    coping behavior, 13–14
    as danger and opportunity, 3–9, 158
    defined, 2–3
    developmental, 10
    drug abuse, 245
    emotional distress in, 10–12
    family, 245
    legal, 246–247
    medical, 245–246
    precipitating events of, 9
    psychological, 247
    situational, 10
crisis hotline, 84
crisis intervention strategies
    ABC model of, 20–21
    development of, 12–14, 17
    for persons with disabilities, 291–293
    related to AIDS and HIV infection,
        279–281
    and suicide prevention movement, 14
    theoretical modalities contributing to,
        17–21
crisis-prone person, 6–7
critical incident debriefing, 20, 157
crystal methamphetamine, 257–259

cultural sensitivity
    development of, 37–38
curvilinear model of anxiety, 10–11
cyberbullying, 120

D

danger
    crisis as, 5, 6–7
    natural disasters, 158
    and opportunity, 18
    to others, 97–99
danger to others, 33
Darwin, Charles, 135
date rape, 203
death and dying, 134–143
    counseling principles and procedures,
        140
    definitions, 135
    determinants of grief, 138–139
    intervention, 139–140
    Kübler-Ross's stages of death and
        dying, 134–135
    losing a child, 140–143
    manifestations of normal grief, 138
    tasks of mourning, 136–137
debriefing process, 169–170
Dederich, Charles E., 253
delayed reaction, PTSD, 163
delusions, 100
denial
    in Alzheimer's disease caretakers, 284
    as defense mechanism in crisis, 5, 7
    as defense mechanism in substance
        abuse, 250
    in individuals with AIDS, 279, 280
    in individuals with HIV infection, 280
    as stage in death and dying, 134
depersonalized feelings, 247
deployment (deployed), 178
depression, 66, 85, 86
    as stage in death and dying, 134
    and suicide, 179–180
    suicide and, 85, 86
    veteran's issues, 179–180
derealized feelings, 247
detoxification, 251
developmental crises, 10, 109–132
    creating grandparental subsystems,
        119
    creating marital subsystems, 116–118

creating parental subsystems, 118
creating sibling subsystems, 118
eating disorders, 124–128
family systems theory, 114
life cycle crises, 110–113
runaway teenagers, 114
teen pregnancy, 121–122
developmentally disabled, 286
development of cultural sensitivity,
    37–38
*Diagnostic and Statistical Manual of
    Mental Disorders (DSM)*, 155, 244
differentiation, 122
disabilities, 285–293
    abuse of persons with, 287
    Americans with Disabilities Act (ADA)
        of 1990, 287
    biopsychosocial model, 271–272
    crisis intervention strategies for
        persons with, 291–293
    defined, 285
    disabled population and ADA,
        287–288
    elderly persons with, 288–289
    history of, 285–287
    persons with developmental,
        290–291
    persons with mental, 289–290
    subgroups with, 288
disabled elderly people, 288–289
disaster mental health, 164
disasters. *See* natural disasters
disengagement, 115, 116
dissociation, 155
Distant Thunder, 73
diversion programs, 246
divorce and separation, 143–146
    children and, 144–145
    crises related to blended families,
        145–146
    intervention strategies, 144
domestic violence, 224–238. *See also*
    intimate partner violence and
    domestic violence
Drug Enforcement Administration, 257
drug use statistics, 244
drunk driving, 246, 247, 250
*DSM. See Diagnostic and Statistical
    Manual of Mental Disorders (DSM)*
dual relationships, 32

E

eating disorders, 124–128
  anorexia nervosa, 125
  bulimia nervosa, 125
  characteristics of, 126
  treatment considerations for, 125–126
economic loss, 146–147. *See also* job loss
Ecstasy (3,4-methylenedioxymetha-
    mphetamine, or MDMA), 261
educational statements, 67, 202–203
  battered women and, 238
Education for All Handicapped Children
    Act, 292
ego strength, 8, 12
elder abuse, 33, 222–224
  intervention strategies, 223–224
  reporting, 65–66
Elder Abuse Reporting Act, 33
Ellis, Albert, 19
EMDR. *See* eye movement desensitiza-
    tion and reprocessing (EMDR)
emergency psychiatry, 83
emic, 38–39
emotional abuse, 236
emotional distress, 10–12, 64, 158
emotionalism, 40
empathy, 56
empowering statements, 68
empowerment model, with sexual assault
    survivors, 202–203
enabler, 254, 255, 256
enmeshed, 115
Erikson, Erik, 110
  psychosocial stages of development,
    112–113
Erikson's eight stages of development,
    128
ethical issues, 27–44
  confidentiality, 32–36
  controversies, 29–30
  countertransference, 31–32
  dual relationships, 32
  multicultural competence, 36–40
  need for ethics, 28
  therapeutic self-awareness, 31–32
  use of paraprofessionals, 30–31
etic, 38–39
etic *vs.* emic issues, 38–39
evolutional crises, 116–119

exceptions to privilege and
    confidentiality, 32
existential theory, 18
eye contact, 53
eye movement desensitization and
    reprocessing (EMDR), 181, 192

F

families
  blended, 145–146
  effects of substance abuse on, 259
families overcoming under stress
    (FOCUS), 182
familismo, 39–40
family subsystems
  grandparental, 119
  marital, 116–118
  parental, 118
  sibling, 118
family systems theory, 114
family therapy, 71, 219, 251
family therapy, structure, 115–116
Farberow, Norman L., 83–84
fatal attraction case, 99
Father of Modern Crisis Intervention.
    See Caplan, Gerald
fix, 262
FOCUS. *See* families overcoming under
    stress (FOCUS)
follow-up and commitment, 73–74
four phases of community disasters,
    158–159
FRAMES, 254
freebase, 258
Freud, Sigmund, 17, 135
functioning, impairment in, 12
functioning level, 4, 64

G

gay, 43. *See also* lesbians, gays, bisexuals,
    and transgenders (LGBT)
general neglect, 212
Gerry House West, 253
grandparental subsystems, 119
grassroots programs, 14
gravely disabled persons, 29, 30, 33, 100
grief, 138–139
  counseling principles and procedures,
    140
  defined, 135

grief (*continued*)
    determinants of, 138–139
    intervention strategies for dealing with,
      139
    losing a child, 140–143
    manifestations of normal, 138
grief work, 13
gun violence and shootings, 160–162

H

hallucinations, 100, 261
Health Communications, Inc., 257
Health Insurance Portability and
    Accountability Act (HIPAA), 29
health maintenance organizations
    (HMOs), 15
Hemlock Society, 94–95
heroin, 262
heterosexism, 43
high-risk suicidal clients, 91–92
HIV (human immunodeficiency virus)
    infection. *See also* AIDS (acquired
    immunodeficiency syndrome)
    client types, crisis intervention, 279–281
    intervention strategies, 281–283
    modes of transmission, 275–276
    progression to AIDS, 276
    social aspects, 278–279
    treatment for, 277–278
homeostasis, 114
homicidal ideation, 97–98
homicidal issues, 65
homophobia, 43
homosexuality, 43
hospice care, 271
hospitalization
    for crystal methamphetamine
      abuse, 259
    involuntary, 83, 91, 100
hotline
    child abuse, 99
    crisis, 84
    suicide, 85
humanistic approach, 18–19
Hurricane Katrina, 157, 158
hypervigilance, 156

I

illicit drug misuse, 257–263
Individuals with Disabilities Education
    Act (IDEA), 292

individuation, 123
infant whiplash syndrome, 215
informed consent, 34–35
intervention strategies, 88–92
    with abused elderly people, 223–224
    Alcoholics Anonymous (AA), 250–251
    for alcohol problems, 254
    for battered women, 232–234
    for batterer, 236–238
    behavior modification approaches for
      substance abuse, 252–254
    child abuse, 217–218, 221
    death and dying, 139–140
    divorce and separation, 144
    family therapy, 251
    job loss, 147
    medical approaches for substance
      abuse, 251–252
    military sexual trauma (MST), 205
    natural disasters, 163
    perpetrators of sexual abuse, 221–222
    with rape victims, 202
    for substance abuse, 248–254
    trauma response, 162–165
    twelve-step facilitation (TSF), 251
    veteran's issues, 191–192
intimate partner violence and domestic
    violence, 224–238
    battered woman syndrome, 230–231
    batterer, 234–235
    battering cycle, 229
    cultural considerations, 226–227
    cultural factors, 225–226
    historical perspective, 224–225
    intervention strategies with battered
      women, 232–234
    intervention strategies with batterer,
      236–238
    prevalence of, 227–228
    reasons why women stay, 228
    universal factors, 225–226
intravenous (IV) drug use, 274
invisible wounds, veteran's issues,
    179–192
    alcohol misuse, 180–181
    anger issues, 180
    college enrolled veterans, 183
    depression and suicide, 179–180
    family issues of veterans, 182–183
    interventions, 191–192

PTSD, 179
   traumatic brain injury (TBI), 181–182
   treatment of, PTSD, 180
involuntary hospitalization, 83, 91, 100
isolation, as stage in death and dying, 134

J

job loss
   interventions, 147
   role of perceptions, 147
Joint Commission on Mental Illness and
      Health, 14
Jones's ABC method of crisis
      management, 20
journaling, 73
Judeo-Christian culture, 43

K

Kübler-Ross, Elisabeth, 133, 134
   stages of death and dying identified by,
      134–1335

L

Lanterman-Petris-Short Act, 29–30
L.A. Scale for Assessment of Suicidal
      Potential, 83–84
Latinos, 39–40
   acculturation rates, issues related
      to, 40
   AIDS and, 274
   ataque de nervios (los nervios), 40
   catholicism, 39
   emotionalism, 40
   enmeshed family structure, 40
   familismo, 39–40
   intimate partner abuse, 226
   machismo, 39
   marianisma, 39
   personalismo, 39
legal issues, 27–44
   confidentiality, 32–36
   controversies, 29–30
   countertransference, 31–32
   defining law, 28–29
   therapeutic self-awareness, 31–32
   use of paraprofessionals, 30–31
legal referrals, 72–73
lesbian, 43. *See also* lesbians, gays,
      bisexuals, and transgenders (LGBT)

lesbians, gays, bisexuals, and trans-
      genders (LGBT), 42–43
life cycle crises, 110–113
   adolescence, 111
   infancy, 110
   maturity, 111–112
   middle adulthood, 111
   preschool and middle school, 111
   toddlerhood, 110–111
   young adulthood, 111
Lindemann, Eric, 12, 49
logotherapy, 163
long-term therapy, 71
Los Angeles County Department of
      Mental Health, 164, 169
Los Angeles Suicide Prevention Center,
      83
loss, crises of, 133–153
   death and dying, 133–143
   divorce and separation, 143–146
   job loss, 146–150
low-risk suicidal clients, 89–90
loyalty issues, 145
LSD (lysergic acid diethylamide), 247,
      261–262
Ludt, Nancy, 140, 142

M

machismo, 39
MADD (Mothers Against Drunk
      Driving), 247
mainstream society, 287
managed care, rise of, 15–17
mandated reporting laws, 216
man-made disasters, 159–160
marianisma, 39
marijuana use, 259–261
   chronic pot use, 260
   intervention strategies, 259
marital subsystems, 116–118
marital therapy, 71
material resources, 7–8, 157–158
MDMA, 261
meaning therapy, 163
means, 91
medical referrals, 72–73
medication
   for emotional distress, 11–12
   for grief, 139
   for PTSD, 170

Mental Health Center of North Iowa, Inc., 158
mentally disabled people, 289–290
Mental Status Exam, 100–102
methadone, 245, 246, 262
Michigan Alcohol Screening Test, 250
middle-risk suicidal clients, 90–91
military culture, 178
military service, 176–179
  culture, 178
  issues, 178–179
  operation enduring freedom (OEF), 177
  operation Iraqi freedom (OIF), 177
  statistics, 178
military sexual assault, 203–205
military sexual trauma (MST), 199, 205
  survivor of, 74–79
Moline, Mary, 20
mourning
  defined, 135
  tasks of, 136–137
MST. *See* military sexual trauma (MST)
multicultural counseling, 36

N

Narcotics Anonymous, 261
National Center for Post-Traumatic Stress Disorder, 159, 170
National Center on Child Abuse Prevention Research, 211
National Child Abuse and Neglect Data system, 211
National Committee to Prevent Child Abuse, 211
National Council on Alcoholism, 244
National Council on Alcoholism and Drug Dependence, 244
National Institute of Mental Health, 289
National Women's Health Information Center, 227
natural disasters, 157–158
  intervention strategies, 163
  opportunity, 158
nonmaleficence, 28
nonperpetrating parent, 218
nonprofessionals, 16–17
nonsuicidal self-injury (NSSI), 95–97
  assessment of, 96–97
  interventions for, 97

no-suicide contract, 90–91
nurturance, 110, 111, 115

O

obsessive-compulsive disorder, 66
OCSAN. *See* Orange County Sexual Assault Network (OCSAN)
OEF. *See* operation enduring freedom (OEF)
OIF. *See* operation Iraqi freedom (OIF)
open-ended questions, 53–55, 61
operation enduring freedom (OEF), 177
operation Iraqi freedom (OIF), 177
opportunistic infections, 274
opportunity, crisis as, 5–6
opportunity, natural disasters, 158
Orange County Sexual Assault Network (OCSAN), 200, 202
Orange County Social Services Agency, 215, 219, 220
organic brain disorder, 66
OxyContin, 179

P

Paddington Alcohol Test, 250
palliative care, 270–271
paraphrasing, 56
paraprofessionals, 15
  use of, 30–31
parental subsystems, 118
pathologic interactions, 114
Pentagon attack of September 11, 160
perpetrator, 218, 221–222
Persian Gulf syndrome, 177
personalismo, 39
personal resources, 8
person-centered counseling, 19
physical abuse, 212, 222, 236
plan, 91
play therapy, 219
Police Executive Research Forum, 288
postdeployment, 178
posttraumatic stress disorder (PTSD), 154–162, 215–216
  battered woman syndrome, 224
  child abuse, 215–216
  demographic information for, 184–186
  invisible wounds, 179–192
  military service, 156, 176–179
  other therapeutic approaches to treat, 170
  overview of, 154–156

symptoms of, 155
treatment of, 180
types of, 156
veterans and, 156, 179–181
veteran's issues, 179–192
Pot Smokers Anonymous, 261
precipitating events, 9, 62–64
preferred provider organizations
   (PPOs), 15
pregnancy, teen, 121–122
premorbid functioning, 100
preventive psychiatry, 13
privileged communication, 32, 33
problem identification, 59–69
   emotional distress and functioning
      level, 64
   ethical checks in, 65–66
   precipitating events and, 62–64
   substance abuse issues, 66
   therapeutic interaction and, 66–69
professional issues, 27–44
   confidentiality, 32–36
   controversies, 29–30
   countertransference, 31–32
   multicultural competence, 36–40
   therapeutic self-awareness, 31–32
   use of paraprofessionals, 30–31
Pryor, Richard, 258
pseudopsychotic condition, 247
Psychiatric Emergency Treatment
   (PET), 15
psychoanalytic theory, 17–18
psychosis, 83, 96, 97
psychotic breakdowns, 100
psychotic decompensation, 82–104
PTSD. *See* posttraumatic stress disorder
   (PTSD)

Q

questions
   clarification and, 55–56
   close-ended, 53–55
   open-ended, 53–55, 61
   soft closed-ended, 55
   wording of, 54

R

rape, 200–209
   date and acquaintance, 203
   defined, 200–201

intervention strategies, 202
   myths of, 200
rape trauma syndrome, 200, 201
rapport, developing and maintaining,
   50–51
Red Cross, 163, 164, 169
reel therapy, 73
reflection of feelings, 56–58
reframing statements, 68–69, 256
   battered women and, 232
relationship breakups, 143–146.
      See also divorce and separation
research study
   of veteran's issues, 183–192
resources, 71
Ritalin abuse, 247
Rogers, Carl, 19
runaway teenagers, 123–124
   interventions, 123–124
   motivations for, 123

S

Sand Tray therapy, 192
San Francisco Child Abuse Council, 213
SAPRO. *See* Sexual Assault Prevention
      and Response Office (SAPRO)
Scale for Impact of Suicidality
      Management, Assessment and
      Planning of Care (SIS-MAP), 86
schizophrenia, 66
secondary PTSD, 157. *See also*
      posttraumatic stress disorder (PTSD)
secondary traumatic stress disorder, 167
   and burnout, 167–169
secondary traumatization, 157, 182.
      See also posttraumatic stress
      disorder (PTSD)
self-advocacy, 223
selfmutilative behavior (SMB), 95–97
serious illness
   AIDS (acquired immunodeficiency
      syndrome), 272–283
   Alzheimer's disease, 283–285
   biopsychosocial model and, 271–272
   human immunodeficiency virus (HIV),
      272–283
   overview, 272
   palliative care and, 270–271
sexual abuse, 124, 236
   adults molested as children, 216, 221

sexual abuse (*continued*)
  children and, 221
    posttraumatic stress disorder and, 157,
      215, 216
sexual assault, 222, 228. *See also* rape
Sexual Assault Prevention and Response
    Office (SAPRO), 204
Shadel, Schick, 252
shaken baby syndrome, 215
shelters, 71–72, 232
  runaway youth, 124
sibling subsystems, 118
  structural dysfunction, 119
Simpson, Nicole Brown, 225
Simpson, O. J., 225
situational crises, 10
  related to adolescence, 119
Smith, Robert Holbrook, 250
snorting, 257, 258, 262
social resources, 9
speed, 257–259
  effects on family, 259
spouse, battering, 229
stalking, 227
Steiner, L., 92–93, 95
stress, 9, 11
stress management classes, 73
structural family therapy, 115–116
  diffusion, 115
  disengagement, 115–116
  enmeshed situation, 115
  rigidity, 116
substance abuse, 243–267
  alcohol, 247–257
  defined, 244–245
  heroin, 262
  issues, 66
  LSD (lysergic acid diethylamide),
    261–262
  marijuana, 259–261
  speed, 257–259
  types of drug abuse crises, 245–247
substantiated, 211
suicidal ideation, 84, 85, 88
suicide, 83–104
  assessment, 83, 85–88
  clues, 84–85
  and depression, 179–180
  high-risk suicidal clients, 91–92
  history of, 83–84

in HIV/AIDS patients, 279
  intervention strategies, 88–92
  low-risk suicidal clients, 89–90
  middle-risk suicidal clients, 90–91
  overview of, 84
  phenomenological aspects of, 92–93
  prevention, philosophies of, 94–95
  rates, 83, 84, 92
  substance abuse and, 247
  symptoms of, 84–85
  teenagers and, 120
suicide check, 65
suicide prevention movement, 14
Suicide Status Form (SSF), 86
suicide watch, 91
Sullivan, H. S., ABC model of crisis
    intervention and, 49, 50
summarization, 58–59
support groups, 71
  divorce, 144
  for grieving parents, 142
  for HIV/AIDS patients, 280, 281
support statements, 61
support systems, 71
Synanon, 253
Szasz, Thomas, 94–95

T

The Tarasoff Case, 34
TBI. *See* traumatic brain injury (TBI)
teenagers
  bullying, 120–121
  eating disorders, 124–128
  life cycle crises, 111
  pregnancy in, 121–122
  runaway, 123–124
  situational crises related to, 119
  suicidal ideation in, 126
  thrown away, 124
TeenScreen National Center for Mental
    Health Checkups, 85–86
terrorist attacks, 159
therapeutic self-awareness, 31–32
thrown away teenagers, 124
tolerance, 244
tranquilizers, 251, 252
transgender, 43. *See also* lesbians, gays,
    bisexuals, and transgenders (LGBT)
trauma response, 164

traumatic brain injury (TBI), 179, 181–182
trigger chart, 253
triple whammy treatment for AIDS, 277
tsunami of 2004, 158
twelve-step facilitation (TSF), 251
twelve-step groups, 71
twelve-step programs, 248
    for codependents, 257

V

VA. *See* veteran's administration (VA)
validation statements, 67
verbal following, 53
veteran's administration (VA), 191, 204
veteran's issues
    college enrolled veterans, 183
    family issues, 182–183
    invisible wounds, 179–192
    military service, 176–179
    PTSD, 179–181
    research study of, 183–192
vets centers, 191

victimization, PTSD and, 157
violence against others, 98–99
violence against women, 227, 228
virtual or e-therapy, 36
virtual reality exposure, 180
vocal style, 53

W

Wellesley Project, 12–14
Wilson, Bill, 250
withdrawal symptoms, 262
Women's Transitional Living Center, 233
women, violence against, 227–228
Worden, W., 136
    tasks of mourning, 136–137
World Trade Center attack of September
        11, 2001, 160
worried well group, 279

Z

Zager, Gary, 124
zidovudine (AZT), 277